PARTY LINES

ED GILLETT

PARTY LINES

DANCE MUSIC AND THE MAKING OF MODERN BRITAIN

PICADOR

First published 2023 by Picador
an imprint of Pan Macmillan
The Smithson, 6 Briset Street, London EC1M 5NR
EU representative: Macmillan Publishers Ireland Ltd, 1st Floor,
The Liffey Trust Centre, 117–126 Sheriff Street Upper,
Dublin 1, DOI YC43
Associated companies throughout the world
www.panmacmillan.com

ISBN 978-1-5290-7064-4

Copyright © Ed Gillett 2023

The right of Ed Gillett to be identified as the
author of this work has been asserted by him in accordance
with the Copyright, Designs and Patents Act 1988.

Photography credits:
Page 7: Homer Sykes / Alamy Stock Photo. Page 35: Alan Lodge. Page 65: Kent Police.
Page 91: Alan Lodge. Page 131: Edward Webb / Alamy Stock Photo. Page 169: Flora and Fauna
International. Page 203: Krown Media. Page 233: Courtesy of Gordon McNamee. Page 263:
Salvör Bergmann / flickr. Page 293: Ed Gillett. Page 329: Ed Gillett. Page 357: Yushy.

All rights reserved. No part of this publication may be reproduced,
stored in a retrieval system, or transmitted, in any form, or by any means
(electronic, mechanical, photocopying, recording or otherwise)
without the prior written permission of the publisher.

Pan Macmillan does not have any control over, or any responsibility for,
any author or third-party websites referred to in or on this book.

3 5 7 9 8 6 4 2

A CIP catalogue record for this book is available from the British Library.

Typeset in Bembo by Jouve (UK), Milton Keynes
Printed and bound by CPI Group (UK) Ltd, Croydon, CR0 4YY

This book is sold subject to the condition that it shall not, by way of
trade or otherwise, be lent, hired out, or otherwise circulated without
the publisher's prior consent in any form of binding or cover other than
that in which it is published and without a similar condition including
this condition being imposed on the subsequent purchaser.

Visit **www.picador.com** to read more about all our books
and to buy them. You will also find features, author interviews and
news of any author events, and you can sign up for e-newsletters
so that you're always first to hear about our new releases.

To my dad, my sister, and my best friend Sally
(and the music I've danced to with each of you)

'Oppressors take very seriously the possibility that culture can be used as a vehicle for the organization of protest or rebellion or, dammit, revolution.'
Cecil Gutzmore

'This is the real bone of contention between civilization and collective ecstasy: Ecstatic rituals still build group cohesion, but when they build it among subordinates – peasants, slaves, women, colonized people – the elite calls out its troops.'
Barbara Ehrenreich

'Carnival is not really a festival given for the people, but one the people give themselves.'
Johann Wolfgang von Goethe

Contents

Introduction   1
'This is a journey'

1. **Beat Down Babylon**   7
   Soundsystem culture, racism and the roots of UK dance music

2. **British Tribal Music**   35
   Free festivals, new Travellers and rural proto-rave

3. **Dance Before the Police Come**   65
   God's Cop, Victorian values and Thatcher's war on vice

4. **Make Some Fucking Noise**   91
   Techno terrorists versus the Criminal Justice Act

5. **Tony and Gordon Go Large**   131
   Big beat manifestos, the 'creative industries' and the rise of the superclub

6. **Some Giddy Rite of Passage?**   169
   Power, profit and prohibition in the global dance drug trade

7. **The Breakdown**   203
   Disrespect agendas and the demonization of Black British dance music

8. **Pirates' Anthem** 233
   Kiss, Rinse and the evolution of dance
   music radio

9. **Real People Doing Real Things** 263
   Broadcast TV, online platforms and the
   visual mediation of UK dance floors

10. **Strictly Business Techno** 293
    Gentrification and resistance in the
    night-time economy

11. **Plague Raving** 329
    Covid-19 and the eternal return of the
    illegal party

12. **Just Like We Never Said Goodbye** 357
    The past, present and future of UK dance
    music

    Thanks and Acknowledgements 387

    Notes 389

    Index 431

Introduction

'This is a journey'

Pick up most books which attempt to cover the full historical span of dance music, and you're likely to be told either implicitly or directly that they're the real thing: the authoritative text, the landmark history, the singular truth. This book is none of those things: it's a thread picked through a culture that's already been extensively catalogued and historicized over the last 30 years, in an attempt to draw out themes and connections which others might have missed, or whose meaning might have changed in the decades since those definitive stories were first written,* and to extend that perspective to more recent events. The narrative thread connecting all of this is, at its simplest, a power struggle: between our collective urge to congregate and dance, to lose and find ourselves on the dance floor, and the political and economic authorities which seek to constrain or commodify those messy and unstable desires. When I look at the history of UK dance music, it's this conflict I see underpinning everything, explaining how and why Britain's political and economic contexts have shaped dance music's form and function, and

---

* To take one small but illustrative example: plenty of early writing about dance music lauds the American anarchist Hakim Bey's theory of the 'Temporary Autonomous Zone' as a means to understand the revolutionary power of the rave. Bey's arguments sit far less comfortably now than in the 1990s, partly due to his pen name – an uncomfortable piece of Middle Eastern

how rave has, in turn, played a critical role in moulding the Britain we inhabit today. Hopefully I'm not alone in thinking this way, but by definition and design this is a subjective and partial perspective.

Why should it be anything else? Of all the cultural disciplines to write about, dance music is perhaps the one most deeply shaped by personal experience. Literature, theatre, even recorded music: each of these at least has some objective form from which we can derive and compare our own personal readings. But what is dance music without physical sensation, the pressure of sound from stacked bassbins, the tang of sweat in the air, the jostling of joyful bodies against yours? While some of this might be overstated – in particular the reliance throughout dance music history on the subjective experience of being on drugs – at some point, you have to accept that the only way to truly understand dance music is to *feel* it, bodily and emotionally, rather than to understand it intellectually. Trying to muscle all of that into a piece of writing capable of being both universally understood and universally accepted would clearly be futile.

Despite this, a canon has undoubtedly formed around the history of UK dance music. The two pieces of writing most responsible for that are the equally superb *Energy Flash* by Simon Reynolds and *Altered State* by Matthew Collin, to which I hope *Party Lines* might be seen as some kind of successor or response. In its simplest terms, and as laid out across those two books, the established narrative of UK dance music goes roughly as follows: house and techno are created in the Black neighbourhoods of Chicago and Detroit in the mid-1980s, gradually spreading to DJs and dance floors around the

---

appropriation for a white man born Peter Lamborn Wilson – but more importantly because of his unapologetic advocacy for paedophilia: extracts from *T.A.Z.: The Temporary Autonomous Zone* were published by US paedophile group NAMBLA in 1993, alongside various other works focusing unambiguously on Wilson's sexual interest in children. The urge to view rave culture through Bey's lens takes on a very different set of connotations when you belatedly realize that the social strictures from which he was seeking autonomy include laws around the age of consent.

world. But it's not until four British DJs – Paul Oakenfold, Danny Rampling, Nicky Holloway and Johnny Walker – go to Ibiza in the summer of 1987 and experience this new electronic music while under the influence of Ecstasy, that things truly make sense. Returning to London, the clubs the 'Ibiza Four' set up – Future, Spectrum, Shoom and The Trip – mark the first spaces in which electronic dance music and Ecstasy combine to form an entirely new cultural form: acid house.

Over the next few years UK dance music, mutating first from acid house into rave, then hardcore and jungle, rewires and revolutionizes British culture, then that of the entire world. Its ballooning popularity sees it expand from basement clubs to vast illegal raves, a wave of mass civil disobedience which eventually forces the government to act. When they do so, with the Criminal Justice and Public Order Act 1994's infamous clampdown on 'repetitive beats', conventional retellings suggest that UK dance music's relevance as a political and cultural force is largely erased. Raving instead becomes a depoliticized and unthinkingly hedonistic leisure activity, of interest only for its shifting sonic and genre qualities; a mere background hum, where once it was the heartbeat of the UK's counterculture.

The opening chapters of *Party Lines* try to deconstruct some of these myths around rave's emergence and early years. Rather than treating the legendary journey of the 'Ibiza Four' and the subjective experience of being on MDMA as the twin sparks which ignite the rest of the story, it also looks at the critical (and still largely underacknowledged) role of Black soundsystem culture in setting out not just the core sonic influences for acid house, but also the social and political landscape which it would come to occupy. The soundsystem is just one of several such antecedents underpinning rave's pre-history from the free festival movement of the 1970s, to the moralistic policing of queer venues in British city centres in the 1980s. These each reveal UK dance music not as the spontaneous, unprecedented eruption it's so often depicted to be, bursting suddenly into rich colour against the bleak monochrome of the Thatcher years, but instead the direct and largely predictable evolution of cultural and political currents which cut across late twentieth-century Britain.

Party Lines also looks to expand that narrative towards the present: where previous retellings tend to lose some of their urgency after the Criminal Justice Act is passed, this book argues that the dance floor continued to be a highly political space, albeit serving diametrically opposed aims: the soft-market economic policy and anti-Black authoritarianism of the Blair governments, but also the burgeoning 'creative industries' which came to include superclubs like Cream and Ministry of Sound. From there, these same forces of corporate capture and underground resistance run through pirate radio, broadcast and visual media, and struggles around urban space and gentrification: a process which ends in Covid-19's violent disruptions and the tentative re-emergence of more equitable possibilities for UK dance music stretching into the future.

That's not to claim that these ideas are new, or exclusive to me. While book-length overviews of UK dance music history still tend to gravitate towards those more familiar and widely-accepted narratives, *Party Lines* also draws on a rich and growing history of writing which challenges and deconstrusts those old assumptions: whether in academic work by Kodwo Eshun, Paul Gilroy, Mark Fisher, Joy White, Julia Toppin, Caspar Melville, Lambros Fatsis and many others, or in more genre-specific journalism and literature by Dan Hancox, Emma Warren, Lloyd Bradley, Ciaran Thapar and Matt Anniss to name but a few. *Party Lines* is an attempt to synthesize several of these ideas (along with my own) into an overarching narrative which, while still inescapably partial and subjective, forms a coherent through-line tracing UK dance music's shifting political, legislative and financial forms over the last forty years. It's the story of power and money shaping how, where and why we dance: the spaces we occupy, the sounds we hear, the people with whom we share the communal rituals of the dance floor, and the people to whom money and privilege accrue as a result. But it's also a story of how our collective desire to dance with each other has built modern

Britain: its social hierarchies, cultural communities, capitalist structures and legal restrictions.

The seed for this story was first planted in a north London flat, meeting the artist Jeremy Deller for the first time before working together on his film *Everybody in the Place*. He explained his concept by loading up two YouTube videos: in one, silent images of the police baton-charging the striking miners at Orgreave. In the other, the audio from the KLF's 'What Time Is Love?', all apocalyptic synth stabs and pounding drums. It's a devastatingly simple juxtaposition: how could this dense, foreboding music have been produced in anything other than the crucible of post-industrial decline and authoritarian violence? If *Everybody in the Place*'s connections between Thatcherite unrest and the birth of acid house was the starting point, then the end of the thread lay somewhere near Housekeeping – a group of aristocrats, landlords and bankers posing as tech-house DJs in the late 2010s, whose industry success laid bare the webs of money, power and influence coursing through the contemporary UK dance music scene, allowing those with privilege and access to get away with whatever they want. *Party Lines* is, in part, an attempt to work out how the former culture ended up producing the latter.

There are undoubtedly going to be things I've missed in the process, whether through the limitations of the written word, the practicalities of managing such a vast story with tendrils stretching into so many different parts of British and political life (the shift in research focus, between dancing at an illegal lockdown rave one day, and battling the Metropolitan Police to release Freedom of Information data the next, has at times been jarring) or just because of my own individual blind spots. I'm a straight, white cisgendered man writing about cultures which, while not exclusive to or defined solely by the experiences of marginalized communities, are undoubtedly rooted in those injustices. What for me feels revelatory or totemic – proto-rave hippies listening to extended synth jams at Stonehenge, police and protestors battling in Hyde Park as the Criminal Justice Act passes into law, or the post-industrial sound-and-light spectaculars of The Warehouse Project – might feel inert or peripheral to others. We all have our own dance music: the wordless rush of anonymous bodies pressed together in dark spaces; lonely nights spent in dimly lit bedrooms, pirate broadcasts emerging from the static; your first kiss in the drum'n'bass room at Fabric; the sun breaking over treetops in a distant, unfamiliar field; dry ice vibrating in the air in front of you as the speakers quake. Each of these moments tells a different story to each of us, every single one of them true. The particular story contained here just happens to be mine.

My earliest experience of dance music – before all of the sweaty basements and the Arcadian fields, the lasers and bassbins and livestreams – came from digging through my dad's CD collection as a curious child in the early nineties. One of the albums I first fell in love with was Coldcut's *70 Minutes of Madness*, a frenetic DJ mix taking cues from the duo's late-night Kiss FM radio shows, swerving deliriously and deliciously between jungle, acid techno, breakbeats and ambient interludes, layered with vocal samples salvaged from the dustbins of twentieth-century cultural ephemera. It opens with an impossibly plummy voice: the post-war actor Geoffrey Sumner, taken from a 1958 LP demonstrating the then-revolutionary technology of stereo sound, sampled previously on tracks by Eric B. & Rakim and Public Enemy. 'This is a journey,' Sumner intones, 'which along the way will bring to you new colour, new dimension, new values, and a new experience' before his voice echoes away into nothingness, and the beat drops. I hope *Party Lines* offers you something equivalent to that rather stiffly expressed sentiment: a sense of expansion and insight, evoking something which is both highly subjective and communally understood; the intuited experience and emotion of UK dance music's political and social history, brought into the light, in a form of words which you and I can share.

NOTTING HILL REVELLERS WATCHED BY POLICE, 1974

1. Beat Down Babylon

Soundsystem culture, racism and the roots of UK dance music

It is 4 a.m. on a Saturday in St Paul's, a neighbourhood north-east of the centre of Bristol known for its sizeable Jamaican community. Deep bass tones throb through the walls of an otherwise unremarkable terraced house, with the sound of reggae and soul tracks cutting through the amorphous chatter of young voices. The year is 1973: a decade since the Bristol Bus Boycott brought systemic racism onto the British political agenda, and seven years before St Paul's would explode into anger and rioting in response to aggressive policing and spurious raids on late-night music venues.

Behind each of these struggles for political and social agency, the blues dance – loosely defined as an unlicensed all-night party held in a house or other impromptu space, catering almost exclusively to Black audiences (more specifically Jamaican, or at the very least Caribbean) – formed an insistent, bass-heavy soundtrack to the forging of Black British identity, and to the birth of UK dance music. The sonic debt owed by British electronic dance music to Black culture and experience is clear and inarguable, from acid house's frantic rewiring of sounds created in the queer Black clubs of Chicago to jungle, garage and grime's stylistic inheritance from dub and reggae. Less regularly discussed are the connections between wider legislative policing or economic pressures affecting Black British lives between the 1950s and the 1980s, and the forms subsequently taken by UK dance music: from immigration and housing to employment and stop-and-search, the sociopolitical forces which first collide in the blues dance create the conditions from which global multimedia brands, lavish superclubs and illegal warehouse raves alike would ultimately be formed. The story of dance music stretches across ethnicities, cultures and identities, and race is not the only lens through which we can view it; however, to fully grasp the complex interweaving between dance music, political power and social history, Britain's complex relationship with race and racism has to be placed front and centre.

One of the young Black men crammed into this small Bristol house is the sociologist Ken Pryce, who is attending to covertly gather research material for his PhD study into the 'lifestyles, attitudes, beliefs and behaviours' of West Indian communities in Bristol, later published in 1979 as *Endless Pressure*. Having been subsumed into the throng, he will go on to provide one of the first written descriptions of what the blues dance looks, sounds, smells and feels like from the inside. On being let into the party, he joins a 'dense, teeming, sweaty mass of humanity' shrouded in weed and tobacco smoke. The atmosphere is shadowy but undeniably sensuous: attendees 'lean their heads and watch, laughing and talking' next to solo dancers 'thrusting their heads backwards and forwards' to the rhythm, alongside couples 'clinging to each other, locked in an embrace'.

Anyone who has been to a nightclub in the past forty years will instantly recognize the combination of shadowiness and sensuality at work here: the thrill of the illicit, the gloom of a windowless room full of vibrating bodies, and the subsuming force of the sound system. But there are seedier connotations also present in this account: Pryce wasn't just a sociologist but also a criminologist, a perspective detectable throughout *Endless Pressure* as he divides the various members of Bristol's Caribbean communities into reputable and disreputable categories, with the blues dance catering almost exclusively to the latter. Pryce identifies 'Something menacing, almost sinister' in the scene he witnesses, describing the attendees as 'the hardcore of the criminal underworld' and drawing direct links between late-night music and criminality which continue to influence discussions around Black British identity and culture half a century later.

Pryce was far from the only observer to draw insalubrious associations between late-night dancing and criminality. Despite this, over the second half of the twentieth century the blues dance would go on to become a vital source of refuge and release for Black and other marginalized people in the face of wider society's hostility and mistrust. Perhaps the clearest example of this spirit could be found at 103 Railton Road in Brixton from the mid-1970s to 1981, at an after-hours shebeen* run by Pearl Alcock. Born in Jamaica in 1934, Pearl would leave her French-Canadian husband and move to the UK aged twenty-five, working as a cleaner in

---

* The term 'shebeen' originates in Ireland and refers to any kind of unlicensed drinking establishment, usual open late at night and located within a domestic space. It includes blues dances but also spaces which didn't cater to Black audiences or focus on music, somewhere closer to a pub than a nightclub.

Leeds before eventually buying a clothes shop in Brixton. Portrayed in Bernadine Evaristo's novel *Girl, Woman, Other* as 'a middle aged Jamaican woman who stripped her basement of furniture, set up a sound-system and charged at the door', Pearl was also a hugely accomplished artist and a proud bisexual woman, with the empty basement of her clothes shop acting as 'the only gay bar in Brixton . . . a space like no other.'

What little oral history has been recorded from those who visited Pearl's shebeen suggests a space in which different Black and queer communities could find some shared measure of peace, pleasure and sociopolitical agency. According to the photographer, artist and historian Ajamu X: 'Pearl's was not . . . an exotic "other" place but one of the very few places in Brixton which comfortably accommodated black queer men in the 1970s.' One anonymous attendee describes a room 'packed with people dancing,' with 'a bar at the end selling Heineken or cocktail type stuff, martinis and so on.' The crowd is described as 80 per cent black, 20 per cent white, and almost exclusively male. 'Of the black guys that would go to Pearl's . . . maybe half of them would be in a relationship with a white person, and half would be in a relationship with a black person.' Another anonymous attendee describes their first visit to the shebeen as 'a terrified little white boy being sensually samba'd around by a gorgeous black man' while at the far end of the room, 'Pearl was ensconced with her little record player playing 45s, seeming so much like some African queen.'

The radical intersections at play in Pearl's shebeen reflect the physical layout of Railton Road itself, and the wealth of communal spaces and political collectives surrounding it, from Olive Morris and Liz Obi's Black feminist squat at number 121 to the UK's first gay centre, founded a few doors down the road by South London Gay Liberation in 1974. In a 2020 video walking tour, covering each of the sites of the Railton Road squats, colourful local personality Peter Bradley walks past 'apparently innocent, inoffensive, uninteresting basement flats' which have, in his words, now been 'gentrified to buggery' before recounting his experiences in Pearl's basement at

103 Railton Road. 'It was just . . . an astonishing time: something that you never would have thought someone of her courage would have been able to open and run.' There's something in Bradley's description which speaks not just to the blues dance or the shebeen, but the entire history of UK dance music: unlit and illicit spaces, built on trust and whispered word-of-mouth, driven by loud music and warm bodies, evading the wider interests of capital and property, existing somewhere between pure pleasure and political revolution.

Unlicensed and ephemeral, the very existence of the blues dance spoke to the marginalization of Black culture and people in twentieth-century Britain. Until the Race Relations Act of 1968 outlawed racial discrimination in the provision of goods and services, the widespread exclusion of Black people from huge swathes of mainstream British society remained entirely legal, with vast numbers of pubs and late-night venues across the UK operating a colour bar of varying levels of conspicuousness both before and after doing so became illegal. It's possible to trace back the British state's restrictions on Black sonic pleasure even further, to colonial systems of control which repressed music of African origin across the Empire. From banning the mbira thumb piano in Zimbabwe over its spiritual associations to the Canboulay riots in Trinidad, which arose in response to the suppression of Carnival traditions, music's power as a unifying force for subjugated people has long seen it treated as a threat, and singled out for especially restrictive treatment. When large-scale immigration began from colonized countries in the aftermath of the Second World War, these same repressive principles were brought back to the motherland too. Denied access to existing late-night spaces, the first generations of Black people arriving in Britain in the 1950s were obliged to create their own, setting the template for acid house pioneers and warehouse rave rabble-rousers of all races to follow in subsequent decades.

Count Suckle, owner and operator of one of the UK's first Jamaican-style soundsystems, describes this as a necessary and obvious response to the formal injustices of racist door policies. 'We come over from Jamaica, and we didn't have no halls of our own. There was no place for Black people to go. They wouldn't let us in club, they say you've got to be a member, but there was no member for Black people.' Duke Vin, whose soundsystem was established a matter of months before Suckle's after both had stowed away on the same banana boat from Kingston in 1952, frames the issue similarly: 'We didn't have nowhere to go. I couldn't find nowhere to go for a dance, so I start me own.'

Despite the passing of numerous anti-discrimination laws over the ensuing decades, informal policies which continued to restrict Black access to and ownership of licensed late-night spaces merely became more subtle or insidious, hidden from view or dressed up in polite bureaucracy – door policies which ban hoodies and baseball caps for example – rather than being truly reckoned with. Mykaell Riley, vocalist for UK reggae band Steel Pulse before becoming an author and academic, describes the racism embedded in British nightlife as common knowledge growing up in 1970s Birmingham: 'We knew we didn't have access to venues, that there was a door policy across the clubs. They'd let a few Black women in, for the gaze of the white men, but Black men were prohibited.' Racial control of space was linked directly to financial ownership and capitalist hierarchies. 'It was an unwritten policy right at board level. The people that own the buildings, own the clubs, made it clear to the managers of those premises that they didn't want Blacks in that room.' Those forces in turn shaped and politicized the music itself, he explains: 'It meant that you had to develop your own space to share and engage with your music. But it also meant that you focused inwards, on your community, and rethought the principal audience for the music you were making: it was about appealing to the Black community first . . . It wasn't that we started out wanting to be political, we just wanted to reflect our experience, and that was our experience as a community.'

In many cases, the persistent exclusion of Black men and women from public space was a direct extension of nakedly racist ideologies:

in 1965 the National Front marched through south-east London in support of the colour bar in operation at a pub called the Dartmouth Arms. At other times, the approach was more subtle. The academic Rob Waters identifies the use of different spaces within purportedly integrated venues as a tool with which racial hierarchies could continue to be enacted: the saloon bar, invented in the nineteenth century as 'a segregated space within public houses' reserved for middle-class drinkers, distinct from the working-class space of the public bar, was reimagined in the post-war years as a space reserved for white customers, while Black drinkers 'were refused service at the saloon bar, and redirected to the public bar'. Anthony Stevens, who ran the Soul Control soundsystem in Manchester during the 1980s, tells the story of a club owner friend, who went on a professional training course, being told by their lecturer: 'These are the three golden rules of venue management, which don't leave here: No blacks, no Pakis, no sportswear.'

While soundsystem operators like Duke Vin and Count Suckle might have been shut out of late-night venues in the immediate post-war years, Black music itself certainly wasn't: indeed, the influence of African and Caribbean music on the UK dates back well before post-war increases in migration or Lord Kitchener singing 'London Is the Place for Me' from the gangplank of the HMT *Empire Windrush*, from the Southern Syncopated Orchestra wowing Edwardian music halls in 1919 to Caribbean artists playing a major role in the British jazz scene of the twenties and thirties. In his authoritative history of Black music in London, Lloyd Bradley identifies 'a veritable flood of Caribbean musicians flowing into London long before the Windrush hove into view'. But both before and after *Windrush* these cultural exchanges would happen almost exclusively on white society's terms, with Black music permitted, let alone celebrated, only when it was played in white-owned spaces, incorporated into white-controlled branches of the music industry, or enjoyed by audiences deemed acceptable to white expectations and fears.

While a number of Black-owned venues were successfully established in the 1960s, they were largely hounded out of existence in the following decades. Despite the popularity of spaces like the Q Club in Soho or the Four Aces in Dalston, Black artists, venue owners and audiences would regularly find themselves at the whim of economic and political power structures from which they were systematically excluded. The Four Aces faced near-constant police raids and threatening visits from the National Front while under Black management. 'It was a struggle to keep the doors open and hold on to the licence,' recalls its owner, Newton Dunbar, who would be personally prosecuted no fewer than fourteen times, each ending without a conviction. Similarly, Count Suckle's foundation of the Q Club in 1962 was the direct result of heavy-handed policing at the previously whites-only Roaring Twenties in Soho. After Suckle's DJ sets there proved so popular with both white and Black dancers that venue management were forced to formally integrate the dance floor, the Metropolitan Police began raiding it on a near-weekly basis. With the space rendered essentially unmanageable, Suckle was swiftly and sharply encouraged to relocate.

More famous still is the Mangrove restaurant in Notting Hill and its owner Frank Critchlow, both targeted relentlessly for years over spurious allegations of drug-selling on the premises. With a clientele that stretched from Black radicals like Althea Jones-Lecointe and Darcus Howe to rock stars and Hollywood actors, the Mangrove was a magnet for countercultural networking and increasingly aggressive state attention. A protest march over police harassment of the Mangrove's customers (white and Black alike) ended in a riot, with Critchlow and others eventually acquitted after a trial which acknowledged, for the first time, racism amongst Metropolitan Police officers. This friction, between interest in or demand for Black culture and white society's fear of Black agency, is a recurrent theme throughout the forty-year history of UK dance music: one research project on blues dances in Nottingham describes the police turning up in force to shut down a party, kicking out the dancers and confiscating the soundsystem equipment – all while conspicuously helping themselves to repeated servings of curried goat.

Waves of police violence targeting Black venues in the post-war years were accompanied by legislative changes intended to further squeeze the civic space afforded to immigrant communities. The Town and Country Planning Act of 1962 and the Licensing Act of 1967 tightened the requirements on premises that sold alcohol, thereby creating new grounds on which they could be shut down. The Noise Abatement Act of 1960 and the Control of Pollution Act 1974, meanwhile, put noise pollution on a statutory footing for the first time, enabling the same aggressive approach to then be taken against venues which didn't sell alcohol. When the late 1950s and early 1960s saw a boom in Black members-only drinking clubs based in basements and back rooms – a replacement for the pub, in much the same way that a blues dance paralleled a nightclub – legislation was promptly utilized to close them. Until the Town and Country Planning Act 1962, these clubs were able to open without prior permission from the council, and would require a formal licensing review before they could be closed. Often, those proceedings would be triggered by complaints from their neighbours, with 'local residents and local papers alike tirelessly [providing] an image of these clubs as dens of vice and iniquity, where gambling, prostitution, drugs and violence were commonplace.' Unlike the Race Relations Act, whose passage clearly didn't bring an end to discriminatory door practices in white-controlled spaces, legislation designed to shut down Black recreation was strictly enforced. As part of the unambiguously named 'Operation Shut Down', the chief of Brixton police announced in 1962 that 'clubs which continue to run after being refused a license will be raided on a warrant, every night if necessary, to let the people running them see they cannot flout the law.' Lambeth Council were similarly enthusiastic, saying that 'the new Act now means we shall have more control over the clubs, many of which have become dens of vice.'

These policies weren't limited to venues specifically, but imposed across all areas of Black British life. With the Commonwealth Immigrants Act of 1962 and the Commonwealth Immigration Act of 1968, the British government moved to exercise control over the previously unrestricted inward movement of its former colonial subjects, with cynical concepts of post-war economic utility phased out and replaced by Enoch Powell's delirious visions of innate Black barbarity. The passage of the Rent Act in 1957 removed state-dictated rent controls, allowing unscrupulous private landlords to charge extortionate sums to Black tenants for properties in slum-like conditions, knowing that they'd be systematically excluded from consideration by others: one 1956 survey of London landlords found that 90 per cent were unwilling to take on Black lodgers. The 'sus' law* empowered the police to stop, search and arrest anyone they suspected of *intending* to commit any other arrestable offence (carrying a maximum prison term of three months) rather than requiring either evidence or reasonable suspicion that a specific offence had already been committed. While 'sus' was restricted to pre-defined areas of concern (these were located primarily in London, which accounted for more than half of all searches conducted under 'sus' powers) its definition of intent was so broad as to essentially give the police unfettered discretion to stop, search or arrest anyone, at any time, for any reason – the antecedent of today's highly controversial 'stop and search' powers, themselves subject to much the same concerns over racial disproportionality as the 'sus' laws once were. These powers were justified by the Home Office as 'one of the few provisions which permits crimes to be prevented, as opposed to being detected after the event' but in practice 'sus' created a free pass for officers to harass and intimidate young Black men without fear of consequence.

When public anger at this heavy-handed policing finally bubbled over in St Paul's, Bristol in 1980, and in subsequent uprisings across Brixton, Toxteth, Handsworth and Chapeltown the following year, 'sus' was formally taken off the statute books. Three years later, near-identical powers were reintroduced via the Police and Criminal

---

* Or to give it its full title, 'An Act for the Punishment of Idle and Disorderly Persons, and Rogues and Vagabonds'. Its passage into law in 1824 preceded the creation of the Metropolitan Police by some five years.

Evidence Act in 1984. Where police raids and noise restrictions were used to shut down licensed spaces, 'sus' and other laws were used to harass unlicensed soundsystems. DJ Dubplate Pearl, interviewed by the author Caspar Melville in 2017 for the Bass Culture Research project, recalls police interference as a constant presence in her life: 'Harassment from the police, we got that all the time: at our functions, any time we went out, even coming from school we'd be stopped, or if we're in the West End we be stopped for whatever reason, with some stupid excuse . . . that was the kind of the thing you were up against.' Steel Pulse would turn police violence at an unlicensed party into the subject of a song itself, with the lyrics to 1982's 'Blues Dance Raid' describing the police storming into a party, smashing up the speakers and turntables, and roughing up attendees.

For centuries, Black art has addressed violence and racism head-on in an attempt to reclaim or find liberatory meaning within those collective experiences: 'To create art amid sorrow or oppression is to insist on excavating meaning from the dull senselessness of pain,' argues the writer Hannah Giorgis. 'Blues Dance Raid' attempts to do exactly this, transmuting the pain and destruction inflicted on the soundsystem and blues dance into beauty, with the song's unstinting lyrics set to sweet melodies and an irresistible rhythm. It's a form of storytelling which connects back to the slave spirituals of the American South, and forward to the anti-authoritarian flex of later UK dance music, from Shy FX's 'Sound of the Beast' to Skepta's 'DTI'. In each case, the violent shutdown of one party becomes the soundtrack for the next: when in 2012 Norfolk Police posted a video of sledgehammer-wielding officers smashing up a seized soundsystem, the footage was sampled and re-mixed within weeks for a promotional video advertising another unlicensed rave. In a live version of 'Blues Dance Raid' recorded in 1993 Steel Pulse gradually slow the bass and drums down to a glacial crawl, as if someone's broken into the party and switched off the turntable, before the full band surges back in, at full speed, utterly triumphant.

Linton Kwesi Johnson's poem 'Five Nights of Bleeding', published in 1974, offers a bleaker response to these political pressures, and a premonition of the violence which would erupt around the blues dance during the late 1970s and early 1980s. Johnson describes not just the 'Babylonian tyrants' of the police, but their aggression becoming internalized by the audience, and turned inward on itself: against the backdrop of a hot, tar-black night, the attendees are driven first to madness, then violence among themselves. Racist policing is depicted as the driving force behind a collective psychological collapse within Black communities, a self-negating anger that kicks back at the state, but also rots disempowered groups from within. Dedicated to Leroy Harris, fatally stabbed at a blues dance in south London and mentioned in the fourth of the poem's five verses, 'Five Nights of Bleeding' reflects Paul Gilroy's assessment that blues dances were increasingly seen by the authorities as 'sources of antipolice violence rather than simply places in which the licensing laws were being broken.' Signed to Richard Branson's Virgin Records in 1978, Johnson would record 'Five Nights of Bleeding' for his debut album *Dread Beat an' Blood* with backing from groundbreaking UK dub producer and musician Dennis Bovell. David McNamee writes that the recorded version '*becomes* its subject' with its 'slinky, stalkerish skank' mirroring the heat and tension of the sound clash itself, while the lyrics 'scan like grave pleas for sanity as carnage erupts.'

Bovell's involvement underlines this sense of paralysing claustrophobia: in 1976, he was imprisoned for riot and affray – common law offences similarly archaic to 'sus' – in relation to an incident occurring two years earlier at the Carib Club in Cricklewood. Police claimed they'd entered the Carib during a soundclash at which Bovell's Sufferer HiFi soundsystem was competing, in order to arrest a man suspected of stealing a car; critics would later point to the fact that the same club had been raided four times before as evidence that the police were deliberately targeting it. According to Bovell, aggrieved dancers freed the suspect in question, whom the police had arrested in the toilets of the club, forcing officers to retreat, running blindly into the toilets and locking themselves inside while 'people hammer[ed] on the door to beat the shit out of them.' After the police extracted themselves, they returned swiftly with reinforcements in the form of 140 officers and a dog team, before sealing off the roads around the club, shutting the party down, and forcing everyone out. Newspaper reports described officers chasing Black youths and 'beating them with truncheons' while a white witness recounted seeing a police dog 'chasing a young black woman and tearing at her clothes.'

Of the forty arrests made in relation to the Carib, few made it to trial and fewer still to a verdict: one suspect, forced to sign a confession after being beaten by the police, was subsequently found not to have left his home at all on the night in question; another, accused of owning a knife which had apparently fallen from the back pocket of his trousers during the raid, modelled said trousers for the jury, revealing them to be 'tight fitting, and without a back pocket'. Bovell's arrest hinged on accusations that he'd used his soundsystem to encourage violence against the police, getting on the mic to shout 'Get the boys in blue!', something Bovell has long denied on both factual and linguistic grounds, the idea of speaking in a 'hardcore Cockney accent' clearly absurd. 'Which black man you know going to refer to the police as the boys in blue? *Never.*' In a prosecutorial approach which pre-empts policing and judicial responses to later genres like grime and drill, Bovell was accused of involvement in that shadowy and most ill-defined of organizations, a 'gang' – thus rendering him violent by proxy, despite his own lack of violent behaviour – and of engaging in a nebulous form of rhetorical violence by merely playing music deemed inflammatory. In Bovell's case, the police alleged he had fomented disorder at the Carib by putting on Junior Byles's 1972 cut 'Beat Down Babylon' during the raid, a tune which combines lyrics about standing up to evil with luridly realistic whip-cracking sound effects: the owner of the Carib recalls a senior inspector telling him that 'by giving him Dennis the rest could go free and I could run the club as I liked.'

Despite the flimsiness of the evidence against him, Bovell was found guilty at a second trial, after a hung jury in the first, and sentenced to three years in prison; six months later, the Court of Appeal overturned the original judgement and freed him.

The attitudes of police officers and judges towards blues dances, soundsystems and Black cultural expression flowed downwards from their political masters. While not mentioning music directly, then Leader of the Opposition Margaret Thatcher's claim in 1978 that 'people are really rather afraid that this country might be rather swamped by people with a different culture' and that 'people are going to react and be rather hostile to those coming in' spoke clearly to the frictions that surrounded Black late-night social spaces. In 1981, Tory MP Jill Knight (one of two MPs who would later introduce the landmark anti-gay legislation Section 28) spoke in the Commons about a blues dance in her constituency, which she described as a 'a seething mass of people, 99 per cent of whom were of the Rastafarian type, who can look a little frightening.' Knight flipped the exclusion of Black people from licensed venues on its head, portraying it instead as favourable treatment. 'I must be frank and voice my fears that because of the race connotation these parties are not treated as they would be if the persons concerned were of a different race. If we tried to cram 200 people into a very small house, charged them £2 a head for entry, smoked marijuana and played music all night, the authorities would be down on us like a ton of bricks.' Knight ended her speech with the same oratorical flourish as both Thatcher and Enoch Powell before her, steeped in foreboding over the potential for simmering white resentment to boil over: superficially concerned with protecting Black people from recrimination, her language in fact pulls simultaneously in the opposite direction, emphasizing white grievances and subtly normalizing the idea of matters being taken into the listener's own hands. 'It must be stated that there will be a serious decline in race relations if that situation continues, because people are beginning to think "It is all right for that group, because nobody will touch them". That must have a very bad effect upon race relations, and eventually it will have a knock-on effect which could be very dangerous indeed.'

Rhetorical allusions to Black soundsystem culture being met with vigilante responses were far from abstract or theoretical. A month after Jill Knight's speech in the Commons, a blaze tore through a teenage house party in New Cross, killing fourteen people and injuring more than fifty. While the precise cause of the fire remains unknown, a fatally bungled police investigation provoked local anger over the apparent lack of concern for lost Black lives, a perception reinforced by Margaret Thatcher's studious refusal to engage with the victims' families: 'Thirteen dead and nothing said' would become the common refrain of those affected. Three weeks after the fire in New Cross, the deaths of forty-five white people at the Stardust nightclub in Dublin prompted immediate letters of condolence from Downing Street and Buckingham Palace, and the adjournment of Parliament. A fortnight after that, and more than a month on from events in New Cross, a representative of the grieving families finally received their first correspondence from the prime minister in the form of a boilerplate letter offering lukewarm sympathies, asserting that the police were investigating to the best of their abilities, and asking for bland condolences to be passed on to the bereaved rather than making any attempt to communicate with them directly.

The destruction of Black musical spaces was not a new phenomenon: as early as 1958, Count Suckle was forced to flee to the roof of a house on Lancaster Road after white youths firebombed a blues dance involving his soundsystem, while the Chicago-After-Midnight club in south London 'was subject to multiple arson attacks in early 1959'. Lloyd Coxsone, the Brixton-based founder of the Coxsone Outernational soundsystem and producer of early lovers' rock anthem 'Caught You in a Lie' recalls bricks being thrown through the windows of his blues dance in the early 1960s. In 1971 an arson attack at a Black house party in Forest Hill, a stone's throw from New Cross, injured twenty-two people, while a scene in the 1980 film *Babylon*, in which a fictional reggae band's studio is vandalized with National Front graffiti, is rumoured to have been inspired by a real incident targeting the band Aswad. NF members were also suspected of petrol-bomb attacks at Black-associated music venues including the Four Aces in Dalston and Acklam Hall in Ladbroke Grove, and happily claimed responsibility for burning down the Albany Theatre in Deptford in 1971. While racism is all too often couched in the bland language of 'legitimate concerns', evidence would suggest that nothing seems to set off virulent white rage quite like the sight and sound of Black joy.

This cumulative weight of bureaucratically enforced exclusion, political disdain and physical violence – the endless pressures bearing down Black British lives in the second half of the twentieth century – is the soil in which UK dance music was first planted. Black British reggae and dub would reach new heights in the 1980s with acts like Steel Pulse and Aswad becoming bona fide pop stars, and countless local soundsytems proliferating across the UK; at the same time, a younger generation would take inspiration from the blues dance culture of their parents, and adapt it for the newer sounds of hip hop and electronic dance music arriving from America. When house music initially crossed the Atlantic from Chicago, its earliest fans were not the overwhelmingly white tastemakers and crowds of Shoom, Future or The Haçienda, but Black teenagers and twentysomethings throwing parties in impromptu and unlicensed cultural spaces, drawing directly on the lineage of the blues dance. 'Soundsystems were the single most important thing for Black music in the UK . . . I was just spellbound by the whole culture of it,' says Anthony Stevens, whose Soul Control soundsystem threw blues dances and semi-legal raves across the Moss Side and Hulme areas of Manchester from the early 1980s onwards. 'When my parents first came here from Jamaica, they weren't welcome in white pubs and clubs, so it made sense that we were always having house parties, where someone would turn their home into a club for a weekend.' When Stevens and his friends wanted to host their own parties, they found themselves subject to the same constraints as their parents' generation, and adopted largely the same strategies in response. 'If we wanted to have our own events then we had to go to local community centres, gyms, or school halls, because we weren't welcome in the city centre. They didn't have music systems there, so you'd have to bring your own,' he explains.

Stevens and others didn't copy every aspect of the blues dances which had catered to their parents' generation from the fifties to the seventies, though bigger crowds and growing ambitions meant shifting from domestic locations to communal spaces, while changing musical tastes saw Motown-era soul, lovers' rock and roots reggae gradually eclipsed by rare groove, electro, hip hop and house. But in their most essential elements Soul Control's parties were still part of the same lineage, rooted in the improvisational use of ad-hoc venues and tight-knit local connections. 'When soundsystems were allied to a specific street or postcode, then that became the collective identity for all the boys in that area, and even the girls, whether they were directly involved in it or not,' Stevens says, underlining the role of soundsystems in not only offering a source of cross-generational learning at a time when Black students were still regularly treated as 'educationally subnormal', or a parallel source of income when young Black men were still disproportionately excluded from the labour market, but also enabling the creation of specifically Black local identities and civic pride at a time when these communities were still treated largely as suspect, invasive and alien. As Paul Gilroy puts it in 'Between the Blues and the Blues Dance': 'Musical culture and the elaborate social relations which eddied around it . . . created that locus and invested it with a precious democratic energy in which audiences and performers could interact and collaborate.'

Video footage from a 1986 Soul Control party in Moss Side perfectly captures this transitional moment, between the inherited forms of the blues dance, the rapidly globalising house sounds of Chicago, and the more UK-specific strains of acid house and rave which were about to burst into life. A young, exclusively Black and seemingly drug-free crowd of British youngsters jack to Adonis's 'No Way Back', their moves ranging from furious proto-rave pulsations to spins and shuffles drawn from northern soul and breakdancing, the latter a deliberate feature of the event courtesy of breaking crew Mastermind Roadshow. The audience's clothes are a spectrum of styles both forward-looking and anachronistic, from scruffy trainers and rave-adjacent sportswear, to luxuriously wet-looked Jheri curls and seventies leather jackets. This connective tissue between the Black musical underground and the birth of UK dance music has largely been sidelined in the latter's most persistent creation myths: while the illegal rave promoters of 1989 are regularly spoken about as if they were the first people to throw parties in abandoned industrial spaces, they were in fact merely iterating on the approach of earlier rare groove promoters like Shake and Fingerpop or Family Funktion. As early as 1985, unlicensed warehouse parties across London, featuring a playlist largely made up of raw American soul and funk deep cuts, set the template which acid house and rave would subsequently adopt; in turn, these rare groove parties were themselves drawn from the ideas and infrastructure of the blues dance, rooted in the soundsystem heritage of scene DJs like Norman Jay.

As the blues dance slowly morphed into something more akin to what we'd recognize today as a rave, tensions between underground credibility and mass-market profit (the former often Black, the latter increasingly white) also became increasingly visible. When DJs like Mike Pickering started playing Chicago house at the Haçienda in 1986, the crowd had been overwhelmingly Black: within a year or two that audience was squeezed out by increasing white interest, even as other clubs continued to exclude Black punters as a matter of course. Newer soundsystems like Soul II Soul occupied the same physical spaces as blues dances, but combined the energy and community of previous generations with more mixed, hedonistic and fashion-conscious crowds, their 'funki dread' stylings inspired as much by David Mancuso's New York loft parties as Linton Kwesi Johnson. Soul II Soul founder Jazzie B describes this shift as an extension of previous Black soundsystem traditions, but also an embrace of a more racially mixed present: 'White people were involved in your sound system, so ideas, equipment, and technology took on a slightly different slant.' His interviewer Lloyd Bradley agrees on the growing cultural alliance between white and Black youth: 'We grew up together, we had gone through school together, we chased the same girls together, we played football together – why not go to clubs together?'

And yet even this expanding interest in and acceptance of Black culture wasn't enough to prevent Soul II Soul being firebombed out of blues parties in Hackney by the National Front. 'We were starting to break down the barriers, because one or two club owners realized there was money in Black music,' says Anthony Stevens. 'There was a club just off Piccadilly that had a white DJ playing house music, because that was the acceptable face of what we played . . . but there was still that element of racism, because we didn't own the means of our own production.' These imbalances of access and visibility persist today, with parties like Soul Control largely written out of UK dance music history. 'The reason people still think house music got invented in 1988 was because that's when white people got on it, having heard about young Black kids playing it in the hood,' says Stevens. Acid house wasn't in fact a sudden, unprecedented cultural revolution that built itself from scratch, but merely one in a succession of musical styles to make use of the blues dance's evolving social, political and cultural infrastructure and ideology.

Alongside the shifts in culture and perspective which accompanied Black soundsystem culture's tentative crossing of colour lines in the 1980s, the blues dance also increasingly became a space in which a multiplicity of Black perspectives and experiences could be explored. Almost exclusively a male-controlled space from the 1950s to the 1970s, by the early 1980s women were forming their own relationship with the soundsystem, using it to explore specific experiences of Black womanhood. Nzinga Soundz, run by DJ Ade and Junie Rankin, describe themselves as 'one of the UK's longest running all-female soundsystems', with their journey intrinsically shaped, but not compromised, by their gender: 'From the beginning of our careers as DJs we were aware that the sound system environment was a highly codified space,' they write, describing a scene in which their presence as women was inherently disruptive to the traditional, predominantly male, soundsystem dynamic, repeatedly 'knocking people off balance whether they were DJs, MCs, Engineers or audience members.'

Ade and Rankin describe their first entry into soundsystem culture (and that of several other female soundsystem DJs including Princess, Sista Culcha and Rasta Queen) as being primarily domestic in nature: bored of being relegated to the back room of family parties with her infant relatives, the young DJ Ade would volunteer to look after the music in the living room, learning the fundamental DJ skills of how to read a room, and knowing when to drop a given tune or switch up the mood. Branching out from this to DJ at blues parties in their teens, which again occupied a domestic space, feels like a natural progression. So too does the specifically female brand of political activism which accompanied Nzinga Soundz's work: lending their support and energy not only to the *Race Today* Collective and the New Cross Fire campaign, but also to the East London Black Women's Organisation and the Nurses Association of Jamaica UK, combining Black liberation struggles with a growing societal awareness of feminist issues, threading the close-knit infrastructure of the soundsystem into these mutual networks of solidarity and support. 'There is a paradox that while as women we're held to a high standard, we're not expected to be successful,' said DJ Ade in a 2020 interview, underlining the critical role played by women within soundsystem culture, in particular women who possess 'a life-time passion for music . . . who relate with and have been actively involved in the struggles of African people, and how those communities have been impacted in response to those struggles.'

There are few places where politics, policing and Black British culture intersect more potently, or with greater effect on the subsequent evolution of UK dance music, than in Notting Hill Carnival. While it's important to distinguish between predominantly Jamaican influences on UK soundsystem culture, and the primarily Trinidadian traditions which underpin Carnival, Notting Hill has functioned for nearly seventy years as Britain's biggest blues dance: a space in which questions of culture, identity and control expand beyond the walls of a basement or youth club, and spill out onto the streets. Carnival was founded against a backdrop across Notting Hill of racist violence, far-right rabble-rousing, and police disinterest in the safety of Black residents. Standing as a candidate in the 1959 General Election, Oswald Mosley flooded Notting Hill with canvassers, but ended up losing his deposit, in part because he'd already been outflanked on the subject of rancid xenophobia by the sitting (soon to be successfully re-elected) Labour MP George Rogers. 'The government must introduce legislation quickly to end the tremendous influx of people from the Commonwealth,' Rogers stated in 1958. 'Overcrowding has fostered vice, drugs, prostitution and the use of knives. For years the white people have been tolerant. Now their tempers are up.' Earlier that year, 400 white youths had rioted through Notting Hill, attacking the homes of local Black residents and going, in their own words, 'nigger-hunting'. It was revealed some fifty years later that senior police officers had dismissed racism as a motivating factor when investigating, despite being attacked themselves by white youths wielding metal bars, and being told, 'Mind your own business, coppers. Keep out of it. We will settle these niggers our way. We'll murder the bastards.'

Similar closed-mindedness also clouded the police's approach to the transparently racist murder of Kelso Cochrane in Notting Hill in May 1959: walking towards Paddington General Hospital in the hope of getting painkillers for a broken thumb, Cochrane was set upon by a gang of six white men and stabbed to death. With eerie similarity to the killing of Stephen Lawrence some forty years later, the police refused to consider racism as a motive, bungled their initial inquiries, mishandled evidence, allowed suspects to collude on their statements, and repeatedly leaked information to the press, including untrue suggestions about Cochrane's drinking habits. Within two days of Cochrane's death, Detective Superintendent Ian Forbes-Leith asserted: 'The stabbing had absolutely nothing to do with racial conflict'. To those targeted, however, the intent was perfectly clear, as was the need for Black communities to stake out civic space and visibility for themselves. In *Policing Notting Hill: Fifty Years of Turbulence*, the area's former Divisional Commander Tony Moore identifies not just anti-Black violence but also the lack of Black community spaces as a key contributing factor in unrest across the late 1950s. What few Black-owned licensed venues or semi-legal drinking clubs existed in Notting Hill had largely been shut down by 1959, with the levels of racist violence in white-owned illegal spaces ('people with their legs shot off with shotguns and axes in their heads and this kind of thing' as one police officer puts it) generating increasing demand for illegal blues dances.

Carnival wasn't only a reaction to white violence, police disinterest and unmet demand for Black cultural space, but also an act of deliberate political praxis. Born in Trinidad and imprisoned in the US for her membership of the Communist Party, Claudia Jones was deported to Britain in 1955. Eager to continue her community activism, she founded the *West Indian Gazette* three years later, using it as a platform from which to campaign for a Caribbean carnival, and tie Black British cultural identity into wider issues on race, gender and class. When the Caribbean Carnival launched the following year, in 1959, Jones subtitled it 'A people's art is the genesis of their freedom' and ring-fenced profits to help pay the fines of both Black and white people arrested in the previous year's disorder. 'Claudia Jones was very much a Communist,' writes Angela Davis, 'who believed that socialism held the only promise of liberation for Black women, Black people as a whole and indeed for the multi-racial working class.' Ashley Roach-McFarlane writes that Jones 'understood the political importance of creating a space to foster discourse that challenged the oppressive nature of capitalism, and to articulate the oppression and violence Back people faced', describing Carnival itself as 'the spiritual and physical representation of Black resistance'. In an enjoyably literal representation of her politics, on her death in 1964 Jones was buried in Highgate Cemetery, slightly to the left of Karl Marx.

The Caribbean Carnival founded by Jones initially took place indoors at St Pancras Town Hall in January and February, to coincide with its Trinidadian counterpart. Despite having been envisioned by Jones as part of her wider socialist worldview, in its early years Carnival largely steered away from political gestures. Nicole Ferdinand and Nigel Williams's study of the roots of Carnival reveals that this friction lasted well into the 1960s, referring to 'an invited group of steel band players . . . who decided to stage an impromptu parade during the event. Some residents of the area mistook their actions for a protest, and shouted abuse at the players.' After Jones's death, the indoors Carnival became amalgamated with a separate outdoor event organized by white activist Rhaune Laslett who, as president of the London Free School, aimed to 'build cooperation and understanding between the different ethnic and religious groups living in Notting Hill' with her Notting Hill Fayre and Pageant combining English folk traditions with Trinidadian music, Irish pipers and New Orleans-style marching bands.

These early attempts to avoid overt confrontation with outside society were themselves highly contentious for some Black people. Speaking in 1978, activist and writer Cecil Gutzmore was intensely critical of these gentler early iterations of Carnival. The event was not in its early years seen as a challenging or disruptive form of culture, Gutzmore says. 'The police participated . . . and they got enormous propaganda out of it: reassurance to the black community that they were nice people.' Gutzmore's argument brings to mind the now-annual photos of Metropolitan Police officers in stab-proof vests dancing with ostentatiously feathered-and-sequinned mas parade dancers, inviting us to question who really benefits most from that exchange. As racial tensions ratcheted up across the UK over the course of the 1960s and 1970s, the idea of Carnival as a cosy jamboree in which Black culture could be enjoyed free of political context became impossible to justify: in 1969, Rhaune Laslett ceded control of the Carnival's organizing committee to a new Afro-Caribbean leadership team. Between 1970 and 1973 Carnival remained largely a peaceful if inconsistently organized affair, catering chiefly to local audiences in Notting Hill and focused primarily on Trinidadian steel bands and masquerade traditions.

By 1975, however, things had changed dramatically: the addition of Jamaican soundsystems increased both attendance and volume levels, with the era's more overtly politicized and uncompromising styles of roots reggae giving voice and focus to the frustrations already embedded within Black communities, from endemic racism to the economic malaise which had defined much of the 1970s. Once that happened, Gutzmore says, Carnival became a form of *'threatening culture* . . . and it had therefore to be suppressed or controlled . . . the state took the view that the cultural gauntlet had been thrown down.' Speaking to Paul Gilroy in 2021, Linton Kwesi Johnson identifies the entrance into adulthood of a new generation of Black people, born on British soil to immigrant parents and growing up entirely within the pressure-cooker of British racism, as a critical turning point: this generation were, he says, 'not prepared to be as reticent about the racism that we were experiencing [or] to put up with what our parents reluctantly put up with.' Just as important was the influx of white residents into a rapidly gentrifying Notting Hill, accelerating tensions with Black communities unwilling to continue being treated as disposable.

In 1976 these frictions – the same contests over space, culture and agency that had underpinned the blues dance, now writ larger than ever – erupted in violence. Caught flat-footed by the dramatic increases in Carnival attendance in 1975, there was a sustained effort by the police to either privatize the event's ownership, and thus gear it towards profit rather than politics, or relocate it. Having failed to either move Carnival off the streets (Chelsea's Stamford Bridge stadium was at one point suggested as an alternative venue, somewhat bizarrely given the reputation for racism afforded to the team's supporters at the time) or reshape its corporate structure, the police instead brought 1,500 officers to the 1976 event, intent on controlling it by force alone. As the event wound down in the afternoon, frictions between police and revellers – the police alleging a spate of pickpocketing, the crowd angry at what they saw as unjustified and over-aggressive arrests – turned into a pitched battle between hundreds of Black youths and massed lines of riot officers. Lord Tokyo's 1978 song 'Ladbroke Grove Riot' would go on to memorialize the sound of bottles smashing and women screaming, set to a calypso rhythm: the violence of the past transformed once more into the dance music of the future.

In the aftermath of 1976's disorder, Carnival's organizers splintered into competing factions, each with conflicting ideas about what Carnival represented, and differing levels of enthusiasm about it functioning as a focal point for militant political action. With Black neighbourhoods from Brixton to Toxteth continuing to witness fierce disputes with police through the early 1980s, it's perhaps unsurprising that the more politically radical factions initially won out in those disputes over Carnival's direction. But when the first death of an attendee in 1987 was followed by an audit which unearthed 'perceived financial incompetence and corruption', the balance of power shifted. By 1989 more conciliatory voices calling for 'an apolitical artistic display' took control, and the event was privatized (just as the police and council had pushed for in 1976) becoming 'widely recognised as a successful hallmark event and tourism product'. By the 1990s, Carnival's global reach saw hip hop stars like Jay-Z and Busta Rhymes appear; today, while the weekend continues to be raucous, occasionally contentious among local residents, and subjected to regular hand-wringing from the right-wing press,* it's now largely been assimilated into our collectively accepted understanding of Britain's multicultural identity, and is seen primarily as a joyous celebration rather than a massed howl of rage.

★

---

* Things have at least improved since a bracingly racist *Daily Express* leader from 1977's edition of Carnival (at which smaller but still notable levels of disorder occurred), which reads: 'War Cry! The unprecedented scenes in the darkness of London streets looked and sounded like something out of the film classic *Zulu*'.

In considering the history of Black British culture, and by extension the backstory to UK dance music, it's important to remember that this narrative isn't rooted solely in oppression, misery and hard-fought resistance, but also in a profound sense of bliss and belonging: one track by Bristol soundsystem DJs Smith & Mighty even declares that 'Bass Is Maternal', the heavy throb of the soundsystem a womb-like cloud of protection and solace. Steve McQueen's acclaimed 2020 film *Lovers Rock* sketches its narrative arc across a night spent at a blues dance, from the giddy rituals of getting dressed up to the fuzzy early morning journey home, via the transcendent joy of surrendering yourself to the sound. Its climax is elegiac rather than euphoric, though: the music drops out entirely, replaced by the low a cappella singing of the crowd. They sway together dreamily, eyes closed, turning the refrain from Janet Kay's blues dance classic 'Silly Games' – written and produced by Dennis Bovell – into something approaching a hymn or a mantra. It is a moment of pure stillness and communion, highly specific to the Black soundsystem culture of the 1970s, but easily comprehensible by anyone who's had a similar dance-floor epiphany during the ensuing decades, felt the nameless bliss of simultaneously losing and rediscovering yourself in the music. In his writing about the blues dance, Paul Gilroy references Jimi Hendrix's concept of the 'electric church' as a space in which 'healing glimpses of an alternative moral, artistic and political order' could be grasped. The dance floor assumes a state of grace, separate from the rough everyday world but shaped entirely by it: not just a temporary escape from the pressure and violence which continually mark and mar the lives of its inhabitants, but also a mechanism by which those degradations might be transcended; a glimpse of some other world which, just by being present together, we're already building.

Step out of Ladbroke Grove tube station in the late August air, weave through the thickening crowds, place yourself in front of a massive speaker stack erected on a residential cul-de-sac, and I defy you to feel like the pliant, apolitical consumer of a 'tourism product'. Even in today's more commodified and sanitized form, Notting Hill

Carnival remains the UK's most visible example of collective ownership being exerted over public space without establishment permission. It is both our biggest blues dance and our longest-running illegal rave, arguably the fulcrum around which Britain's entire history of defiant pleasure-seeking (or pleasure-flecked defiance) can be seen to turn. From the throbbing bass of the blues dance to the picket lines at Orgreave, Covid lockdown parties to pirate radio broadcasts or druids massing at Stonehenge – everything connects here. 'Massive in size, working-class in composition, spontaneous in form, subversive in expression and political in nature – the ingredients for carnival are explosive,' wrote Gary Younge in 2002, in words which might equally apply to all UK dance music, and the urge it embodies to throw off the oppressive weight of everyday existence. 'It soon becomes clear why so long as there has been carnival, the authorities have sought to contain, control or cancel it.' It's in this sense of the carnivalesque – a concept first coined by Mikhail Bakhtin to describe the festivals of the nineteenth and early twentieth centuries, with their inversion of the normal social order and opposition to systems of control – that dance music's unspoken political meaning begins to be revealed. From soundsystem to superclub, neither police officer nor politician can deny that these are ultimately *our* streets, *our* spaces, or that we can be prevented from occupying or reimagining them only to the extent that we collectively consent to be.

In this, the blues dance and the wider carnivalesque set the template for every moment of euphoria and conflict within UK dance music to follow: Black soundsystem culture would soon crash headlong into the birth of acid house, involving not only the familiar disruptive influences of Ecstasy and electronic rhythms, but also the political and cultural battles already being waged across the 1980s within parallel British subcultures, from New Age Travellers and anti-capitalists to football casuals and queer Soho club kids. For each of these groups, just as for Black communities before them, the dance floor would rapidly become not only a site of hedonism and excess, but also one in which new social structures could be envisaged, and new forms of resistance enacted.

A CELEBRATION OF THE SUMMER SOLSTICE AT STONEHENGE, JUNE 1984

2. British Tribal Music

Free festivals, new Travellers and rural proto-rave

It is late in the summer of 1973, and the sun is beginning to set over the trees of Windsor Great Park. Several thousand young hippies have congregated in this verdant corner of crown-owned land, lured to drink, dance and dream by flyers declaring: 'We want a new society... We want to replace the family with the commune... We want to widen the circle of human love... We want to bring God down out of the sky and put him where he belongs.' Others have assumed baser motives on the part of attendees, with *The Sun* featuring photos of scantily clad 'hippy chicks' on page 3 and urging 'sensible young people' to stay away. As dusk approaches, Hawkwind perform on an ad-hoc stage made from a single large sheet of plywood laid flat on the grass, the seated crowd forming a circle around them while others perch on van roofs and lampposts in the fading light. Orange sunbeams glint off singer and saxophonist Nik Turner's silver cape and facepaint, as he makes theatrical gestures, outstretches his limbs and spins into an elegant pirouette; a knot of freaky dancers, some topless, one fully naked, kick yellow dust up from the parched ground; a woman in a crimson skirt writhes ecstatically and grasps at the air. Elsewhere, sun-dappled leaves cast moving shapes on tents pitched among the trees, while in the distance, out of focus, a Union Jack flaps listlessly above the ramparts of Windsor Castle. The following morning, as the festival site clears, grey rain falls on a man lying face down, alone, in the middle of a field.

Depictions of the early 'golden years' of British dance music (measured largely from early acid house club Shoom opening in the autumn of 1987 to the passing of the Criminal Justice Act in November 1994) tend to lean heavily on how revelatory they were: a wide-eyed Terry Farley recounts his first experience of Shoom by saying: 'It's just not like anything I've ever seen.' But the earlier popularity of Chicago house in Moss Side, or Notting Hill Carnival's musical embodiment of Black British unrest, each suggest that the birth of British dance music wasn't a moment of individual creative genius or an instantaneous cultural realignment, but a fluid extension of preceding social and political struggles. Just as Black soundsystems of the 1970s and 1980s – and the ways they were policed, legislated against and politicized – were pivotal in shaping the forms dance music would subsequently take, so too were the pressures surrounding a predominantly white subculture over the same time period: the growing circuit of free festivals, and the group of regular attendees who would eventually become known as new Travellers.*

---

* While the travelling communities discussed in this chapter are most commonly referred to as New Age Travellers, this term was both media-created

Alan Lodge is a sprightly, mischievous figure who sits at the heart of multiple British post-war countercultures as participant, activist and documentarian. Having experienced a political and musical awakening at the Windsor free festivals of the early 1970s, he would go on to organize festival welfare services for the new Traveller communities of the 1980s, and campaign against the Criminal Justice Act on behalf of early nineties rave soundsystems, all while acting as one of the most important investigative photo-journalists embedded within those groups, documenting their shifting tensions with the police and wider state forces. Camera permanently wedged between a ubiquitous woollen beanie and the bushy facial hair which gave him his nickname of Tash, Lodge represents a direct link between the free festival hippies of the 1970s and acid house ravers in ensuing decades, and resistance to the shared authoritarian pressures facing them.

Lodge sees the treatment dished out to these different groups by police and others in the second half of the twentieth century as merely one chapter in a much deeper conflict which dates back millennia: between a nomadic relationship with the land, in which it belongs simultaneously to no one and everyone, available at any moment for temporary collective use by whoever happens to be passing through, and a settler mindset in which each patch of soil is parcelled up for individual ownership and control. Lodge talks about free festival hippies, new Travellers and illegal ravers as the descendants of those first itinerant tribes, making use of England's communal spaces for ephemeral pleasure. However, since time immemorial that approach has aroused the distrust and frustration of settled communities, who see those same spaces as belonging exclusively to themselves, and view their use without permission or payment as an affront. 'It's the hunter gatherers versus the farmers, it's five or six thousand years old. We still haven't decided how to

---

and unpopular with Travellers themselves. Following the lead of researcher David Christopher, this book uses the collective term 'new Travellers' preferred by those to whom it refers.

deal with the fact that some people want to set up camp, build fences and houses, and farm things, while some people want to stay on the road. What happens when a nomadic group are passing through, and the settlers' fields are in the way?'

This same friction is visible in even our earliest societal myths: the Old Testament story of Cain and Abel, in which the farmer Cain murders his sheep-herding brother after the latter drives his flock across the former's fields, has been described as a parable for conflicts between agricultural and nomadic communities during the Bronze Age. Those same frictions would be repeated in later English struggles over the control and use of land: where peasants once exercised collective use of commonly held land on which anyone was free to graze their flocks, from the 1200s onwards these open fields would increasingly be 'enclosed' and handed over to individual landowners, then rented back for a profit to the people who previously used them for free. This process of privatization consolidated power and money in the hands of the already-wealthy few, set the conceptual template for colonial expropriation of foreign land, and eventually drove the urbanization of a formerly agricultural working class: between 1760 and 1870 one-sixth of England's common land was enclosed, pushing the people it had once supported into rapidly industrializing cities. The enclosure of the commons also sparked repeated peasant and proletarian revolts: folk-rock band The Levellers, heavily associated with new Travellers in the late 1980s, would take their name from a seventeenth-century dissident group known for flattening the hedgerows used to cordon off previously open fields. Alan Lodge, meanwhile, compares the Traveller and free festival communities of the 1970s and 1980s to another earlier group: the travelling players of the Elizabethan era. 'You don't have a theatre in every village, but if you have a travelling show, then you can bring that entertainment to more remote parts of the country'. From these early modern traditions of itinerant play and commerce – not just the touring theatre but also the market and the fair – would spring the Victorian circus, the music festival and the illegal rave. Barbara Ehrenreich's book *Dancing in the Streets: A*

History of Collective Joy makes the historical connections between physical space, political control and communal pleasure even clearer, tracing a thread from society's earliest tribal rituals and Bacchanalian rites through the secularisation of religious festivities in the Middle Ages, to the 'carnivalization' of sporting events and the birth of rock 'n' roll.* 'The repression of festivities and ecstatic rituals over the centuries was the conscious work of men, and occasionally women, who saw in them a real and urgent threat,' she writes. 'When one class, or ethnic group or gender, rules over a population of subordinates, it comes to fear the empowering rituals of the subordinates as a threat to civil order.'

By the early 1970s this inherited combination of the radical, collective, nomadic and carnivalesque had coalesced in the form of the UK's first free rock and pop festivals. The inaugural Windsor Free Festival in 1972 was tiny, chaotically disorganized and met with sardonic bemusement by onlookers. The event was launched with a press conference in Holland Park: 'Gathered around a withered tree at sunset', reads one report from the *Kensington Post*, 'the 100-odd with hair, ponchos, kaftans and coats-of-many-colours limp in the still summer air looked not impressive . . . the whole thing seemed quite laughable.' The report goes on to note that none of the bands scheduled to appear had shown up, presumably on the basis that the event's emphasis on total freedom meant they wouldn't be getting paid. In another vignette from the same article, reminiscent of nothing so much as *The Young Ones*' resident downtrodden hippie Neil, an impassioned attendee chants the refrain 'Give Us Freedom!' and exhorts others to join him, before eventually realizing that no one else can be bothered.

Yet by 1974 the Windsor Free Festival had grown from these

---

* Curiously, considering it was written in 2006, *Dancing in the Streets* makes no mention at all of electronic dance music, despite rave culture being arguably the single most important form of 'collective ecstasy' in the world at the close of the twentieth century. If this book is an attempt to build on or fill in the gaps around writing by people like Matthew Collin and Simon Reynolds, then Ehrenreich's work can also be added to that list.

inauspicious beginnings to attract thousands of people. Watching Super 8 footage of the 1973 edition, the music, rhetoric and style – all long-haired jams, handmade kaftans and hippie earnestness – feels utterly distinct from footage recorded at Sunrise and Energy raves fifteen years later, with their laser-lit sensory overload and bug-eyed velocity. And yet despite these stylistic differences, what feels striking about the 1970s free festivals is their similarity to later dance music in atmosphere and intention: the illicit social interactions at play, the freeform and loosely politicized sense of transgression, the intangible feeling in the air, glimpsed fleetingly on old home-movie footage. After all, both of these events are interested in many of the same things: the occupation of rural space without state approval, using music to create spaces outside normal social expectations and restrictions, as well as a dedication to sensory pleasures and chemical excess. A band like Hawkwind feels easy to dismiss today, with their noodly guitar solos, interpretative dancing and endless references to wizards and spacemen: an archaic midpoint between naive hippie psychedelia and cringeworthy prog rock posturing. Place a motorik space-rock jam like 'British Tribal Music' – a squall of spiralling synthesizers, heavy riffs and propulsive drums included on Hawkwind's 1980 LP *Levitation* – next to the dubby proto-house tracks emerging from the clubs of New York and Chicago at much the same time, like the Peech Boys' 'Don't Make Me Wait' from 1982, or the sleekly futuristic acid tracks which would follow by the middle of the decade, and Hawkwind feel like they come from a different era or universe altogether. But if we set aside each track's purely sonic attributes, and focus instead on their social function, those stylistic differences start to dissolve. Both the archaic chug of 'British Tribal Music' and the robotic futureshock of DJ Phuture's 'Acid Tracks' are ultimately doing the same thing: using music as a tool for the listener to lose their mind while dancing in a field somewhere in rural England, along with several thousand other freaks all sticking two fingers up at authority.

For a young Alan Lodge, the urge to veer away from polite society and into the free festival scene was driven not by this idea of countercultural debauchery but a sense of civic duty. 'I was originally interested in joining the Royal Air Force, but then I went to a couple of free festivals at Windsor Great Park, and I turned left. I joined the London Ambulance Service . . . I'm interested in public service, I think people need to do things for their society. But at the same time I was interested in the development of these free festivals.' In 1972 Lodge helped found Festival Welfare Services, a group providing medical support for 'these folks in the festival scene that were breaking arms, falling under trucks, having babies, doing drug overdoses and half a dozen other things'. In doing so, Lodge was inspired in large part by Middle Englanders claiming that the emerging free festivals were 'a drain on society', overwhelming local health services in whichever area they took place: the formation of a parallel support system within the festival's own infrastructure was intended to head off such criticisms.

Lodge's political engagement reflected the broader free festival scene's roots in radical collective action: the Windsor Free Festival's main organizers included Bill 'Ubi' Dwyer and Sid Rawle, both major players in the squatters' rights movement of the early 1970s; the former managed the festival from a squatted commune in Holland Park, choosing Windsor Great Park in part for the provocative political symbolism of its proximity to the Queen's residence, and subtitled its first edition 'Rent Strike: The People's Free Festival'. As the number of squatters across the UK increased dramatically during the early 1970s, so too did attendances at free festivals; by the end of the decade, the hardcore festival goers moving from weekend to weekend had begun to solidify into a more permanent new Traveller community, even if they were (to varying degrees) distinct from the generations of Gypsy and Roma travellers which preceded them, both in terms of not constituting a distinct ethnic group, and their retention of 'extremely elastic ties with settled society, sometimes preferring to return for shorter or longer spells as the need arose.' Lodge says:

> Sometimes the travellers came from Gypsy stock but more often than not, they were squatters in the inner city; with the advance

of Thatcherism, they were starting to get excluded in large numbers, with no work, no home, no prospects . . . It became obvious that if people got together and pooled resources, they could punch above their weight. If eight people put in 60 quid each, they could get a bus, put a mattress in the back, then they've got shelter and a support network. And as that became a more obvious thing to do, more people did it.

Squatting and the burgeoning new Traveller movement continued to function as an extension of centuries-old disputes between private and communal land ownership: the enclosure of the commons re-enacted in a post-industrial landscape. While the authorities of the 1970s and 1980s didn't go as far as their fifteenth-century predecessors – who eventually sent the leaders of the Levellers to the Tower of London – they nonetheless pushed back with increasing force against contemporary threats to private property, social order and traditional peace and quiet. Scheduled to last for ten days, the Windsor Free Festival of 1974 was swamped by Thames Valley Police six days in, after the crowd had swelled to more than 2,000 people. Penny Rimbaud – born Jeremy Ratter, then a key member of the free festival counterculture, later a founder of the punk band Crass – describes police 'dragging away a young boy, punching and kicking him', quoting another attendee who apparently witnessed 'a pregnant woman being kicked in the belly, and a little boy being punched in the face' before being himself attacked for questioning the police's behaviour. Organizers including Dwyer and Rawle were imprisoned for a month the following year, after merely handing out flyers advertising a putative 1975 Free Festival on the same site: an incredibly harsh sentence given their alleged crimes. *The Times*'s coverage of events was vastly more muted, but tacitly acknowledged that the police may have overreached: 'Accusations of unduly rough tactics will have to be inquired into' they admit, accepting that the police's actions appeared to inflame rather than diminish tensions, and that even those without previous cause for anti-police sentiment 'may today be nursing a disillusionment that will not fade rapidly or make the relations of the police with the public any easier.'

Following criticism of the police's actions at the Windsor Free Festival, and accepting on some level that the popular demand the event reflected had to be directed *somewhere*, Harold Wilson's government attempted to transfer proceedings to an abandoned RAF base at Watchfield in Oxfordshire. However, in doing so they missed the crucial point that free festivals, just like illegal raves, derive their cultural cachet and popular appeal in large part from their emergent, unpredictable and illicit nature: a government-run illegal party is by definition an oxymoron. With meagre attendance and a muted atmosphere at Watchfield, whose barren concrete flatlands were also far less enticing than the wooded groves of Windsor, the free festival crowd instead chose to align themselves with preexisting nomadic networks of ritual, celebration and protest, and shifted their attentions to the solstice celebrations at Stonehenge. This felt historically and culturally apposite: Stonehenge has long been of deeper historical significance to nomadic groups in British life – 'a site of social centrality, a shrine around which their lives as well as the stories they told about their lives revolved' – while research published in 2020 suggests that part of its original purpose may well have been rooted in music, with the stone's acoustics focusing sound within the circle and blocking outside noise. A tiny, largely undocumented gathering appears to have taken place at the stones in 1972, echoing both ancient Neolithic ceremonies and the reconstruction of English folk rituals in the eighteenth and nineteenth centuries, but in 1974 rock fans started to gather in numbers at the stones, with many arriving as a direct result of the police's violence at Windsor.

They were inspired to varying degrees by the enigmatic and puckish figure of Philip Russell, another organizer of the Windsor Free Festival better known as Wally Hope. Born into a wealthy Hertfordshire family, the death of Hope's father generated a sizeable trust fund which afforded him space and time to cultivate his creative and anti-authoritarian interests: he 'wanted to claim back

Stonehenge – a place that he regarded as sacred to the people and stolen by the government', said his close friend Penny Rimbaud in a biography of Hope titled *The Last of the Hippies*, 'and make it a site for free festivals, free music, free space, free mind.' Arriving at Stonehenge in June 1974, Wally's brand of impassioned, evangelical zeal and disarming naivety is summed up in his letter to a local landowner:

> *Dear Sir,*
> *With all well meaning respect, our LORD GOD and his son Jesus Christ, have ordained a spiritual pilgrimage to Stonehenge on 20th June, 21st etc to fulfill the TWO COMMAND MEANTS:*
> *LOVE GOD*
> *Love your neighbour*
> *You are and will be our neighbour. We beg of you for help, friendship and trust, if the gathering is overflowing big, we will give you any help you need, but you must respect we are to GOD's law, and trying to balance the violence, corruption, ensuing 3rd world war, oily energy crisis, to manual farming love Peace and Freedom.*
> *Your best mate WALLY*
> *For the Kids x*

When the 1974 attendees at Stonehenge – described as 'a group of drop-outs [setting] up a sordid encampment' by the government – were forced off the site and prosecuted, Wally ensured that proceedings quickly descended into farce. He appeared in court wearing a Cypriot National Guard officer's uniform, and described the charges as 'a cannon ball bouncing backwards and forwards in blancmange'. His co-defendants gave their names as Sir Wally Raleigh and Wally Woof The Dog, and their address as 'Fort Wally, c/o God, Jesus and Buddha, Garden of Allah, Stonehenge Monument, Salisbury, Wiltshire'. Penny Rimbaud, meanwhile, credits Wally with truly miraculous powers, from magicking up a flurry of snowflakes on a summer's day, to '[cutting] up a rainbow and [throwing] the pieces into the air, where they hung in strange random patterns.' His tribute speaks poignantly both to the optimism and beauty Wally regularly seems to have catalysed in the people around him, and his quasi-sacramental use of industrial quantities of hallucinogens. 'Drugs, to [Wally], were not something to "drop out" with', says Rimbaud, 'but a communion with a reality of colour and hope that he actively brought back into the world of greyness and despair.'

This description explicitly distances the new Travellers from preceding hippie counterculture (which Rimbaud and Hope both loudly disdained) but also harks forward to the abstractly politicized 'colour and hope' later injected into the drab monochrome of late Thatcherite Britain by acid house and Ecstasy. Indeed, Wally Hope's political and cultural interests position him as a kind of proto-raver: retaining the anti-authoritarian and carnivalesque urges of earlier hippiedom, but replacing its florid, utopian earnestness with something more sharply hedonistic, more politically volatile, and more clearly laced with postmodern self-awareness. In Hope's letter to the farmers around Stonehenge, something stands out along with the writing itself: a single visual motif scrawled repeatedly around the text, with which Hope attempts to express and underline his intentions. The symbol he chose would not only reflect the free festival and new Traveller scenes, but eventually become synonymous with dance music: a mischievous, inscrutable smiley face.

But this isn't a simple inheritance: Wally Hope's story would also mark a dividing line between the Arcadian daydreams of the 1960s, and the increasingly violent treatment subsequently experienced by itinerant subcultural groups, from new Travellers to ravers. It would also reflect the ravaging effects of drug use, which would play an increasingly important political role during the 1970s and 1980s (albeit medically induced in this case, rather than recreationally indulged in). Arrested ahead of the 1975 Stonehenge festival, after a spurious raid on his squat led to the discovery of three tabs of acid, Hope was forcibly sectioned and – according to Penny Rimbaud's account – so vastly over-medicated that he developed chronic dyskinesia, a movement disorder more often associated with long-term use of the antipsychotic substances he was being prescribed. Two days after the last reveller had left Stonehenge, and without his family or friends being informed, Wally was quietly released onto the streets: drugged into insensibility and without any financial or practical support, it took him two days to drive the seventy miles home. Two months later, Rimbaud writes, as 'the realisation that he was doomed to live in a half-world of drug induced idiocy made its way into what was left of Wally's brain', he took an overdose of sleeping pills and died at the age of twenty-eight. Rimbaud maintains to this day that Hope's neutralization was a deliberate policy undertaken by Westminster politicians and the police, humiliated by his regular appearances in the papers playfully thumbing his nose at their authority.

Despite Wally Hope's death, within a few years Stonehenge would become the central point in a network of festivals stretching across the country, from May Hill each spring to Sizewell in the early autumn. By 1976, free festival attendees moving from event to event had coalesced into the first semi-permanent new Traveller convoys: as with the rave-centred nomadic crews which followed them in the early 1990s, this consolidation of resources both fostered a coherent, empowering group identity, and provided logistical and physical resistance against attempts to prevent them gathering. 'Between '74 and '77 as the Stonehenge festival started getting bigger, it took on the mantle of the People's Free Festival,' explains Alan Lodge. 'The rest of the year got argued about, but Stonehenge was absolutely central.' By the early 1980s, attendance numbers were dwarfing even the biggest free festivals of the 1970s. 'Stonehenge was expanding exponentially: 1982 was huge, 1983 was twice as big again, and 1984 was actually humungous,' says Lodge. The best guesses put attendance numbers at 60,000 people, but with the festival lasting six weeks, and Glastonbury just down the road, the total numbers passing through are likely to have been much higher. 'People were *commuting*,' says Lodge, 'they went to Stonehenge, then to Glastonbury, then they went back again. I mean, if there were 60,000 in the field at any one time there might have been a quarter of a million passing through over six weeks.'

As the numbers at Stonehenge swelled from 1982 to 1984, the music on offer broadened to accommodate them. Bands like Hawkwind or the potently named Wystic Mankers continued to represent the core free festival sound, rooted in whimsical folk-rock and acid-tinged prog excursions, but something else was stirring too: while dance music's integration into the new Traveller movement would take on critical importance in the early 1990s, its seeds can be detected far earlier. Roots reggae band Misty In Roots and the Coxsone Outernational Soundsystem would both play at Stonehenge as early as 1981, with stages and festival infrastructure from Stonehenge being used in Brockwell Park the following year for a 'Cultural Herb Festival' campaigning for the legalization of cannabis. By 1984 a number of club soundsystems found their way to the stones, spinning disco, rare groove and hip hop alongside more standard protest-folk and space-rock fare. One of these nascent Stonehenge soundsystems may even offer a direct connection between the aggressive policing of Britain's post-hippy Traveller counterculture and the similar experiences of Black communities around the blues dance. While details are scarce, one of the acts listed on the Stonehenge Free Festival line-up for 1984 appears to have been the North London outfit Galaxy Soul Shuffle, owned and run by a DJ named Winston Silcott: just over a year after the festival at Stonehenge, Silcott would be arrested for the murder of PC Keith Blakelock during the infamous Broadwater Farm riots.*

---

* The product of mounting tensions between Black estate residents and police, the riot in Broadwater Farm on 6 October 1985 had been triggered by the death of Cynthia Jarrett during a police search of her home. A demonstration outside Tottenham police station turned violent after police attempted to clear the streets, and led to wider unrest: PC Keith Blakelock, responding to a fire away from the main area of disorder, was attacked by a group of around fifty people and brutally stabbed to death. With the police under immense pressure to secure convictions, Winston Silcott and two other men

One early outlier in the gradual process of sonic expansion visible over the course of the 1980s was the first 'proper' Stonehenge festival in 1974, at which the *only* music on offer was electronic, performed by a group called Zorch. Billed as England's first all-synthesizer band, they played burbling arpeggios and meditative drones on a set of three EMS Synthi AKS synths deep into Saturday night, followed by a solo set from band member Basil Brookes on Sunday, 'during which he completely freaked out a guy in the audience who thought he was conjuring up Dark Forces', according to one anonymous account of proceedings. Zorch's only LP, recorded in 1975, offers a loose and incomplete approximation of these live performances: on the 24-minute 'Return of the Elohim' triangle-wave pulses and discordant tones sweep across the stereo field, growing slowly in intensity, building to an almighty climax, then dissolving into ambient washes of soft pad sounds, submarine pings and muffled voices. What limited other evidence remains from Zorch's brief three-year existence between 1972 and 1975 suggests sonic connections between the earlier synth experiments of US groups like Tonto's Exploding Head Band and British synth-rock pioneers Gong, contemporary European synth auteurs like Vangelis and Jean-Michel Jarre, and the dreamier elements of UK rave sounds to follow – from later electronic-Traveller crossover bands like Eat Static or Ozric Tentacles to more prominent names in the UK house and techno pantheon.

Much like Hawkwind, while Zorch's wigged-out repetition and the fantastical allusions of their song titles suggest the terminally

---

were convicted in 1987 on the basis of confessions made without a lawyer present, despite evidence that they had been nowhere near the scene of Blakelock's murder; subsequent forensic analysis of police notebooks found them to have been altered. Silcott's conviction was overturned in 1991, although he remained in prison until 2003 having been found guilty of a different murder, for which he'd been on bail at the time of the Broadwater riot: he maintains that this was an act of self-defence, and that his continued imprisonment was an act of revenge for successfully overturning his conviction for Blakelock's murder.

unhip hinterlands of prog rock, a surprising amount of the sonic character of this free festival proto-rave has survived into later UK dance music. The unlicensed nature of events at Stonehenge is critical to this: with no legal curfew to adhere to and no one to tell them what to do, Zorch's synth meditations could run as long as six hours, accompanied by a mind-meltingly complex light and laser show dubbed the Acidica. Far closer in form and function to an all-night DJ set than a rock show, these performances arguably represent the very first illegal electronic music events in the UK, some fifteen years before acid house exploded and twenty years before the Criminal Justice Act was passed. Listen to fellow EMS Synthi enthusiasts The Chemical Brothers, for example, and the genetic traces of Zorch's burbling electronic reveries remain entirely detectable, from the dizzying oscillations of 'The Private Psychedelic Reel' to the cover artwork of *Surrender*, in which faded photos of free festival hippies are given a retro-futurist makeover, and daubed in hyper-saturated rave colours. There are also more telling, practical connections between free festival proto-rave and later dance music culture: not just the influence of the Acidica system on club visuals, but also Zorch's bespoke sound system, designed by a young man called Tony Andrews. In the late 1980s and early 1990s, Andrews's Turbosound rigs would become a mainstay of outdoor raves, with their presence regularly used on flyers as a mark of sonic quality; in the early decades of the twentieth century, having sold Turbosound, Andrews's newer generation of Funktion One systems became the global industry standard in underground and corporate dance music venues alike.

While the increasing size and musical heterogeneity of the new Traveller and festival scene in the mid-1980s offered exciting new creative possibilities, they also generated complex social issues within and beyond the convoys. In 1980 a group of new Traveller bikers, offended by the presence of punk bands including Crass and The Epileptics on that year's line-up, had spent their Saturday night attempting a kind of cultural coup. Throwing 'a hail of flour-bombs, cans and bottles' at the stage, attacking band members and damaging the festival generator, they declared that punk music and its fans weren't welcome at 'their festival'. Penny Rimbaud describes gangs of bikers armed with makeshift weapons, marauding across the festival site and attacking any punks they could find; he recalls 'screams of terror as people were dragged off into the darkness to be given lessons on peace and love' while others, oblivious, carried on partying around them. The emergence of the 'brew crew' as a distinct group of 'mainly angry young Travellers, feeding themselves on a diet of Special Brew and developing a penchant for nihilism, blagging and neighbourly disrespect' would deepen these intra-community tensions, establishing frictions between older, more idealistic Travellers and a younger generation more interested in letting loose: a dynamic which would only be exacerbated by the arrival of rave later in the decade. In the early 1980s John Pendragon, one of the event's original founders, attempted to establish an 'Alternative Free Festival', or a community within the community, seeking a return to the smaller scale and more whimsical sentiment of the 1970s. He was unsuccessful.

While drugs had long been sold and consumed openly at free festivals, the increasing availability and visibility of heroin during the 1980s had a similarly corrosive effect on longer-standing hippies' Arcadian ideals, much as Wally Hope's death had a decade before. 'It's a bit controversial, this,' says Alan Lodge, 'but I think we were attacked with chemical weapons, in the form of heroin. I think it was made more easily available and cheaper to some sections of the community . . . You'd sell bits of the bus to buy another fix, and eventually it'd end up as scrap metal, which you'd leave on the side of the road.' Those responsible for bringing heroin into the community would often (though not always) face community justice: 'There was a certain amount of site violence every so often . . . turfing heroin dealers off the site was done with extreme prejudice,' notes Lodge, arguing that the free festival crowd's attitude towards hard drugs often belied their reputation as fluffy hippies. Dealers caught at Stonehenge in 1984 had their cars overturned and torched, the vehicles' burned-out shells left to rot on Salisbury Plain. The police's own attempts to arrest two festival goers in 1981 had been met with collective resistance, in the form of a large crowd who swarmed the officers and freed their suspects, before destroying a police operations centre.

While acting as evidence of the Travellers' commitment to self-regulation, these incidents also served as ammunition for their adversaries among the wider public. 'They hang around for a month, living rough, playing music and leave the place in a hell of a mess,' said Michael Beaumont of the National Trust in 1984, before announcing that 'the land in its care surrounding the monument at Stonehenge cannot be used for a festival in 1985 or thereafter,' with the sheer size and environmental damage of the 1984 festival cited as key issues in their decision. In 1985 the newly formed English Heritage, who had recently taken over custodianship of the site, took out an injunction alongside the National Trust against fifty named organizers of the festival, including Alan Lodge. 'The welfare services I provided were deliberately misunderstood as part of the organisational DNA of the festival, so I was one of the people named in the High Court and forbidden from going to Stonehenge,' he says. Emblematic of authorities' misunderstanding of how free festivals operated, the injunction defined all 60,000 attendees as the 'agents' of Lodge and others, as if mindlessly under the command of some centralized command structure.

In allowing the festival to continue at Stonehenge for over a decade, however, the National Trust were in fact vastly more tolerant than several other elements of the British establishment. While the political and social implications of the free festival scene had always been apparent – allowing thousands of people to set up temporary enclaves in which laws could be openly flouted was hardly likely to go unnoticed – and governments of all stripes had treated nomadic communities poorly for centuries, Margaret Thatcher's election in 1979 marked a step-change in efforts to crowd these evolving subcultures out of British life. Thatcher's aggressive dismantling of the post-war consensus, replacing communal bonds of support, reciprocity and identity with notions of pure self-interest and self-reliance, was entirely antithetical to the collective responsibility and un-rooted freedom to which the new Travellers aspired, even as her government's gutting of British industry and slow bleeding of the welfare state served to swell the number of people drawn to life on the road. One of Thatcher's favourite slogans during her successful general election campaign of 1983 was an emphasis on 'Victorian values', which she defined as 'You [don't] live up to the hilt of your income; you respect other people's property; you save; you believe in right and wrong; [and] you support the police'; hers was a vision of Britain rooted in private property rights, Puritan meagreness and a deference to establishment institutions. New Travellers were rapidly identified as a key incubator of perceived moral degradation, and their very presence portrayed as fundamentally incompatible with British life.

Home Secretary Douglas Hurd famously described the new Traveller convoy as 'a band of medieval brigands who have no respect for the law', while the local MP for Salisbury, Robert Key, announced to the *Salisbury Journal* that he was personally investigating the role of new Travellers in spreading hepatitis and AIDS. Thatcher declared herself 'only too delighted to do anything I can to make life difficult for such things as hippy convoys', while the media regularly depicted new Travellers as 'giro gypsies', 'scum' or 'Hordes of Marauding Locusts'. This underlying animus towards alternative cultures was perhaps best embodied by infamous right-wing scandal-merchant Kelvin MacKenzie who, while editor of *The Sun* in 1980, reacted with horror when colleagues suggested that the paper cover debates over the legalization of drugs. MacKenzie dismissed the idea with a splenetic rant about who his paper was really speaking to, and by extension the people Britain was now being run for: 'He's the bloke you see in the pub – a right old fascist, wants to send the wogs back, buy his poxy council house, he's afraid of the unions, afraid of the Russians, hates the queers and weirdoes and drug dealers. He doesn't want to hear about that stuff!' MacKenzie's crowd of 'weirdoes' would undoubtedly have included the free festival audiences of the time, and certainly came to encompass new Travellers and ravers alike over coming years.

One particular rhetorical trope used to disparage both groups was an emphasis on uncleanliness: a sense of dirtiness and pollution came to define Travellers and ravers in the popular imagination, and in existential rather than literal terms. 'All large crowds have a tendency to leave a mess behind them whether they be tourists, football supporters or religious pilgrims,' notes Kevin Hetherington in his study of new Travellers. 'However these crowds might be described, it is rarely through images of dirt . . . dirt is a moral category rather than a physical one.' By contrast, Stonehenge would be seen as 'disfigured', 'despoiled' and even 'raped' by the presence of new Travellers. In 1986, Hampshire's chief constable, John Duke, would say of those attempting to reach the stones: 'Frankly, they're foul-mouthed, they smell foul, and they're soiling a treasured part of this community.' The same mindset and vocabulary would be directly transplanted to the nascent dance music scene within a matter of years: a *Daily Mail* article in June 1989 would describe an acid house party 'bearing down on an unsuspecting piece of gentle England', while the MP Stuart Randall would speak in Parliament the following year about the 'garbage and filth' inherent to illegal raves.

From the 'New Age' label to the implied hypocrisy of 'the "so-called" Peace Convoy', politicians repeatedly sought to define Traveller communities in mainstream terms, infuriating those who rejected such categorisation. 'What the fuck is a New Age traveller? It was a sneer,' sputters Alan Lodge, outraged at attempts to rhetorically sever the Traveller convoys of the 1980s from their nomadic ancestors. 'It wasn't what we called ourselves. It was an attempt to delineate us from those older stories: another way for the press to throw rocks at you.' The 'Peace Convoy' term originated in 1982, but the group to whom it referred would form the year before, when a subset of new Travellers left that summer's Stonehenge festival and made their way en masse to protest camps surrounding the NATO nuclear missile base on Greenham Common in Berkshire, in an act of solidarity; a handful spray-painted the words 'Peace

Convoy' on their vehicles as a marker of their pacifist intentions. Like so many of the sites chosen for free festivals and raves, Greenham Common was formerly public land, subjected to enclosure by way of a wartime requisition order in 1941 before being sold to the Air Ministry. When NATO announced a deal to station American personnel and nuclear missiles there in early 1981, a group of forty women and children marched 100 miles from Cardiff, setting up a protest camp at the base's gates. They, and those who joined them, would stay until the early 2000s, outlasting the missiles and even the base itself (removed by 1991 and closed in 1997, respectively). While the Peace Convoy was 'less a considered political event or zone than a regular irritant to majority culture' its presence at Greenham Common offered not just passive solidarity but active engagement, sharing knowledge and skills developed from the new Travellers' preceding years on the road.

That influence and encouragement ran both ways: held on the spring equinox of 1982, a Cosmic Counter-Cruise Carnival merged the colour, noise and hedonism of a free festival with the political aims of a protest, a precursor for rave's elision with the protest movements of the 1990s. Late on the Saturday night, as the Androids of Mu blasted out a set of raucous heavy rock in the Tibet Ukrainian Mountain Troupe Tent, members of the Peace Convoy began taking bolt cutters to the wire fence of the base. Sneaking across the moonlit ground, they crept silently up to a group of military vehicles, and poured paint into their fuel tanks. The next morning, base authorities responded by uprooting dozens of trees near the edge of the base, denying cover to anyone thinking of making further incursions. Outraged by this act of ecological vandalism, the Peace Convoy reacted in turn by tearing down large sections of the fence with sledgehammers. Evidence of the motivating force of music within their activism can be seen in the fact they set up a PA on a flatbed truck to provide a soundtrack for their demolition; following the Peace Convoy's initial assault on the base's infrastructure, the wider peace camp's use of direct action would become increasingly fearless, from protestors chaining themselves to fences to dancing on top of missile silos.

The actions of new Travellers also influenced the direction of the Greenham Common protest in less edifying ways. Their presence drew inevitable media attention, with the *News of the World* declaring that 'Hippies flout law in missile base rave-up' alongside lurid stories about orgies around the campfire and freely available drugs, eliding the boundaries between the protest and the party. This treatment of the party and the protest as interchangeable was a smear on all peace camps, writes David Taylor, 'in the same way tabloids later called all new age travellers a "peace convoy" in an attempt, by implication, to smear the peace movement as a whole.' More importantly, the bacchanalian impulses of the free festival proved to be a turn-off for the main group of Greenham Common protestors, who subsequently refocused their campaign away from a carnivalesque free-for-all and asserted the peace camp as a female-only space. Brig Oubridge, who helped convince the convoy to make their initial trip to Greenham in 1981, describes the convoy members' destruction of MoD property as 'extremely controversial within the peace movement' and ultimately 'instrumental in reinforcing the determination of a majority of the Greenham Women to keep the protests there strictly all women.' As with dance music's later political activism around the Criminal Justice Act 1994, a principle is laid down here which repeats in subsequent decades. Free festivals, illegal raves – indeed any social or musical gathering which challenges the status quo – are inherently political in their upending of traditional power relationships. But trying to corral that energy into the rigid messaging and structures of traditional political sloganeering or activism is like trying to nail fog to a wall. Partying's emergent, chaotic and elusive nature invariably makes it too slippery a thing to exploit as agitprop, and often actively undermines the political intent in trying to do so. 'It was an action conceived in a spirit of solidarity', says Oubridge, 'whose effects were almost entirely divisive.'

However messy the interactions between the new Travellers and protestors might have been internally, from the outside mainstream society saw them as a single radical bloc, and increased political awareness of free festival audiences hardened opposition towards them. 'The politics of the situation started to change,' says Alan Lodge, 'because suddenly people realized that this wasn't just a bunch of hippies who take drugs and listen to Hawkwind. They had a political worldview, and ideas about how other people should be, not just themselves.' The author George McKay quotes one convoy member who sees their targeting by the government and police as revenge for puncturing the Conservatives' reputation for maintaining law and order: 'a whole troop of crazy people going out and rejecting everything they believe in and encouraging others to join them.' In a private July 1984 speech to the Conservative backbench 1922 Committee, Thatcher spoke of 'the enemy within' – a sinister nexus of striking miners and Labour-led councils, the domestic equivalent of General Galtieri and the Argentinian army's 'enemy without', which Britain had just defeated in the Falklands. She had planned to use the phrase publicly for the first time at October 1984's Conservative party conference – declaring that 'our country is not to be torn apart by an extension of the calculated chaos planned for the mining industry by a handful of trained Marxists and their fellow travellers' and decrying the Labour party as a threat to the very principle of democracy – before the IRA's bombing of her Brighton hotel the night before her speech prompted a retreat from such volatile rhetoric. Despite this, the underlying sentiment of those words – that Thatcher and her government were engaged in a vicious war of attrition for Britain's very soul against a shadowy coalition ranging from political opponents to militant trade unions to radical activists to the morally unsound – remained critical to Thatcherism as an ideology. Travellers (and later ravers) were merely one part of this 'dangerous and oppositional culture of resistance' which posed an existential threat to British society, justifying increasingly harsh measures to quash the disruptive and destructive forces their activities threatened to unleash.

Frustrated by complaints over noise, mess and damage, the police argued for increased powers to shut down unlicensed events and move new Traveller convoys on. Conscious of the destabilizing forces which could be generated by massed gatherings, driven by a commitment to 'Victorian values' and a fear of 'the enemy within', Thatcher's government introduced a swathe of legislation designed to limit the new Travellers' ability to operate. The Highways Act of 1980 created an offence of 'wilfully [obstructing] the free passage along a highway', which was subsequently used as a catch-all charge with which to disrupt the activities of new Travellers, anti-apartheid protestors and miners' pickets alike. This was followed in 1986 by the Public Order Act, which centralized and expanded the ways in which people involved in mass gatherings could be criminalized. These powers were inspired not only by new Travellers, but also by violence at Orgreave in 1984 and the uprisings which began in Brixton in 1981; they would also go on to become the primary set of powers used to clamp down on the early rave scene in the late 1980s. But the free festivals and Traveller convoys were undoubtedly a central target: Section 1 of the law put in place a four-mile exclusion zone around Stonehenge; a steel-reinforced ring of police vehicles, roadblocks and guard dogs.

It's deep into the night in the sleepy village of Netley, Hampshire, shortly before midsummer in 1986. In the vast, sterile atmosphere of a concrete-walled police training centre the stentorian voice of the county's chief constable, John Duke, booms out over a muddy PA. 'Is everyone getting a clear, uncomplicated message?' he intones, over the insistent buzz of fluorescent lights. In front of him, ranged at long trestle tables, are hundreds of rank-and-file officers, their riot gear stashed politely under their wooden benches, helmets placed neatly on the tables in front of them; within a few hours, these men will aggressively evict a nearby camp of new Travellers, on their way to Stonehenge for the solstice, from a disused RAF base in Stoney Cross. The scene is bleakly comic: the hulking officers look like nothing so much as naughty schoolchildren, assembled in a nondescript sports hall to be lectured by an elderly headmaster. Duke's elongated vowels and upright manner make the analogy feel even more apt, and reflect the stiff-upper-lip attitude of a generation raised during the Second World War. 'Let's remind ourselves of an event nearly a year ago today,' he begins gravely, 'where some of the things that police officers did weren't quite the credit they should be.' Duke turns to a flickering cathode-ray TV, from which fuzzy images can be discerned of vans and other large vehicles moving across an open field, lines of police officers moving to intercept them, before a school minibus is stormed by a riot team wielding truncheons and shields. 'If there are any here tonight with concepts of revenge, if there are concepts of disorderly policing, I invite you to leave us now,' he intones, with almost Shakespearean gravitas.

Duke's sentiments of fair play and policing feel wooden, somehow performative, and are clearly informed by the presence of a BBC documentary crew filming his speech. Little by little, however, that mask starts to slip, and his rhetoric moves away from notions of restraint and proportion to focus on a profound clash of cultures. 'The real threat from the warriors in that convoy is substantial . . . They've shown, those invaders, a completely reckless disregard for peace . . . by subterfuge, and by moral and immoral blackmail, they're seeking to impose their self-appointed freedoms. The solution is to be found by us; it's up to you now. The setting is there, the plan is there. The dialogue has ended.' The footage of unchecked police violence, still rolling on the TV screen to Duke's right, begins to feel less like a warning and more like a tacit acknowledgement of what's required to maintain order. The footage itself dates from the previous summer, and an eruption of violence which would permanently alter the cultural and social fabric of the UK: the Battle of the Beanfield.

As demonization of the new Travellers ramped up from both the media and politicians in the first half of the 1980s – in tandem with the Travellers' own increased politicization – violent skirmishes between the police and the Travellers became increasingly common. A tiny festival at Nostell Priory in Yorkshire in the summer of 1984 ended with all 360 attendees arrested – a tactic of collective detention which would be repeated at the Love Decade warehouse rave in Leeds five years later. More tellingly in relation to the new Travellers, their vehicles would also be damaged and tents burned by the same riot police who, eight months earlier, had been bludgeoning the striking miners at Orgreave: this wasn't just about prosecuting individual offences, but destroying the infrastructure which allowed 'the enemy within' to function. The following February, CND supporters and Peace Convoy members protesting at RAF Molesworth in Cambridge were met by a phalanx of 1,500 soldiers from the Royal Engineers and 1,600 police officers, led by the Defence Secretary, Michael Heseltine, in the largest peacetime mobilization of troops in modern British history. At a cost of £6.5 million, this sizeable force swiftly erected a line of steel-and-barbed-wire fencing, and violently evicted a group described by *Spitting Image* as '100 hippies and one dog.'

The message was clear, and entirely in keeping with John Duke's address to his officers some eighteen months later: the time for dialogue was over. 'It was a complete step change in what happened to most of us', says Alan Lodge, 'but not to all. There were travellers like me who were on the road in the summer months, but liked to spend the winter in a house. But there were travellers who stayed out on the road for winter after winter: they'll tell you about being taken down slip roads of the M25 in the middle of the night, where coppers and assorted thugs would come over the embankments and give them a pasting, out of view.' Following their eviction from RAF Molesworth, the Peace Convoy 'shifted uneasily around the country for the next few months, persistently harassed by the police and regularly monitored by planes and helicopters.' Just as with the free festivals of the 1970s and the illegal rave scene in the late 1980s and early 1990s, the new Travellers' cat-and-mouse games with police across the English countryside was just one part of a larger, deeper and longer-running battle for control over the very soil of England: between a communitarian vision of common land, free for all to use and transit through; and a hierarchical one in which private ownership ruled supreme, enforced physically by the state. And yet the differences are stark, too: the new Travellers making their way inexorably towards the Beanfield weren't toying with police for the weekend thrill of it; many had families on board; most considered the convoy their only real home. While the violence dished out to illegal ravers and free festival hippies might have been inexcusable, the treatment of new Travellers in June 1985 as they neared Stonehenge was truly dystopian.

There's a photograph taken in the Beanfield which captures the chaos of that day perfectly: in the foreground, a woman named Rose Brash, dressed in a white smock, cradles a tiny infant as she walks through a field of knee-high plants; she is hunched, vulnerable, her eyes barely open, her arms bare. There is a rough discoloration of unclear provenance on her cheek; her baby daughter stretches an arm out, helplessly. Brash appears broken, terrified, utterly in shock. Behind her, snaking back through the field, stand thirty to forty riot police: the sun reflects sharply off their visors, rendering them anonymous and implacable (in the subsequent legal action brought by twenty-four Travellers for wrongful arrest, assault and criminal damage, it would be revealed that the police had hidden their identification numbers). One appears to be looking down at the crops, as if lost in thought; others mill around aimlessly in the middle distance. Beside them, stretching back into the far distance, are dotted a variety of buses: they are immobilized, emptied of passengers, their windows smashed, soot flecked around their engine grills. On the horizon, next to a low, grey clump of trees, sit a cluster of vehicles: black smoke billows ominously from their midst.

Around 140 vehicles had been met on the morning of 1 June 1985 by police blockades and lorryloads of gravel tipped across the road, preventing them from getting any closer than seven miles from Stonehenge. Alleging that the lead vehicles in the convoy had attempted to force their way through a roadblock, police began smashing their windows and hauling people out for arrest. Those further back in the convoy responded by turning through an adjacent hedge, and driving into a field abutting the road, looking either for an escape, or an alternative route toward Stonehenge.

It is here that the footage shown by John Duke to his officers, and the actions which 'weren't quite the credit they should be' began. In a piece to camera for ITV, removed from its coverage before broadcast, the journalist Kim Sabido describes the scene in front of him:

> What we've witnessed in the last half an hour has been surely some of the most brutal action by police forces in Britain for a long time. Whatever the causes, the end product seemed to be just hitting out wildly by the police, with babies in those trucks and in those buses . . . The people in those coaches who were trying to escape from the police were just grabbed, their windows were smashed, and they themselves were beaten sometimes senselessly on the floor.

Visiting the ITN footage library the following week to review the rushes of material filmed at the Beanfield, Sabido found that much of the most incriminating footage of police violence had been removed. Nick Davies of *The Observer* described the police as 'flies around rotten meat . . . There was glass breaking, people screaming, black smoke towering out of burning caravans and everywhere there seemed to be people being bashed and flattened and pulled by the hair. Men, women and children were led away, shivering, swearing, crying, bleeding, leaving their homes in pieces.' Speaking in 2016, Rose Brash describes the experiences which led to her harried, haunted appearance in front of the press cameras: 'I was pulled out of the bus, even though I had my daughter Kaya in my arms. The copper with me in the photograph looks as if he's helping, leading me to safety, but he was only doing it for the sake of the cameras.' Once they were out of sight of the press, Brash says, she was shoved into a line-up with the other Travellers awaiting arrest.

The legacy of the Beanfield was fundamental for the new Traveller movement, marking the final suppression of any hope that they might find space to create a truly alternative, self-sustaining society: the dreams of Wally Hope, Ubi Dwyer and others ending in a mass of blood, smoke and broken glass. The ramifications for wider British underground culture were similarly profound: much like the defeat inflicted on the miners at Orgreave, here was evidence that, when push came to shove, the police were willing and able to impose order by use of force. This understanding would fundamentally colour the forms subsequently taken by UK dance music, even though illegal raves would occupy much the same landscape of convoys and roadblocks, injunctions and soundsystems as the free festivals. Rather than loudly declaring themselves a utopian alternative to mainstream society, illegal raves would (for the most part) operate far more secretively, evading rather than confronting the state (at least, until they ultimately became too big to ignore).

The late 1980s saw the new Travellers conduct a similar retreat from popular attention: while a smaller core continued to traverse the country lanes and common land of England, harried to ever greater extents by the newly passed Public Order Act, they largely dropped off the media and public's radar. Many of those who'd previously attended free festivals turned their attentions to licensed, permitted events instead, with the rapidly growing Glastonbury festival largely taking the place of celebrations at Stonehenge by the end of the 1980s. When a small crew of hardy (or foolish) new Travellers attempted to revive the People's Free Festival at the stones in 1987 and 1988, they were met with baton charges by the police. For other veterans of the free festival circuit, the violence and destruction of the Beanfield meant that giving up a life on the road became the only viable option: Alan Lodge moved into a flat in Nottingham, and began a degree in photography. And yet the underlying emotions which the new Travellers and free festivals had represented were to remain merely dormant, rather than fully extinct; within a handful of summers UK dance music would begin to reoccupy many of the same spaces in British social and political life, reinvigorating the new Traveller scene and creating strange new cultural forms of its own. Alan Lodge and others waited quietly in the wings, sketching out new tactics to evade the clutches of the law, and anticipating new opportunities to reoccupy the commons in pursuit of collective pleasure. 'The interesting bit was Section 39 of the Public Order Act,' says Lodge of the legal pressures facing the new Travellers, and the opportunities soon to be offered by the more ephemeral thrill-seeking of acid house and rave. 'The law said that we committed an offence if we occupied a piece of land "with the common purpose of residing there" . . . But then, we asked ourselves: what if we don't *reside* there?'

UNOFFICIAL LOGO OF KENT POLICE'S ANTI-RAVE SQUAD,
THE PAY PARTY UNIT, 1989

3. Dance Before the Police Come

God's Cop, Victorian values and Thatcher's war on vice

'I was doing the late show,' says Paul O'Grady, his thick Tranmere accent instantly recognizable from the thirty years he's spent at the heart of Britain's light entertainment establishment, whether appearing under his own name or that of his drag persona, the 'blond bombsite' Lily Savage. He's talking about the night in January 1987 when police raided the Royal Vauxhall Tavern. 'The door burst open and this copper comes in. Of course, I thought he was a stripper.' O'Grady describes being told to leave, and asking the officer 'Who the fuck do you think you're talking to?' before realizing that the entire pub was swarming with police. Led out into the main hall, O'Grady saw the Tavern's regular Thursday night crowd – a collection of 'perfectly nice people, rent boys, drunks and the mentally unstable', as O'Grady describes them – being lined up against the walls by an almost incomprehensible number of officers. A year and a half after the Battle of the Beanfield, six months before Paul Oakenfold et al. touch down in Ibiza, and just over a year before Section 28 would pass into law, Thatcher's war on deviance and disorder, from the blues dances of Bristol to the new Travellers of rural England, had also reached the queer venues of south London. The same winter of 1987 also saw the peak of confusion and scaremongering over the AIDS crisis:* as O'Grady watched his patrons being bundled out of the room by the police, he noticed that every single officer was wearing an identical pair of bright blue rubber gloves, as if mere contact with the Royal Vauxhall Tavern's patrons represented a mortal threat of contamination and corruption. 'Well, well,' he said, grabbing a mic and addressing the assembled throng, 'looks like we've got help with the washing up.'

Of all the ways in which the Thatcher government inadvertently laid the foundations for acid house and rave to take over Britain – the masses of unemployed and antagonized young people desperate for some form of release, the deindustrialized spaces waiting to be reappropriated for collective pleasure, or the mercantile ambition of a newly post-industrial British economy – none is as important as its attitude and approach to public order and moral vice. While 'the enemy within' was originally embodied by Arthur Scargill and Militant left-wing councils, the definition came to include any groups which sought to gather together, so long as either the

---

* Princess Diana would open the UK's first dedicated HIV ward three months later in April 1987. Her gesture of basic human decency to the patients she met – shaking ungloved hands with them, aware that HIV wasn't transmitted through skin contact – was viewed as a watershed moment, underlining the leper-like ostracization otherwise afforded at the time to those with HIV/AIDS.

people or the pastimes involved fell outside a narrow, archaic and morally conservative sense of propriety and British identity: Black soundsystems and new Travellers, as we've seen, but also queer communities, football hooligans, striking miners and various others on the fringes of society. The running battles between illegal rave promoters, sweat-drenched crowds and police Acid Squads which followed weren't unique, but merely an extension of that same lineage.

If there's one individual who embodies these connections between Thatcher's reheated Victorian morality and the origins of UK dance music, then it's James Anderton, chief constable of Greater Manchester Police from 1976 to 1991. His biography reads like that of someone born a century earlier, from the 'square Victorian courtyards, bleak slag heaps, horse-drawn hearses, milk floats and coal delivery carts' of his interwar childhood in Wigan, to the ferociously retrograde Christian morality installed in him from birth: 'He doesn't believe in kissing, he thinks it's sinful,' one school friend remembers being told. Even the Manchester constable who first inspired him to become a policeman, his great-uncle Nehemiah Occleshaw, sounds like a character pulled straight from the pages of a Dickens novel. From the moment Anderton took charge of the second-largest police force in the country in the late 1970s, he would focus relentlessly on vice, immorality and godlessness as the fundamental causes of crime, a highly weaponized extension of the 'Victorian values' Thatcher would later come to eulogize. Indeed, when Anderton faced a wave of public outrage over his comments regarding AIDS patients, sex workers and addicts – that they were all 'swirling around in a human cesspit of their own making', comments he later claimed to have been dictated to him by God – Thatcher herself would secretly intervene to block a public inquiry into Anderton's behaviour.

Formerly a lay preacher, Anderton's fire-and-brimstone evangelism and fondness for the media were hugely controversial at the time, and come across as positively barbaric now. The legalization of homosexuality was, in his words, 'one of the worst changes in legislation ever enacted in this country . . . an abomination. How anyone can say it is not sinful or against the law to engage in practices of that kind is beyond my comprehension.' Anderton's own daughter would subsequently come out as a lesbian, to the barely concealed delight of the tabloid press. According to Anderton, patients dying of AIDS 'had a choice, they chose to ignore the risks and, therefore, suffered the consequences. That is part of the natural order of things in God's creation,' while young people in Manchester were treated as quasi-demonic for merely going out and dancing: 'they prefer the dark night to daylight, they dance like there is no tomorrow, and they spread the virus of drug abuse wherever they go. They are not of this world, they believe in very different things to you and I, and like many young people, they arrogantly believe they can make their own laws.'

The treatment Anderton advocated for such heathen immorality was similarly uncompromising: appearing at an international policing conference in 1987, he blithely declared his support for the mandatory castration of sex offenders. Later the same year, he articulated his view of criminals as a whole to the unsuspecting readers of *Woman's Own* magazine. 'Corporal punishment should be administered so that they actually beg for mercy . . . They should be punished until they repent of their sins. I'd thrash some criminals myself, most surely. I could punish people quite easily.' Rather than educating his officers on AIDS, he issued every member of the Manchester Police force with an 'infectious disease briefcase' containing a mask, gloves, a hazmat suit and a canister of disinfectant spray. When the 1981 riots spread from Brixton to Moss Side, Anderton refused to cooperate with an inquiry into allegations of police violence, and refused to allow his officers to testify. Anderton's moral disdain was highly selective, though: in 1977 he 'entered a secret pact' with the National Front, arranging police protection for their march through Levenshulme, while conspiring to keep the march itself secret from the local community, ensuring that the far-right could take over the streets unopposed. Such sentiments would see Anderton lauded by conservative media – *The Sun* declaring in 1986 that 'what Britain needs is more men like James Anderton – and fewer gay terrorists holding the decent members of society to ransom' – but reviled by others as 'God's Cop', an autocratic bogeyman and the purest embodiment of hollow Thatcherite sermonizing. 'No City Fun', a piece written for a Manchester fanzine by Liz Naylor in 1978 and credited knowingly to 'James "Don't Call Me Scarface" Anderton', embodies something of that mutual hostility: 'The city is terrifying, it is frightening, it is a prison . . . I think I hate the city. I think it hates me.' The Happy Mondays would later name one of the tracks on 1990's *Pills 'n' Thrills and Bellyaches*, after Anderton: 'God's Cop' sees Shaun Ryder free-associate around themes of divine providence and police corruption, backed by the Mondays' endearingly ramshackle funk-rock, before imagining an afternoon spent sharing a cheeky spliff or two with the esteemed chief constable. Ryder's infamous chemically loosened grip on reality might make the precise meaning of his satire a little tricky to parse, but the totemic place Anderton occupied in the minds of Mancunians comes through loud and clear.

Anderton's wholly unreconstructed attitudes may have attracted attention, but they were far from unique: 75 per cent of respondents to 1987's edition of the British Social Attitudes Survey declared that they found gay sex between consenting adults 'always or mostly' wrong. In December 1986, less than a month before the Royal Vauxhall Tavern was raided, Bill Brownhill, the Conservative leader of South Staffordshire Council, responded to the screening of an educational film about AIDS by declaring, during a council meeting: 'I should shoot them all . . . those bunch of queers that legalise filth in homosexuality have a lot to answer. It is disgusting and diabolical. As a cure I would put 90% of queers in the ruddy gas chambers.' Brownhill faced no formal censure for his comments from the Conservative party: the following autumn Margaret Thatcher would declare to an approving Party Conference that 'Children who need to be taught to respect traditional moral values are being taught that they have an inalienable right to be gay . . . all of those children are being cheated of a sound start in life' shortly before her government introduced the notorious Section 28. Brownhill's comments were also immediately welcomed by the leader of the local Labour opposition, who replied that 'Everyone of us here will agree with what has been said' before the council as a whole voted to block future licence applications from gay pubs in South Staffordshire wherever possible: nightlife once again was the first in line to be targeted in response to perceived social decay.

This principle extended from the licensing of late-night queer spaces to their treatment by police. During their 1987 raid on the Royal Vauxhall Tavern the Metropolitan Police arrested eleven people, including the landlord's wife, upstairs watching TV with her children at the time. As with countless other incursions into late-night venues over the years, the police justified the raid on the RVT with reference to suspected drug use – specifically allegations that poppers were being sold under the counter by the pub's staff. A reasonable topic for police interest, you might think, except for the fact that neither the possession nor sale of amyl nitrite was illegal at the time, and indeed still isn't today despite repeated government attempts to ban it. O'Grady describes wanting to chin the female police officer bundling him off the stage, his anger underpinned by the wider hostility facing gay communities: 'there was a new Chief Constable in South London who was extremely homophobic, AIDS was at its peak and all the stigma that went with that'.

The first annual report of the Gay London Police Monitoring Group (GALOP) in 1984 revealed that nearly twenty years after the legalization of homosexuality late-night venues were still regularly being used by the Metropolitan Police to entrap gay men. Plain-clothes officers are described loitering outside gay clubs and bars, propositioning customers as they leave, then arresting them for 'persistently importuning for an immoral purpose' if they express any reciprocal interest. GALOP would refer to this as a new 'gay sus law': just as with the use of the 1824 Vagrancy Act to target Black men, the police's repurposing of an archaic and vaguely worded piece of legislation (originally enacted to protect Victorian show-girls from being hassled at the stage door) left them free to arrest and harass gay men at will, often on extremely spurious grounds. In terms which recall arguments levelled against police treatment of blues parties or new Traveller convoys, GALOP argued that these tactics were 'used not to enforce the law or to stop crime, but to regulate social behaviour in public that the police do not approve of'. The 'persistent' nature of the offence required at least two instances of soliciting to have been identified by police: GALOP described countless arrest records using identical language to claim that a member of the public had reported the suspect behaving suspiciously prior to their conversation with undercover officers; none of these witnesses were ever produced in court, or even identified by name.

Attempts to associate late-night queer spaces with rampant criminality and disease, or to 'quarantine the city' from the threats they presented, would persist throughout the following years, overlapping with the early years of acid house and rave. Paul O'Grady would himself join the ranks of those arrested as a result of the raid on the Royal Vauxhall Tavern: with his microphone still connected, and his prominent position onstage accentuated by the spotlights and his tottering heels, he called on punters and staff to riot. Unlike Dennis Bovell, imprisoned a decade earlier on near-identical charges of 'conspiracy to commit a breach of the peace', O'Grady was ultimately released without being charged. If this was supposed to constitute some form of progress, it felt extremely meagre.

In 1991, *The Guardian* published an article by gay writer Rupert Haselden which positioned queer nightlife as the underlying force destroying the nuclear family and, by extension, society itself: without the purpose of raising a family, he argues, 'we invite an indulgent outlook on life and literalise this in the clubs and bars, in casual promiscuous sex.' For Haselden, AIDS was the symbolic endpoint of this process of moral decay, 'a flashing neon sign in the midst of the gay community, becoming a metaphor for the self-destructiveness and the self-indulgence that accompanies it.' As late as 1994, the Metropolitan Police could be found raiding a gay sauna in London, taking twenty-seven men into custody on suspicion of gross indecency, and seizing as evidence a book containing the names of a thousand of its patrons. In April 1988, five men were arrested after they 'punched and kicked people in the queue' at London gay nightclub Heaven while shouting 'Kill the queers!', rendering one victim unconscious – the judge at their trial directed the jury to acquit them. Four months later, in August 1988, *The Sun*'s very first acid house scare story also centred on a scandalized trip to Heaven, this time in its guise as the venue for Paul Oakenfold's Spectrum night. Viewed through the lens of preceding attitudes, this feels less like a coincidence than a form of continuity.

Nowhere was the overlap between emergent late-night culture and establishment homophobia more visible than in James Anderton's patrician rule over Manchester: pursuing a relentless campaign against what he saw as the ills of the modern world, his heavy-handed policing and moral censoriousness had a chilling effect on the city's night-time venues, including those connected to the emerging dance music scene. 'Bad luck', reads a student advice column from *City Life* magazine in 1984, 'You've chosen to live in Manchester, so you'd better behave yourself'. Officers would spend the late 1970s and early 1980s stalking the back streets of the city at closing time, expressly tasked with exposing incidents of behaviour that Anderton considered indecent: lovers in alleyways or youths loitering on corners would be hauled into the station; police motorboats would crawl along the canal bordering Manchester's gay quarter, and men spotted on the banks or under bridges would be frozen in high-powered police spotlights.

Gay venues themselves remained a consistent and conspicuous target, often on extraordinarily flimsy grounds, regardless of their customers' propriety: in 1978 Anderton attempted to use yet another antiquated by-law (this time a prohibition on 'licentious dancing' dating back to Victorian anxieties over the 'repulsive pantomime' of cancan dancers) to demand that the gay venue Naps (or Napoleons) prohibit its patrons from dancing with each other. Six years later, the same venue was forcibly raided by twenty officers, its membership list seized and attendees ordered to give their names and addresses before being allowed to leave. This didn't mean that other spaces were safe, though: in 1990, the year before Anderton retired, Greater Manchester Police launched a concerted campaign, via submissions to the magistrates' courts, to revoke premises licenses for the Haçienda and several other dance music venues. While another Happy Mondays song might have eulogized Manchester's '24 Hour Party People', in reality the city's legal venues were hamstrung by outdated licensing laws and moral unease from those responsible for enforcing them, with even the famed Haçienda only remaining open until 2 a.m. This might have been acceptable to punters prior to 1987, when DJs first started playing imported Chicago house records to more sedate pre-Ecstasy crowds, but once the pills kicked in such archaic curfews became meaningless, whether James Anderton approved or not. Faced with hostile terrain in the city centre, the party relocated itself to alternative zones less susceptible to police attention or control. Dub and soul soundsystems, including Anthony Stevens's Soul Control, continued to host blues parties in the Black youth clubs and living rooms of Moss Side, rather than confront the de facto colour bar in operation at licensed venues or risk harassment from Anderton's goon squads. Next door in Hulme, enterprising ravers smashed through the internal walls of a dilapidated brutalist block in 1987 and set up a squatted venue called The Kitchen.

Hulme Crescents was a near-perfect example of paternalist mid-century urban planning gone horribly wrong: its 3,200 homes had been envisioned as a post-war utopia of modernist curves and green spaces, and 'a solution to the problems of twentieth-century living', as its architects put it. It was more accurately described by *The Guardian* as 'a morass in which design faults and tenants' revulsion at their environment have combined to produce a staggering number of maintenance demands and angry howls of neglect.' Opened in 1972, within two years the entire development was deemed unsuitable for children to live in, after a five-year-old fell to their death from one of the numerous unprotected concrete balconies. Pervasive damp, sewage leaks, malfunctioning heating and cockroach infestations meant that by 1975 a full 96 per cent of residents said they wanted to be relocated. Unable to afford the cost of demolishing the blocks, Manchester City Council simply stopped charging rent in 1984, creating a vacuum which was gladly filled by members of society less perturbed by the spectre of urban decay.

From 1987 to the Hulme Crescents' demolition in 1994, The Kitchen brought together all-night ravers, post-Beanfield free party crusties, rain-sodden punks and political radicals. 'The whole area was full of travellers' buses, dogs-on-a-rope types, junkies, squatters, freaks, outsiders,' reads one memorial by John Robb of Mancunian punk band The Membranes. 'It was also full of ex-cons, muggers, and mini gangsters, but you can't have everything can you?' The space itself was grim and intimidating, a sharp rejoinder to the artfully designed industrial chic of The Haçienda: the walls separating individual flats, and in some cases the floors between them, had been smashed through to form a single cavernous space, lit by naked light bulbs, with a bar hidden in a thick fog of weed and tobacco, and a soundsystem set up in the main room. The crowd, according to Robb, were 'E'd up, [with] gonzoid-eyed and scrunched-up faces leering into the dark haze' while the music consisted of 'booming acid house' which reverberated around the estate, 'a beacon to every leering crazy in town.' The refusal of local police officers to patrol Hulme Crescents' sinister warrens of raised walkways and brutalist barriers meant that The Kitchen operated largely free of state intervention. It was, in Robb's words, 'a concrete wilderness with no control, a virtually independent freak scene run by the freaks for the freaks . . . It was a ten-minute walk from The Haçienda, but it may as well have been a million miles away.'

For those willing to venture a little further outside Anderton's moral orbit, even greater pleasures awaited in the abandoned mills of Blackburn, a short drive away: from the autumn of 1988 to the summer of 1990, the white-hot core of Britain's rave culture could be found in the post-industrial gloom of this very specific corner of the North West. With Greater Manchester Police 'harassing anyone who attempted to stage an illegal rave inside the city limits', as Matthew Collin explains, 'so Blackburn became the focus.' While the Blackburn warehouse scene has generally been granted a place in canonical histories of UK dance music, most notably *Altered State* (albeit as a secondary storyline alongside more familiar narratives from London and the South East), it's also benefitted from renewed interest and historical reappraisal in recent years. This has included the Arts Council's *Acid House Flashback* project, which recorded and published the recollections of those who organized and danced at the parties. And yet it remains difficult to overstate Blackburn's importance in the development of UK dance music as a social and political force. Where other early acid house parties like Shoom or The Trip were radical largely by accident, their politics a side-effect of bringing people together and creating new social and cultural communities, the Blackburn scene marks the first point at which confrontation with the state, and the ability of the rave to reshape wider society, become an intentional part of how UK dance music functions and is organized.

In focusing on Blackburn as an alternative to the conventional history of early acid house, it's worth outlining exactly what that canonical narrative consists of. If we adhere to that more established version of events, acid house is discovered by four London-based DJs – Paul Oakenfold, Danny Rampling, Johnny Walker, and Nicky Holloway – on a lads' holiday to Ibiza in the summer of 1987. More specifically, the moment of inspiration occurs when they take Ecstasy and dance to DJ Alfredo's 'Balearic' sets at the nightclub Amnesia, the drug sparking a transcendental new understanding of Alfredo's eclectic mix of synth-pop, afro-cosmic drums and Black electronic music imported from Chicago and Detroit. Returning to the UK, the 'Ibiza Four' are inspired to set up their own club nights channelling that same energy: Rampling is the first, launching Shoom at a fitness centre in Southwark in the autumn of 1987; Oakenfold follows with Future in the back room at Heaven, a gay club under the railway arches at Charing Cross, before rapidly growing demand sees him expand to the main room with Spectrum;

Holloway joins the party in the spring of 1988 with Trip at the Astoria, on Tottenham Court Road. Powered by the growing popularity of Ecstasy and its transformational effect on listening to electronic music, these clubs trigger a cultural and social revolution over the course of 1988, dubbed the 'Second Summer of Love'. Acid house spreads from London to Manchester via The Haçienda (other northern venues remain largely secondary in this canon) and from underground clubs catering to in-the-know hipster crowds to a mass youth phenomenon. Parties start taking over abandoned warehouses, airfields and other post-industrial spaces around London's urban periphery, convoys of ravers circling the M25 in search of drug-fuelled abandon.

But this spike in popularity also brings about the demise of acid house's Arcadian first phase, from multiple fronts: mercantile promoters like Tony Colston-Hayter of Sunrise take advantage of this massively expanded market for dance music by running enormous, highly lucrative rave spectaculars of dubious legality in brownfield sites around the M25, which overwrite the intimacy of earlier acid-house nights so beloved of the original Balearic cognoscenti. Organized crime groups spot an opportunity to muscle in on the ballooning profits being made by unlicensed party promoters, while the demand for Ecstasy sees increasing numbers of unscrupulous dealers cutting it with other substances: between the growing violence on and around the dance floor, and the dilution of Ecstasy's unifying energy, the vibe shifts precipitously.

UK dance music's increases in both scale and disorder also pique the interest of the tabloid media, who begin running hysterical scare stories about the acid craze, and painting its originators as new folk devils; politicians get involved too, with Thatcher's government taking steps to shut down acid house parties and raves of all sizes through new policing strategies and legislation; the golden era of acid house ends sometime in the early 1990s (depending on who you speak to) with the music corralled into licensed venues, the pills less potent than they used to be in 1987 and the crowds less friendly: the utopian transcendence of the 'Ibiza Four' replaced by something infinitely more pedestrian.

This sequence of events is both true and consequential, but the extent to which it's become embedded in our collective understanding as *the* story of UK dance music's formative years risks obscuring other narratives, experiences, and connections. Blackburn wasn't the only regional scene exerting a critical influence at the turn of the nineties – the birth of 'bleep techno' in Sheffield is also hugely important, not least for establishing that London wasn't necessarily ahead of the rest of the country. But in terms of UK dance music first finding its feet as an overtly politicized force, shaped not just by electronic music and drugs but also by the aggressive and antiquated policing of perceived vice, government decision-making and radical collective desires, Blackburn plays a unique and pivotal role.

The city's position at the epicentre of early dance music culture in the North West was partly a question of geography: close enough to Manchester, Liverpool and Leeds to draw in cultural influences and potential audiences, yet far enough away for the city's policing of unlicensed parties to lag behind that of its bigger neighbours. James Anderton's moralistic crackdown on unlicensed Manchester venues – with the exception, perhaps, of the unpoliceable Kitchen – meant that when The Haçienda and other legal spaces closed at 2 a.m., those who'd been turfed out but wanted to keep dancing had little option but to head down the M66. Officers in Blackburn, by contrast, were initially bamboozled by the illegal rave scene, and struggled to keep up: between February and August 1989 the average Blackburn warehouse rave went from a few hundred attendees to a couple of thousand. Blackburn's long-running economic torpor meant that the city lacked the licensed clubs which might have accommodated the crowds of ravers now flooding into the city: when The Haçienda launched an offshoot night in Blackburn, it took place not amidst the artful straight lines and minimalist cool of its carefully designed parent venue in Manchester, but in Manhattan Heights, a chintzy 1950s-themed American bar with carpet on the dance floor, a pink Cadillac hung over the entrance and bartenders in bootleg New York Yankees T-shirts.

While Blackburn might have struggled to produce decent legal venues for dance music, its post-industrial decline made it almost preternaturally suitable for illegal warehouse raves, with local police regularly overwhelmed by the sheer number of empty industrial spaces available to party promoters. One of the most interesting conversations from *Acid House Flashback*, the 2019 Arts Council-funded project which interviewed dozens of people involved in Blackburn's warehouse scene, comes from David, a uniformed officer tasked with responding to illegal raves in the late 1980s and early 1990s. He describes the city as a policing 'nightmare', with decoy cars and false reports of mass brawls in the city centre leading officers on countless wild goose chases, while the party kicked off elsewhere. 'The [wider] policing of Blackburn went by the board, there wasn't the manpower to deal with both sets of situations,' he says. David's descriptions of the parties themselves are also notable for being largely even-handed, entirely out of keeping with James Anderton's Old Testament sneering. While he emphasizes the dangers inherent in people flocking to abandoned mills and warehouses, and the police's duty to try to keep them safe, David also acknowledges that 'there was some enjoyment from the people that went.' Just as the zero-tolerance approach of the police in Manchester had served to relocate the North West's acid house scene, so the less militant or coordinated response of east Lancashire's officers helped it to flourish in Blackburn.

Local pub the Sett End – known as the Sweat End by locals – became both the centre of the city's licensed acid house scene, and the meeting point for after-hours convoys from across the North West to congregate once all the legal venues closed. 'You'd be racing through the town on your way to the warehouse, you'd probably have the police on your tail,' recalls Jane Winterbottom, one of the leaders of regular rave convoys from Manchester. 'You'd get to the party after about half an hour, you'd lock your car, run down the street, and get into the warehouse as quick as you could.' The doors would be locked, leaving the police stranded outside, helpless to prevent the party. 'Then the lights would go out, you'd wait about 30 seconds, it'd be complete silence, you'd have 10,000 people in the party . . . and then you just see one light where the Technics decks were, [illuminating] where the needle was going on the record and then just as the needle started crackling on the record, you'd just feel this wave of people cheering. For me, that moment, them few seconds, was the best part of the whole thing.' The idea that the police's attentions merely added to the thrill of early illegal parties is mirrored elsewhere: in a 1992 BBC documentary one raver admits that 'there was a buzz to getting busted, when the police used to come along and turf everyone out.' He describes a party in 1988, in which the police set dozens of sirens blaring on their vans, in an attempt to clear the venue through sheer force of volume. An enterprising DJ simply mixed into 'Can You Party' by Royal House – one of the biggest tunes of the moment, with an eerily similar-sounding siren running through it – the sound of the rave suddenly augmented rather than undermined by the police's unwitting accompaniment. Where the police might have hoped that a clampdown would dampen the party, in fact it often served to do the opposite. Over the summer of 1988, thousands of ravers took over an abandoned Tizer factory, the Albion Mill, and even a disused abattoir. 'Every weekend it just got better and better and better,' said Tony Creft, a central member of the city's most prominent rave collective, The Self Help Group. 'You could never turn around after one of them and say it was the best – well, you did at first, but the week after that became the best one. They were all the best one, the best one, the best one.'

The city's rave scene wasn't just the product of spatial expediency, though. Deindustrialization ripped the heart out of communities across the UK, but Blackburn was undoubtedly one of the longest and most profoundly affected: with an economy based almost entirely on cotton and textile production, the increase of globalized trade from colonial India and the United States had seen mill closures and heavy job losses in east Lancashire as far back as 1908, and consistently from the 1960s through to the late 1980s. That historical and economic context not only dictated the physical spaces Blackburn's parties occupied, but the energy with which the liberatory opportunities they offered were seized. 'Coming off all that angst: the miners' strike and football violence, all the stuff in the 80's that weren't great, the smashing of the unions and racism,' recalls John, another local party organizer and DJ. 'Then suddenly, hang on a minute . . . [you realized that] all that's nonsense, this is something real, tangible that we can do.' This was reflected in The Self Help Group's ferocious commitment to making their parties happen by any means necessary: on one occasion ram-raiding a DIY store to steal a generator, on another jacking a power cable from a set of temporary traffic lights rather than risk cancellation. Their no-frills productions and egalitarian principles meant that once essentials like the generator had been secured by fair means or foul, sensory pleasures didn't stretch much beyond a decent soundsystem and a couple of lights. This in turn kept ticket prices down, and ensured that the parties remained financially accessible to anyone tempted by the idea of losing themselves for a night. A forty-five minute road-trip from Manchester, a bit of cat-and-mouse with the police on the way to a disused industrial space, two quid on the door, and a willingness to put up with the smell of axle grease, fizzy pop or animal carcasses, and you'd be granted access to the greatest party in the world.

But the situation in Blackburn couldn't last: just as the city's emergence as a hotbed for illegal raving had been shaped by the nature of its policing, so changes in policing strategy would ultimately bring an end to its eighteen-month flurry of warehouse parties. The trigger for this would be Westminster's first attempt to legislate against UK dance music: the Entertainments (Increased Penalties) Bill, tabled by backbench Conservative MP Graham Bright. Despite not creating any new offences, the new law increased fines for unlicensed party promoters and empowered police and local councils to take more aggressive action against them. The Bright Bill, as it became known, was merely the British state's first attempt to clamp down on 'pay parties' – its immediate effects on the illegal rave scene, and the wider path it created for increasingly aggressive anti-rave legislation, culminating in the Criminal Justice Act of 1994, would fundamentally alter the development of UK dance music. Bright was not a lone voice: one month before he tabled his bill, Blackburn MP Jack Straw – later to become an infamously heavy-handed Home Secretary under Tony Blair – wrote to his predecessor in that great role of state, David Waddington, to demand legislative action. 'Blackburn has become the North West centre for Acid House parties,' he argues, claiming that 'the existing law is quite inadequate effectively to deal with the organisers of these parties, especially given the determination of these organisers to refuse to accept any kind of social constraint.' In Blackburn itself, the Bright Bill's impact could be seen in the formation of Operation Alkali, a specific anti-rave task force which targeted east Lancashire's illegal party scene with growing intensity. 'The presence wasn't that severe at first, but it was still there and it was uncomfortable,' said Jane Winterbottom. 'You'd go to the shop for a pint of milk and somebody would stop you in the streets, it'd be a policeman asking you questions . . . They broke into the house opposite us and they were filming us . . . They wanted us to know they were there.' This increased police attention was prompted in part by local organized crime groups muscling into the raves. As early as August 1989, brothers Anthony and Christopher Donnelly – Mancunians with close familial ties to one of the city's most prominent gangs – had attracted 4,000 ravers to an unlicensed party on the moor near Edenfield. Six months later another key member of The Self Help Group, Tommy Smith, found himself in the basement of The Haçienda with a gun in his face, being told: 'You work for us now.'

The Sett End closed in early 1990, riddled with accusations over infiltration by gangs and officers from East Lancashire Police alike. Tensions between ravers and the local constabulary reached a peak in February 1990, when 200 officers stormed a 10,000-strong rave just outside Burnley, and shut it down by force. One attendee, the DJ Drew Hemment, recalls 'a double line of police in full riot gear, marching shoulder to shoulder, striking their linked shields in time with the beat of their hobnailed boots.' As the police started clobbering anyone in their way, writes Hemment, ravers fleeing the building were met with another line of riot police stationed outside, truncheons raised. This shift in policing didn't just target the parties themselves, but the infrastructure around them, as one of the anonymous interviewees in Bob Balraj Singh's academic research into the Blackburn raves recounts. 'They had identified all the main organisers, and by now they had extra resources, they were making it impossible to get into Blackburn. Any major route into the town was now getting road blocked and people were getting turned away. You couldn't have a party without the people.' Where one of 1991's biggest club hits by Shut Up and Dance would go on to urge people to 'Dance Before the Police Come', it felt like – in Blackburn at least – the time to do so was already running out.

As more aggressive policing tactics in Blackburn squeezed the activities of The Self Help Group and others, promoters attempted once again to relocate the party outside the reach of the authorities. In July 1990 the Love Decade warehouse party took place in Gildersome, just outside Leeds, over the county border with West Yorkshire. Taking place the week after Graham Bright's Parliamentary Bill became law, Love Decade was shut down with unprecedented force, resulting in the largest mass arrest in British history. Rave crews forced out of Blackburn might have naively hoped that the West Yorkshire Police would be slower on the uptake than their East Lancashire counterparts, but the reverse was true: hardened by their experiences in the miners' strike, officers arrived at Love Decade with riot shields and truncheons drawn. 'I remember seeing the police coming down the hill like Romans, banging their shields,' recalls Leeds promoter Dave Beer, who describes the police 'dealing with us just like the miners. They were blatantly attacking all of the partygoers. Everyone was pilled-up and loved-up and just wanted to dance.' While only 8 of the 836 ravers arrested at Love Decade were ever charged with anything, the message was clear: what had been allowed to happen in Blackburn was not going to be repeated. Another of the people interviewed for *Acid House Flashback*, referred to solely as Damo, was amongst those charged, eventually becoming the first person in the UK convicted for attending an illegal rave. 'When you're taking something like what you had [in Blackburn] and moving it into somewhere like West Yorkshire, where they've got the resources, the money,' he explained of his arrest, 'the police turned around and said, "That's not happening here."' Like both Dennis Bovell and Lily Savage before him, Damo was arrested on suspicion of riot and affray, convicted and sentenced to two months in a young offenders' institution. With crowds and organizers alike exhausted by the mounting pressures on illegal raves, Blackburn's warehouse parties had almost entirely fizzled out by late 1990. Instead, parties were steered towards licensed, bricks-and-mortar venues where crowds could be controlled, drugs seized and profits fully taxed. The increased penalties and restrictions of the Bright Bill had been accompanied by a loosening of restrictions around legal venues, with the 1988 Licensing Act belatedly enabling pubs to open in the afternoon (repealing the 1914 Defence of the Realm Act, originally passed amidst fears that afternoon boozing might hamper the war effort). More importantly for the rave scene, the magistrates responsible for licensing decisions became increasingly willing to let legal venues stay open late: when Ministry of Sound launched in September 1991, it did so with the country's first twenty-four-hour dancing licence (albeit one that forbade it from selling alcohol).

As the Blackburn warehouse scene was entering its terminal phase in early 1990, similar battles over urban space, public morality and the illicit pull of drugs and dancing remained very much alive at the other end of the country, courtesy of Ken Tappenden's infamous Pay Party Unit: a specialist team of police officers based in Gravesend, tasked with monitoring and disrupting illegal rave networks across the UK. Tappenden was in many ways the polar opposite of James Anderton: affable and unassuming, after retiring in 1993 he established a second career as an after-dinner speaker and toastmaster, trading in elegant tributes and formal pleasantries rather than

Anderton's ongoing tendency for quasi-messianic ranting. But on a professional level Tappenden was utterly implacable, easily the equal of his counterpart in Manchester. Through him, the same concepts of public morality, 'Victorian values' and 'the enemy within', which had underpinned Anderton's reign over Manchester, the relocation of after-hours partying to Blackburn and eventually the violence of the Love Decade bust would again dictate the police's attitude to UK dance music. Under Tappenden's command the Pay Party Unit proved hugely effective at stemming the rise of illegal parties between its formation in 1989 and closure in September 1991, with all the steeliness and dedication to duty you'd expect from a man who'd been the senior investigator on over thirty murder cases, and who oversaw repatriation of the bodies of Britons killed in the Zeebrugge ferry disaster of 1987. Just like his peers in Leeds, Tappenden's attitude towards the policing of illegal raves had been forged in the violence and anger of the miners' strike in the spring of 1984. Tappenden had been the supervising officer responsible for setting up police barriers at the entrance to the Dartford Tunnel, preventing a convoy of miners based in Kent from joining their comrades on the picket line in Nottinghamshire and threatening them with arrest them for breach of the peace if they travelled any further. The uproar from unions and civil liberties groups was instant and vociferous: how on earth could Tappenden justify such heavy-handed restrictions, they quite rightly demanded, when the miners in question were travelling over a hundred miles away, and the police didn't even know precisely where they were heading? The High Court agreed: having hauled Tappenden in to explain himself, they found Kent Police's actions had been undertaken without proper legal authority and underlined that an 'imminence or immediacy of the threat to the peace' was required to arrest someone.*

---

* Tappenden's connection back to the miners' strike was also shared by one of his best-known adversaries, Paul Staines, who handled PR for Tony Colston-Hayter's Sunrise promotions and ran a short-lived campaign against the Bright Bill in 1990. Now better known as the right-wing blogger Guido Fawkes, Staines cut his teeth in the 1980s working for property developer and

Fast-forward five years, and a seemingly unrepentant Tappenden could be found recycling precisely the same strategies – mobile roadblocks and spurious threats of arrest – to prevent would-be ravers from reaching their intended destination and disrupt party promoters' infrastructure. Tappenden would later admit that his tactics had regularly 'overstepped the mark' in terms of the law. 'I visited lots of firms who hired out heavy plant machinery, and told them I'd do them for conspiracy if they hired [them out] to party organisers. I couldn't, but that's what I told them.' Again, he relied on laws around breach of the peace – 'I scanned the Public Order Act and pulled out stuff most lawyers had never even heard of,' he said – stretching those powers to the brink of legality, or beyond. When not busy with clumsy attempts to describe acid house to the Home Office and senior police officers as 'a combination of black dance music, electronic effects and weird vocals', the Pay Party Unit's confidential internal reports appear to back Tappenden up, revealing that their primary sources of intelligence came not from a broad spectrum of detailed evidence-gathering, as claimed at the time, but by leaning on the companies supplying marquees, lighting rigs and sound equipment to party organizers. Just like the blue-gloved officers storming the Royal Vauxhall Tavern, or the violence and violations meted out to the striking miners, the end goal – stopping acid house parties – was automatically assumed to justify the legally murky means. You can perhaps even detect a glimmer of insouciant pleasure in the Pay Party Unit's approach: their logo,

---

shadowy Conservative fixer David Hart, tasked by Thatcher with funnelling cash to strike-breaking miners as a means of driving a wedge between different unions. Interviewed by Matthew Colling in *Altered State*, Staines dismisses his involvement in the rave scene as a bit of harmless fun, entirely separate from his more serious political career, but an article he wrote for the *Libertarian Alliance* newsletter in 1991 connects the early rave scene more directly to Staines's ultra-libertarian agenda. 'This is truly a regime of which Stalin or Hitler himself would be proud,' he claims of the government's anti-rave efforts. 'If ever there was an area crying out for Thatcherite deregulation, it's the archaic system for the licensing of music and dancing.'

unearthed in the National Archives during my research having been hidden away in confidential reports to the Home Office for thirty years, reflects Tappenden's single-minded focus: set within the flared sunburst of a police badge sits the smiley face so beloved of Shoom, Wally Hope and countless others, complete with a thick black line crossing it out. Even for the extremely literal tendencies of the police, it feels a bit on the nose.

Tappenden's generous interpretation of the powers available to him would play a vital role in shaping the evolution of UK dance music, as satellite Pay Party Units were set up across the UK by other forces, including Operation Alkali in Blackburn. 'Slowly but surely, they went to work on everyone,' says Joey Wieczorek, the puckish East End promoter who pre-empted many of his peers in the illegal rave scene by curtailing his unlicensed Labyrnth parties in the autumn of 1989, tired of the attentions of the Pay Party Unit and the wider Metropolitan Police. 'I'd say September or October 1989 was when we got battered: they'd followed us one night, we had a backup venue and another venue and they'd just been on us completely. They obviously had the resources now: in the beginning, you'd get two flatfoots walking in with their helmets on and their long coats, and they'd just walk around with their hands behind their back, looking fucking amazed, then they'd walk off and you'd never see them again.' Wieczorek was perhaps more of a target than most, being known to the police from his days as a prominent member of Tottenham Hotspurs' hooligan firm. 'I'd probably be in prison or dead now, if it hadn't been for the rave parties. That's certainly the way I was going. I was tooled up, I was game as a beigel, I *hated* other football teams, hated Northerners. I was Tottenham, and no one else mattered. God knows what I was thinking, but that's how it was.' Given his previous CV, the police coming down on him for throwing parties felt wildly excessive. 'At the time, I felt – why they've got it in for us? My home got raided seven times in something like a year and a half. Eventually they're going to find something whether they "find it" or not . . . we felt that things were changing. There was a lot more pressure now.'

Wieczorek set up legally at the Four Aces in Dalston instead, and watched from the sidelines as the rest of the illegal party scene got squeezed out of existence by Tappenden and his colleagues over the following four years. 'They had my blessing without a doubt, but I did feel at the time that that would have led us into some serious shit,' he says. Much as the police were forming networks to share best practice and intelligence, though, so were the ravers. Penny Anderson, a journalist at the *New Musical Express* and a Haçienda regular in the early 1990s, remembers hearing from a friend that Rough Trade in West London had received a bulk order for tie-dye Happy Mondays T-shirts, billed to Scotland Yard of all places, information which duly filtered its way across to the door staff and venue managers in Manchester. 'And then some suspiciously sensible looking people in Happy Mondays T-shirts, and the sort of leather jackets you'd see in your aunty's catalogue, turned up,' Anderson says. 'They were going round asking if people had any "ecstasy tablets" but they wouldn't even know how to phrase it properly. They were being so obvious that people were walking around doing rabbit ears behind them.'

Wieczorek's roots in football hooliganism weren't just relevant to his own personal experiences, but to the wider containment strategies adopted by police across the nascent UK dance music scene. The Public Order Act 1986 — the very same piece of legislation used to curtail the actions of the new Travellers and to break up the UK's first illegal raves — also created the UK's first football exclusion orders. They enabled the police, on production of a court order, to bar anyone convicted of any crime committed at a football match (for which by definition they would have already been arrested, tried and punished separately) from entering any football ground in the country for a minimum of three months. Hooligans were, of course, yet one more group contained within the broad umbrella of 'the enemy within', justifying the same legal restrictions to prevent them from fomenting disorder. The pre-emptive and expansionist principles behind the Public Order Act's football exclusion measures were fundamentally the same as those used against Travellers elsewhere in the same legislation: judicial sanctions acting not as a response to a specific crime being committed, but as an open-ended preventative measure targeting so-called undesirable groups. In this, they also harked back to the mass dispersal orders of the miners' strike and the use of 'sus' laws to harass Black communities, as well as point forward to the Criminal Justice Act, and grime DJs getting ASBOs. Whether football-related violence or acid house euphoria, it's the same Thatcherite moralism and fears of societal decay: the idea that specific groups of people, whether football supporters, nomadic communities, young Black men or fans of 'repetitive beats', deserve a greater burden of legislative and policing attention than their neighbours and friends. The large-scale surveillance operations which would subsequently be brought to bear on illegal rave promoters and pirate radio also have their roots in the police's response to hooliganism: in 1987 'Operation Fulltime' saw coordinated police raids at thirty properties across the South East and the Midlands, based on rudimentary CCTV footage of violence at matches involving West Ham and Millwall. Precisely the same tactics would be used two years later when members of West Ham's hardcore Inner City Firm discovered pills, started promoting raves, and set up rave pirate station Centreforce FM; following a five-month surveillance operation their homes were raided in November 1989. Both cases ended with the suspects acquitted, after it became apparent that whole swathes of the police's circumstantial evidence was inadmissible or impossibly weak.

The same month as the Centreforce FM raid, Robert Darby and Leslie Thomas became the first rave organizers to be convicted of a serious crime – 'conspiring to manage premises where drugs were supplied' after a raid on a Thames party boat. Darby and Thomas were sentenced to ten and six years in prison, broadly equivalent to the jail terms handed out to rapists. 'Six and ten's a lot of fucking bird for putting on a boat party, poor cunts. That resonated with a lot of people, certainly with me,' says Wieczorek. Referring to Albert Patrick, the detective chief inspector responsible for the arrests, Wieczorek says, 'He was a fucker. You could tell he wasn't having any of us. I got whooped off the street not long after doing [a party at] Paddington Bowl, and was told very clearly: you fucking try that again you're going, son.' Perhaps inspired by the radical collectivism of the Blackburn scene, the officers who collared Wieczorek were intent on establishing whether Labrynth had any wider agenda. 'The first question they asked me was "Is this political?" and I looked at them thinking, are you stupid? We want to go and get off our tits somewhere and you think I'm Jeremy Corbyn? Leave me out.' The ensuing shift from illegal raves to licensed venues allowed both sides to claim a moral victory of sorts: for the police, more aggressive action meant restoring some semblance of public order, cutting off a trend for mass civil disobedience, and snatching back financial oversight of the events on behalf of the mainstream economy rather than ceding them to organized crime. For dancers and DJs, the relaxing of licensing laws meant that they could carry on dancing all night, at parties which didn't carry anything like the same risk of being shut down and would, if you were lucky, now have working toilets. With the Pay Party Unit haemorrhaging colossal amounts of money, and a reduction in the number of illegal parties making the headlines, political pressure saw it close in late 1991.

But any hopes that a two-year surge of aggressive policing might fully heal the social wounds rave had temporarily sought to salve were clearly optimistic: pursued relentlessly by police following his move to the Four Aces, Wieczorek would be charged with evading the payment of some £1.25 million in VAT, spending eight years awaiting trial before being found not guilty. He describes Robert Darby, subject of those initial raids, as 'a lovely fella from the Isle of Dogs . . . of course, he's dead now, got fucking stabbed up in a row over in Essex.' Albert Patrick, the man who'd pursued them both, would end up being removed from the Met's investigation into Stephen Lawrence's murder following allegations of police corruption. The illegal rave scene would respond to this clampdown by splintering into harder-to-detect units, operating under the radar, waiting for a chance to expand again: an echo of the same process undertaken by the free festival circuit a few years earlier. Almost immediately, though, both tribes would find their energy and ambitions rekindled through closer collaboration with each other.

At the time of their arrival, acid house and rave were depicted as harbingers of previously unimaginable futures, an electronic ritual to welcome in the twenty-first century, powered by alien sounds and mind-altering drugs. Looking back some thirty-plus years after the Pay Party Unit was shuttered, what's striking is instead how deeply embedded that moment seems in its immediate past, from the last remnants of centuries-old institutional homophobia and James Anderton's antediluvian values, to Ken Tappenden's strike-breaking expertise. Whatever the canonical histories say, the birth of UK dance music and the Second Summer of Love owe as much to the picket lines, policing tactics and moral panics of the earlier 1980s as they do to the global adventures of superstar DJs and the formative experiences of those first pills. Rave's supposed halcyon days between 1987 and 1991 were inarguably possessed of a unique and unrepeatable beauty and meaning – certainly for those ten thousand people held rapt in the gloom of an anonymous Blackburn warehouse, waiting for the future to begin – but they were not, despite what we're so often told by the generation who experienced these events first-hand, some transcendental leap into the beyond. They were merely one iteration of the same struggles over power, money and space which preceded them and were, in the re-emergence of the new Travellers, the road to Castlemorton and the powers of the Criminal Justice Act, about to repeat themselves once again.

POLICE AND PROTESTORS AT THE FINAL DEMONSTRATION
AGAINST THE CRIMINAL JUSTICE ACT, OCTOBER 1994

4. Make Some Fucking Noise

Techno terrorists versus the Criminal Justice Act

Open the CD case of the Prodigy's second album, 1994's *Music for the Jilted Generation*, and you're confronted with a visual representation of arguably the most pivotal moment in recent British social history. The album's inner-sleeve artwork, hand-drawn in comic-like style, depicts a wide, seemingly bottomless canyon, spanned by a rickety rope bridge. On the left-hand cliff, thousands of heavily armoured police officers are amassing; some are piling out of blacked-out vans, others are holding back snarling Alsatians. Their transparent riot shields and visored helmets are instantly recognizable from Orgreave, the Battle of the Beanfield and the Love Decade warehouse bust. Behind them, the horizon is dominated by a hulking industrial structure, belching smoke into the night air and tinting the sky blood red. On the opposing precipice, a mass of bodies are thronged around Volkswagen camper vans and two massive speaker stacks, dancing in unencumbered joy. The long grass of the field they occupy is dotted with wildflowers. In the foreground, a man wearing ripped jeans and bovver boots raises a middle finger to the cops across the ravine. In his other hand is a machete, which he's using to slice through the rope holding the bridge up, cutting the dancing masses off from their dystopian pursuers. In one fell stroke, The Man is defeated, and rave nirvana is attained.

Between the album's artwork, and its liner notes declaring, 'How can the government stop young people having a good time? Fight this bollocks', the average Prodigy fan listening to *Music for the Jilted Generation* at the time of its release would have had no doubts about the target of the band's ire: 1994's most notorious piece of legislation, the Criminal Justice and Public Order Act. Reforming huge swathes of the criminal justice system, the act served to fundamentally rebalance power relationships between the individual and the state, just as the defeat of the miners' strike had done for economic relations nearly a decade before. Described by Mark Fisher as an act of 'psychic privatisation', the Criminal Justice Act is best remembered today for its restrictions on protest, squatting and other forms of public assembly, inspired in no small part by populist moral panics over rave culture. Most famous of all remains the clauses which banned any events involving more than a hundred people (later revised down to twenty), taking place at night in the open air, and which included 'sounds wholly or predominantly characterised by the emission of a succession of repetitive beats' – the first time lawmakers had attempted either to define dance music in law, or indeed prohibit it on the basis of its sonic characteristics.

The seeds of this unprecedented collision between the dance floor and the statute book had been laid four years earlier.

Constrained by increasingly sophisticated policing strategies, the aggressive interests of organized crime, and the expanded powers of the Bright Bill, by the middle of 1990 UK dance music had retreated to some extent from the massive orbital raves and warehouse parties which had defined the Second Summer of Love. But behind the scenes a new coalition of outdoor rave organizers was being forged, between a second wave of house and techno soundsystems on the one hand and the Traveller and free festival communities who'd lain dormant since the Beanfield on the other. From the summer of 1990 onwards, the 'free party' emerged as rave's new dominant form: massive outdoor gatherings powered by electronic music and drugs, as had been the case in previous years, but this time knitted into the new Travellers' annual festival calendar, and making use of their inherited knowledge of English byways and remote green spaces. Generally featuring a collection bucket rather than an entry fee, free parties attracted substantially more idealistic and radical promoters than earlier raves: the post-Thatcherite opportunism of Tony Colston-Hayter and others replaced by overtly anti-capitalist crews like the self-proclaimed 'techno terrorists' of Spiral Tribe or the 'house music anarchists' of DiY. The mass civil disobedience embodied in the free party scene, and its increasing connections to a wider radical counterculture running from new Travellers to environmental protestors and direct action groups, brought the liberatory potential of collective dancing into ever-sharper focus. For those involved in running or attending these events, it was as if the doors of a truly alternative society were slowly creaking open: one where the communal world-building of the dance floor might no longer be limited to the weekend.

As attendances and media attention grew, and with government ministers increasingly anxious over this new alliance of different anti-establishment groups, free parties became the target of sustained political and policing pressure. The pivotal moment arrived on 22 May 1992: the first day of the infamous free party on Castlemorton Common, near Malvern in Worcestershire. Police attempts to harry and disrupt various rave-powered Traveller crews instead squeezed them together into one mega-convoy, which eventually pitched up in Castlemorton on the Friday of a swelteringly hot late May bank holiday weekend. The ensuing free party, in which somewhere in the region of 30,000 people danced to dozens of soundsystems for an entire week, became the biggest illegal rave in British history, scandalizing Middle England and giving the Conservative government a populist folk devil with which to justify the swingeing reforms of the Criminal Justice Act. The entire history of UK dance music, if not modern British social history as a whole, hinges on that one blissfully stretched-out weekend in 1992. From the centuries-old nomadic rituals on which it was built, to the legislative repercussions it unwittingly helped to usher in, Castlemorton was the fulcrum around which both ancient and modern danced together.

In the shadow of the Criminal Justice Act, UK dance music took on a wholly different social and political identity: transitioning from an incubator of potential revolution to a highly regulated and lucrative cultural product. Revisiting *Music for the Jilted Generation*'s artwork three decades after its creation, the most striking thing about it isn't the sense of defiant rebel energy it's so unambiguously courting, but how anachronistically earnest that sentiment feels, verging on simplistic agitprop or utopian caricature. Both the Prodigy themselves and Les Edwards (the renowned comic-book artist who drew the inner sleeve) would later deny that they intended to directly criticize the Criminal Justice Act, claiming instead that *Music for the Jilted Generation* was merely an abstract paean to the general concept of rebellion. Between their carefully depoliticized disclaimers and the album itself topping the UK album charts in the autumn of 1994, we can see in miniature dance music's broader realignment: towards commercial and social acceptability, and away from anything which might threaten more profound unrest or upheaval. Today, with UK dance music comfortably nestled in the bosom of global capital, it feels almost impossibly quaint to suggest that the simple act of dancing in a field might genuinely spark a revolution of the masses. But if you were there at the time, the idea might not have seemed quite so fanciful.

It begins with a soundsystem, a field on the fringes of Glastonbury, and Bez from the Happy Mondays standing motionless on the dance floor, staring deeply into the eyes of a horse. Earlier that week, members of Nottingham rave collective DiY had turned up at the festival gates with a set of Technics turntables, a DJ mixer and a crate of records, hoping to blag their way in: their approach as appealingly ramshackle as their name suggests. Formed in Nottingham in the autumn of 1989 but hailing from every corner of the UK, DiY were ravers first and foremost, throwing their first squat parties largely out of dissatisfaction with the alternatives then on offer: impersonal and overpriced orbital mega-raves occurring in the South, or violently policed and unpredictably organized warehouse parties in the North. Instead, they took inspiration from Nottingham's rich history of blues parties, treating the soundsystem not just as a temporary portal to a night of pleasure but as a tool for collective and cultural community-building. 'What we had experienced was great individually but there had to be a better, more idealistic whole,' writes DiY founder Harry Harrison in his autobiography *Dreaming in Yellow*. 'If the rave scene had lost its way and its idealistic origins, then someone needed to put them back . . . we could book a venue, and try to do it ourselves.' From their first events in the autumn of 1989, DiY expanded rapidly and somewhat haphazardly from house parties to club nights to warehouse raves, interspersed with trips down to London for the Poll Tax riots, before they found themselves at Glastonbury the following June, turfing up with turntables and records but no speakers, like travelling Elizabethan players in hope of a stage. They were directed towards the unfenced and largely unregulated Travellers' field, which abutted the more formalized and boundaried zones of the festival proper: Harrison recalls meeting up with another member of the collective who informed them with delightful serendipity that 'some Travellers he knew had set up a marquee at the bottom of the main drag in the free zone. They had a sound system, he had records, but did we know anyone with decks and a mixer?'* The stage had been set: between the efforts of DiY and another of the UK's pioneering acid house soundsystems, the Cambridge-based Tonka crew, by the end of the weekend an alchemical bond had been formed between the travellers and the ravers, and between the autonomous spaces of the nomadic convoy and the sensory rush of Ecstasy-assisted electronic music. The Happy Mondays came down to the Travellers' field on Saturday night, fresh from playing the Pyramid stage, and were met at sunrise by a Traveller riding a horse onto the dance floor: 'as Bez and the horse stared telepathically into each other's eyes', writes Harrison, 'a new paradigm was born.'†

DiY's immersion into the egalitarian organizing of the new Travellers expanded their sense of what their parties could or should be. The music industry 'could never understand why we didn't charge and make a fortune', Harrison told *Vice* magazine in 2014. 'If you didn't get it – well, then you just didn't get it.' But adopting the mentality of the free festival and the blues dance, viewing their events as a collective good rather than a business endeavour, had strategic as well as ideological benefits: both the Bright Bill and pre-existing anti-rave policing tactics had targeted business-minded rave

---

* In an enjoyable nod back to the free festival circuit, the soundsystem in question belonged to none other than Nik Turner of Hawkwind, while the pyramid-shaped marquee it sat within, also belonging to Turner, had previously been used at Stonehenge, and at earlier, smaller iterations of Glastonbury, inspiring the latter's own famed Pyramid stage.

† Despite DiY and Tonka's pivotal role in kickstarting what would become the free party scene, they were neither the first people to play acid house at a free festival – Harrison credits the Sweat soundystem with this at the Avon Free Festival in 1989 – or the first to bring all-night dancing to Glastonbury. Interviewed by the journalist Joe Muggs in 2019, the post-punk bassist Youth of the band Killing Joke recalls that dub reggae, courtesy of soundsystems like Jah Shaka and Saxon, had in fact been playing until sunrise from the early 1980s – 'the only music you could go dance to all night long that wasn't acoustic around a bonfire'. Just as blues dances had set the template for all-night raving across the UK, so it seems that Black soundsystem culture also laid the same cultural foundations in the fields of Worthy Farm, before both were obscured from the canon.

moguls through fines and seizures (it was the *Pay* Party Unit, after all). If the organizers weren't charging on the door, then the powers available to the state lost much of their purchase. 'The police were all looking for a Mister Big with a Samsonite full of fivers,' recalled fellow DiY organizer Jack in 2014. 'They didn't really have an idea about why some people would be doing it for free and what the point behind that was.'

Simultaneously, the new Travellers began to understand the symbiotic possibilities offered by free parties: these vast new crowds, lured into the countryside by the promise of unfettered debauchery and all-night dancing provided a new injection of energy, manpower and money with which to support life on the road, while the free party promoters' hit-and-run tactics – using a given piece of land as a site of temporary entertainment rather than semi-permanent residence – offered a means by which to circumvent the restrictions of the Public Order Act 1986. While the new Travellers' dreams of a permanently sustainable nomadic counterculture might have died at the Beanfield, the free party scene afforded something approaching an alternative: the vast majority of attendees spent the working week living 'normal' lives rather than remaining on the road, but their temporary pleasure-seeking provided economic sustenance for a smaller core of permanent Travellers, and helped to rebuild their collective identity. Alan Lodge, who'd left the convoy in 1989 and settled a stone's throw from DiY's squat in Nottingham, was one of those former nomads who saw a tantalizing new opportunity in rave's reinvigoration of travelling communities, and in particular in DiY's lithe, listenable deep house rather than more aggressive rave or techno. 'It turned out that the next generation weren't frightened to bring their kids with them,' he says of the free parties which began to dot the English landscape following Glastonbury 1990, 'so suddenly it's not just seventeen-year-olds hanging out and listening to something that sounds like a drill bit, it's families that felt they could hang out for a few days and regenerate those tribes.'

These sentiments didn't apply to everyone in the convoy,

however. 'The older ones hated it,' explains Roger Beard, a stalwart of the new Traveller convoy who would go on to become a resident DJ at Paul Oakenfold's foundational acid house nights Future and Spectrum. 'There was an element that loved it, and an element that hated it . . . [Windsor Free Festival founder] Sid Rawles's son stormed off the site, because he wanted to be playing dance music and they [the older hippies] wouldn't let him do it.' Beard was one of the first people to try and bridge the gap between the early acid house clubs and post-Beanfield Travellers, with grand plans to transport the entire crowd at Future up to Stonehenge for the spring equinox in 1988. 'The idea was that everyone would show up at the club, they'd get put on a coach like the Magical Mystery Tour, we turn up at Stonehenge and put on a big party.' Their plans fell apart when the police raided Future promoter Ian St Clair's house, and started leaning on the club's suppliers. 'We tried to hire coaches and none of the coach companies would do it, because of the injunction around travelling to Stonehenge,' explains Beard. Despite these setbacks, Beard would continue to act as a conduit between the acid scenes of the 1970s and the 1990s, inviting his Traveller contacts into the clubs and his DJ friends out to the fields; three years later, the conditions for forming more substantial alliances between ravers and Travellers would become vastly more amenable.

With the mothballing of the Pay Party Unit and its national coordination of anti-rave operations (which had been geared towards static locations like warehouses in any event, rather than the constantly moving target of a convoy) no longer available to local police forces, there was little to restrain the growing coalition between ravers and free Travellers as the 1991 festival season began. A huge rave on Hungerford Common in May of that year embodied this new symbiosis: 'The Travellers took the site during the week,' explains Roger Beard, 'and they had a marquee, but none of them had a soundsystem. So a soundsystem came down on the Saturday. They were called Sweat, they came with the full MC thing, going on about "We ain't gonna play until you make some noise!"' Five minutes of hazy camcorder footage shot that weekend offers a brief glimpse into this new paradigm: an old diesel engine, seemingly removed from its parent vehicle and now used as a generator, sits next to a green lorry repurposed as a Traveller family's home. A man weaves between cars cradling an infant; a boy in his early teens cringes at his mum's dancing. This is clearly a space in which social and familial connections run deeper than mere partying, where whole lives are ongoing around and throughout the mayhem of the weekend. Elsewhere, though, the crowd feels wholly alien from those who would have flocked to Stonehenge a decade earlier, the transitory and transactional nature of their engagement far clearer. 'Morning ravers!' calls an unseen camerawoman to a group of impossibly fresh-faced friends, all dressed in stylish club clobber: one grins back with gleaming teeth, while another tousles her peroxide hair. The driver of the Ford Escort parked next to them is slumped forward in blissful exhaustion, while his passenger gurns furiously and bobs his head to the beat. 'Free party people in the area!' shouts an unseen MC.

The summer of 1991 saw similar scenes repeated up and down the country. Video from the fortnight-long White Goddess free festival, held on Bodmin Moor in Cornwall in August 1991, shows a group of children no older than seven or eight bopping self-consciously in the early morning gloom to an absolutely relentless selection of distorted breakbeat techno blaring from Spiral Tribe's rig. The footage cuts to later in the day, once the sun has burned the mist off the ground and the clouds out of the sky: a woman dances on the roof of a 1970s Volvo estate, shouts, 'Can you feel it? Then you've got it, let's go!' and encourages the same children from before to join her, clambering over a man slumped unconscious on the bonnet as they do so. 'Bank holiday bender!' shouts the woman, as she cuts shapes in the late summer air to the distant thud of kick drums. This amalgamation of the hedonistic with the parental feels oddly wholesome and unexpectedly transgressive: earlier UK dance music had to be sought out and journeyed into, a full-body escape from the normal expectations and constraints of everyday life, laced with faintly sordid and unambiguously grown-up connotations; emphatically *not* something that you brought your kids to. The free party marks the point at which the pounding beats and chemical experimentation of the rave first begin to be assimilated into the wider patterns and responsibilities of everyday British life, informing everything from the superclub's mass-market week-to-weekend cycle of production and consumption, to trendy mid-morning parent-and-toddler raves in the gentrified neighbourhoods of the early 2020s.

Consistently behind the curve as the first wave of acid house promoters had enriched themselves between 1987 and 1989, police and politicians were initially outflanked by those now eschewing the profit motive entirely. Little over a year after the Bright Bill had promised an end to illegal raves, the renewed surge in free parties (and the increasing crowds drawn to the them) also returned the subject to the political agenda. The Home Office, led by future Conservative leader Michael Howard, tried to stem the tide by issuing new guidance to police forces in May 1991 on how the existing powers of the Public Order Act 1986 could and should be used to disrupt or remove new Travellers and their raving comrades, but he was met with a lukewarm response from the police: the parties kept coming, and public clamour over them continued to grow.

Just as Tony Colston-Hayter had become the media's primary bogeyman during the initial rush of outdoor raves in 1988 and 1989 – 'Acid's Mr Big' as the *Daily Mirror* dubbed him – so press and political attention focused on one soundsystem in particular during the free party era, a motley crew of radical techno-hippy troublemakers called Spiral Tribe. The Tribe's core members had, like those from DiY, grown up going to free festivals and blues dances, before moving on to The Haçienda, Blackburn warehouse raves and witnessing the same scenes at Glastonbury 1990 as punters (albeit dancing in Tonka's tent rather than DiY's). They were possessed of a similarly utopian approach to rave as a social force, but their rhetoric and ideology went beyond the affable acid pranksterism of Harry Harrison and friend, tipping over into earnest declarations of all-out sonic warfare. 'The party is every day, every minute of every day,' declared DJ Terra Technic uncompromisingly, in a 1992 interview with the BBC. 'The music's on 24 hours a day. When it's off, we're not in the area.' Dressed in identikit black bomber jackets, shaved heads and army boots, Spiral Tribe's 'techno terrorists' were destined to send Middle England into palpitations even before you got to the music itself: a rigid and utterly unforgiving selection of monolithic techno stompers, brain-mangling acid tracks and riotously aggressive breakbeats, the Spirals priding themselves on going further, faster and harder than anyone else dared. 'People quite often leave their jobs, pack up and run away from home to come and join the Spiral Tribe, like they're joining the circus,' said the softly spoken but piercingly intense Mark Harrison, the crew's unofficial spokesperson and figurehead, in the same BBC interview. 'They contribute whatever skills they have, and they love doing it, and that's why it's grown so big. The number of people on the road, that creative vibe, is contagious. That's what sets us apart from the straightforward, commercial, run-of-the-mill nightclub event, which is really just music and leisure, industry and entertainment; it never goes any further than that.' Harrison's choice of the circus as a metaphor for the free party scene mirrors Alan Lodge's comparisons between free festival hippies and troupes of Elizabethan actors: rave acting as merely the latest iteration of a centuries-old collective urge to find solace and solidarity, and reconnect with half-remembered rituals buried deep in the soil, by escaping outside everyday societal norms and the physical boundaries of the city. 'London was no longer big enough to contain our parties, so we went west,' writes Harrison of their expansion in late 1990 from urban warehouse raves to outdoor free parties. 'It was there, out in the wilds, that we discovered the scattered remains of the free festival movement. By then we'd developed a clear notion that our mission was to unlock and open up spaces – take back the commons – or, if they wouldn't give them back, we'd just set up new ones.'

A 'calendar of police harassment' collated by Tribe members

over the course of 1991 and 1992 tracks the escalating police tactics deployed in response to their activities, and the soundsystem's increasingly noisy and defiant responses: a cycle of polarizing and pressure-raising forces which would lead inexorably towards Castlemorton. Initially, the police appear to follow the disruptive but largely non-confrontational tactics practised by Ken Tappenden in previous years: bending the law with the use of 'lies and threats' according to Spiral Tribe, but focusing primarily on drug-related arrests rather than detaining rave organizers. This approach proved largely unsuccessful at stopping the parties, and instead lapsed regularly into farce: at one event, several attendees were arrested for possession of substances that turned out to be vitamin pills, before being released without charge. At another rave held in the then-abandoned husk of the Roundhouse in Chalk Farm, the police attempted to confiscate the crew's sound equipment, before giving up after it turned out that they'd forgotten to bring the necessary paperwork. In December 1991 the Spirals squatted an empty property in Surrey, only to discover that it was part of the eye-wateringly wealthy gated community St George's Hill: home over the years to everyone from pop stars and multimillionaire businessmen to footballers and Formula 1 drivers. Despite Spiral Tribe having stumbled over it accidentally, St George's Hill represented a cosmic link back to earlier generations of radical English protest. Its sprawling mansions had been built over land once occupied by the Diggers: religious dissidents and collectivists of the mid-1600s, an offshoot of the similarly intentioned Levellers, who'd challenged their feudal landowners by re-taking a strip of formerly common land in St George's Hill following its enclosure, and using it to grow food. This was a place invested with symbolic meaning and historical resonance, perfect for challenging the staid landowning hegemony of the 1990s, and reasserting the right to collective pleasure. Alerted to the historical and political significance of their location by swarms of paparazzi, Spiral Tribe stuck to their guns: what else was there to do but party?

If Harrison and others had hoped that their incursion into

enemy territory might prick the consciences or pique the curiosity of their new neighbours, they were sorely mistaken. Instead, by striking out from their usual surroundings of dingy warehouses and remote rural idylls, bringing the rave instead to the doorsteps of judges, politicians, investors and other establishment powerbrokers, Spiral Tribe did little more than draw a massive target on their own backs. Almost immediately, the treatment afforded to them by the police stepped up a gear. 'The moment everything changed, which we didn't realize at the time, was when we squatted St George's Hill, even though it was a fairly small party,' says Mark Harrison. 'Our amps were stolen immediately after that from the main Spiral Tribe squat, and it's always been a mystery: we're well connected with all the people in the area, and we've never had even a hint of where they went. We'd discovered undercover police watching us just prior to that. They must have been watching the house.' If all this sounds vaguely paranoid, the 'calendar of police harassment' suggests that police attitudes did indeed shift at that moment, with raids on Spiral Tribe events ramping up in frequency and intensity in the early weeks of 1992. Just over a month before Castlemorton, the Metropolitan Police deployed their most fearsome public order unit – the Territorial Support Group, more often seen dealing with riots and massive protests – to deal with a Spiral Tribe party on Acton Lane in West London. 'All of a sudden you peered out of a crack in the wall, and the place was surrounded by every kind of police vehicle you can imagine,' recalls one attendee, describing the scene shortly before the police sealed the building, and a lengthy stand-off between the TSG and ravers developed, broken only when officers clad in riot gear stormed the building. 'Sledgehammers and a JCB digger were used to collapse walls in on the people trapped inside,' reads a Spiral Tribe statement published in the event's aftermath, which goes on to allege that the police 'indiscriminately beat up men, women and children', destroyed Spiral Tribe's soundsystem, injured upwards of 700 partygoers and arrested five people (none of whom were Spiral Tribe members) for assaults on officers and breaches of the peace. Tribe member Simon later recalled the 'horrible experience' of being manhandled to the floor. 'Really, what were we doing that was so disastrously wrong? Occupying empty buildings, playing music and dancing.'

Where politicians and the police lacked insight into the motivations or methods of Spiral Tribe's DJs and dancers, they projected their fears of mob rule onto them. 'The authorities couldn't understand how this many people could assemble in one place, in pre-internet, pre-mobile days,' recounted crew member Cyrus in 2014. 'That loss of control hammered them into cracking down much harder than they might otherwise have done.' Coming off the back of a decade defined by civil unrest from Toxteth to Brixton, politicians 'understandably became nervous about the potential emergence of a politicised underclass,' as Matthew Collin puts it. In particular, the Poll Tax riots of March 1990 – in which somewhere in the region of a quarter of a million people marched on Whitehall, ending in pitched battles with the police running into the night – had shown that such conflict would not be consigned to the 1980s (more pertinently for career-conscious types in Westminster, the riots also contributed directly to Margaret Thatcher's removal from office). In the 1998 policing textbook *Policing Public Disorder: Theory and Practice* the academic David Waddingon castigates officers' rigid and fatalistic thinking when confronted with the spectre of the mob, and their collective tendency to 'pathologise the motives and actions of the crowd as fundamentally irrational, or prone to "manipulation" by ill-intentioned individuals or subgroups.' In this model of policing, anyone on the dance floor – indeed within a crowd of any kind – can be effortlessly moulded and controlled by the most unsavoury or antisocial person in attendance, becoming little more than an unthinking tendril of some greater malevolence. These 'theories of disorder' defined a generation of British public order policing, from the violent clashes at Notting Hill in 1974, to the burning streets of Brixton and Toxteth in 1981, the mounted cavalry charges on the fields outside Orgreave, carnage in the stands at Hillsborough, and indeed a JCB crashing through the walls of a rave; officers from the Territorial Support Group would go on to be repeatedly accused of beating up suspects in their care to their involvement in the death of newspaper vendor Ian Tomlinson during the G20 protests.

The shock and awe tactics deployed by the Territorial Support Group to deal with Spiral Tribe were not universal, however, with different regional police forces adopting inconsistent and largely avoidant approaches to managing, containing or disrupting free parties occurring on their respective patches. Where Spiral Tribe faced riot squads and tear gas in West London, other forces around the UK preferred to redirect the rave rather than confront it head-on. Roads leading to a suspected free party site would be blocked off, a cordon of police vehicles would prevent the convoy from pulling over, and outriders would gently but forcefully escort the assorted mass of ravers and Travellers to the nearest county border, where they'd be shunted into the remit of a neighbouring police force, to become somebody else's problem.

It's this approach which led directly to Castlemorton: the previous spring's Avon Free Festival had seen between 2,000 and 4,000 people descend on Chipping Sodbury, enraging everyone from the village's Conservative chairman to local golfer Kevin Dunn, who complained to the *Western Daily Press* that 'they've taken over four holes and some of the greens are in the middle of their camp.' Anticipating a repeat of scenes in Chipping Sodbury the following year, Avon and Somerset Police launched Operation Nomad ahead of the 1992 festival season: a coordinated attempt to prevent free party convoys from settling anywhere within their area of responsibility, with internal police documents confirming that 'dedicated resources will be used to gather intelligence in respect of the movements of itinerants and Travellers, and deal with minor acts of trespass . . . resources will be greatly enhanced for the period Thursday 21st May to Sunday 24th May inclusive in relation to the anticipated gathering of Travellers in the Chipping Sodbury area.' Chipping Sodbury had itself been chosen as a venue in 1991 only after the police prevented the convoy from reaching their preferred location on Inglestone Common: repeatedly blocked off from more familiar festival sites, free party convoys were forced to relocate to less and less desirable spaces, closer to civilization, where the noise and disruption of the party would be felt more acutely, and local anger would intensify, which in turn put more pressure on the police to act more assertively. The cycle of mistrust and mutual antipathy would then repeat itself, cranking up an already febrile situation to unsustainable levels.

Throughout the spring of 1992, free party crews and police forces across the South West played an elaborate game of cat-and-mouse with each other, the overall effect of which was to gradually limit the space in which events could take place, and to corral different Traveller groups together, intensifying the simmering ill-feeling on all sides. With the bank holiday approaching, Avon and Somerset Police finally managed to get this combined mass of ravers off their patch, and escorted them over the border to West Mercia, a decision that would prove fateful. Where the officers from Avon and Somerset had spent decades handling Traveller groups and free festivals, their West Mercian colleagues were relative novices: caught flat-footed, they put up little resistance when convoys – many of them hardened by previous conflict and unwilling to play nice with the police after their harrying by other forces – gravitated towards Castlemorton Common.

This isn't to say that West Mercia welcomed free parties, as local Chief Constable David Blakey made clear. 'This spring has seen the formation of an unholy alliance between new age travellers and ravers . . . the Traveller is a dropout, a descendant of the hippie, while the raver is a party-going young person of any and all social class and employment. They have little in common except music, parties, perhaps drugs, and a willingness to defy authority.' But as the vans and soundsystems converged on Castlemorton, it became clear that West Mercia's police didn't have the resources, know-how or inclination required to resist what was rapidly becoming inevitable. 'One lone policeman in his car asked why we were there, so it was said that we were waiting for some friends that we had lost en route,' DiY crew member Emma told *DJ Mag* in 2014: scouting ahead of the main convoy for potential party sites, she'd been one of the first people onto the Common. 'The copper drove off, and the festival appeared.' Within hours, a critical mass of vehicles and people had assembled, too large to be removed by force. 'Under current circumstances, we are clearly obliged to adopt a low-key approach on the site in order to avoid unnecessary conflict with members of this huge gathering,' said Assistant Chief Constable Philip Davies. 'Many of them have already displayed an extremely aggressive attitude towards the police, and the safety of officers must be one of my priorities. This is already a difficult situation, but I do not wish to provoke things further by sparking off large-scale disorder.' A post-event report written by David Blakey concludes that 'given the geography of the area and because nothing could prevent the travellers stopping at Castlemorton or on any of the surrounding commons, it was a hopeless attempt.'

While the police clearly had their reasons not to risk even greater disorder, to outraged locals, anxious politicians and an incensed media their stance looked like nothing more than capitulation. 'I have never seen such filth and degradation,' fumed local Councillor Alex Stewart-Cleary. 'These people have turned Castlemorton into a cesspit, a human rubbish tip.' One local resident told *The Times* that 'they're just useless bastards, the lot of them, and they belong in a zoo', while another nearby landowner told *Newsnight* that the festival represented 'a total breakdown of law and order within this country . . . we do not want these people returning to Castlemorton Common, however I fear for other rural areas that such an invasion should be deposited on them.' In a House of Commons debate conducted in the days following the end of the festival, the Conservative MP Michael Spicer, in whose constituency Castlemorton Common sits, describes the event as an 'invasion . . . new age travellers, ravers and drugs racketeers arrived at a strength of two motorised army divisions, complete with several massed bands and, above all, a highly sophisticated command and signals system' – the free party transformed in starkly non-metaphorical terms into a foreign paramilitary force, violently annexing a pristine piece of rural England.

In one particularly bizarre piece of reportage, broadcast as the party began to wind down, a suited TV reporter mediates a discussion between three local housewives, all dressed in spotless white frocks, and three festival attendees wearing muddy plaid, boots and ramshackle dreadlocks. 'After finding these . . . *drug* equipment in my front garden . . .' sputters one of the locals, so knotted with outrage that she can barely get the words out, 'people must understand that a gathering such as this is an umbrella for the drug-dealing and drug-pushing of the people up *there*.' The camera zooms in on the clear plastic bag she's holding, which appears to contain a syringe. When pressed on the issue of noise, one of the free Travellers can do little more than puff his cheeks out, shrug, and claim entirely unconvincingly that, 'Well, the noise is being kept to a minimum now,' while another leans in to opine woozily that 'the Government needs to legalise all drugs . . . I don't think that sort of thing is very good myself, but it happens in every town.' Each group's position seems guaranteed to stoke the others' antipathy and mistrust, ratcheting up the tension between them further. Whatever positives the free parties strived for, and whatever hyperbole and snobbery were contained in wider discussions about Travellers and ravers, Castlemorton clearly involved incessant noise, property damage – smashing fences for firewood and Travellers' dogs harassing or savaging local livestock were both common themes – and some measure of environmental impact on potentially sensitive ecosystems (Castlemorton Common had been declared a Site of Special Scientific Interest in 1985). Allegations of antisocial, destructive or self-indulgent behaviour levelled against those involved in the free party scene might have been exaggerated, but they were not imaginary. At the same time, it's easy to see why a marginalized community such as the new Travellers, singled out for violence and demonization from police forces and governments stretching back decades if not centuries, subject now to increasingly restrictive policing tactics and demeaning media portrayals, may have felt no urge for deference or politeness towards the world of privet hedges, pristine tea rooms and twitching net curtains which so clearly disdained them.

The breathless media coverage afforded to Castlemorton had another unintended side-effect: while tales of unhinged debauchery might have incensed the conservative tastes of Middle England, they also unwittingly acted as a colossal recruiting campaign for young people with the time and wherewithal to get themselves to Worcestershire. Loud music, sex, drugs, the wholesale upending of social norms and staid hierarchies, and it was all free? No wonder people kept pouring onto the Common, and remaining there long after the bank holiday had ended. 'It wasn't helped by the media to be honest – if they hadn't said anything it would have just stopped as it was,' one unnamed attendee told the BBC, which had helped to bring Castlemorton to national attention by making it their lead item on the *Six O'Clock News*. 'But as soon as you start putting it out on the television that there's this huge party everyone jumps in their car and just turns up.' For many of those who were there, Castlemorton would be spoken about in reverential tones. Harry Harrison of DiY describes the scene in his autobiography as less a 'drug-crazed dystopia' than something approaching a village fête, the sun beaming down on children laughing and adults luxuriating in 'some kind of English Shangri-La'. The same sense of untrammelled bliss and communion ran into the night, with Simon Reynolds describing his experiences dancing to Spiral Tribe's soundsystem in *Energy Flash* as akin to 'a pagan gathering' in which the crowd evolves 'into a single, pulsating organism', while Reynolds himself is swept up in 'a frenzy of belligerent euphoria'. His description unwittingly mirrors David Waddington and the wider policing establishment's assessment of the psychological forces underpinning large crowds: from both perspectives, the knot of people on the dance floor becomes a singular, undifferentiated mass, their consciousness merged into one; the only difference being that it's viewed with transcendental glee by Reynolds, and unspeakable dread by the police.

As sure as a comedown follows a high, though, it quickly became apparent that the scale and audacity of Castlemorton was unsustainable and would have to be answered for: 'not only the peak but also the death of free rave culture', as one anonymous commenter put it. Some of this had been visible in the moment – Harry Harrison of DiY describes news crews from as far afield and Japan and New Zealand filming proceedings – but it was when the party began to wind down that things started feeling inescapably real. DiY managed to avoid the attention of police officers surrounding the site by spiriting their soundsystem away under cover of darkness, hidden in a horsebox. Others weren't so lucky: Spiral Tribe were one of the last soundsystems to leave the site after hanging around for the clean-up operation, at which point they were arrested en masse, on suspicion of devising and masterminding the entire event.

Subsequently prosecuted for 'conspiracy to commit a breach of the peace', the thirteen-person Spiral Tribe trial at Wolverhampton Crown Court became the most expensive criminal case in British history. It also turned into the site for yet another unlicensed party, when hundreds of supporters turned up to the committal hearings wearing T-shirts which read 'Make Some Fucking Noise!' and stood shouting and cheering outside the courthouse. 'What the fuck else are you going to do?' says Harrison. 'You've just been wrongfully accused of organising the whole of Castlemorton. We had to embrace our outlawness, because otherwise we'd just be victimised. If this is the route we're going down, then let's enjoy it.' Harrison describes the 'gammon-faced' magistrate overseeing the hearing as 'all your worst headmasters rolled into one. When he saw everyone coming in, and the whole place full with these Make Some Fucking Noise T-shirts, he went absolutely mental.' Things descended immediately into some kind of bizarre Benny Hill farce. 'He was livid, so he made a court order – "By order of the court, take those T-shirts off!" Of course all the girls obliged, and had nothing on underneath. "By order of the court, put those T-shirts back on!" It was great. We knew at that moment that things were going our way.' During the trial itself, Harrison and others realized that they could spring the locks on the massive, steel-and-bulletproof-glass doors to their cells with nothing other than a plastic coffee stirrer. 'So we freaked out the guards for a long time by moving everyone around in the cells, so they weren't quite sure if they'd left that person there. Eventually they found us all together in one cell, so they just left all the doors open.' Halfway through the trial, the Tribe's supporters started squatting on land directly behind the courthouse and playing techno at earbleeding volume during proceedings. The sense of the state losing control was palpable.

Other aspects played into Spiral Tribe's hands too, most importantly the objective facts of the case. Despite their reputation as fearless techno rabble-rousers, Spiral Tribe had in fact only played a peripheral part in proceedings at Castlemorton, having been forced to borrow other crews' equipment after so much of theirs had been destroyed at Acton Lane. Alongside this, the prosecution's case that Spiral Tribe had single-handedly directed and controlled the convoy was palpably unsustainable, given that so much about Castlemorton had been emergent and unpredictable rather than the product of a centralized, identifiable conspiracy on the part of any one group or individual. Surprisingly, the star witness turned out to be a senior West Mercia police officer, a Superintendent Clift, who'd been left off the prosecution witness list but was tracked down by defence lawyers in hospital. His statement turned out to be dynamite, completely eviscerating the prosecution's entire case: Spiral Tribe couldn't have conspired to organize a rave on Castlemorton Common, he said, because the decision to divert the convoy there was made by him. At the commital proceedings in early 1993, he'd found Mark Harrison and whispered: 'I just want you to know that I don't agree with what is happening to you here. This is a political stitch-up.' When it came to the criminal trial, he proceeded to publicly absolve them of responsibility by insisting that he'd allowed the convoy through on humanitarian grounds.

As the trial progressed, it also became clear that the 'techno terrorists' label the Tribe had cultivated in the press, and the quasi-satanic reputation foisted on them by the police, were going to be similarly difficult to reconcile with the facts. Maybe part of this is the softening effects of nostalgia, but for a group decried as the most dangerous people in Britain, both in their statements at the time and their recollections today, Spiral Tribe come across as earnest, well-spoken and deeply unthreatening. 'I wouldn't say that we're just a reactionary kick against society,' Harrison said in a 1992 interview. 'If you don't like things about society, we don't go out and petrol bomb the place . . . we're not confrontational, we're not violent, we're not just rejecting everything . . . we take a very creative and positive approach to what might be bad in society.' Reminiscing later on the legacy of Spiral Tribe, he sounds far closer to the placid hippies of the free festival scene in which he grew up than the drug-fuelled wreckers of civilization Spiral Tribe were regularly portrayed as at the time: 'Having the ability to be able to be in a space and then to kind of gravitate as human beings into collectives into groups, to be able to express your creativity without rules is a very interesting thing,' he says. 'Because it doesn't necessarily mean that it's all going to just collapse into an apocalyptic mess.' While the Tribe's sonic palette and anti-establishment rhetoric were decidedly more abrasive than those offered by DiY, or Wally Hope and the free festival hippies, they clearly all existed on the same continuum, inspired by much the same utopian principles, which meant that prosecutorial attempts to pin them down as confrontational, nihilistic troublemakers fell flat. As a result, it was far less shocking than it should have been, given the expense and attention lavished on the trial, when it ended in the acquittal of all thirteen defendants. This was a colossal humiliation for the police and prosecutors, and a vindication for Harrison and others, but any euphoria had already been snuffed out: their cards marked, Spiral Tribe would find it next to impossible to continue operating in the UK after Castlemorton. They attempted one final free party in June 1992, on a brownfield site in the heart of mid-regeneration Docklands, under the totemic glare of the newly built Canary Wharf: temple to the neoliberal reshaping of Britain's economic and political cultures under Thatcher. While the audacity of their location was admirable, with only two roads leading to the site the party would be successfully shut down by the police after only an hour. By the time the 1993 festival season started up, and with the Castlemorton trial looming, the

Spiral Tribe convoy instead decamped to Beauvais in France, coining the term 'teknival' for their new wave of European free parties.

By the time of Spiral Tribe's acquittal in late 1994, the wider political landscape around free parties had shifted even further, with the trial conducted against a wider backdrop of ratcheting unease within Westminster, and a Conservative government increasingly determined to make sure that nothing on the scale of Castlemorton could ever be allowed to happen again. A set of confidential Cabinet Office memos released to the public in 2018 charts the increasingly hostile thinking amongst senior Conservatives towards ravers and travellers over the course of 1992. 'The police are reluctant to use the powers available to them,' complains Michael Heseltine, the Environment Secretary, in a policy paper produced by his department early that year, noting that the Traveller population remained higher at the beginning of the 1990s than it had been in 1981, despite the violence of the Beanfield and the extended powers to remove or arrest Travellers given to the police by the Public Order Act of 1986. Over the course of February and March 1992 – the period immediately preceding Castlemorton, Spiral Tribe's Acton Lane raid, and an election the Tories were widely expected to lose – Heseltine tried to push through proposals which would remove local councils' obligation to provide Traveller sites, with the intention of pushing nomadic communities into permanent housing. John Major's policy advisor Carolyn Sinclair convinced the prime minister to delay any announcement of these proposals, highlighting the lack of existing sites for Traveller communities and warning that 'gypsies and travellers will simply be moved around the country in a game of "pass the parcel"': precisely the same issue that would lead within weeks to events at Castlemorton.

Major's surprise election victory in April 1992 and the sight of 30,000 ravers congregating over the May bank holiday swiftly brought the issue of nomadic pleasure-seeking back to the top of the political agenda. A succession of more hawkish voices came to the fore in Cabinet discussions over the course of 1992 and 1993, moving the conversation beyond Heseltine's proposals to broader and more draconian legislation being developed by the Home Office. One of the most aggressive voices was a young Damian Green – then a policy advisor to Major, later Theresa May's de facto deputy prime minister. 'This issue is one which greatly exercises our supporters in rural areas,' he expounds in a letter to the prime minister in February 1993, arguing that Heseltine's renewed proposals 'would combine great weakness, compared to what landowners are expecting, and be a public relations disaster . . . You have raised expectations of a tough response to these irritating problems. A [sic] announcement of a thin set of measures which do not even attempt to cope with Raves will be greeted with little enthusiasm.' At the Conservative party conference in September 1992 Major declared 'New age travellers? Not in this age. Not in any age . . .' to rapturous applause from the Tory faithful. A year later, newly appointed Home Secretary, Michael Howard, would use his maiden conference speech to announce a new piece of legislation to deal not only with the issue of ravers and Travellers, but indeed reshape the British state entirely: the Criminal Justice and Public Order Bill, later to become the Criminal Justice and Public Order Act 1994.*

One of the most common misconceptions about the Criminal Justice Act is that it was specifically or solely an 'anti-rave' law. While its mention of 'repetitive beats' was clearly designed to bring an end to free parties, and despite images from Castlemorton embodying the licentiousness and disorder the government sought to legislate against, the roots of their desire to restrict public assembly stretch back further than Operation Nomad, the free party scene, or even UK dance music as a whole. If nothing else, the explosion of dance music's mainstream popularity in the second half of the 1990s demonstrates that it wasn't the dance floor itself which most vexed those responsible for drafting and passing the Criminal Justice

---

* A piece of legislation remains a bill while it is debated in the Commons, Parliamentary committees and the Lords; at the point that it becomes law, it is referred to as an act.

Act, but the contextual elements of the free party scene: promoters who didn't pay their taxes; Conservative-leaning homeowners in the shires, anxious about noise and disorder; the collective decadence of widespread drug-taking; and the potential for raves to stoke popular discontent when allied to wider radical activist networks.

Throughout the 1980s Thatcher had raged against 'the enemy within' and its nebulous alliance of striking miners, homosexuals, new Travellers, left-wing activists, trade unions, football hooligans and (in the decade's latter stages) acid house ravers. Despite measures like the Public Order Act of 1986 and the Bright Bill in 1990, the idea that British society was rotting from the inside, emboldened by a sinister creep of left-wing permissiveness and sloth, became an article of faith for Conservative politicians and voters. The party's 1992 election manifesto leant heavily on tropes of safety and security; at the following year's Conservative Party conference, Major unveiled his Back to Basics campaign, a focus on 'neighbourliness, decency, courtesy'. The Criminal Justice Act wasn't just trying to shut down illegal parties, it was a concerted attempt to defeat this entire shadowy coalition of subcultural groups and radical ideas, which in the minds of the Conservatives represented an existential threat to British decency and order. Indeed, out of the hundreds of pages of legislation eventually passed as the Criminal Justice Act, only two paragraphs mention raves. Even the clauses targeting other public order offences – squatting, hunt sabotage, environmental protest and so on – still make up a minority of the Act's clauses. Elsewhere, the legislation banned prison officers from going on strike, abolishing their trade union in the process; it removed criminal defendants' right to silence; and transferred decisions on bail from the magistrates to the police. It expanded and formalized the state's ability to retain DNA and CCTV evidence, and created new powers by which the police could stop and search people without suspicion of a crime having been committed – a descendant of the hated 'sus' laws. The Criminal Justice Act represented a dramatic expansion of state power across the criminal justice system as a whole, indeed the entirety of British society. The spectacle of

Castlemorton merely provided colour and simplicity to the government's argument, with ravers positioned as the most visible scapegoat for an extraordinarily broad incursion into the rights of the individual: a convenient entry point through which the Home Office could rein in the wanton decadence of the 1990s as a whole, and bring all of the varying groups seen as responsible for it to heel.

It was clear early in the passage of the Criminal Justice Bill that this broad, dystopian attempt to curtail individual liberty was deeply flawed. In their extensive legal analysis of the proposed legislation Richard Card and Richard Ward state that the bill is likely to have limited effect on crime prevention, 'assumes that social evils can be cured by creating new offences and by increasing maximum sentences or police powers' and 'displays no coherent approach to the problem of crime'. Amongst several other logical inconsistencies and haphazardly defined concepts, Card and Ward note that the bill's specific anti-rave powers apply only to events which take place at night, but that no definition of 'night' is provided. 'Is it sundown to sunset, or some other variable period related to the sun?' they ask, noting that the bill's powers would thus be broader during the winter, despite raves predominantly taking place in the summer. Even filtered through the starched formalities of legal academia, one can feel the authors' teeth grinding at the clumsiness on display. As the bill passed through the House of Lords in the summer of 1994, Michael Howard was subjected to a similarly polite form of rhetorical vivisection by Liberal peer Lord Wigoder: 'I begin to think of the Secretary of State as a sort of "Coco Pops" Home Secretary. I visualise him eating his breakfast cereal every morning surrounded by the tabloid newspapers, and almost every morning what he thinks is a bright idea flashes across his mind. Lo and behold, by lunchtime the same day he has tabled it as an amendment to the Criminal Justice Bill, without any reflection, discussion, consultation or research.' Despite this, criticism from the Opposition benches in the Commons was muted; the Labour party (in particular the Shadow Home Secretary, one Tony Blair MP) remained acutely conscious that sticking up for drug-addled ravers and loony left-wing protestors would see them once again painted by the Tories as soft on law and order. In the bill's second reading in the Commons, Blair's response was rooted in uncertainty about whether the new measures would reduce crime, rather than defending those most at risk from its immense new powers. At the bill's critical third reading, Labour abstained, allowing it to pass unamended.

In the Labour party's absence, responsibility for challenging the government was left to a patchwork coalition of campaigning groups, called the Freedom Network, which ran from Westminster insiders to free festival dog-on-a-string types. The human rights charity Liberty were a key part of the coalition, providing legal research on the bill's myriad shortcomings. 'We believe it offends the basic principles of justice, and that it's likely to increase discrimination against groups who are already marginalised, and to increase harassment and intimidation,' reads their information pamphlet on the legislation as a whole. Of raves, they 'believe that it will be counter-productive to criminalise raves and festivals, and a heavy-handed approach will exacerbate rather than reduce the problems it's trying to address.' But this was not an entirely united front. Camilla Berens – the editor of *Pod* magazine, which covered the UK's free party networks, protest groups and political radicals throughout the early to mid 1990s – criticized the scale and visibility of Spiral Tribe's activities for putting raves back in the establishment's crosshairs. 'It screwed the whole thing up for all the other outfits who wanted to perpetuate the free festival scene,' she said in 1992. Speaking thirty years later, it's fair to say that while acknowledging the stitch-up Spiral Tribe were faced with after Castlemorton, her views on the counterproductive nature of the era's big, confrontational raves haven't mellowed:

> A lot of people that I knew in the London squat scene really felt that they brought it on themselves. When you work in the grey areas of legality, you've really got to keep your head down; and if you're doing free parties in that world you've got to be careful about where you do those parties. And Spiral Tribe just didn't

seem to get that. I think one of their press releases boasted that their system could be heard 12 miles away, like that was something to be proud of, whereas most people who had any experience in that culture knew that was just a stupid thing to do, because it wasn't sustainable.

Alongside the organizing efforts and campaign groups, artists and soundsystems played their own part: compilations were produced and benefit concerts staged to raise funds, while artists folded the debate around the bill into their work. Orbital's 'Are We Here' is a dreamy fifteen-minute slice of breakbeat techno, released five days after the Criminal Justice Act became law. As the track draws to a close, dissolving into a plaintive wash of ambience and muted drum loops, a collage of sampled voices exclaim: 'We never see him, he treats his home like a hotel . . . he's a promiscuous, long-haired, work-shy, drug-taking layabout who ought to be in the bloody army'. There is an unmistakable sense here of the censorious proponents of the Criminal Justice Act emerging to take back control, as the party winds down and the drugs start wearing off. Included as a B-side on the CD single is 'Are We Here (Criminal Justice Bill?)', which consists of exactly four minutes of total silence – a dance remix of John Cage's 'silent' avant-garde piece 4'33", and a wry comment on the government's suppression of free rave soundsystems. More ambitious still is 'Flutter' by Autechre, released as part of the *Anti* EP in 1994, with all proceeds going to Liberty's anti-CJA fighting fund. Under a wistful, looping synth line a mesh of constantly shifting rhythmic patterns stretches and strains, their drum programming designed to at least theoretically sidestep the act's proscription of 'repetitive beats'. 'Flutter has been programmed in such a way that no bars contain identical beats and can therefore be played under the proposed law', reads the liner notes. 'However we advise DJs to have a lawyer and musicologist present at all times to confirm the non-repetitive nature of the music in the event of police harassment.'

These campaigning efforts culminated in a series of direct actions in central London over the course of 1994 – the best known of these are three protest marches in May, July and October, but anti-CJB campaigners also occupied buildings in Westminster (dubbed 'New Squatland Yard' after its proximity to the Met Police's headquarters), and worked with existing squats in Brixton and Kentish Town, using these both as organizational bases and venues for benefit gigs. The first protest, held on May Day and organized by the Advance Party – a coalition which included Camilla Berens of *Pod* magazine, in her capacity as the Freedom Network's de facto press officer – passed largely without incident. Various soundsystems were even able to relocate from Hyde Park to Wanstead Flats for a free party without disruption: 'All those involved in the alternative culture, ravers, protestors, squatters, travellers and all sorts, came together . . . it was a jubilant display of people power,' wrote *Frontline* magazine. By the second protest in July, the drearily omnipresent Socialist Workers Party, unable to pass within two hundred miles of a protest movement without parasitically taking it over and sucking all the joy from it, had muscled their way in. 'They got wind that this was the new big thing coming in, which is what they do – sort of bandwagon onto other people's campaigns so they can promote themselves,' says Berens. 'They called themselves the Coalition Against the CJB, which was weird because we *were* the coalition against the CJB, so we thought "Who the fuck are you?" and then did some digging and it turned out they were the SWP.' Berens says that for the second march, the SWP essentially held the rest of the movement to ransom. 'That was a really difficult dialogue. I was really opposed to going along with them and doing another march, but then other people said if we don't, they'll just hijack it and misrepresent us. So we were kind of forced into tagging along for the ride.'

More unsettling still are suggestions from Mark Harrison that two of the people heavily involved in coordinating opposition to the Criminal Justice Bill are now widely assumed by members of Spiral Tribe to have been 'spy cops': undercover officers who lived under entirely fictitious identities (using the names of children who died in early infancy) in order to infiltrate a variety of predominantly left-wing groups from the late 1960s to the early 2000s. 'It was very odd . . . when I was introduced to them, one of them gave me the darkest, weirdest look. It's haunted me all across the last thirty years, like she *knew* me,' says Harrison. 'And what's even weirder is that across every single person I've spoken to, no one's ever been able to trace who they were, or where they came from.' After speaking to Harrison, I try to follow the thread back or find some information relating to the two names he gives me. They appear repeatedly in contemporary coverage of the opposition to the Criminal Justice Act, including their arrest in 1993 for conspiracy to commit a breach of the peace (the same charge as faced by Spiral Tribe, although in this case the prosecution gave up before things reached the courtroom). But neither of these two people have any digital footprint today: no Facebook accounts, no quotes or appearances in subsequent writing about the free party scene, no matching records in the phone book. No one else I speak to about them, from Alan Lodge to Camilla Berens to Matthew Collin to the solicitor who represented the pair in 1993 have any recollection or record of them from any later than the end of 1994: it's as if they disappeared off the face of the earth the moment that the Criminal Justice Bill was passed into law.

In March 2015 the then Home Secretary, Theresa May, announced a public inquiry into the use of deep-cover officers, following press scandal over multiple spy cops fathering children with women they'd seduced while operating under their false identities, and others spying on the family of Stephen Lawrence in the immediate aftermath of his murder in 1993. More than 1,000 organizations are confirmed to have been infiltrated by undercover officers, from the Animal Liberation Front to the Socialist Workers Party, Greenpeace and Reclaim the Streets; the inquiry is working slowly, chronologically through the evidence, with witnesses from the 1990s not expected to appear for several years. While there's been no public acknowledgement of any deep-cover officers operating within the illegal rave scene, its close proximity to and overlaps with groups which were undoubtedly targeted (not to mention its associations with drugs, organized crime and disorder) mean that the possibility is hard to discount entirely.

Had there been deep-cover spy cops operating at the upper levels of the anti-CJA movement, then they would have disappeared suddenly when their undercover assignments ended, as happened with other confirmed undercover officers, as if they'd suddenly ceased to exist. Amongst all of this, one small detail from the publicly available information on deep-cover policing tactics stands out, part of the elaborate cover story used by 'Mark Kennedy' (the undercover officer whose whistleblowing first sparked the spy cops scandal) to infiltrate various political groups in the early 1990s. He was, amongst other things, a bedroom drum'n'bass DJ.

While the existence of deep-cover spy cops remains unclear, what is certain is that the police used large numbers of more temporary undercover operations to infiltrate individual raves around the time of the Criminal Justice Act. Neil Woods was an undercover officer for fourteen years, with his assignments including a DiY rave in 1994: 'The drug squad were very keen for my colleague and I to infiltrate this particular party, because they'd heard that a big hitter, a gangster from Nottingham would be there. So we went in, and in no time at all we'd been offered some pills. But they were offering them for *free*.' Woods describes his and his partner's mounting unease at the idea of arresting a bunch of free party hippies. 'My colleague eventually said, "Fuck this, I'm not gathering evidence against these people," and I said I didn't want to either, and asked what we should do. She said: "Let's get stoned," so we scored some cannabis and got stoned and danced and ignored the whole thing, then went back to the drug squad afterwards.'

Despite the stultifying influence of the Socialist Workers Party and shadowy suspicions of undercover cops being embedded in the heart of the anti-CJA movement, the second mass protest against the proposed legislation in July 1994 still carried some trace of rave-like vitality and fun. Videos from the day show a young lad with a speaker stack lashed to the back of his Sinclair C5, and shirtless ravers dancing in Hyde Park – the mirror image of hippies dancing to Hawkwind in Windsor Great Park twenty years earlier – but the blank uniformity of thousands of SWP-issued 'Kill The Bill' placards suggests a more generic approach to defending the right to party. 'The SWP wanted to do it by the book,' writes a commenter on the website urban75: 'Trafalgar Square march, "Kill The Bill" slogan, turn it into a protest against the government, not an affirmation of anything at all. Largely because they hadn't the faintest idea what might be affirmed, or what culture, let alone DIY culture, is about.' Friction began to mount: there was particular disquiet about Advance Party literature which included quotes from police officers, arguing that passing the bill would make their work harder, a campaign strategy which pissed off the more radical left for whom making cops' lives easier was emphatically not part of the plan. 'One thing I noticed,' recounts a review of the second, SWP-diluted march in the dance zine *Eternity*, '[is that] there was hardly any raving contingency – where were you all?'

As the march passed Downing Street, crowds rushed the gates at the junction with Whitehall and began throwing bottles, placards and other objects at the police beyond. Camcorder footage shows the front line of protestors violently rocking the gates back and forth in an attempt to break through, creating a relentless, metallic 4/4 pulse, soundtracked by thousands of whistles from the masses beyond – the sonic palette of rave and techno directly repurposed as tools of civil disobedience. Mounted police charge the crowd from behind; a protestor's head snaps back as he's grabbed by the scruff of the neck; we hear glass smashing, screams, loudhailer instructions to clear the area. At the gates, masked ravers in ripped jeans and checked shirts spit through the railings at Territorial Support Group officers in riot gear, who charge forward and ram their shields and truncheons into the wrought iron. Despite the arrest of fourteen protestors at the gates of Downing Street, the march ended with protestors splashing about gleefully in the Trafalgar Square fountains, their anger dissolved by the blazing summer weather.

Things were very different by the time of the final march in October, conducted against an increasing backdrop of frustration and impotence as Commons opposition to the bill withered: the inevitable comedown after four or more years of free partying.

Activists from the anarchist group Class War handed out pamphlets advising on the correct technique for throwing unspecified large objects (they also kept their potential targets tactfully unmentioned) and urging protestors to 'Keep It Spikey'. This was a rejoinder to The Freedom Network's calls for the July march to remain 'fluffy' and their pamphlets urging attendees to 'keep it sweet, keep it right, remember this is a peaceful fight', inspired by the non-violent direct action principles of the anti-roads movement and fears of police provocation. 'That's how we saw change, that's how you change things. You don't attack the cops, you go out and physically obstruct wrongdoers or you lock yourself onto something. It's a very different ethos,' says Berens. 'There's probably only about three people in Class War anyway.'

Noble plans to engage non-violently were scuppered, however, when the police moved in to get rid of post-protest stragglers in Hyde Park. 'I think the police got really pissed off because there was an incident earlier on where we had soundsystems at the front of the march, they'd been told not to go into the park. Then by accident or design one went the wrong way, towards the park, there was a bit of a tussle, and the police had to acquiesce,' says Berens.

> It was only about 5.30, a nice day, people were sitting around the bandstand, listening to a bit of music. Next thing we knew, from the far end of the park half a dozen police horses came charging at us, from out of the blue, no warning. There were kids there, there were animals. And quite naturally some of the group, blokes particularly, started remonstrating with these mounted police, who just turned round and galloped off. And then they started telling us to move out of the park, but people were really upset and fucked off, and it just deteriorated.

News coverage in *The Independent* of the violence which followed, as Hyde Park was cleared by force, quotes a Liberty protest observer who describes the policing as a 'shambles' and says 'she had seen several unprovoked attacks on demonstrators by the police.'

The *Daily Mail* took a rather different tack, in an article headlined REVOLT OF THE RAVERS, decrying 'the ravers who call the tune – behind a front of legitimate protest' along with 'the underground party organisers who have spread misery throughout the country' and 'music that became a rallying cry for violence'.

In his documentary *Everybody in the Place*, the artist Jeremy Deller describes rave culture as 'a death ritual marking the transition of Britain from an industrial to a service economy', a sense of finality and rupture which feels especially tangible in images of ravers being chased across Hyde Park by massed lined of riot police in October 1994. If police violence at Orgreave a decade earlier came to symbolize the death of industrial Britain, and the end of a post-war consensus in which workers' solidarity rather than market forces dictated political possibilities, then we should consider this final suppression of anti-CJA protests as a similar kind of requiem. This was not just the last full-scale free party in Britain, but the end of a far deeper and more meaningful lineage of anti-establishment revelry, in which the British working class could assert control over common land and reclaim it for their leisure regardless of upper-class disapproval: a funeral knell for British counterculture, and any lingering hopes that post-industrial Britain might be built on anything beyond narrowly capitalist and morally conservative interests. When one of the squatted anti-CJA communes on Claremont Road in East London was forcibly evicted a few weeks after the October protest, a TV report opined that 'everyone living in this time-warped street of the 60s knew the rave had to end sometime.'

In the aftermath of the Criminal Justice Act becoming law, the coalitions which had formed around opposing it returned to their own individual areas of concern. Environmental groups refocused on anti-road protests – most famously around the Newbury bypass – their direct action setting the groundwork for Extinction Rebellion a generation later. Other campaign groups evolved into Reclaim the Streets, then the anti-globalization protests of the early 2000s, opposition to the war in Iraq and the Occupy movement; the

Socialist Workers Party would, with grim predictability, attach themselves parasitically to each of these. The police, meanwhile, moved on to more important matters. 'I recently received a Christmas card', huffs the Chief Constable of Gloucestershire in a letter to John Wadham, Liberty's director, in December 1996, 'which depicts the three Wise Men being stopped by a number of uniform officers' and then searched, on suspicion of attending an illegal gathering. 'The clear implication from the card is that the police are oppressively using the powers enacted by Parliament in the Criminal Justice Bill,' thunders the chief constable, adding that, 'it does not dignify your organisation by making somewhat cheap comments at a time of deep religious significance to many people by a generalised slur on the British Police Service.'

Despite the Criminal Justice Act's enduring association with Castlemorton and rave culture, the first people arrested under its expanded powers (on Sunday 5 November 1994, two days after the bill became law) were in fact two hunt saboteurs named Jamie Shaw and Tim Spencer. Described as 'thugs, wreckers, and bullies' by Michael Howard in a speech later the same month, hunt saboteurs made up more than 90 per cent of arrests conducted under the new legislation in the first few months of its existence. In 1996, the clearing of an anti-road protest camp blocking the construction of the Newbury bypass saw more than 300 environmental campaigners arrested, but the overall numbers remained surprisingly low: by the beginning of 1997 the government had mounted a mere 470 prosecutions for aggravated trespass, and a further 42 for 'trespassory assembly'. Ascertaining how many of these arrests related to free parties is difficult, due to the specific wording of the clauses which deal specifically with raves. Under the powers of the Criminal Justice Act, potential attendees commit an offence only if they refuse to leave a piece of land *when directed to do so* by a police officer. If the police tell them to leave and the person complies, then no crime is committed, meaning that no record needs to be made of the Criminal Justice Act's powers being used. This allowed the police to stop raves going ahead merely by threatening potential attendees with arrest, while keeping the true extent of the Criminal Justice Act's chilling effect on free parties unrecorded and unverifiable. In this, the law pulls in two directions – vastly expanding the powers of the police and the state to dictate how people behave, while also cloaking those powers in uncertainty and deniability.

With a similarly depressing sense of inevitability, the legal concerns raised by Liberty and others over the law's draconian powers would also be proved entirely justified. Far from its restrictions being confined solely to the most dangerous or demonized elements within British society, as promised, the Criminal Justice Act instead became moulded by the more restrictive ideologies and priorities of the police – the same process which saw James Anderton repurposing Napoleonic-era dancing laws to shut down gay clubs in 1980s Manchester. In 2009, Devon Police scrambled a helicopter and riot van to shut down a thirtieth birthday barbecue involving fifteen attendees, based on a Facebook invite saying the party might run through the night, while in 2015 the Criminal Justice Act was invoked during attempts to shut down an 'eco-village' camp in Runnymede. With no little irony, attendees had come together to celebrate the 800th anniversary of the signing of Magna Carta – the 1215 charter of rights described 'as the foundation of the freedom of the individual against the arbitrary authority of the despot'.

More important and insidious than such individual incidents, however, was the Criminal Justice Act's more generalized effect across the criminal justice system, and its impact on civil liberties at a collective level. It significantly lowered the threshold for taking samples such as hair and saliva from suspects without their consent, and for the first time dealt with the DNA profiles drawn from those samples: the police were allowed to keep these indefinitely, regardless of whether or not someone was subsequently charged or convicted. This laid the foundations for the UK to develop one of the most intrusive DNA databases in the world, which by 2020 contained 6.6 million profiles, including data from a disproportionately high number of Black men. It wasn't until 2012 that a European Court of Human Rights ruling forced the government to set time limits on retaining DNA data, and only then for profiles taken from victims and witnesses (whose details had previously been stored alongside those of suspects). The Criminal Justice Act also provided expanded powers for the police to stop and search people without suspicion – provisions which harked back to the hated 'sus' laws, and their disproportionate use against Black youth in the 1970s and 1980s, both in specific relation to shebeens and blues parties or more broadly. Much like 'sus', CJA powers have also been consistently used to target Black and Asian men during the thirty years since they came onto the statute books: in 2020, *The Guardian* reported that Black people were still nine times more likely to be stopped and searched by the police than their white compatriots. In addition to their highly discriminatory application, these powers continue to be of near-negligible use in stopping crime: the same 2020 *Guardian* data revealed that of the 18,000 searches justified under powers granted to police in 1994, a paltry 4 per cent led to an arrest. Justified in the early 1990s by urgent appeals to moral panic around bug-eyed ravers and filthy hippies, these powers now form a key part of the incessant background hum of intrusive surveillance, unnecessary harassment and mutual mistrust which underpins young Black Britons' daily interactions with the police.

Within UK dance music itself, the effects of the Criminal Justice Act lacked quite the same levels of dystopian mission-creep, but were no less transformational. One last attempt at a Castlemorton-scale free party in June 1995, dubbed the 'Mother' festival, was shut down aggressively by the police; with illegal raves retreating into the shadows, UK dance music's focus shifted to the booming market of superclubs and festivals – dancing not as a form of antisocial defiance, but a fully regulated leisure activity. After a fallow year in 1991 – prompted in large part by clashes between Travellers and festival security in 1990 – Glastonbury returned in June 1992 with a far meatier security apparatus and a massive steel wall around its perimeter, unambiguously severing its connection to the free festival circuit (notwithstanding the persistence of those who continued to dig under or climb over such barriers). Its embrace of rave culture had also become noticeably more centralized, with the Experimental

Sound Field marking the festival's first official provision of a space dedicated to electronic dance music: as opposed to the situation in 1990, where it had merely been the passive gathering-point for an amorphous and unsanctioned network of external operators. Moving away from the non-hierarchical patchwork of ramshackle free party systems, and towards the technologically advanced sonic spectacle which would come to define dance music in the twenty-first century, the ESF boasted a state-of-the-art 360-degree surround sound system, and a quadrophonic mixing desk inherited from one of Pink Floyd's 1970s stadium tours, all designed and installed by Tony Andrews of Turbosound and Funktion-One fame: in addition to running Zorch's speaker rig at Stonehenge, Andrews had also been a key figure at Glastonbury ever since its foundation, even helping to build the first Pyramid stage.

The creation of the Experimental Sound Field was highly conditional – Glastonbury founder Michael Eavis agreed to its existence only so long as it was excluded from the printed festival programme and exiled to the fringes of the site – but its success laid the foundations for an official Dance Tent in 1995, and eventually an entire Dance Village. Underworld, soon to become one of the biggest dance acts in the world, played for a reported twelve hours over Saturday night and Sunday morning, but it's another of the artists who appeared in the Experimental Sound Field in 1992 who would go on to embody the cultural and social changes embedded within it. Two summers later, at the very moment the Criminal Justice Bill was making its way through the Commons, brothers Paul and Phil Hartnoll – better known as Orbital – stepped out onto the *NME* Stage, their signature headlamps piercing the midnight gloom, and began the first headline set by a dance act at a major British music festival, cementing dance music's rapid ascent from fringe concern to main-stage draw, and closing a circle which began with Zorch's performance in front of Stonehenge some twenty years earlier. When the fizzing single-note synth line and off-beat handclaps of closing track 'Chime' kick in, and a feral roar goes up from the crowd, it's as seismic an instant as Dylan going electric: the precise moment at which dance music becomes fully absorbed into mainstream British pop culture.

This, traditionally, is also where narratives of UK dance music's political meaning tend to start drawing to a close, with the crushing of the free party scene and rave's co-option by more commercially palatable interests; transformed into big business by the Criminal Justice Act, what had been a quasi-revolutionary force becomes by the end of the 1990s just another pastime, defined by the meaningless extravagance of the superclub, the dance floor left creatively neutered and politically inert. Stark distinctions can certainly be drawn between the antisocial spikiness of the unlicensed parties around the M25 from which Orbital drew their name, or the quasi-revolutionary lineage of illegal partying to which they arguably owed their entire existence, and the mass-market spectacle involved in headlining Glastonbury. Where crews like Spiral Tribe spent 1994 exhorting dancers to 'Make Some Fucking Noise' in both a sonic and political sense, Orbital's objectives were far less contentious: 'Hi! Enjoy', says one of the Hartnolls affably and a little self-consciously as they take to the *NME* Stage.

An alternative and equally telling point of comparison might be the Hartnolls' own appearance four years earlier on that other great British pop music institution: *Top of the Pops*. Booked to perform 'Chime', but hamstrung by BBC producers' insistence on miming to a pre-recorded backing track rather than playing live, their appearance instead became a surreal piece of cultural satire. Wearing anti-Poll Tax T-shirts, the Hartnoll brothers bop half-heartedly behind a desk of sequencers and samplers, each of which is very conspicuously not plugged in, occasionally prodding limply at a button or fader and grinning inanely at the cameras. Next to them a solitary on-stage dancer makes a resolute but doomed attempt to bring the energy of the rave into the TV studio, weaving and twirling to minimal effect. The audience, consisting mainly of men wearing suits and women with artfully volumized hair, remain almost entirely unmoved, clapping along listlessly and looking increasingly bemused by the baffling anti-spectacle on display.

There's an overwhelming sense here of a vast cultural gulf between the formalized expectations of pop music and early evening TV, and the untranslatable power of the rave.

And yet by the time Orbital headlined Glastonbury four years later, that expanse had been comprehensively bridged: 1994 was a turning point not only because Orbital brought rave to the main stages, but because it was the first year that substantial portions of the festival were broadcast live on British TV. When the Hartnolls sheepishly asked the crowd to 'enjoy' the music, they weren't just speaking to 20,000 people in the field with them, but millions more watching on Channel 4 as Saturday night prime time ended, into whose homes these approachable techno reveries would now be beamed. Those opening bars of 'Chime' and the cheering Glastonbury crowd undoubtedly mark the end of rave as a monolithic countercultural force, and the beginning of something else entirely. UK dance music would never again threaten or promise the single-handed overthrow of society. But the received wisdom of its retreat into the apolitical hinterlands doesn't tell us the whole story: its constriction via the Criminal Justice Act and absorption into the cultural mainstream didn't render it devoid of political or social energy, or reduce it to a mere hedonistic indulgence, they just focused its political energies in different and less obvious directions.

Where prior to 1994 dance music had been a flag around which anarchists and revolutionaries might gather, it would now become an equally potent signifier for an entirely different constituency, from New Labour politicians and local council decision-makers to leisure industry empire-builders, inner-city property developers and global financial players: the free party might be over, but the notion that dance music ceased to function as a political force after the Criminal Justice Act would be swiftly and repeatedly proved false.

LABOUR SUPPORTERS CELEBRATE THE PARTY'S ELECTION VICTORY, MAY 1997

5. Tony and Gordon Go Large

Big beat manifestos, the 'creative industries' and the rise of the superclub

There are any number of iconic images associated with the Labour party's landslide election victory on 1 May 1997, from Michael Portillo's hideous pallor as he finds out he's lost his seat, to Tony Blair walking past the flag-waving masses* on his way into Downing Street. But one particular moment sticks in the memory more than

* Perhaps indicative of Blair's knack for political optics, it should be remembered that these were not spontaneously impassioned members of the British

any other, even for those of us too young to have been any more than dimly aware of events at the time. It's late in the evening, shortly after the enormity of the result has become clear; former party leader Neil Kinnock, under whom the party had begun its 'long trek back towards electability', is flanked by senior MPs Robin Cook and John Prescott, soon to become Foreign and Home Secretaries respectively; alongside them stands Blair's oleaginous campaign director, former spin doctor and all-round political svengali Peter Mandelson. Behind them, filling the cavernous space of the Royal Festival Hall, a joyous throng of Labour election staff, volunteers and party members are singing, smiling and swigging from cans, all soundtracked by a thumping 4/4 beat. Kinnock, Cook, Prescott and Mandelson are making a game but mesmerically awful attempt to join the fun: like countless career politicians before and since, their attempts to behave like normal human beings lapse immediately and inevitably into the uncanny.

Kinnock beams and sways in a blissful and ungainly fashion, appearing to be gripped less by a sense of political vindication than the synapse-fizzing blast of a decent pill. Prescott scowls and mutters to himself, as if seven pints deep at closing time and spoiling for a fight. Mandelson claps half-heartedly to the beat, loses interest, and grins superficially at various off-camera acquaintances, his actions unintentionally mirroring the skittish self-regard of someone who's been railing lines of coke in the toilets. Cook is ramrod straight, his eyes bulging: he appears to be trying to dance solely with his eyebrows, as if ketamine has rendered every other part of his body immobile. The music soundtracking this bizarre spectacle is, of course, D:Ream's 'Things Can Only Get Better' – a Northern Irish gospel-house belter adopted by New Labour as the soundtrack to their election campaign and, tonight, the euphoric rush of victory. After a decade spent in the political wilderness, UK dance

---

public, but hand-picked Labour volunteers who'd worked on the election campaign.

music is now the official soundtrack for the establishment to get right on one.

First released in 1993, but only lightly grazing the Top 40 on its initial foray into the charts, a poppier remix of 'Things Can Only Get Better' spent four weeks at Number 1 the following January. Two years on from that, it was co-opted for the launch of Labour's five 'pre-manifesto' pledges – a series of promises on key topics like education and healthcare, written largely by Tony Blair himself and mailed to two million marginal voters. Something in the song's message clearly resonated with Labour apparatchiks, or tested well with the party's army of focus groups: by the time the election came around in May 1997 'Things Can Only Get Better' had displaced 'The Red Flag' as New Labour's election anthem, the feel-good sonic backdrop to rallies, photo opportunities and campaign adverts alike. The purest distillation of its communicative power can be found in a party political broadcast which aired shortly before polling day, which uses 'Things Can Only Get Better' as its soundtrack, and which now feels so gauche as to verge on self-parody. We see the letterbox of an anonymous front door flap open: onto the doormat drops a polling card, and a copy of *The Sun* declaring 'ELECTION: 3 DAYS TO GO'. A man in a pale blue-green shirt picks up the polling card and turns it over thoughtfully: the camera never shows his face, but we are given the distinct sense of him musing on the card's meaning and importance. A calendar ticks forward to election day: mind made up, our faceless hero strides out of the door, as if propelled by destiny, to be greeted by a carefully choreographed fever dream of English archetypes and aspirations just as the song's thumping bassline kicks in. A middle-aged man in a red Ford Mondeo* nearly runs him over, then offers us a grinning thumbs up;

---

* The semiotic choices made here are not remotely accidental: of course *The Sun* is used as a prop, given that the flagship Murdoch paper's decision to endorse Labour, and break from its decades-long Tory support, was a critical part of Blair's success with swing voters. Likewise the appearance of a Ford Mondeo: of all the various demographic segments and social stereotypes identified by pollsters as key constituencies for New Labour to connect with

a Black woman selling flowers smiles pliantly and then, mesmerized, follows our hero down tree-lined Victorian streets while carrying a bunch of roses; alfresco diners at a kerbside restaurant stand and applaud as the camera tracks across them; a man carrying a massive bunch of balloons and a woman wearing rollerskates join the procession; D:Ream's chorus of gospel singers guide us towards aspiration and redemption. It is Jesus's triumphal entry into Jerusalem, reimagined for a world of centre partings, chunky mobile phones and England losing to Germany on penalties.

In *The Century of the Self*, the documentarian Adam Curtis maps out the influence of Freudian psychoanalysis on twentieth-century society and meaning, from Sigmund Freud's earliest exploration of unconscious desires to advertising pioneer Edward Bernays (Freud's nephew, inventor of the term 'public relations' and the world's first spin doctor) who weaponized those buried urges to drive political and marketing campaigns of uncanny power and foresight. Curtis's narrative culminates with Labour's 1997 election victory, and in particular the use of focus groups by campaigners like Philip Gould (who had been, like Bernays, an advertising executive) and Matthew Freud (a PR guru and Sigmund's great-grandson). The open-ended conversations and bubble-like intimacy of the focus group offered pollsters a glimpse into the subconscious desires of swing voters – 'eight people sipping wine in Kettering', as fellow party employee Derek Draper puts it – insights which in turn profoundly shaped New Labour's policy positions and messaging. Curtis argues that the ascent to power of Tony Blair and Gordon Brown marked the end of democracy as a process guided merely by voters' inherited tribal identities, notions of active citizenship, or cost-benefit analyses of the manifestos on offer; instead, in 1997 the democratic process becomes a Freudian expression of the electorate's

---

and win over, 'Mondeo Man' remains amongst the most familiar. Even the light blue shirt of the lead character feels painfully on the nose: the traditional colour of the Conservatives shifting subtly in hue, suggesting the changing views of a wavering Tory voter.

unconscious desires, a reflection of how each candidate makes them *feel*. That sentiment is captured no more potently than in the climax of 'Things Can Only Get Better' and the electoral campaigns built around it: as the club-ready beats thump and a mass of choral voices drive us into hitherto-undiscovered realms of bliss, voting for Labour becomes not only a way to fix the ills of the country, but a way to transform *ourselves*, the transcendental power of the dance floor transfigured to the ballot box. Labour's last-minute party political broadcast is steeped in this: by the time the crowd reaches the polling station, led by the faceless man in the pale aqua-blue shirt, the atmosphere is positively carnivalesque, a hallucinatory vision of some new Albion; the flower-seller gives the Tory candidate, a grey-haired old fogey standing stiffly by the door, a pinch on the cheek; voters stand back and gasp as our faceless Everyman makes his way to the ballot box. After casting his vote, the camera pans up to at last reveal this latterday John Bull, the embodiment of the renewed spirit running through these sceptred isles. It is – shock horror – none other than Tony Blair himself, grinning inanely back at us as the hi-hats lift us higher and the chorus hits.

With the music still pounding away, the screen fades to white. Where Blair stood, we're now left with a two-word instruction written in his own handwriting – 'Do it'. A few seconds later, his autograph appears beneath. There's a heady mix of connotations at play here, from the uneasy lure of Freudian desire-baiting to the gentle platitudes of self-help literature, and a quasi-messianic reliance on Blair's personal charisma. But this combination of short, blunt imperative and euphoric overload also harks back unexpectedly to the earliest days of Chicago house. From Phuture's 'Work It' to Farley 'Jackmaster' Funk's UK chart-topper 'Jack Your Body' or 'Free Yourself' by Virgo, it's noticeable how much of this music repeatedly iterates on precisely the same rhetorical template borrowed by Blair: a short, abstracted demand set to a thudding 128bpm kick drum; dance floor catharsis and urgent command working hand in hand. There's even a 1995 house pumper by Chicago producer Glenn Underground titled 'Do It'. If New

Labour's campaign materials had instead spent 1997 asking the electorate 'Can You Feel It?' no one would have so much as batted an eyelid.

That linguistic similarity isn't accidental. New Labour weren't just hitching their wagon to dance music in a vague appeal to youthful credibility, but because the emancipatory energy of house music – from its roots in the queer Black clubs of Chicago to its latterday expression in the form of 'Things Can Only Get Better' – spoke directly to the British voting public's most powerful unconscious desires. However different the sweat-drenched walls of the Warehouse in 1987 and the ballot boxes of the 1997 General Election might seem, and however distinct the indignities of ingrained American racism and homophobia might be from the upheavals of the Thatcher years, both of these versions of house music speak to similar emotional states: a collective weight being cast off, sallow moral orthodoxies being defied, and disenfranchised communities belatedly emerging from the shadows of an oppressive superstructure. 'It's difficult to remember now what Thatcher's Britain felt like,' DJ Fabio told *The Guardian* in 2008, describing the birth of acid house in terms which could just as easily be applied to New Labour's ascent to power. 'A lot of people were searching for something, for a way out'.

After staying up through the night to witness the 1997 results coming in, veteran Labour campaigner John O'Farrell details his journey home as a kind of spectral, rainbow-flecked reverie, with 'the dawn sun shining on the Houses of Parliament, the new gold paint glistening and reflecting in the Thames . . . it really did look like a completely different place'* – a dreamlike scene which is likely to be instantly recognizable to anyone who's rolled out of the Stygian gloom of a nightclub at 6 a.m., only to find the sun blazing

---

* O'Farrell's book, which details his experiences as a stalwart Labour party member through the electoral doldrums of the 1980s before climaxing with Blair's victory, is of course called *Things Can Only Get Better*. The sequel, published a decade later as the Blair government unravelled, would be called *Things Can Only Get Worse*.

and the everyday world resuming around them. After eighteen years of Thatcher's Victorian values, is it any surprise that by 1997 the British public felt like throwing their hands up in the air? Or, indeed, that New Labour would gravitate towards the emotive power of dance music, right down to its most granular stylistic tics, in an attempt to leverage that popular sentiment for their own electoral purposes? Forget about the myopic parochialism and performative nostalgia of Britpop, with which Blair and others are far more regularly and erroneously associated:* the 1997 election was won by house music. 'I would have liked to walk around the streets of England', writes O'Farrell, speaking as much to the early hours hedonist as the constituency Labour party member, 'to soak up the euphoria on that scorching spring morning.'

Similar traces of the unifying energy of dance music can be found in the Blair government's greatest domestic policy achievement: the Good Friday Agreement of 1998, which largely brought to an end the violence which had plagued Northern Ireland for generations. Made possible only by the collective will of Northern Irish communities to leave behind years of sectarianism and mutual suspicion, the peace process reflected rapidly changing social attitudes, with the flowering of acid house playing a small but symbolic role in dissolving social barriers between young Catholics and Protestants. 'The Troubles manifested themselves in your psyche in ways that you cannot even understand,' the DJ and producer David Holmes said of Sugar Sweet, the acid house night he started in Belfast in December 1989, describing rave's ability to break down sectarian barriers. 'These communities fucking hated each other but among them you had groups of people whose religion was music.'

---

* The same goes for 'Cool Britannia' – a phrase which wasn't coined by New Labour at all, but by the flailing Conservative government in 1996, and from which the former tried consistently to distance themselves. 'I would point out that the words Cool Britannia were used by Virginia Bottomley in five different press releases in 1996 and 1997', Chris Smith MP, New Labour's first Culture Secretary, told *The Guardian* in 2007. 'I defy you to find a reference to Cool Britannia in a press release I released. I hated it!'

A 1995 documentary titled *Dancing On Narrow Ground* by the Derry-born film-maker Desmond Bell, commissioned by Channel 4 but never broadcast, captures some of that same optimism, even if it ultimately comes to more measured conclusions amongst the drudgery and greyness of working-class Northern Irish life in the early 1990s. 'Dance music's the only thing in Northern Ireland that brings different cultural communities together,' says one interviewee, amidst shots of gurning ravers from both Catholic and Protestant communities: 'there's no animosity, no fighting, nobody cares what your religion is, where you're from, or what background you are.' Bell himself would later acknowledge that rave 'encouraged some young people to reach out towards a political settlement that would tackle sectarianism' even if dancers ultimately returned to their divided communities at the end of the night, and despite the fact that a generation later Northern Ireland is 'still stuck with the same shower of political bigots ruling us.'

If the ravers, radicals and other subcultural groups targeted by the Criminal Justice Act had hoped that New Labour's electoral pact with dance floor transcendence during their 1997 campaign might translate to legislation of a similar hue once they were in office, they were to be sorely disappointed. There was to be no rolling-back of the CJA's expanded policing powers, and no return to the halcyon days of M25 orbital raves or free festivals; the Blair government's commitment to the sesh was to remain strictly presentational. Instead, their attitude to dance music would be formed the year after their election in a white paper published by the Creative Industries Task Force (an arm of the newly formed Department for Culture, Media and Sport) and snappily titled 'The 1998 Creative Industries Mapping Document'. The creation of DCMS was itself instructive, dismantling and rebuilding the Conservative-created Department for National Heritage: after 1997, culture would no longer be a staid and under-appreciated political backwater, useful only for keeping the electorate pliantly nostalgic, but a critical part of New Labour's renewal of British identity. According to the man who drove this concept within government, Blair's first Secretary of

State for Culture, Chris Smith MP, the repositioning of DCMS was undertaken 'not because heritage is unimportant, but because we wanted something more forward-looking, a name that captured more accurately the spirit of modern Britain' – culture as a proxy for the wider message New Labour were selling to voters at home, and observers and investors abroad.

This required smooth alignment between the 'creative industries' – divided into thirteen categories from film and music to software design and architecture – and the most fundamental tenets of New Labour's politics and economics. Art and culture would no longer be viewed merely in aesthetic terms, but with increasing emphasis on the contribution they made to the wider economy: GDP and tax revenues; national and local place-making and branding; educating young people, offering creative outlets for marginalized communities, addressing inequality or supporting social mobility; and providing the loosely defined 'creative' skills necessary to modernize British industry, making it fit for a rapidly globalizing and increasingly digitized marketplace.

In explaining what characterizes the 'creative industries', DCMS's mapping document is bluntly and revealingly financial in its outlook. '[They] have their origin in individual creativity, skill and talent and . . . have a potential for wealth creation through the generation of intellectual property'. Dance music was perfectly placed to profit from this shift in focus: sleekly modern, and with its global expansion led by a vanguard of British entrepreneurs, it pointed forward to a bright new future in which the UK's cultural production and intellectual property might generate the same wealth and envy as its steel and cotton had done centuries before. The vast crowds flocking to abandoned warehouses and moonlit fields offered copious evidence of the music's market appeal, while the hardscrabble DIY ethic of white labels, pirate radio and impromptu parties pre-empted the increasingly precarious and atomized economies of the twenty-first century. Where swathes of UK dance music prior to 1994 had been built on the protection or resurrection of principles crushed by Thatcher – working-class solidarity, a commitment to the common good rather than private profit, and mass defiance of social norms — as the 1990s progressed the prevailing mood became increasingly defined by a far narrower, more lucrative and less politically contentious set of neo-liberal ideals.

Concepts of the 'creative industries' applied equally to Britain's film and TV sectors, whose evolving fictional depictions of UK dance music over the course of the 1990s offer an example in microcosm of rave's wider political and cultural rehabilitation: from a seedy and malevolent source of moral decay in the era of Castlemorton, to an integral part of the country's creative economy by the end of Blair's first term in power. A 1992 episode of *Inspector Morse,* in which a baffled Morse ends up at an illegal rave on the hunt for a killer, perfectly captures that earlier, more censorious, mindset. Directed by Danny Boyle two years before he found fame with *Trainspotting*, the episode's scriptwriters position rave firmly within a shadowy underworld corrupting Oxford's young people, and define it entirely through its relationship to illegal narcotics. 'Youth culture's a bit of a mystery to you, isn't it, officer?' asks a shady venue owner when Morse quizzes him on late-night goings-on. 'When young people say parties,' he says with a villainous smile, 'what they mean is *drugs*.' Despite hiring up-and-coming rave promoters Fantazia to give the show's climactic party scenes a gloss of verisimilitude, *Morse* largely treats dance music as unknowable and senseless, little other than a cipher for chemically induced nihilism and social decay. Sergeant Lewis's tearaway daughter spends the entire episode locked defiantly in her bedroom, muffled beats thudding through the door, while the episode's primary narrative is driven by Morse's suitably angelic niece taking a substance called Seraphim at the illegal rave which opens the episode: within minutes, we find out that she's killed herself. 'That's what's really wicked,' opines Morse. 'To make you think you've seen everything there is to see, at [the age of] sixteen. That you've had the best of life, before it's even begun. To make you think you've got nothing more to live for.' In *Morse*'s world, the joy and transcendence of the dance floor becomes its own inverse: euphoria is in fact self-abasement, ecstasy is in fact despair, the communal experience of the dance floor terminally isolating.

Broadcast three years later in 1995, a matter of weeks before the death of Leah Betts would bring moral panics around Ecstasy back to the front pages, BBC Two's *Loved Up* comes to largely the same philosophical conclusions as *Morse* – perhaps unsurprisingly, given the production's origins as an anti-drug PSA. Drawn into a world of pills and partying by a new boyfriend, Sarah (played by a pre-fame Lena Headey) narrowly avoids being beaten up by one dealer and raped by another, before her mother's suicide attempt (strongly implied to be the direct result of Sarah's absence) convinces her to return to the straight and narrow. Sarah's rejected boyfriend, by now deep in the grip of addiction, is left to hoover up another two pills and dance alone on an empty rooftop, the very picture of wretchedness. However, by the mid-1990s dance music's pop culture associations and fictional representations were already changing at pace: within a year of *Loved Up*'s broadcast, the illegal rave went from den of iniquity to comic relief when *Men Behaving Badly* – perhaps the archetypal 1990s sitcom – sent its main characters to a warehouse filled with smoke and lasers. 'Right, we're going to a rave,' declares Martin Clunes's character Gary, in a misguided attempt to bring some youthful zest back into his life. By the end of the episode he's crawling around the dance floor and vomiting onto the camera, the trauma of chemical overindulgence played not as tragedy, but as farce.

When the Channel 4 sitcom *Spaced* devoted an entire episode to its cast of characters going clubbing in 1999, they dispensed with even this thin veneer of moral disapprobation. It's made as clear as possible, without actually showing characters necking pills and snorting lines, that they're all higher than the sun and loving it: the cast gurn and rush to the sound of irrepressible hard house thumper 'Let Me Show You' by Camisra, gabble lovingly in the chill-out room, and eventually collapse in a heap on the sofa, their feet still tapping instinctively to a half-remembered beat as they fall asleep, all of their tensions soothed and narrative frictions reconciled.

Where drug-induced psychosis drives Inspector Morse's niece to her death, *Spaced*'s pathologically twitchy cycle courier Tyres – so addled by Ecstasy use that he regularly hallucinates dance music emerging from everyday sounds, like a kettle boiling or a clock ticking – ends the series blissfully cutting shapes to the sound of a pedestrian crossing in Hammersmith. Released the same year as *Spaced*, *Human Traffic* stretches broadly the same narrative arc – a group of young hedonists drink and dance their way through a big night out – into a feature-length film, and reaches largely the same conclusions. Despite an unspeakably morose tableau from the fag end of the afterparty – all grey-skinned faces and crushed beer cans, the downbeat arpeggios of 'Belfast' by Orbital perfectly evoking that moment when the weary, desaturated grind of the real world begins to reassert itself – its general atmosphere is overwhelmingly one of joy and connection. 'You lucky, lucky people,' declares John Sim's Jip as the film begins. 'The weekend has landed. All that exists now are clubs, drugs, pubs and parties . . . this could be the best night of my life.'

However, there's a one fictional depiction which sums up dance music's political, cultural and economic transformation more potently than any other: the unmistakeable and largely incomprehensible *Kevin & Perry Go Large*, released in 2001. Fortysomethings Harry Enfield and Kathy Burke dress in Kappa tracksuits to portray gurning teenagers, whose primary narrative motivation involves going to Ibiza and 'shagging all the birds we want'. Rhys Ifans's superstar DJ Eye Ball Paul arrives with the immortal words 'Tits up, Big Baz! 'Avin it large!' – things still somehow manage to go downhill from there. In the film's sole concession to factual accuracy its climax is filmed at Amnesia, the original Ibizan home of DJ Alfredo, repurposed by 2001 as the decadent and aspirational Balearic outpost of Liverpool superclub Cream. As our two heroes' trance anthem 'Big Girl' sends the crowd into raptures, Perry's camcorder video of Kevin's parents having sex is broadcast on the big screen to thousands of unsuspecting ravers. It's *Carry On Clubbing*, only with more smut and less wit, a film that simultaneously treats dance music as something aspirational and glamorous – Kevin handles the white label of his debut single as if it was a holy relic – and everyone involved in it as a venal, drug-addled moron. Where illegal narcotics and sinister machine music were in 1992 depicted as a malevolent force corrupting Britain's innocent suburban youth, here it's Kevin and Perry's priapic gormlessness which instead corrupts the harmless fun of the dance floor. Extravagantly deranged and in retrospect almost completely unwatchable, *Kevin & Perry* is also the logical conclusion of the 'creative industries' run amok, from shamelessly slapping a thin British veneer on the US gross-out comedies which had dominated box offices in preceding years, to the film's absolutely relentless product placement, from the extremely conspicuous cans of Coke dotted throughout the film, or the lingering exterior shots of the plane on which Kevin and Perry fly to Ibiza, courtesy of Virgin Airlines' short-lived budget sub-brand Virgin Sun, to Cream's own pivotal place in proceedings.

The concept of the 'Culture Industry' (from which the slightly broader category of the 'creative industries' was subsequently derived) was first coined by the German philosopher Theodor Adorno in a 1947 essay subtitled 'Enlightenment as Mass Deception'. Like many of his peers in the Frankfurt School, Adorno sought to understand how the political and cultural revolutions of the Enlightenment could have ended with the senseless barbarity of the early twentieth century, from the dogmas of Nazism and Stalinism to the horrors of repeated global war. Guided by a rigid reading of Marxist theory, Adorno saw mass popular culture, and its wholesale co-option by capitalist interests, as a fundamental part of that process. The 'culture industry' served to flatten out human expression, subjugate it to the needs of the market, and churn out an undifferentiated slurry of meaningless mass-produced content: this kept the proletariat amused, distracted them from their oppression and curtailed their revolutionary aspirations; culture instead becoming a 'dreamless art' which 'denies its audience any dimension in which they might roam freely in imagination'. Adorno, who died in 1969, would have had only a fleeting glimpse of the electronic music and synthetic drugs which would later catalyse dance music, but he appears to have seen enough to form a view on the social impact of popular music at least, expressed in hilariously stuffy terms. 'Individuals of the rhythmically obedient type are . . . most susceptible to a process of masochistic adjustment to authoritarian collectivism', he wrote sniffily in 1941, suggesting that our enjoyment of repetitive beats merely reflects a deeper unspoken desire for the top-down imposition of order, whether dictated to us by a DJ or the state.

Adorno's arguments about the stultifying and reactionary nature of industrialized culture might not have seen him invited back to the afterparty with any regularity, but would be repeated near-verbatim by opponents to Blair's reforms in the 1990s and beyond: 'Culture is not industry, it's culture,' argues one contributor to a 2018 academic seminar on the impact of the DCMS mapping document. 'It's a ridiculous reductionist exercise to try to work out what the British theatre is worth to the British economy, because it's not about the economy, it's about human spirit.' Others saw the lauding of 'creativity' under New Labour as so broad and abstract a concept that it became meaningless – 'If everything can be creative – a management model, a kidney dialysis machine, package holidays – then wherein lies the specific value of the creative industries?' At the end of his time in power in 2007, Blair would deliver a speech to the great and the good of the art world, lauding the contribution of the creative and cultural industries, which embodies all of these shortcomings and more. Standing in the cavernous, gleaming void of Tate Modern's recently repurposed Turbine Hall – along with the Millennium Dome perhaps the most powerful architectural symbol of New Labour's cultural politics – his words turn to mush. 'Dynamism in arts and culture creates dynamism in a nation,' he asserted. 'A nation that cares about art will not just be a better nation. In the early twenty-first century it will be a more successful one.' Adorno himself, some sixty years earlier, had pre-empted Blair's verbiage with withering accuracy: 'in the culture industry, the subject matter itself, down to its smallest elements, springs from the jargon into which it is absorbed'.

While Blair's reforms gave the commodification of culture in general and dance music in particular political heft, the economic forces underpinning those policies predated his election, and have continued long after his departure from Downing Street. Between the passing of the Bright Bill in 1990, the convictions of Robert Darby and Leslie Thomas the preceding year and the emergence of licensed venues like Ministry of Sound, rave's assimilation into mainstream British public and economic life had begun by the summers of 1991 and 1992, even as crews like Spiral Tribe and DiY were busy overseeing the peak of the free party scene. The first wave of acid house promoters had included a number of extremely savvy businessmen – Tony Colston-Hayter and his Sunrise crew being the most famous example – but for many their unsavoury associations with unlicensed events made it harder to pivot into more respectable operations. Instead, those who'd laid the foundations during UK dance music's lawless years were largely overtaken in the early 1990s by younger upstarts with less baggage, who took the massive open-air events pioneered by Sunrise and legitimized them, securing temporary event licences from local authorities and working pre-emptively with the police to avoid getting shut down. In March 1992, the BBC broadcast a half-hour documentary which went behind the scenes of a legal, licensed rave in Cramlington, run by the promoters Nocturnal. Despite leaning heavily on the moral panic which had greeted earlier illegal raves – '12 hours of non-stop frenzied dancing . . . the pushers are there, and drugs change hands,' intones the narrator gravely, before a local councillor decries the event as a threat to local youngsters – there's also a clear sense of perspectives shifting. The event is described as 'the first sign that a suspect underground culture could be gaining respectability' while its promoter, Graham Auld, is characterized by the police as 'an honest type of person who's keen on doing things the right way.'

While the style and sound of these events were broadly contiguous with those run by Sunrise or even Spiral Tribe, their underlying structure was diametrically opposed: contained within the licensed and taxable framework of the creative and leisure industries rather than the vestigial remains of Britain's post-hippie counterculture; condoned rather than challenged by the state; and privately owned rather than collectively generated. Where all-night dancing and a laissez-faire approach to drug-taking at Castlemorton had apparently threatened to tear society apart at the seams, dance music's incorporation into mainstream capitalist enterprise saw it swiftly repositioned as good, clean fun. 'It was Britain's biggest ever rave,' the *Daily Mirror* cheered breathlessly after a licensed Fantazia event at Castle Donington, a little under a month after Castlemorton had sent the tabloids into fits. '10 hours of non-stop grooving which made Saturday nights at the local disco seem as quaint as a Victorian tea party.' Speaking to *DJ Mag* in 2020, Fantazia founder James Perkins says that his success was 'all about the brand' and his own smart, professional presentation: concepts which would no doubt have thrilled the authors of the DCMS mapping document. 'To get these 8am licenses I needed to go in there and be taken seriously. I didn't look like somebody from The Prodigy,' he says. Along with Fantazia an increasing number of legal rave promotions – Raindance, Dreamscape Visions, and Tribal Gathering amongst others – served both the burgeoning demand for events with the scale and spectacle of 1988's warehouse raves or 1992's free parties, and the authorities' increasing acceptance of such events, as long as they happened in appropriately licensed and regulated form.

Ten years and one month after Castlemorton, a very different type of free party would embody these shifting values and mercantile aspirations in crushingly literal terms. Fresh from securing TV rights to English Test cricket matches, and with a home Ashes series scheduled for the summer of 2001, Channel 4 embarked on an ambitious plan to set up huge public screens, stages and speaker stacks at a succession of scenic locations around the UK, on which they would then air the day's sporting action; once the day's play had concluded, free music events would take place using the same infrastructure. For the Brighton leg of this national tour they booked

Norman Cook, aka Fatboy Slim; borrowing from the weekly Big Beat Boutique club night run on the seafront by Cook's label Skint, this outdoor party became known as the Big Beach Boutique. Squeezed in after stumps on a Friday evening, with minimal advertising or fanfare ahead of time, a very substantial (but still manageable) 65,000 people showed up in July 2001, families picnicking in the afternoon sunshine, ravers dancing until a respectable 11 p.m., and fireworks launching from the West Pier at dusk. 'It was quite a short lead in,' explains an anonymous source close to the event, 'and that made it feel quite joyous and spontaneous.'

Despite being three times the size of Castlemorton, and superficially functioning in much the same way as the free parties which had caused such uproar a decade earlier – a site is taken over by a DJ and a soundsystem, without fences or entry charges, and a crowd of people listen to amplified dance music for hours on end – the Big Beach Boutique had instead been actively welcomed by local politicians, and engaged with collaboratively by the local police. 'All the places we went to were delighted that Channel 4 wanted to bring a screen and put the cricket on,' my source continues. 'We started with the cricket, and then kept adding ideas for expanding the events and they kept saying "marvellous."' Event organisers from Channel 4 engaged in detailed planning with the council over several months: intriguingly, given the extent to which the government and police had used drugs as a stick with which to beat free parties in the early 1990s, there appears to have been a much greater level of realism about the inevitability of an event like the Big Beach Boutique attracting the same kind of behaviour, with Brighton Council focusing on harm reduction measures like the ready availability of free water, rather than the scaremongering which dogged events like Castlemorton.

Throughout the 1990s, clubbing had remained one of Brighton's most recognizable cultural exports, specifically the genre of 'big beat' in which the city had played a crucial incubatory role. Merging hip hop-inspired sampling, the thumping electronic rhythms of house and a laddish irreverence which sat somewhere between

Loaded magazine, punk rock and the *Carry On* films, big beat was — along with jungle — one of the first distinctively British subgenres to emerge from the post-rave melting pot of the mid 1990s. Unlike jungle, however, big beat is now looked back on largely as a fad and an embarrassment, undone by obnoxious 'avin-it-large posturing, Kenny Everett-style zany antics and the same air of national self-importance which eventually caused Britpop to curdle.* Jeremy 'Jez' Usbourne, protagonist of the mid-2000s sitcom *Peep Show*, pledges half-hearted allegiance in one episode to the Big Beat Manifesto. It reads, in full, 'Big Beats are the best, get high all the time': as precise an encapsulation as you could ever hope to find of the inchoate lairiness and optimist-hedonist bravado which defined late 1990s British pop culture. Before long, the likes of Norman Cook, Skint and the Big Beat Boutique had become proxies for Brighton's cultural identity, even unofficial civic role models. Skint began sponsoring Brighton & Hove Albion FC in 1999, their logo splashed across the team's shirts, while Cook's inescapable second album as Fatboy Slim, *You've Come a Long Way, Baby* (which remained at Number 1 for what felt like the entirety of 1998), features a song called 'You're Not from Brighton': its titular refrain is chanted over and over again, somewhere between a terrace sing-along, devotional mantra and tourist board catchphrase. The Big Beach Boutique was the apotheosis of this cultural and civic collaboration, and New Labour's concept of the creative industries made flesh: music not just as abstract artistic expression, but something to

---

* There's even a direct parallel to the soft nationalist iconography of Noel Gallagher's infamous Union Jack guitar: a Ministry of Sound big beat compilation titled 'The Future Sound Of The United Kingdom' whose artwork is stuffed to the gills with vintage photos of Beefeaters, pearly kings and swinging Carnaby Street groovers, all collaged and overpainted in the style of 1960s Pop Art, a mash-up of various British iconography (even the Ministry of Sound logo itself, nicked wholesale from the real-life Ministry of Justice) which no doubt felt energizing at the time, but reads as grimly parochial now. '[Big beat] started as a breath of fresh air', wrote Skint's founder Damian Harris in 2008, 'and ended up like the loud, annoying drunken bloke you really wish would leave the party.'

be seamlessly integrated into national and local branding strategies, bringing in thrill-seeking outsiders with money to spend, and creating cultural moments which were memorable and (perhaps more important) marketable.

Of course, where an idea proves lucrative, capitalist rationale dictates that it must be repeated and expanded. Following its lowkey success in 2001, the Big Beach Boutique returned to Brighton in bigger and noisier form the following summer, underpinned by several important changes: this time, it was Skint and Cook's management who were in charge, rather than Channel 4, subtly shifting the emphasis from a TV broadcast with some music to a rave with some TV cameras; the date was also moved from a Friday afternoon, wedged in after the cricket, to a day long party taking up all of Saturday. Where the first event had been defined by low-key promotion and word-of-mouth buzz, there would now be a full-scale marketing blitz, from adverts on the side of London buses to Radio 1 DJ Chris Moyles telling his drive-time listeners to head down to the South Coast – a strategy which does not appear to have been fully communicated to everyone involved in the event itself. The result was bedlam: a quarter of a million people, equivalent to Brighton's entire existing population, poured into the city over the course of a sweltering 28-degree day and packed the seafront. Towards the end of the event, it became apparent that stewards stationed at the water's edge were being pushed into the sea by the sheer weight of numbers, forcing organizers to remove them from their positions. As the tide came in, the crowd instinctively pushed back up the beach towards the concrete promenade, and a very serious public safety incident was only narrowly avoided: a scarily similar situation at the 2010 Love Parade in Duisburg ended with 21 people crushed to death and 500 injuries. Local residents, meanwhile, ended up trapped in their homes for hours on end, while ambulances and paramedics became unable to reach those requiring attention and disorder ran rife. Local police, expecting a repeat of the previous year's good-natured and manageable crowds, had assigned a mere fifty officers to the event. 'The volume of the crowd was such that someone was robbed just six metres away from one of my staff, but he was physically unable to get there to help,' Chief Inspector Peter Mills told *The Guardian* a week later. 'The officer had his own handcuffs and baton stolen as he tried to get through.' Post-event debriefing documents show just how precarious the situation was: 'It didn't end up as a catastrophe', wrote one officer in 2007, 'but I think everybody involved realised how close we were to that happening.'

After the music stopped, the chaos continued at Brighton station: with the last London-bound train scheduled to leave shortly after Cook's set finished, there was a surge towards the platforms; numerous people fell onto the tracks, and Railtrack were repeatedly forced to switch off electrical power to the lines to avoid casualties. There were two deaths over the course of the day, though neither were directly attributable to the event itself: one man died on the beach during Cook's set, having suffered a heart attack, while twenty-five-year-old Australian nurse Karen Manders fell to her death from the seafront railings in the early hours of Sunday morning, long after the music had finished. Of the ninety other serious injuries, including two people with broken legs, many were ferried by lifeboat to Brighton Marina for treatment, when it became clear there was no way to get them to help on land. The relatively low number of serious injuries or deaths can be attributed in part to the decisive action by event organizers and the emergency services (Norman Cook successfully argued, as the crowd swelled, that cancelling the performance completely would cause a riot, but agreed to finish his set thirty minutes earlier than planned). Perhaps counter-intuitively, it's also been suggested that the crowd's drug-taking may have helped: massive bar queues across the city limited the crowd's drinking, replaced to some extent by the more placid effects of Ecstasy, making things easier to de-escalate than might otherwise have been the case.

Speaking to my source, it's clear that the emotional impact of what unfolded in Brighton was substantial, and continues to weigh heavily on everyone involved: in the weeks after the Big Beach

Boutique, they were offered police counselling, set up in the event's aftermath to support officers traumatised by their experiences. Norman Cook – himself no stranger to the terrifying power of an unpredictable crowd, having been present at the chaotic unravelling of Woodstock '99 three summers earlier – has voiced similar sentiments. 'I didn't enjoy it as much as last year,' he told *The Guardian* in the days after the event. 'I never thought it would turn out like this. I've created a monster.' In an interview with local paper *The Argus* shortly before the first Big Beach Boutique in 2001, Cook admits that he'd woken up in cold sweats, having had a nightmare about that year's Roskilde Festival in Denmark, where nine people had been crushed to death during a Pearl Jam show. 'It started me thinking', he says, with eerie relevance to events in Brighton a year later, 'about how important it is for people to look after themselves and each other.'

As the sun rose on a litter-strewn and urine-soaked Brighton beach, the postmortems began. The reaction of the local and national press was predictably scathing, with the *Daily Mail* describing 'chaotic scenes as revellers clung to ambulances to escape the crush, and scores of people had to be plucked from the sea.' And yet, where popular outrage over illegal raves had led swiftly and repeatedly to political intervention in the early 1990s – with the far less destructive events on Castlemorton Common sparking a particularly frenetic bout of national soul-searching – the broader reaction from local and national policymakers in the wake of the second Big Beach Boutique remained curiously muted. There were no exasperated debates in the Commons, no attempts by the tabloids to hold individual organizers personally responsible, and no clamour for new legislation banning local councils and international superstar DJs from producing events 'characterised by the emission of a succession of extremely big beats.' This was, to be clear, a good thing: rather than immediately reaching for the statute book or puritan soundbites, political actors instead focused on keeping attendees at big outdoor raves safer from harm. Despite the mayhem of July 2002, by the end of the year Brighton Council felt confident enough to establish a roadmap for putting on *more* Big Beach Boutiques, dependent on proper health and safety plans being written up. The 2003 edition would be cancelled, wrote *The Independent*, but 'Brighton and Hove City Council has said the party . . . can return in 2004 once procedures for coping with the crowds are in place.' As it turned out, Cook would only return to Brighton on New Year's Day in 2007, with the council insisting on him performing in the depths of winter to reduce attendance numbers. 25,000 people still showed up anyway.

In his 2009 book *Capitalist Realism*, Mark Fisher argues that neoliberalism's seepage into all forms of modern life has convinced us that it's the only game in town, constraining and controlling all other forms of social, cultural or political activity – 'the widespread sense that not only is capitalism the only viable political and economic system, but also that it is now impossible even to imagine a coherent alternative to it' – a line of thinking which helps to explain why the reactions to Castlemorton in 1992 and the Big Beach Boutique in 2002 differ so starkly. The former's largely self-contained noise and inconvenience represented 'the total breakdown of law and order in this country' precisely because they acted in opposition to the wider interests of capital – an unthinkable transgression in a world where cultural value and economic productivity are deemed to be inseparable.

A decade later, the far greater levels of noise, disorder, property damage and physical injury caused by the Big Beach Boutique were subsumed by the economic imperatives of Fatboy Slim's global DJ career and Brighton Council's civic branding: no longer a threat to the very fabric of British society, but merely the regrettable costs of doing business. There's a bleak irony here: Thatcher and Blair's neoliberal monoculture was built in large part on the rave-related legislative enclosure of the Criminal Justice Act, narrowing the spaces and contexts in which alternative or emergent communities could gather and celebrate, on the basis that doing so impinged too much on their neighbours. And yet the ultimate effect of that process has been to *increase* the disruption caused to British society by large-scale raves, on the basis that the associated economic benefits now trump everything else. Where Spiral Tribe were dragged through the courts and effectively exiled from the UK for their peripheral involvement in Castlemorton, Fatboy Slim and Skint were able to build an entire global brand off the back of the first two Big Beach Boutiques, pivoting to hugely lucrative events in Australia, Japan and Brazil. While Cook's regret over the disorder and damage of 2002 feels absolutely genuine, the magnitude of what unfolded has also served to memorialize it in our collective imagination: in September 2022, Cook announced a lavish anniversary box set featuring a remastered recording of his set from 20 years earlier, and a coffee-table book commemorating the event. In *Capitalist Realism*, Mark Fisher quotes Fredric Jameson and Slavoj Žižek's maxim that 'It is easier to imagine an end to the world than the end of capitalism.' While it's unlikely that Fisher was thinking directly of the quasi-apocalyptic scenes on Brighton Beach in 2002 or their highly commercialized aftermath, the sentiment feels relevant nonetheless.

Where Fantazia, Tribal Gathering or the Big Beach Boutique represented a profound shift in the form and function of outdoor dance music events as the 1990s progressed, indoor venues underwent similarly seismic changes with the rise of the superclub. While venues like Ministry of Sound and Cream opened before the Criminal Justice Act was passed, it's only after the outdoor raves of the free party scene were outlawed, and demand for massive dance spectacles was redirected back towards licensed venues in the centre of Britain's cities, that superclubs truly seized control of the zeitgeist. Prior to 1994, licensed party promoters had been forced to contend with numerous competitive advantages held by free parties of the kind run by Spiral Tribe, or the earlier illegal outdoor raves of Tony Colston-Hayter. Where illegal raves were free to get into, they out-competed venues with rent to pay and door charges to impose; where illegal promoters sold tickets, or passed round a collection bucket, they paid no tax, and didn't have to spend money on tedious bureaucratic necessities like working toilets or fire escapes. Illegal raves also offered the illicit thrill of transgressing social norms and breaking the law – the romance of following convoys down the M4, connecting to secret phone lines and insider networks, or outfoxing the police – with which more passive forms of cultural consumption were unable to compete. But it's not like superclubs didn't have their own unique charms: when illegal parties diminished in both scale and prominence following Castlemorton and the Criminal Justice Act, clubbers drawn to the glitzy excess of the superclub found a form of UK dance music brighter, bolder and more overwhelming than any before it. From the designs of the flyers to the lighting to the music to the big-name DJs to the fashion on the dance floor, the superclub was slick, aspirational and utopian, retaining the hedonistic lure of earlier raves while rejecting the illegality, seediness and all-round *otherness* with which so many of them had previously been associated, slotting dance music with perfect seamlessness into the everyday lives of millions of young Britons. 'A generation gleefully lost itself in a maelstrom of disco euphoria and house music', wrote the journalist Dom Phillips, 'and clubbing became the defining sound and lifestyle of 1990s Britain.'

Two bits of archive video shot inside Cream embody the processes at play here, and the subtle shift from club to superclub. The first was recorded in early 1993 for ITV's clubbing magazine show *BPM*: here, the pre-Criminal Justice Act version of Cream feels like a direct extension of the original acid house clubs of 1987 or the free parties of 1991 and 1992, with a vibe that's hedonistic but unpretentious, dancers rocking largely the same floppy hair, T-shirts, bandanas and dungarees you might have caught at Shoom half a decade before, or at Castlemorton the previous spring. Two years later, and the other side of the Criminal Justice Act passing into law, a *Granada Reports* crew visited Cream and captured a profound transformation. The venue itself was unrecognizable, having changed its name from the Merseyside Academy to Nation, as part of a £50,000 refurbishment paid for by Cream owners James Barton and Darren Hughes in exchange for a share of its ownership, expanding its official capacity from 400 to 1,800 people. The dingy, anonymous warehouse feel of proceedings in 1993 is replaced by something infinitely glitzier, mirrored by the crowds now in attendance: lads in collared shirts and slicked-back hair, girls in shimmering dresses and immaculate make-up pouting for the camera. Bouncers in matching Cream-branded black bomber jackets outline the dress code: 'no moustaches, no gold teeth, no gold necklaces, no plaits with beads, and no sequins on the front of their frocks.' In an interview to camera, Barton expounds on Cream's appeal – 'It's the atmosphere we create which helps bring great people here, and then those people bring other great people.'

Word of mouth only tells part of that story, though: in reality it was also marketing and industry networking that drew people in. In the two years between these different TV broadcasts, Cream had launched their newly refurbished venue with a glossy advert in fashion bible *The Face*, for which they'd designed a suitably futuristic logo: three droplet shapes, somewhere between a Nike swoosh and a sperm, arranged in a triangle. They'd also released the first Cream CD compilation, which featured mixes from Pete Tong and Paul Oakenfold amongst others, selling a quarter of a million copies, beginning the evolution from simple nightclub promotion to global media brand. Barton had also been hired as an A&R at Deconstruction – Sony BMG's dance sub-label, and at the time one of the biggest-selling dance labels in the country. For Cream's second birthday in 1994, Barton convinced new Deconstruction signing Kylie Minogue to come up to Liverpool and play a set for 1,800 bemused but delighted clubbers; by the time he left BMG in 1998 he'd signed acts including Robert Miles, Deep Dish and Way Out West, selling millions of records, and using those connections to further expand Cream's empire. 'James and Darren were the only two people who understood that a club brand was as valuable to their audience as the brands on their shirts, jeans and trainers', wrote Pete Hadfield, the head of Deconstruction, in a glossy book marking the club's tenth anniversary. Cream's brand became near-ubiquitous, a wholly integrated media empire from club nights to CDs to T-shirts. 'Cream was the first UK club that pulled people in from a huge radius rather than appealing to people in the immediate area,' wrote Judge Jules.

'[They] would pull people in from South Wales to Cumbria, we saw ravers who would travel 200 miles on one night just to go to Cream.' In 1994, Barton booked acid house renegade Andy Weatherall to play in the club's second room: 'When I played, Cream was a fledgling global brand and wasn't rampantly commercial', he later recalled, 'but I saw the seeds sown.'

Much as Fatboy Slim would do for Brighton later in the 1990s, Cream became the physical embodiments of their home city's civic and creative identity, a unifying and standard-bearing role equivalent to that of a local football club. 'It's why I studied in Liverpool' beams the John Moores University graduate 'Libby' on a poster for Cream in 1999. Under her graduation gown and chalkboard hat, she's fully glammed up for a night out, effortlessly combining three key Blairite touchstones: the cultural pleasures to be found in the 'creative industries' (tinged in this case with mild hedonism), regional placemaking as a reaction to Thatcher's abandonment of the post-industrial North, and the knowledge economy being built by Labour's widening university access. Other entries in the same series of adverts knit Cream into the rhythms and repetitions of late-1990s urban British life: 'It's why we go shopping on Saturday,' beam a pair of young, carefree women hitting the high street; 'It's why I had this done,' says a topless lad with the Cream logo tattooed on his chest. Things occasionally lapse into the mundane, or the unintentionally depressing – 'It's why I save up all year,' says a guy washing dishes in the dingy, indistinct back room of a restaurant; 'It's why I do this every week,' grins a woman in a stand-up tanning station – but for the most part the picture painted of Cream's role in Liverpool's civic regeneration and cultural reinvention is flawlessly positive. 'I remember being in Liverpool aged 17 and being pissed off with everything going on in other cities,' wrote Cream founder James Barton in 2002, placing local pride at the centre of the club's creation myths. 'For years London and Manchester had grabbed the headlines, and we thought Liverpool needed to get back in the game.'

This emphasis on civic identity wasn't just an abstract daydream, but a critical part of Cream's growth. When the ecstasy-related death of Leah Betts in 1995 sparked tabloid hand-wringing over dance music's seedier side, direct engagement with the political process became key to their survival. Barton and Cream co-owner Darren Hughes made an expedient decision to join Liverpool's Centre of Commerce, recruiting Jayne Casey to lead on engagement with local politicians and senior police officers. 'There was a massive cultural shift needed for dance music to move into the city centre, which meant it was under more observation from the police and needed to be carefully navigated. It was a difficult move to become a legal culture,' Casey recalled in 2022. 'Once the opinion formers and the leaders of the city supported Cream, it altered the way the police viewed us,' she wrote. 'If it wasn't for Jayne, we would have got closed down,' agreed Hughes: 'Her relationship with the city got us through.' Cream not only rode out the turbulence caused by a renewed political focus on dance music's proximity to drug use in the mid to late 1990s, but continued to grow. In 1998 they launched the outdoor festival Creamfields as the newest outpost in their brand empire, returning rave to the fields and green spaces from which it had fled in 1994. Local interests were key once again: the first Creamfields took place in Winchester in 1998, but was swiftly moved back to the club's home in the North West – 'great news to the city council, who were baffled that it hadn't happened in Liverpool in the first place.' The city's Lord Mayor would turn up to the 1999 instalment, photographed somewhat awkwardly alongside gurning ravers while wearing his chain of office. By the turn of the century, Cream were running similar events in Argentina, Uruguay, Barcelona, Moscow and Tokyo: within six years of the Criminal Justice Act, dance music had mutated from a malevolent force corrupting society, to a flag-bearer for local Liverpudlian identity, and finally into a vector through which soft British power, cultural influence and creative industry could be projected to the rest of the world.

Ministry of Sound – the pre-eminent clubbing brand in the UK, if not the world, at the moment Tony Blair arrived in Downing Street – built its success on much the same proximity to political processes, policymakers and powerbrokers. It owed its foundation in 1991 to a relaxation of licensing laws introduced the year before as a counterweight to the Bright Bill's clampdown on illegal party promoters, becoming one of the first clubs in the UK to open throughout the night, albeit with licensing conditions which prevented it from serving alcohol. In the first of many sharp marketing moves, however, this was swiftly turned into a positive: Ministry of Sound had been inspired in large part by the Paradise Garage, a New York club home to the legendary DJ Larry Levan, whose purpose-built dance floor and soundsystem, focus on music and dancing rather than conversation, and disinterest in dressed-up disco glam fundamentally altered popular understanding of how a nightclub should function. Its licence was similarly restrictive, with punters drinking fruit juice all night from a communal punch bowl ('Odds were it was spiked', wrote one regular in 2018) – Ministry's initial licensing setbacks merely aligned it more closely with the legendary Garage, and became part of its own mythos.

The similarities were finite, however. Where the Paradise Garage had emerged organically from New York's overwhelmingly queer and Black post-disco nightlife scene, Ministry of Sound was the creation of an entirely different constituency. James Palumbo, one of its three founders and the man most closely associated with it today, was an Old Etonian and a highly successful property banker for Merrill Lynch before getting into the nightclub business. His father was Conservative peer, property developer and Arts Council chairman Peter Palumbo – a helpful background when looking to ingratiate oneself within the corridors of power. 'He was looking for some great idea to create a new empire. He didn't really have one,' recalls Justin Berkmann, the only Ministry of Sound founder with any kind of background in dance music, and the only one – having moved to New York in 1986 – to have actually visited the Paradise Garage. Earlier acid house promoters like Sunrise's Tony Colston-Hayter and Equinox's Quentin Chambers had been lambasted for their perceived upper-middle-class roots – the *Boy's Own* fanzine had even invented a character called 'Tarquin Posh-Facker' to satirize the 'zany kids with double-barrelled names and single-cylinder brains, who liked to dip a tentative toe into the waters of working-class youth culture' – but Palumbo was on another level entirely. Estranged from his father since the mid-1980s, in 1994 he and his sister sued Palumbo senior over allegations that the latter had mismanaged the £70 million trust fund set up for his children by James's grandfather. By the time the 1997 election rolled around, Palumbo was sufficiently embedded in the establishment to lend his chauffeur-driven car to Peter Mandelson; following Labour's victory he was handed a cushy seat on a panel overseeing applications for new corporate Charter Mark applications.

From this well-connected position, Palumbo and Ministry of Sound would play a pivotal role in another signature piece of New Labour cultural policy – the much-maligned Millennium Dome. Having been handed the project in a chaotic state by the Tories in 1997, there were serious misgivings within government for what increasingly felt like a colossally expensive and extremely public white elephant: 'I had two ambitions when I took that job,' Chris Smith told *The Guardian* in 2007 of his appointment as culture secretary. 'The first was, "Can I change the name of the department?"; the other was, "Do we have to go ahead with the Dome?"' As with so much New Labour policy, the solution lay in private investment, with the Dome offering up advertising space (and editorial control, in many places) to a variety of corporate sponsors. Each of its abstractly themed zones soon fell under the patronage of a specific corporation: Boots jumped at the chance to sponsor the Body Zone, the Talk Zone was snapped up by BT and the Journey Zone by Ford. With somewhat more dystopian overtones, the Mind Zone was sponsored by arms manufacturer BAE Systems, the Money Zone by a consortium of City of London banks, and the Home Planet Zone by British Airways. The Faith Zone, however, proved substantially less attractive to corporate interest, at a time when attendance at churches around the country was in terminal decline. 'If the Zone was going to attract major sponsorship, to some extent it would have to reflect the interests of individuals or organisations that might provide the money', writes the academic Sophie Gilliat-Ray. To the bemusement of the faith leaders responsible for the Dome's religious content and the frothing incandescence of the *Daily Mail*, James Palumbo made a brazen pitch for Ministry of Sound to step in, on the unconvincing grounds that 'Dance was the religion of the new Millennium'. This offer was turned down emphatically,* but Palumbo remained closely involved with the project: when the government's initial Millennium Experience drew to a close at the end of 2000, its final event was a 15,000-person New Year's Eve rave promoted by Ministry of Sound. Where rave – and the countercultures which birthed it – had spent the preceding decades harried by the police, targeted by politicians, and exiled to the fringes of polite society and urban space, it entered the twenty-first century clutched tight to the government's bosom, hosting a party in their most treasured landmark, with the full permission of those at the very top.

In the following months, as the government solicited bids for long-term ownership of the Dome, Palumbo even teamed up with the project's former chief executive Pierre-Yves Gerbeau to mount an ambitious and ultimately unsuccessful bid to take over the entire thing. Despite once again being unsuccessful, Palumbo would continue to work with the Blair government before switching sides in the late 2000s and joining the Liberal Democrats. Appointed to an advisory role in 2010 by the incoming coalition government, he would be handed a seat in the House of Lords three years later. Spun in places as the victory of a scrappy underdog, rising from the grimy back streets of Elephant and Castle to the red leather seats of the upper chamber ('being an outsider, Palumbo felt comfortable in changing the rules', runs one puff piece), this was in fact little more than a member of the wealthiest stratum in society retaining his inherited privilege; dance music had only ever been a brief interlude,

---

* Funding would be found from a patchwork of smaller sponsors, including the Hinduja brothers, whose financial links to Peter Mandelson (at the time the Minister for the Millennium Dome) would trigger a political scandal and Mandelson's first resignation from government.

the modern equivalent of an upper-class Victorian taking his Grand Tour around the continent, before settling down to the proper business of exerting power. In 2016, Palumbo finally bowed out of the dance music industry, selling Ministry of Sound to Sony for £67 million.

The fact that Ministry of Sound were even vaguely considered – or indeed considered themselves – a suitable match for the Millennium Dome's faith-based content might seem absurd, but it also encapsulates another thread running through UK dance music's realignment during the Blair years. Just as the Church played a foundational role in the creation of UK dance music, its influence running back through Chicago house to disco, soul, the blues and gospel, so it also underpinned Tony Blair's own moral philosophy. Despite the assertion early in his leadership of the Labour party that 'We don't do God' Blair's convictions were steeped in religious rhetoric and Christian ethics. His 2010 memoir *A Journey* describes an Anglican priest named Peter Thomson as his foremost guiding light, having 'influenced Blair to take his faith more seriously as a comprehensive social vision informing his politics', while his conversion shortly after leaving Downing Street to Roman Catholicism (not to mention his predilection for spiritual healers while in office) undercuts any professed disinterest in the ethereal: indeed, it's easy to see Blair responding not only to the club-focused euphoria of 'Things Can Only Get Better' but also the ease with which its lyrical exhortations to a higher power could take on spiritual as well as secular connotations.

This elision of the banging and the beatific wasn't limited to Blair himself: during the early 1990s a number of explicitly rave-influenced church services sprung up around the UK, attempting to harness the transcendent power of the dance floor to ecumenical ends. The most influential and ultimately infamous of these was the Nine O'Clock Service in Sheffield, which formed out of a commune of radical evangelical Christians founded in the late 1970s by charismatic (and Charismatic, in terms of his specific style of ministry) preacher Chris Brain. The young, artsy commune members spent the early 1980s using youth culture as a vector to smuggle religious messages into the minds of young audiences – they formed a subtly evangelical synth-pop band called Candescence, appearing on line-ups with Cabaret Voltaire and The Fall, and turning down a support slot with U2 on the basis that the latter's lyrics were too *overtly* Christian.

But it was with the commune's first experiences of acid house and Ecstasy in late 1988 that Brain and others in the Nine O'Clock Service truly saw the face of God. Sheffield was by that point the epicentre of forward-thinking UK dance music, with the stripped-down, bass-heavy 'bleep techno' of LFO and Forgemasters representing the very first distinctly British[*] take on the sounds of Chicago and Detroit, at least a year before breakbeat hardcore would stake a claim to that title. Candescence broke up, and the Nine O'Clock Service was formed, running late on a Sunday night in their local parish church. Fusing the hedonistic and sacrosanct in previously unimagined ways, the Nine O'Clock Service's 'experimental worship, which resembled a state-of-the-art nightclub with film loops, projections, [and] multi-track mixing desks' sat alongside a hugely progressive and disruptive theology, writes the author and journalist Roland Howard. NOS addressed everything from ecological collapse to racial injustice, topics which at the time tended to be kept at arm's length by the wider Church: 'reaching out intelligently to a "godless generation", bringing them Christianity with a passion for, and commitment to, their issues.' The reaction from young people in Sheffield was extraordinary: within months the NOS commune members were having to act as makeshift bouncers, turning churchgoers away at the door. The response of the Diocese of Sheffield was even more unexpected: rather than

---

[*] As with big beat, this wasn't just a UK-wide form of cultural association but specifically regional. Forgemasters' name was taken from the crumbling steel mill which had, in 1971, provided 50 per cent of Sheffield's employment: just as techno had been born in the post-industrial hinterland of Detroit, so it resonated particularly with the former home of Britain's steel industry.

clamping down on this unruly and radical new form of worship, they instead put substantial financial and political weight behind it, sensing an opportunity to connect with a generation for whom religion felt increasingly irrelevant, and arrest sliding church attendance numbers. Brain claimed that during a meeting with George Carey in 1991, the then Archbishop of Canterbury-elect had told him that he 'would be happy to see a Nine O'Clock Service in every city and town in the country' while Brain himself was fast-tracked into the priesthood – why serve an apprenticeship under a more senior vicar, the reasoning went, if he was already in charge of one of the city's biggest and most ardent congregations? NOS itself was given a sweetheart deal by Sheffield City Council later that year, moving out of the local church they'd long outgrown, and setting up in the 2,000-capacity basement rotunda of a newly built leisure centre for a peppercorn rent.

What fragments of video footage and other ephemera still exist from the NOS archives suggest that the commune's late-night services were entirely deserving of such a reaction: a stunning sensory and spiritual overload, a million miles away from the trendy vicar cringe most people would expect. NOS wasn't just theologically ambitious but profoundly credible as dance music, rooted in commune members' backgrounds as DJs, designers, artists and musicians, all driven forward by Chris Brain's laser-focused leadership and charismatic vision. A 1993 audio recording of the Nine O'Clock Service's Planetary Mass – a 'weekly celebration of life, and our joint ritual of celebration and repentance on behalf of our culture' which combines rave, early Christian mysticism and ecological activism – is nothing short of astonishing. A buzzing mesh of Arabic horns fade into ambient synth pads: over the top floats a sample of the theologian Thomas Berry, asking, 'What are we looking for in life?' The music shifts into pulsating, irresistible deep house, as Chris Brain steps forward, and introduces the service before a chorus of voices join behind him, singing 'Let your life come on! Let your life come on through me!' over a surge of electronic sound. The service rushes, expands, peaks, and then flows seamlessly into the 'body prayer' – described by Roland Howard as 'a sort of Christianised yoga, focusing on bringing together the bodily chakras with spiritual absolution'. A woman takes over leadership of proceedings from Brain. 'Breathe in – hope – and out – death', she instructs. The first Amen break drops nine minutes in, under a vocal sample taken from an Indian raga. 'Stay . . . stay with me, O Jesus, stay with me', sing the congregation in perfect unison. Without them, you could easily mistake the music for an out-take from Leftfield's contemporaneous progressive house masterpiece *Leftism*, so impeccably produced are its sub-bass pulses and sampled grooves. The sharing of the Eucharist is accompanied by a squiggling 303 acid line, before overtly anti-capitalist prayers for a broken world are offered to God over chugging mid-tempo techno. From moment to moment it teeters on the brink of cheesiness, but between NOS's absolute commitment to their message and the pinpoint precision of their medium it is instead completely beguiling.

Howard describes the Planetary Mass as 'a work of corporate genius. Truly postmodern religious art of the highest order' and it's hard to disagree with him, or question why thousands of young people from around the UK might have flocked to Sheffield to experience it for themselves: from my own conversations with former NOS members, all of whom insisted on speaking off the record, it's clear that those present viewed these events as some of the most powerful, transformative moments in their lives. The Planetary Mass offers us a tantalizing glimpse of a lost future, in which Anglicanism (still a hugely influential force in early 1990s British life despite waning church attendance) could have fundamentally reinvented itself in collaboration with rave culture. Imagine a world in which the Nine O'Clock Service *did* spread to every town and city of the UK, as the Archbishop of Canterbury had once envisioned: we would have witnessed an entirely new form of dance music, allied to deep-rooted but non-dogmatic Christian spirituality and profoundly radical and eco-centric ethics; a mass musical-political movement underpinning the anti-CJA coalition, Reclaim the Streets, Occupy and Extinction Rebellion, as well as offering a powerful bulwark to the Blairite co-option of youth culture via the 'creative industries'.

And yet, of course, none of this came to pass. In August 1995 it emerged that the Nine O'Clock Service had in fact been little more than a terrifyingly abusive cult of personality centred on Chris Brain. Commune members had handed over their life savings to fund Brain's opulent habits; dissenters had been subjected to collective humiliation and then ostracized; vulnerable young women brought into the commune had been groomed by Brain, under the pretext that their sexual awakening would help bring them closer to God; and several were subsequently drafted into a 'Home Base Team' stationed permanently at Brain's house, where they were dressed in identical black Lycra uniforms, and tasked with giving Brain what were euphemistically referred to as 'late night massages'. By the time NOS collapsed in disgrace in the autumn of 1995, it's estimated that Brain was simultaneously sexually involved with anything between twenty and sixty different women within his congregation: one of the biggest sexual abuse scandals to have taken place within the Church of England in its history. And yet only a short-lived media scandal resulted, which saw Brain flee into obscurity and resign the priesthood shortly before a BBC documentary featuring testimony from survivors aired in late 1995. The Diocese of Sheffield refused to pay for counselling or accept responsibility: in that same BBC broadcast, then-Bishop of Sheffield, David Lunn, responds haughtily to the suggestion that more should have been done when allegations were raised directly with him in 1992. 'I don't think you remotely realize the number of complaints about congregations that bishops get,' he mutters, arms folded. 'You follow them up and . . . I don't quite know what one could have done. One hasn't got a reason for assuming that *everything* that *everyone* says has to lead to instant action.' His grumblings were contentious at the time, and feel offensively insensitive now: a perfect encapsulation of the disinterested attitudes that allowed sexual abuse to run rampant through institutions of all kinds throughout the twentieth century. It remains frustratingly unclear whether any of the information Lunn and others gleaned from NOS members was ever passed to the police: despite Brain's widespread psychological abuse and sexual grooming of his congregation being common knowledge, along with numerous more serious allegations not made public at the time, neither Brain nor anyone else was ever arrested or charged when the commune collapsed in 1995. It was only in April 2021 that former NOS members approached the Diocese of Sheffield to call for accountability and compensation, prompting South Yorkshire Police to quietly reopen their investigation: in August 2022, they announced that a man and a woman had been arrested in relation to allegations around NOS. Survivors of the group continue to meet in secret once or twice a year and keep tabs on Chris Brain, who now lives in Manchester under an assumed name.

Following the collapse of the Nine O'Clock Service, all that remained of rave Anglicanism was the superficial, half-hearted trend-chasing that those in Sheffield had so successfully avoided. On Christmas Day in 1995 and 1996, Channel 4 broadcast a pair of special programmes entitled *God in the House*, an overview of the various NOS knock-offs who were still trying to merge the club and the church, with far less compelling and at times unintentionally hilarious results. In its first episode, painfully 1990s digital graphics spin over a nondescript rural church, before the camera crash-zooms frantically onto a stained-glass window, soundtracked by generic house beats. We cut to a graveyard: the comedian Adam Buxton, a year before finding fame with *The Adam and Joe Show*, stands solemnly next to mildewed stonework, a parish spire looming behind him. 'Say the word "rave" and most people think of a bunch of *kids* jumping around all night in a *club* in 1989,' Buxton intones, with precisely the same mixture of earnestness and ridiculousness you'd expect from a lost episode of *Brass Eye* or *Father Ted*. 'But now people are raving in churches, combining house music and visuals to create a completely new form of worship,' he continues, before introducing an ecclesiastical hip-house outfit rapping about the Holy Spirit to the secondary school children of Cheadle,

Greater Manchester. Between Buxton's presence, the terrible music and the shonky production values, you have to rewatch the whole thing a couple of times just to make sure it's not an elaborate piece of satire. The following year's edition of *God in the House* is, if anything, even weirder – 'If [famed Victorian hymn-writer] Charles Wesley had been alive today, you'd probably find him plugging in his drum machine here!' suggests Buxton jauntily, before cutting to a service which features a woman dressed as an angel, replete with white robe and ramshackle tin-foil halo, chanting Gregorian plainsong over terrible Robert Miles-adjacent Eurotrance. All of the radical intensity and sensory overload which made NOS so powerful has been leached out, leaving behind something hollow and ultimately doomed to irrelevance. The collapse of NOS and the failure of its peers instead leaves us with the uncomfortable impression that – like so many other cults – its revolutionary world-building was impossible to sustain without the focus and self-abnegation demanded by a ruthless, charismatic and ultimately abusive leader like Chris Brain.

By the turn of the century New Labour's optimistic, evangelical lustre had also begun to ebb away, as a slew of major and minor controversies from the invasion of Iraq to Tony Blair's holidays with Silvio Berlusconi eroded the rave-like euphoria which first greeted their election, drawing them further and further away from the utopian possibilities glimpsed on that spring morning in 1997. In the weeks after Princess Diana's death, some six months after his triumphal entry into Downing Street, Tony Blair's approval ratings topped 90 per cent. By February 2003, shortly after a million people marched through the streets of London to protest against the impending Iraq War, they had dropped to somewhere around 38 per cent. At much the same moment that dance music completed its post-Criminal Justice Act realignment – from the alternative anti-capitalist society of the free party or the Nine O'Clock Service to the commodified leisure pursuits of Creamfields and the Big Beach Boutique – the last remnants of Blairism's emotional and spiritual fervour were also draining away. For each dodgy dossier or near-asphyxiated raver on Brighton beach, a little of the allure and potential glimpsed earlier in the 1990s was chipped off, replaced by the supposed necessities of realpolitik and free-market economics: dance music not depoliticized, but refashioned by degree into a tool for neo-liberal interests and personal power trips. Where we were promised the stuff of our wildest dreams, a Freudian-meets-Anglican revolution of desire and transcendence, we instead got only its most superficial signifiers, fiddling gently at the edges of the status quo. If there's a lesson to take from the Blair years, whether for dance music or indeed for society as a whole, it's that when someone excitedly promises you that things can only get better, the most important question to ask in response is: better for *whom*, exactly?

A CAMBODIAN ANTI-DRUG OFFICER DESTROYS A STASH OF SAFROLE OIL, 2008

6. Some Giddy Rite of Passage?

Power, profit and prohibition in the global dance drug trade

Chimay is a quiet city of ten thousand souls in the south-west of Belgium, known largely for its elegant castle, historic motor-racing festival and artisanal breweries. Beyond the walls of the old town is an agricultural complex, and within that a collection of run-down brick and concrete farm buildings. A faded, rotting wooden sign advertises fruit and veg, while poorly tended hay bales spill out of their plastic wrapping. Weeds can be found growing around the foot of a large barn, its boarded-up windows exuding a distinct air of menace. In the distance, you can hear a dog barking anxiously. At the entrance to the barn, men in white hazmat suits and gas masks file outside carrying sealed boxes: evidence recovered in the police operation they've just undertaken, one of the largest drug busts in European history. As part of a coordinated series of raids across Belgium, the Netherlands and Poland, this single building has offered up almost a tonne of Ecstasy – enough to manufacture 36 million pills – along with 18 tonnes of safrole oil, the substance from which MDMA is manufactured, otherwise known as its 'precursor'.

Chimay's mayor, Françoise Fassiaux, speaking shortly after the raid and the arrest of nine people in August 2013, expressed surprise that the overgrown backwaters of her sleepy constituency could form a critical node in global drug production networks: 'Rural communities are no longer protected from organised crime,' she told Belgian reporters. Two months after the raid in Chimay, another police operation in Opglabbeek, in the north of Belgium, uncovered 35 tonnes of precursor materials and a colossal manufacturing site hidden across a thousand square metres of unassuming farmhouses, barns and stables. Photos released by Europol reveal a labyrinthine mass of wires, pipes and tanks, set against crumbling concrete walls and overhead strip lights.* Given these two mammoth drug busts in quick succession, it's reasonable to wonder whether Mayor Fassiaux should really have been quite so surprised by the existence of a gigantic Ecstasy lab right under her nose. 'The landscape here is sparsely populated and very dispersed: sometimes two adjacent farms don't have any contact because of vacant land separating them,' she also told reporters, perhaps beginning to understand the attraction of such a location. Indeed, it's clear that ever since ravers across the UK and mainland Europe first began

---

* There's an eerie synthesis here between the post-agricultural spaces reclaimed by makeshift chemists and used for producing Ecstasy, and the post-industrial spaces reclaimed by promoters and DJs in which it is ultimately consumed; at every stage of the process, rave remains elusive and opportunistic, operating in the atomized and abandoned zones left behind by wider society.

dropping pills, there have been shadowy crews in quiet pockets of the Low Countries happy to produce and supply them: in a 2008 study the UK Drug Policy Commission quoted the opinion of the Serious Organised Crime Agency (now the National Crime Agency) that 'Almost all of the ecstasy consumed in the UK is considered to be manufactured in Holland or Belgium.'

All of this feels a world away from the context in which we're normally introduced to the knotty connections between dance music and Ecstasy: the romantic velocity of the dance floor, the surge of empathetic oneness and sensual overload, the fireworks behind your eyes as serotonin floods your pleasure centres. Traditionally, it's this *subjective* experience of being on drugs which is taken as the starting point, with its introduction to the UK traced to the other side of Europe, the island of Ibiza, and the first pills taken by Paul Oakenfold, Danny Rampling and others in the summer of 1987. Twenty years earlier, Barbet Schroeder's cult 1969 film *More* had set the template for these dreamy myths of Balearic excess: a man and a woman gaze out across the Mediterranean, sitting cross-legged and watching as the sun dips gently behind the horizon, bathing the coastal inlets and the hillsides which flank them in a deep pink. As our view stretches back towards the sunset, the rugged landscape becomes little more than an abstract series of undulating forms, sensual and inviting, shrouded in darkness near to us and softening to a light peach towards the sun. The couple beside us inhale deeply, drinking the moment in, before letting out a solemn, rapturous Om: before long they'll be dashing in chemically induced bliss down the island's hillsides and across its beaches, lounging against the rocks, and dancing lithely in the evening air next to whitewashed walls. On its initial release, *More* scandalized audiences with its depictions of heroin addiction and free love, and helped to embed the idea of Ibiza as a bohemian paradise in the popular imagination, while also serving as an inadvertent tourist marketing manual for the White Isle. In the wake of Schroeder's 1960s hippies would come the long-haired rockers of the 1970s, Hollywood superstars lounging opulently at KU Club in the early

1980s, crimson-and-orange-robed sannyasin cultists (thought to be the first to bring MDMA to the island) offering meditation and medication in equal measure, and ultimately the epochal moment in 1987, when four British DJs have their brains rewired by pure MDMA and the selections of DJ Alfredo.

In the popular history of UK dance music, that instant instructs everything which comes afterwards, underpinning how we've written, spoken and thought about UK dance music ever since. The opening chapter of Simon Reynolds's *Energy Flash* (re-named *Generation Ecstasy* for the US market) is titled 'Everything Starts With An E' in a nod to the evangelically pro-pill track of 1989 by E-Zee Possee. Matthew Collin's *Altered State*, meanwhile, is subtitled 'the story of Ecstasy culture and acid house', as if the former entirely circumscribes the latter.* DJ and promoter Nicky Holloway recounts his first trip to (and at) Amnesia in terms which have largely become an article of faith: '"On E", he says, 'it all made sense.' There's even a control group, forgotten in most retellings: jazz-dance DJ Gilles Peterson, later of Kiss FM and BBC Radio 1, went on the same Ibiza trip as Holloway, Oakenfold, Rampling and Walker in that feted summer of 1987, but didn't do any pills. On his return to London, he continued to play the same soul and rare groove tunes he'd done before, rather than pivoting to baggy T-shirts and acid tracks like everyone else: proof, surely, that Ecstasy was the key to unlocking the whole thing. A full thirty years after the event, Sky Arts' 2017 documentary series on the history of UK dance music – titled, wearingly, *The Agony & The Ecstasy* – opens with a verbatim retelling of Oakenfold's Damascene conversion on the dance floor of Amnesia: fans of dance music have heard the same story so many times over the last thirty years, and circumscribed so

---

* In fairness, both Reynolds and Collin treat the subject with far more nuance than can be contained in these brief snippets. 'This begs the question of whether the meaning of rave music is reducible to drugs, or even a single drug, Ecstasy . . . I don't believe that for a second,' writes Reynolds, while nonetheless claiming that 'rave culture as a whole is barely conceivable without drugs'

much of our understanding of the scene within its limited framing, that it too takes on the same eerie gloss of unreality as the images in *More*. 'Though it is based on real events', writes the academic Caspar Melville of the myth surrounding the Ibiza Four, 'the repetition of this story also serves an ideological function.' It gives us heroes to venerate as the sole progenitors of an entirely new cultural form, instead of a knotty mess of interlinked subcultural influences to untangle, from the blues dance to the free festival. It serves financial interests by cultivating desire: you too can have your very own Balearic experience, for the low low price of a ticket to see Paul Oakenfold DJing. And it also arguably serves a social or political function, stripping out dance music's associations with Black, queer or marginalized cultures, enabling a larger and more lucrative mainstream audience to claim it as their own. While drugs have clearly played a huge role in shaping UK dance floors over the past thirty-five years ('By calling this story a myth', writes Melville, 'I do not mean to suggest that it is false') we should be wary of narratives in which Ecstasy is the sole catalyst for its miraculous birth under the Ibizan sky: a story which is equal parts seductive, historically entrenched and potentially distorting.

The most obvious reason to rethink the accepted wisdom about UK dance music's mythical creation on the shores of the White Isle is a coldly statistical one: whatever the recollections of those first Balearic trendsetters, the vast majority of the millions of people who've attended clubs and raves since 1987 haven't been on Ecstasy. This is not an absolute science, as is to be expected when trying to keep tabs on illicit and illegal practices: 88 per cent of respondents to a 1996 survey of Scottish workers in the 'dance drug scene' (i.e. DJs, producers, promoters, and drug dealers) said they'd taken Ecstasy in the preceding year. But wider studies reveal those sorts of figures to be potentially misleading. Even as drug usage increased dramatically in the late 1990s, and dance music went from niche concern to mass-market spectacle, figures from the British Crime Survey – the UK's largest and most reliable source of data on illegal behaviour – show that the proportion of adults in England and

Wales who reported taking Ecstasy in the preceding year never got any higher than 1.8 per cent. Even if we focus solely on those aged between fifteen and thirty-four, the so-called 'chemical generation' whose entire cultural identity was apparently defined by their relationship with Ecstasy, the figure tops out in 2001 at an unexpectedly meagre 4.5 per cent. This still equates to nearly half a million people a year doing pills at least once during that period, but it's worth putting that figure in context: it's roughly equivalent to the numbers who would have passed through the doors of a single large club over the same fifty-two weekends. If the entire crowd at Cream or Ministry of Sound were taking Ecstasy, while the rest of the country remained studiously MDMA-free, I'm not sure we'd afford drugs quite the same hallowed place in our understanding of UK dance music. Clearly the numbers were still substantial, and more than enough for drugs and drug-taking to play a key role in how the sounds and subcultures of UK nightlife evolved, but using the first-person experience of taking MDMA as our keystone to understand this story in its totality feels limiting.

Within the numbers who reported taking pills, it's also worth noting that only a subset of those people would have actually been ingesting Ecstasy. By the mid-1990s, numerous studies indicated that fewer than half of the pills sold as such contained MDMA as their primary active ingredient, while another MDMA drought in the late 2000s saw the drug largely disappear from UK dance floors. Collin and others get far closer to the truth when they talk in terms of a 'polydrug culture' rather than framing dance music as specifically and solely dependent on Ecstasy. It's clear that pills exploded in popularity in the early 1990s, with confidential research produced for the Home Office in 1995 showing seizures of Ecstasy tablets skyrocketing from 768 incidents in 1989 to 3,500 half a decade later. But then so did pretty much every other party drug over the same time period: seizures of amphetamines went from 3,000 a year to just under 13,000, and cannabis from 44,000 to 89,000. The police seized more cocaine than MDMA even at the latter's peak, and have continued to do so ever since. One 1996 survey by teen magazine

Sugar suggested that cannabis, amphetamines, solvents, LSD and magic mushrooms were all more widely used amongst mid-1990s youth than Ecstasy, despite these attracting a fraction of MDMA's attention both at the time and since. Whatever a given member of the great British public was on during rave's golden era, odds are that it was something other than Ecstasy, or indeed nothing at all. The journalist and author Emma Warren, whose decades of dancing include blagging her way into the last ever Shoom party as a teenager, offers a perspective far more in keeping with these statistics, but largely excluded from the prevailing recollections or romanticization of that era. People who conflate dancing and drugs 'have clearly never experienced what happens to your body when you've been moving together in time with other people for hours and hours', she writes. 'Many people had, of course, discovered the kinetic glow initiated by MDMA, but it's not true to say that *everyone* was on drugs. Myself and my best friends weren't.'

This is also a generational question, given the steady decline in drug usage since its peak around the turn of the millennium. For journalists writing about rave in the mid 1990s or early 2000s, it must have felt like a fistful of Doves or Mitsubishis (particularly potent batches of pills identified by the logos stamped into them) were essential to understand this terrifying new techno-futurist ritual. And yet the quarter-century's worth of younger dancers and DJs who've followed them have operated with less reliance, collectively speaking, on the use of narcotics as a mediator; not least because they've been far less able to actually get hold of proper MDMA even if they wanted to. Where Reynolds dots *Energy Flash* with dizzying and delicious tales of his own chemical explorations, from lost nights in enticingly sordid basement clubs to blissed-out dancing under the stars at Castlemorton, my first pill was handed to me perfunctorily in the mud and rain of Glastonbury in 2004, shortly before Orbital headlined the Other Stage. Like the set itself, an underwhelming re-tread of their groundbreaking performance a decade earlier, the pill was a dud. My experience might have been infinitely less romantic than Reynolds's but it's no less true or reflective of dance music's history. For those of us unlucky enough to have come of age after rave's supposed halcyon days, a history which begins and ends with an E offers us noticeably less than our forebears.*

Most importantly, though, positioning the experience of being on Ecstasy as the central feature of UK dance music also serves to marginalize the racialized contexts in which it has played a less pronounced role over the years. Emphasizing the predominately white dance floors like The Haçienda or Cream, where Ecstasy undoubtedly had its most profound epiphanic powers, has meant sidelining the Black and Asian dancers, producers and DJs for whom it's been less widely used, and less collectively revelatory. Take the Daytimer scene centred around Bradford in the mid 1990s as one example: this network of venues and DJs played a critical role in the development of specifically British Asian dance music subcultures, but was far less dependent on drug-taking than its white equivalents; if 'dance music' and 'Ecstasy culture' are treated as synonymous, parties such as these end up excluded from the canon. Similarly, MDMA's infamous loosening of emotional rigidity is largely applicable to specifically male forms of social interaction: 'tens of thousands of previously uptight Brits – even heterosexual footy hooligans – ecstatically embracing each other', as one *Mixmag* article puts it. While it would be foolish to assume that no female or non-binary thugs existed in the 1980s, the emphasis on E's role in dissolving terrace violence serves to refract it through a specific and almost exclusively masculine lens. As dance music has mutated and evolved, the Ecstasy-laced adventures of its disproportionately white and male first-generation gatekeepers feel less and less reflective of its history as a whole, affording disproportionate weight to the

---

* In case I come off like too much of a curmudgeon here, I should mention that I've also had spectacular, life-changing experience with Ecstasy, and on the dance floor. But the two have largely been separate: amongst my social circles, MDMA use has largely been a feature of the houseparty rather than the rave, while my most transcendent dance floor experiences have been almost exclusively drug-free.

subjective perspectives of those lucky enough to experience Ecstasy's first flushes first-hand. This is not to say that the epiphanies we experience when under the influence, and the insights they carry into the 'normal' world, are not real and meaningful. But by focusing on the world as seen through those eyes, we make it harder to factor in the unconscious biases and power imbalances at play, and risk losing sight of other equally vital stories. Quite apart from anything else, the core function of MDMA, its primary chemical attribute and clearest psychological effect, is that it engenders a profound sense of empathy and identification with others around you. Of course if you're on a good pill you're going to feel like everyone else in the room is having precisely the same experience: *that's the whole point*.

Instead of continually harking back to the familiar memories of first-generation ravers, it's possible to look at the relationship between drugs and dance music from another angle: not as a rainbow-flecked journey into our inner selves, but as a global system of power, money and chemical substances, exerting wider contextual pressures on Britain's sonic and political cultures. What matters is not so much the first-person experience of someone taking drugs, but the cumulative third-person effect of that decision, from the shifting tastes and energies of the dance floor to the reaction from DJs, drug squads and the *Daily Mail*. If you are to reframe the question in that way, then the starting point has to shift: away from the sensory recollections of ageing superstar DJs, to a team of hazmat-suited anti-narcotics officers picking their way through the drug factories of the Low Countries, including the unassuming farm building and outhouses on the outskirts of Chimay.

Among the first people to synthesize MDMA in the Netherlands were existing amphetamine manufacturers like Robert Hollemans. Ever since the International Opium Commission of 1909 kickstarted efforts to regulate and prohibit narcotics, the Netherlands' numerous and well-established connections to global trade networks, the country's geographic position at the heart of Western Europe, and its particular history of smuggling across its southern borders with Belgium and Germany, have all made it 'one of the most important sources of synthetic drugs such as MDMA and amphetamines, [and] a major transit hub for other drugs' such as cocaine on its way from South America. Even in pre-MDMA days, Dutch drug labs were responsible for a disproportionate volume of Europe's drug supply: more than half of the LSD seized by police forces across the continent between 1988 and 1992, and over 80 per cent of the amphetamines seized between 1985 and 1989, originated from Dutch laboratories. By the mid-1980s, MDMA started to appear on the radar of Dutch university research chemists, and from there it began to seep inexorably into the criminal underworld.

Robert Hollemans was one of those responsible. His interest in MDMA piqued, he sought out a copy of Californian biochemist Alexander Shulgin's infamous psychopharmalogical memoir-cum-cookbook *PiHKAL* in his local library to discover more. *PiHKAL*, or 'Phenethylamines I Have Known And Loved', was an exhaustive documentation of Shulgin and his wife Ann's explorations into the outer realms: synthesizing strange new psychoactive compounds in their home laboratory on the West Coast, dosing themselves up, and then extensively describing the ensuing experiences. Originally discovered in 1912 by German pharmaceutical company Merck as a by-product of research into new blood-clotting medicines, then largely ignored for over half a century, MDMA had begun to re-emerge in psychedelic circles around 1970. Shulgin heard about its psychoactive potential in 1975 and developed a more straightforward synthesis method for it: impressed by its disinhibiting effects, he began recommending its potentially therapeutic effects to psychotherapists in and around San Francisco, from where it filtered slowly into countercultural and hippie circles. Hollemans skipped to the section which featured Shulgin's instructions for synthesizing MDMA, and got to work.

He and other Dutch chemists had also been pushed towards MDMA by the fall of the Berlin Wall, which opened up huge swathes of Eastern Europe to cross-border trade for the first time in decades, allowing cheaper amphetamines produced in post-Soviet countries to flood the market. Increasing numbers of Dutch producers switched to Ecstasy: more complex to produce, it initially remained beyond the reach of their new Polish or East German competitors, and as such held its street price, while the Dutch government's sluggish approach to legislation meant that MDMA wasn't officially prohibited until 1988. When police raided Hollemans's lab on suspicion of amphetamine production earlier that year, they instead found it packed to the rafters with MDMA; on the basis that the latter was still legal, there was nothing they could do.

From the Netherlands, the flow of drugs and money connects us back briefly to the balmier shores of Ibiza, via the elusive devotees of the controversial Indian guru Bhagwan Shree Rajneesh. Familiar to viewers of the 2018 Netflix documentary series *Wild Wild Country*, Rajneesh founded his first ashram in the Indian city of Pune in 1974, encouraging his followers – known as sannyasins – to celebrate the liberating powers of free love and psychedelic drugs, and to 'bring what was repressed and unconscious to the surface, [using] meditation as a tool to develop a different attitude towards the thoughts and feelings that had been exposed.' Where Freud had used psychoanalysis to achieve these goals (with an eventual and tangential connection back to UK dance music via New Labour's electoral co-option of Freudian principles) Rajneesh's acolytes went straight to the source. Their collective practice, termed Dynamic Meditation, combined mind-altering drugs, repetitive electronic music and freaky dancing in an attempt to create trance-like states of pure being. 'The music begins – electronic, repetitive, insistent – and so do I, inhaling and exhaling deeply', writes one sannyasin of these group rituals, in language that uncannily mirrors the energy and emotion of a rave. 'The music changes . . . the beat is more insistent than before . . . the screams and shouts fill a room that is hot with effort . . . the music seems to carry my body as if it were a suit of clothes and the music, moving within, were flesh and blood.'

Listening to a mix of sannyasin music broadcast on independent UK radio station NTS in 2018, what's most striking is its similarity to the 'afro-cosmic' approach popularized by Italian DJ Daniele Baldelli and the Balearic styles of DJ Alfredo, both of which heavily influenced the first generation of UK acid house DJs: in the sannyasins' strung-out jams, all undulating Afro-Cuban drums and eerie electronic drones (German new age musician Deuter, photographed in his sannyasin robes surrounded by reel-to-reel tape machines, sitars and an EMS Synthi, began following Rajneesh in 1973 and composed all the music for the commune's meditations until 1981) you can absolutely detect the genetic forebears of later dance music. From Pune, Rajneesh's acolytes connected fluidly to the hippie communes on the beaches of Goa, with LSD, sex and parties acting as a shared currency between the two groups. In 1981, Rajneesh reacted to increasing pressure from the Indian government by purchasing a massive plot of land in rural Oregon, relocating huge numbers of his followers to create Rajneeshpuram: an entire city in their own image. With MDMA circulating freely within West Coast countercultural and psychotherapy circles by this point, the two having been introduced to each other by Alexander Shulgin in preceding years, the drug quickly made its way into the commune at Rajneeshpuram, featuring in both the sannyasins' out-of-body rituals and, allegedly, the deliberate spiking of Rajneesh's enemies. When things in Oregon went sideways in 1985 – resulting in the scandalous stories of guns, abuse and mass poisonings detailed in *Wild Wild Country* – and Rajneesh was arrested, the commune collapsed and sannyasins scattered across the globe. Several pitched up in Ibiza, by now established on the global hippy trail via its connections to Pune and Goa, in the process opening up a meditation centre and bringing MDMA to the island for the first time. Others landed in the Netherlands; within a few years they would set up a direct connection between the growing supply capacity of local MDMA producers, and increasing demand for the drug in Ibiza, setting the stage for the drug's discovery by curious Brits on holiday.

As acid house and then rave took hold in the UK, the Netherlands became the primary source of Ecstasy flowing into the country. It was responsible for three quarters of all pills seized in Britain in 1994, while a single Dutch laboratory busted the same year was found to have been capable of churning out half a million pills a day. The global nature of these supply chains, and attempts by international drug enforcement bodies to disrupt them, would remain largely hidden from those attending raves, while simultaneously exerting an influence on UK dance music more profound than any DJ or record label. Between 1990 and 1995 a succession of UN conventions and European Community ordinances obliged national governments to monitor and restrict access to MDMA's precursor chemicals, including safrole oil. While this had minimal impact on drug enforcement within the UK, it did have substantial effects on manufacturers in the Netherlands, forcing them to source their raw materials internationally rather than domestically. Over the same period, larger Dutch organized crime outfits spotted the profits being generated by amateur underground chemists, and began muscling into the industry – in a particularly enjoyable Scorsese-esque detail, one man responsible for the supply of dimethylformamide (an essential solvent for synthesizing MDMA) was known only as 'The Snail'. Between 1992 and 1995, these global pressures on precursor supply chains and the harder-nosed profit motives of Dutch organized crime saw the purity of Ecstasy sold in the UK drop precipitously. As the percentage of MDMA in pills decreased, it was increasingly replaced with cheaper and more easily synthesized chemicals to meet still-growing demand: caffeine, infamously, but also good old-fashioned amphetamines or MDMA-like compounds including MDEA and MDA.*

Each of these alternatives replicated MDMA's adrenalin rush and late-night energy, but they lacked its tactile, empathetic fuzz. While only a subset of clubbers might have been taking pills on any

---

* Alexander Shulgin warns against precisely this phenomenon in *PiHKAL*: 'Unprincipled charlatans can always add mineral oil and butter yellow to otherwise white solids to make them into yellow oils,' he says of the white precursor to MDA and the yellow equivalent for MDMA. 'Caveat emptor.'

given dance floor at any given time, changes in their chemical make-up were enough to alter the atmosphere and sounds experienced in basement clubs and free parties across the UK. In his book *Drugs 2.0*, Mike Power details the arrival of Snowballs on the UK market in 1992: synthesized in Latvia after the fall of the Iron Curtain and marketed as Ecstasy, they in fact contained no MDMA whatsoever, instead consisting of its less euphoric cousin MDA. 'These strange pills that made the atmosphere and users edgier,' as Power describes them, coincided with a move away from the slinky 120bpm grooves of acid house, and towards the 130 to 140bpm freneticism of breakbeat hardcore and early jungle. While the precise interactions between drug supply and dance floor sounds are impossible to fully untangle – it's entirely possible that changing drug trends are as much a reaction to shifting musical tastes as a cause of them – the synchronicity here is hard to ignore.

Between 2006 and 2008, the actions of a few politicians and law enforcement officers on the other side of the world would exert a similarly profound effect on UK dance floors. Mike Power describes an abandoned poachers' campsite high in the forested Cardamom Mountains of Cambodia as 'a bizarre mix of charnel house and war movie . . . husks of a tree beside a vast cauldron over the embers of a large fire.' These trees, felled shortly before authorities raided the ramshackle camp, are known in English as camphor wood; the fire, over which a gigantic metal drum and makeshift distilling apparatus have been arranged, would have been used to extract sassafras oil from shredded piles of camphor roots and bark; vacuum-distil that sassafras oil, and you end up with safrole, the precursor to MDMA, and the same chemical seized in huge quantities during the raid in Chimay. As illegal logging of the highly endangered camphor wood ramped up over the mid-2000s, the Cambodian government made the connection between deforestation and the international drug market, and subsequently banned the import and export of all safrole-rich products in 2007: a photograph taken the following year by Fauna and Flora International, the UK-based NGO which had tracked much of the illegal logging to begin with, shows a Cambodian official throwing blue plastic jerry cans of sassafras oil onto a large, smouldering bonfire. With the assistance of Australian police and UN anti-drug squads, some thirty-three tonnes of sassafras oil were destroyed in one colossal burn in the summer of 2008: enough to manufacture 260 million Ecstasy tablets, or one high-strength pill for every Ecstasy user in the UK every single Saturday night for the next ten years.

Over the same period, the Chinese government also began clamping down stringently on the manufacture and export of piperonyl methyl ketone, or PMK, the only other widely used MDMA precursor. The combined effect of these actions on the global availability of Ecstasy was colossal: where 16.5 tonnes of MDMA were seized around the world in 2007, within a year that had dropped to a measly 6 tonnes. As supplies dried up, UK clubbers began to look elsewhere for their intoxicants: many went for mephedrone, a newly synthesized compound similar to crystal meth; its novelty meant that it initially remained legal, sold as 'plant fertilizer' and pounced on by grey-market Chinese manufacturers, who soon began shipping fifty-kilo consignments of the drug direct to the UK. Others turned to ketamine: legal until 2006 and remaining a Class C substance (the lowest rung of the UK's prohibition system) until 2014, a 2009 report by the Independent Scientific Committee on Drugs indicated that 68 per cent of clubgoers had used ketamine at some point in their lives, up from 25 per cent seven years earlier. Again there's a potential blurring here of cause and effect, between the drug's sedative, dissociative effects and the sluggish, bass-heavy sounds of dubstep which had risen to prominence in the preceding years: a precise breakdown of who was taking the drug to enhance the music, and who was using music to enhance the drugs, remains lost in each individual user's intensely private desires.

In 2009, Simon Reynolds used a *Guardian* article to reach for a link between ketamine usage and 'wonky' — an emerging dubstep subgenre combining acid-bright synth lines and clattering, off-axis percussion. 'K heads are a fucking nightmare', according to a message board user quoted by Reynolds. 'They fall into everything, break stuff, don't move out of the way of incoming traffic, slobber over bouncers . . . and just look at you in confusion when you ask them to do anything.' In the particularly ketamine-saturated environs of Bristol, notes Reynolds, ravers infuriated at this mass dance floor zombification resorted to printing 'Dubstep Against Ketamine' T-shirts to voice their disapproval. While there are undoubtedly parallels between the lopsided beats of artists like Hudson Mohawke and the limb-loosening effects of ketamine, a more convincing connection is made by Philip Sherburne to the minimal techno scene, perhaps the largest and most lauded dance music genre of its day. Identifying a sub-strain of 'ketamine house' as early as 2005, Sherburne notes the music slowing down, extraneous melodic material being swept away, and the euphoric peaks and troughs of earlier techno being instead flattened out to a horizontal, mirror-like sheen stretching away pacifically to the horizon. Each of these changes, of course, reflect the mindset of someone zonked on the sedate charms of ketamine, rather than riding the euphoric rollercoaster of MDMA. Ricardo Villalobos, credited by Sherburne with pioneering this new sound, would take ketamine-influenced minimal to its logical conclusion: one of his tracks, *Fizheuer Zieheuer*, unfolds languidly over a generous thirty-eight minutes, its nagging melody unchanged throughout, orbited by a subtly shifting web of aluminium-light drums, rubbery sound effects and dub echoes. Over the course of the late 2000s and early 2010s Villalobos would become one of the biggest DJs in the world, his rise owing as much to dingy farmhouse labs in the Low Countries, faceless bureaucrats in UN offices, and anti-drug agents following the tyre tracks of illegal loggers through the Cambodian jungle as it did to the packed dance floors of Fabric and Berghain.

In the early 2010s, just as Ecstasy began returning to the UK drug market, the country's musical tastes also started shifting back towards the euphoric peaks and propulsive rhythms of more 'classic' house and techno sounds: formerly sedate 'chill out' artists like Bonobo and Four Tet repositioned themselves as purveyors of tasteful stadium-sized dance tunes, underground acts like Disclosure or

Bicep ascended to the status of bona fide pop stars, and the hipster fringes were dominated by scuzzy all-analogue 'outsider house' jams, recorded on vintage synths onto hiss-saturated tape decks, looking to recapture the raw energy of the earliest Chicago house records. 'I'm the information', chants a down-pitched vocal sample on one of the era's biggest tunes, 'Sicko Cell' by Joy Orbison. 'Cocaine powder . . . Too much, too much . . . I'm so addicted.' There's been plenty of dance music made over the years which either extols or attempts to replicate the experience of being on drugs, but something in the tenor of UK dance music clearly shifted at the start of the 2010s: the product of not only the decommissioned and gentrified former warehouses and factories in Hackney or Brooklyn where this music was being made, but also their still-functional equivalents in Shenzhen, China, where the drugs being taken on UK dance floors now originated.

Having spent several years following the Cambodian safrole burn and Chinese PMK clampdown scrabbling around for alternative precursors from which to synthesize MDMA, Dutch chemists eventually realized that PMK-glycidate, a legal derivative of PMK which forms into a yellowish solid rather than clear liquid, was the answer. Used extensively in the perfume industry, and thus impossible to fully prohibit, PMK-glycidate could both circumvent Chinese export restrictions and be converted easily back into PMK liquid, and from there into MDMA, once it reached the Netherlands. Despite being subject to increasing attention from Chinese authorities over the past decade, the country's grey-market distributors remain happy to sell PMK-glycidate to European producers today. By 2011, the Ecstasy being sold on UK dance floors was the strongest it had ever been; by 2016, purity levels had doubled again on top of that. Brexit, the Covid-19 pandemic, and a shortage of qualified lorry drivers able to bring both legal and illegal cargo into the country saw the purity of MDMA arriving on British shores dip again before once more hitting record levels in 2022.

Systematic, detailed information about what happens once these Ecstasy shipments enter the UK is harder to come by, given that the distribution networks in question are run by organized crime groups – primarily British but with as many as thirty nationalities represented across the UK drug trade as a whole – which are by definition opaque and impenetrable. In general, though, there appear to be four hierarchical levels within the UK drug trade: large-scale importers with international networks, who manage the incoming shipments (largely from Belgium and the Netherlands in the case of Ecstasy); national wholesalers and distributors who move the drugs between cities (from a port of entry to a major local metropolis, say), then sell smaller packages on to regional distributors who operate within a specific city; and then finally street-level dealers, who buy from city-wide distributors and supply individual users. These processes and relationships are highly flexible, with connections cutting across hierarchies and roles often combined – import and wholesale might be managed by the same person, say – meaning that the map of drug distribution across the UK often looks less like a pyramid and more like a web: 'A large jigsaw', explains a joint 2001 study by the LSE and the Home Office into the middle tiers of the UK's drug market, 'in which each particular piece comes from a different set.'

For many years, the primary route by which Ecstasy made its way into the club itself was through bouncers: a 1998 government report concludes that one Liverpool gang used 'intimidation and bribery' to seize control of the city's market for door staff, then 'used their position to facilitate and dominate drug dealing within the premises they were charged to protect.' While subsequent political attention has focused on regulating and accrediting door supervisors, to ensure the industry can't be so openly manipulated, neither this nor increasingly aggressive security measures on the door, from sniffer dogs to airport-style scanners, have stemmed either supply or demand; for the most part it just means that people now take their drugs before getting to the club, rather than once they're inside. Or, indeed, bring the atmosphere of the club back home: taking the same drugs and listening to the same music (the former supplied by better-connected friends, 'social dealers' who make up the majority of street-level sellers) in unlicensed, unofficial and often entirely unassuming spaces.

Ask the average Briton of a certain age what comes to mind when they think of Ecstasy, and it's a decent bet that they'll picture a photo of eighteen-year-old Leah Betts in a hospital bed, chin slumped back towards her chest, mouth lolling open, a grotesque array of tubes and wires running across her face and chest. Leah had taken a single Ecstasy tablet at her eighteenth birthday party in November 1995, given to her by a friend, the embodiment of a 'social dealer', having bought it at a local club. Conscious of guidance at the time that focused on ravers at risk of dehydration, Leah then drank twelve pints of water in a little under ninety minutes: with the MDMA in her system making it harder to process or expel urine, this massive influx of fluid meant that her blood sodium levels dropped precipitously. As a result, some of that fluid began to cross the blood-brain barrier, causing her brain to swell and crushing itself against the inside of her skull. 'When I saw her eyes I knew there was something wrong. They were so big, they were enormous. It was like something out of a horror film . . . she was clawing and screaming at me to help her,' Leah's mother told the inquest into her death. 'Her head was near to exploding,' said her father '[then] she just slowed down and stopped struggling'. Within minutes, Leah slipped into a coma from which she would never recover; five days after her arrival in hospital, her life support machine was switched off.

While she wasn't the first or last person to die in the UK after taking Ecstasy, Leah's death marked a watershed in Britain's social and political relationship with drug-taking, and sparked one of the most profound moral panics in living memory. Where the use and abuse of Ecstasy had previously been confined in the popular imagination to seedy underground clubs or morally dubious Traveller sites in some anonymous field, Leah died in her suburban home just outside Chelmsford, at a sedate party where the music was quiet and alcohol had been banned, taking the pill which led to her death while her parents sat upstairs. Ecstasy was no longer something that happened to *them* over *there*; if it could kill Leah, then no one was safe. If the trajectory of UK dance music between Castlemorton in 1992 and Tony Blair's election in 1997 was largely one of increasing popular demand and mainstream acceptance, then Leah's shocking death was the dark inverse of that process of assimilation. Her death saw Essex police crack down aggressively on the local drug trade, with violent repercussions across the criminal underworld, including the 1995 murder of local drug kingpins 'The Essex Boys'. This sudden re-association between dance music, drug-taking and mortal danger underlined why integrating rave culture into the 'creative industries' was always going to be fraught with difficulty, undercut by the same primal fears about the corruption of England's youth which had dogged rave's earlier countercultural years. In the aftermath of Leah's death, UK dance music would arguably be shaped less by the subjective experience of taking Ecstasy than the media narratives and state interventions sparked by these fears: what you're on in the moment ultimately matters less than what the *Daily Mail* thinks you're on, and the government's attempts to stop you getting on it.

The press did their usual job of ratcheting up the tension, from leading with photos of Leah on her deathbed to their lurid descriptions of her final moments ('Leah Betts died in agony . . . as her brain literally twisted out of shape', reported the *Daily Express* with morbid voyeurism) and grimly following the daily agony of her parents as they decided whether or not to switch off her life support. 'She could be declared clinically dead as early as tomorrow', ran one front-page leader in the *Daily Mail*. Leah's father, a retired police officer, and her mother, a nurse, were the perfect moral and emotional figureheads for the months of press indignation which ensued.* Seemingly endless column inches were devoted to tales of

---

* A secondary scandal, largely forgotten now, erupted across the tabloids in relation to the medical donation of Leah's organs: not because the NHS had squandered the opportunity to make use of them, but because her liver had ended up being used for a transplant in Spain, rather than the UK.

Ecstasy rotting the brains of Britain's children, or to inchoate outrage at its continuing availability and popularity; a short film about Leah's life and death was produced by Granada, broadcast on BBC Two, and sent to every secondary school in the UK. In one particularly uncomfortable piece of media-induced agitprop, ITV flew Paul Betts out to Amsterdam to rail helplessly against the country's drug distributors; the *Daily Mirror* dutifully gave prominent print coverage to the thoughts he'd amassed on street-level dealers during the trip. 'Part of me wanted to go over and flatten him, take justice into my own hands and end his evil trade right there,' he writes, watching a man sell drugs on the streets of Amsterdam. 'It's their sheer callousness that fills me with contempt. But even in my anger I knew that this overwhelming desire to sort him out would do no good and I would be the one who would end up in court.'

'Was it an experiment? A dare? Some giddy rite of passage?' asked the *Daily Mail* rhetorically of Leah's decision to take that fateful pill. 'The young will always be vulnerable to their own insouciance,' they conclude, before railing against 'the pushers and dealers who wickedly adulterate their wares.' The idea that Leah had been poisoned by one of many dodgy tablets on the market (potentially laced with 'Vim, aspirin [or] dog worming tablets' as the *Daily Express* speculated) took hold of tabloid rhetoric in the immediate aftermath of her death, only to be conclusively rejected as a factor in her death at the inquest. 'Unscrupulous drug dealers who dilute Ecstasy tablets with killer chemicals to make more money pose a massive threat to youngsters,' raged the *Daily Star*, quoting an un-named police officer who insists that 'Nobody knows what the drug barons are putting into it. Sometimes there is heroin' – an assertion which would require dealers, not a group normally known for their philanthropy, to replace MDMA with a vastly more expensive substance, then sell it at a loss. However understandable the Betts' unfathomable grief or moral zeal – the latter encouraged by the popular press – might have been, the sum total of this all-out media blitz on the dangers of Ecstasy was negligible, undermined by the increasingly forthright language in which it was conducted. Young people aren't stupid: they compared the absolutist rhetoric from the government and media with the real-life evidence in front of them, in the form of huge numbers of their peers going out raving without incident, and drew their own conclusions. Between 1994 and 1996, the years either side of Leah Betts' death, self-reported Ecstasy usage among fifteen- to thirty-four-year-olds roughly doubled.

As with UK dance music more broadly, aspects of the moral panic over club-related drug use quickly became steeped in racialized imagery and rhetoric. Where the rising prevalence of MDA had accompanied the birth of breakbeat hardcore in 1992, and ketamine the pacification of minimal techno in 2008, the birth of jungle and the arrival on British shores of crack cocaine have similarly endured a long and uncomfortable association. 'COCAINE MAKES A COMEBACK AS RAVERS HEAD FOR THE JUNGLE' reads one *Times* headline published in 1994; while the article doesn't explicitly mention race, the connections it forms between drug-related criminality and a music genre largely understood and depicted as Black are unambiguous. The word 'aggressive' crops up repeatedly, describing the psychological effects of cocaine, the music itself and the atmosphere on the dance floor alike: inside the club 'young men jostle each other in time to the stomach-wobbling bassline, stopping only to sway during the reggae interludes'. The question of cocaine's affordability for inner-city youth is raised, then discarded hamfistedly on the basis that 'small-time dealing' is endemic amongst audience members. 'Crack was the new drug,' says Julia Toppin, a full-time jungle raver in the mid-1990s before becoming an academic focusing on the under-acknowledged role of women in the scene, 'and so people were trying it in raves, and people will talk about that horrible crack smell. But it was only a very specific time period: you tried it because it was the new thing, there weren't, like, crack addicts in the raves.' This sense of crack being a temporary and peripheral aspect of the jungle scene, rather than a fundamental force corrupting it, makes far more sense. Not least because Toppin's research shows that 'no-one can evidence it at any point, ever, not even through the number of drug busts. But, obviously, that was the discourse the police put out. I really feel like it was an excuse to just over-police Black people as usual, keep them in line, and stop them earning.'

More than twenty years later, the same tropes remained grimly prominent. When Louella Fletcher-Michie died in 2017 after taking the synthetic psychedelic 2C-P at Bestival, and her boyfriend Ceon Broughton was arrested on suspicion of manslaughter, the media was sent into a feeding frenzy. Like Leah Betts, Fletcher-Michie was a bright, popular, young white woman, the daughter of beloved TV actor John Michie. Broughton, on the other hand, was Black and had been previously arrested for carrying a knife. Fletcher-Michie was depicted by the *Daily Mail* with 'long, blonde hair flowing from beneath a headscarf, and shades shielding her eyes from the late summer sun' while Broughton 'produced violent rap music' and was 'a fully-fledged member of skateboarding gang Laigon Life.' The facts of the case were undoubtedly damning: Broughton had not only supplied the drugs, but also failed to seek medical help as Fletcher-Michie's condition worsened, instead filming her on his phone. By the time Broughton finally sought assistance, it was too late. Media coverage duly depicted Broughton as taking 'sadistic pleasure in giving women drugs then filming them' while his rap videos, social media and the contents of his phone were mined for further evidence of his degeneracy. He was 'a sadistic drug dealer' who had an 'obsession with death' and led a 'despicable life', the possibility of anything more nuanced or humane remaining unaddressed in the reams of tabloid coverage churned out during the trial. Quite apart from anything else, none of the coverage displayed even the slightest curiosity about whether Broughton had — as one might quite reasonably expect — taken the same hallucinogen as Fletcher-Michie, and if so how that might have impaired his judgement or affected his actions as her condition worsened. 'The reason I feel so bad for him is that that could have been me or any of my friends,' the *Times* quoted one friend of Fletcher-Michie as saying after Broughton was found guilty (his conviction would be subsequently overturned on appeal). 'People say he watched her lying on the floor, looking as if she was dying but every time I go to a festival I see at least one of my friends lying on the floor, looking like they're dying. You don't really acknowledge it as a life-or-death situation. Everyone is doing that. It's just festival antics. Ceon is being portrayed as some kind of drug-dealing gangsta rapper but he's a very nice, honest guy. He wasn't a drug-dealer. It was literally unlucky.'

Where the tabloid media led public debate, politicians were quick to follow: from 1995 onwards, the prohibitionist zeal of the Bettses' media appearances largely set the constrained terms on which political discussion of drug harms could take place. 'The government is not in the business of testing illegal drugs to find out which ones are "safe",' reads the government's talking points on its new Drugs Strategy, rushed out in late 1995. 'Resisting drugs [an early draft has 'abstaining from drugs' crossed out and replaced] is the only risk-free option.' When Tony Blair came to power, he made a specific point of meeting with Leah's parents to promise them that Ecstasy would not be reclassified, but remain a Category A drug alongside heroin and crack. Divergence from that line, or questioning whether Ecstasy's relatively modest harms merited that classification, would not be tolerated. When in April 1996 Mary Hartnoll, director of social services in Glasgow, wrote in an internal memo that Ecstasy causes fewer deaths than aspirin, and was therefore 'a relatively safe drug', her opinion was leaked to the press to be greeted by a wave of vitriol and demands for her resignation. Paul and Janet Betts were once again wheeled out to claim that Hartnoll 'has done a wonderful advertising job for Ecstasy. She has given users and dealers the get-out clause to get away with what they're doing'.

In 2009, the government's chief drug advisor Professor David Nutt wrote a rigorously researched scientific paper for the Centre for Crime and Justice Studies, in which he attempted to compare the varying harms associated with every major drug; everything from heroin to glue-sniffing was included, assessed against criteria from the ease with which people could get addicted to the burden created by each substance on healthcare systems. Ecstasy received the third lowest score of all the drugs assessed, determined to be only a hair's breadth more harmful than poppers or khat, and substantially less damaging than either tobacco or alcohol. Nutt had earned the ire of Labour's waspishly authoritarian Home Secretary, Jacqui Smith, the year before, when he compared the thirty ecstasy-related deaths recorded in 2008 with the hundred deaths caused by horse-riding, but this new heresy was beyond the pale; within twenty-four hours of the report's publication, he'd been sacked. Outraged at the government's refusal to listen to facts, or accept that scientific advisors should be guided by objective evidence rather than political expediency, three more advisors resigned in protest. 'Politics is politics,' remarked Nutt phlegmatically, 'and science is science'. The think tank that commissioned Nutt's research was more direct: 'The message is that when it comes to the Home Office's relationship with the research community', wrote Richard Garside of the Centre for Crime and Justice Studies, 'honest researchers should be seen but not heard.'

One of the final pieces of legislation passed by the Conservative government before their election defeat in 1997 was the Public Entertainments Licensing (Drugs Misuse) Act, which gave local authorities the power to close, without warning, any clubs where drug use on the premises had been reported to them by police. Barry Legg, the Conservative MP who'd tabled the bill, paid tribute to Paul and Janet Betts in introducing it to the Commons, but neglected to mention that the pill which killed Leah hadn't been ingested anywhere near a club, and that his bill would have therefore done little to prevent her death. The thing which would actually have helped her – credible, widely publicized and evidence-based advice on how much water to drink when you've taken Ecstasy – was quietly adopted by the Health Education Authority only after another teenager, Janet Cousins, narrowly avoided death in circumstances unsettlingly similar to Leah's in early 1996. Much like the media blitz which preceded it, Barry Legg's bill utterly failed in its intent to 'help save young lives . . . [and do] something constructive to help crack down on the drugs menace'. It instead merely created a new scapegoat for societal drug use, in the form of late-night venue owners; under these expanded powers, extremely dubious prosecutions relating to a number of venues would lay bare the tissue-thin nature of the government's commitment to public safety. Early in the Commons debate, Legg asserted boldly that young people across the UK 'want to hear the "No to drugs" message' – rather than, as anyone of school age at the time will doubtless remember, being bored to tears by regular and endlessly dreary post-assembly presentations. When Labour MP Paul Flynn, the only person to speak against the bill, shook his head sadly, Legg chastised him, and invited him in schoolmasterly fashion to share his opinion. 'I shook my head because although "No to drugs" has been the message sent out in this country and America for the past thirty years, the use of illegal drugs has increased in every one of those years,' replied Flynn. 'It increased last year, and it will increase next year. Is it not time we look at new policies on drugs?' The official transcript of parliamentary proceedings records the response as coming from 'The House' as if every other MP is speaking with one unanimous voice: 'No'.

Rarely has the old adage that 'hard cases make bad laws' felt truer than in this case. Passed in the febrile atmosphere following Leah Betts's death, the placing of specific legal responsibility on nightclubs to prevent drug use would subsequently be used to shut venues from Niche in Sheffield to Fabric in London, with scant regard for their cultural value or, in many cases, the actual reality of drugs being dealt or taken on the premises. Perhaps the most egregious example of this is the Dance Academy in Plymouth, also known as the Palace Theatre: forcibly closed in 2006, its manager and owner ended up imprisoned for 'permitting the sale of a Class A substance' despite complying fully with the terms of their licence and in the absence of any evidence suggesting their direct involvement with drug dealing. The biggest UK nightclub south of Bristol at the time of its closure, the Dance Academy played a central role in the South West's rave scene: 'If you wanted to make it, this far down, you had to play Dance Academy,' recalls one of the clubs' resident DJs. It had been purchased in 1997 by Manoucehr Bahmanzadeh, an Iranian exile who'd made his fortune running cab companies in his adopted home of Brighton, with his friend Tom Costelloe appointed as manager.

Despite being reassured in 2005 by a local licensing officer that their upcoming licence renewal was a formality, behind the scenes both Bahmanzadeh and Costelloe had been targeted by Devon and Cornwall Police, who ran a twenty-five-man undercover operation briefed specifically to 'look for links between management and the sale of drugs.' Subsequently warned by licensing officers that he risked prosecution, Bahmanzadeh wrote to the police offering to upgrade the Academy's security, but in April 2006 the club was raided, along with Bahmanzadeh's and Costelloe's homes. At their subsequent trials, the prosecution's star witness was a man named Gareth Grimes: a bouncer at the club, he was the only member of staff to testify that Bahmanzadeh and Costelloe had turned a blind eye to drug use. Only during Bahmanzadeh's appeal did it transpire that Grimes had himself been accused of trying to sell drugs to undercover officers, had witnessed the murder of another local dealer and had lied about being a Royal Marine (a small point, but one likely to have played well with a local jury given the large Marine base located just outside the city).

Despite the flimsiness of the evidence against them, and a local drug support organization testifying that dealing at the Academy was 'no worse than in other clubs', Bahmanzadeh and Costelloe were sentenced to extraordinarily punitive prison terms of nine and five years respectively. Summing up, the judge suggested that the defendants could have put on '*Strictly Come Dancing* or line dancing' music to prevent drug use on the premises. Bahmanzadeh's lawyer described his conviction as 'one of the most extreme miscarriages of justice' she'd seen, while Bahmanzadeh himself maintains that he was targeted because he stood in the way of council plans to redevelop Plymouth's waterfront. In 2006, the same year that the Dance Academy was raided, a Plymouth Council spokesperson told a local paper that there were 'lots of exciting ideas for the building';

internal council documents from 2007 stated that 'The Palace Theatre will be regenerated and be a key landmark on Union Street' as part of their redevelopment plans.

Twenty-five years on from the passage of Barry Legg's anti-drugs bill, the continued demand for drugs, and increasingly strident attempts to suppress it, have resulted in a kind of legislative arms race. Rather than stepping back to ask the same questions as Paul Flynn did in 1997, politicians on all sides have instead doubled down relentlessly on cutting off demand, whatever the costs of doing so. When the UK's supply of MDMA slowed to a trickle in the years following Cambodia's safrole burn and China's clampdown on PMK in 2008, it should have been a victory for prohibitionist sentiment. Instead, UK ravers just switched to substances like mephedrone. When mephedrone was banned in 2010, another 'novel psychotropic substance' popped up to replace it, then another, and another, each less clearly understood and therefore potentially far more dangerous than the drug they replaced. As soon as the latest of these compounds was identified by police and legislated against, someone would tweak the formula, create a legally distinct chemical with broadly similar effects, and the cycle would repeat. Theresa May's government responded in 2016 with the Psychoactive Substances Act, as incoherently authoritarian a piece of law-making as could possibly be imagined. Under its powers, every single psychoactive substance currently in existence or yet to be discovered – defined as any material which 'produces a psychoactive effect in a person if, by stimulating or depressing the person's central nervous system, it affects the person's mental functioning or emotional state' – was to be banned, unless it could be categorized as food, medicine, alcohol, caffeine or tobacco. Where the Criminal Justice Act of 1994 represented the enclosure of public space, the Psychoactive Substances Act was an enclosure of the periodic table: a blunt object which once again shifted British society from one in which anything was possible unless expressly forbidden, to one in which everything is banned unless it's been permitted in advance.

The Daily Telegraph, not normally known for its ardent defence of drug users, ran a piece entitled 'Theresa May wants to ban pleasure' which castigated the government's 'bizarre piece of farcically bad drafting' and noted that the law's strictest reading would render illegal everything from whiteboard markers to the smell of a bonfire on Guy Fawkes Night. Imagine the scene: the late summer sun drifts gently below the horizon in some becalmed pocket of the deep English countryside, crickets chirping softly in the verdant haze. Your sweetheart hands you a bouquet of freshly picked meadow flowers; drinking in the sweet, nectar-laden scent of their soft petals, endorphins flood your body, filling you with bliss. You are immediately arrested, and put in jail for a maximum of seven years.

Of course, the Psychoactive Substances Bill failed in its aims, as all prohibitionist legislation throughout human history has done. In 2016, the year of the act's passage into law, there were 2,593 deaths attributed across the UK to drug misuse; the following year, the government's fearless legislative assault on every single psychoactive molecule in the universe had reduced this number by less than a hundred. By 2020, the figure had gone up again by almost a quarter to 2,996, the highest total since records began. The response from Home Secretary Priti Patel was a proposal to 'name and shame' middle-class drug users, with chief constables encouraged to 'make public examples of business owners and wealthy users to change the perception that Class A drugs can be taken without consequence'. The policy was quietly shelved, once it had served its purpose of throwing some red meat to core Tory voters and *Daily Mail* leader writers.

What makes all of this wilful incuriosity, institutional buck-passing and political self-preservation even more infuriating is its largely performative nature. While the idea of a front-bench politician advocating for anything other than blanket prohibition remains taboo, it's telling how many public servants – from Tony Blair's flatmate and former Lord Chancellor Charles Falconer to one-time Tory leader William Hague – have become suspiciously keen on decriminalization the moment they retire, no longer answerable to voters or responsible for toeing the party line. Instead, throughout the last thirty-five years of moral panics and useless political grandstanding, the work of keeping Britain's drug users safe has fallen on a patchwork of underfunded, overstretched social and medical workers, alongside charities relentlessly pushing back against the political establishment's own crippling addiction to burying its head in the sand. The basic premise of harm reduction – that given society's enduring and unbreakable desire to regularly get off our collective faces, attention should be focused on mitigating risks and providing a safe context for people to indulge – has been proven repeatedly correct. In 2012, Amsterdam appointed Mirik Milan as its first Night Mayor, tasked with pulling together various aspects of the night-time city including drug safety. 'As a starting point, you consistently see in countries that have the most progressive drug laws, and policies for harm minimization and testing, that they have the least amount of people dying,' he told me. The numbers back him up: in 2019 the Netherlands recorded a grand total of 250 drug-related deaths: roughly 5 per cent of the UK's total, in a country with one-quarter the population. The message is clear: when you build drug policies around harm reduction principles, fewer people die.

For Milan, the key tool in ensuring that drug use doesn't lead to drug-related deaths has been the public provision of drug-checking facilities, so that people can be sure of exactly what substances they're taking. 'Because of the testing we can provide really good information, so people are aware that there's a risk and they need to be particularly careful. This has led to our red alert system for particularly potent batches: it's not mandatory for clubs and venues, but a lot of them will put up the signs we produce, warning about specific pills or powders'. And yet it was only in the summer of 2022 that approval was finally granted for the UK's first public drug-checking service, run by the country's foremost drug safety organization The Loop, to be set up in Bristol. The Loop's highly experienced volunteers had previously operated in something of a legal grey area, given that possession of the substances they were testing remained illegal. Embedded within police units or festival security teams, testing drugs after seizure but before they were destroyed, The Loop could stay informed about potentially dodgy batches circulating amongst the UK club scene, but were unable to engage directly with users and warn them of potential dangers. Ongoing political squeamishness over accepting the realities of mass drug-taking meant that The Loop remained stuck, with neither police forces nor the Home Office willing to make the first move towards creating a legal exemption for public-facing drug-testing.

Ultimately, it took a global pandemic and multiple avoidable deaths for things to change. As the Covid-19 pandemic eased and lockdown restrictions began lifting, Fiona Measham, director of The Loop and leading authority on drug safety, identified a perfect storm of intersecting issues. 'We know from all sorts of different surveys, including The Loop's, that people haven't been taking party drugs during lockdown,' she told me in August 2021, 'so that combination of people wanting to party hard for the first time in a year and a half, but having a lower tolerance, is something that causes us concern. Adding to that, we've got a cohort of 850,000 young people who turned eighteen during Covid, who are all suddenly able to go to clubs and festivals, but who are relatively inexperienced and potentially more naive around both clubbing and drug use.' This unusually susceptible cohort of drug users crashed head-on into a black market stretched thin by eighteen months without access to their core consumers. 'We know there's disruption to legitimate supply chains due to Covid, Brexit or road haulage shortages, whether it's McDonald's running out of milkshakes or Nando's running out of chicken,' said Measham, 'so it's realistic to assume that there are disruptions to the illicit supply chains too.'

The result was an influx of wildly unpredictable substances, with The Loop's behind-the-scenes testing at the Lost Village festival in August 2021 revealing that fewer than half of the pills being sold as Ecstasy contained MDMA. Terrifyingly, several contained eutylone, a chemical whose short period of MDMA-like euphoria immediately gave way to extended bouts of paranoia, insomnia and psychosis. Within days of clubs reopening, three people had died after taking what they believed to be Ecstasy. And yet these deaths could have been avoided: when the Culture, Media and Sport Select Committee published a report on the post-Covid future of UK music festivals in May 2021, one of its core recommendations was for the Home Office and police forces to sort out the legal ambiguity around public-facing drug-checking, and ensure its availability at summer festivals and other large-scale events, whenever the lifting of lockdown restrictions might enable them to take place. This did not happen: raves went ahead as normal, drug-testing facilities remained as legally murky as ever, and thus not directly accessible to the public, leaving people with no way to check what was in their drugs before taking them.

For want of political will, UK dance music fans continue to be left largely to fend for themselves. 'It's quite clear that the Home Office is going for a full assault on drug possession, that they think this is a metropolitan issue that won't lose them any votes,' said Ant Lehane of drug reform charity Volteface in 2021. As for the Labour party: '[They] won't want to be pinned on the issue or step up and challenge them, for fear of being seen as soft on crime or loony lefties who want to legalise all drugs.' Instead, the same old cycle continues indefinitely: clubs and festivals remain primarily driven by the constant fear of closure embedded in Barry Legg's 1997 act, with millions of pounds in both public and private money continuing to be spent on security staff, airport-style scanners, sniffer dogs, police overtime, and other largely ineffective attempts to clamp down on drug use. Thousands of tickets to raves across the UK are printed each weekend with disclaimers about zero-tolerance drug policies, for events at which it's widely understood that drug-taking will inevitably occur, without the measures which could make that drug-taking safer. Faced with all of this, those in charge will continue to ignore reality, or fall back on the same tired soundbites they've defaulted to for generations.

When I asked the government in the autumn of 2021 whether

they planned to implement the Select Committee's recommendations for public-facing drug tests, their response might as well as have been drafted in 1995, or 1955. It reads, in full: 'There is no safe way to take illegal drugs, which devastate lives, ruin families and damage communities. Any policing arrangements around festivals are an operational matter for Chief Constables.' Asking the National Police Chiefs' Council for details of these 'operational matters' and whether ravers could expect any kind of help in the near future was met with a similarly depressing reply, laying bare the grim, facile disdain for those at risk and the infuriatingly circular logic which has made progress so achingly slow to achieve, from the arrival of Ecstasy in UK nightclubs to the present day. 'Testing illegal drugs is obviously not a role for the police, and is not something we would be involved in at all,' their email reads. 'I guess the simplest thing to do would be to not take illegal drugs.'

POLICE ATTEND THE FILMING OF A DRILL RAP VIDEO IN NOTTINGHAM, 2018

7. The Breakdown

Disrespect agendas and the demonization of Black British dance music

'Every fourteen minutes a blade is used in an offence in England and Wales,' intones the narrator of the documentary series *Cops UK: Bodycam Squad*, 'and gang violence in major cities is escalating.' In between the show's hyper-dramatized collage of stabbings, domestic raids, pixellated faces, sinister ambient music and low-level dogwhistles about the decay of British society, UK dance music makes a cameo appearance. 'We have our own gang problems, and youths out on the streets carrying knives,' says PC Karl Browne, inviting us to join him on a patrol around the St Ann's neighbourhood of Nottingham. We see the view from Browne's dashboard camera, as he rolls down a nondescript inner-city residential street, grey skies hanging low over a terrace of red-brick houses. On the opposite pavement a group of young men, mostly clad in black, are clustered together outside a newsagent. A 'gang of youths' according to the narrator, 'reported to be causing disorder.'

These fears prove ill-founded, when it turns out that the young men in question are merely filming a music video for up-and-coming Nottingham rappers Glockamoley and Lil Danny. Both work in the UK drill scene, a genre originally imported like house music from the streets of Chicago, and defined by sluggish, bass-heavy production and lyrics which focus unstintingly on the grim everyday realities of violence and intra-community conflict. Like many drill rappers, several of the men around the video shoot have balaclavas on to obscure their faces. The police and TV cameras are treated with a broad lack of deference (PC Browne's suggestion that the young men in question 'Grow up, and stop swearing' is resolutely ignored) but things remain entirely good-natured, with nothing even remotely illegal going on. 'Karl knows the local gang members and what they're doing,' explains the narrator, blithely erasing the boundary between guilt and innocence, before noting generously that the activity of young men such as these 'doesn't *always* involve being up to no good.' PC Browne's affable and authoritative demeanour serves to reassure viewers of *Cops UK*: these young men are clearly at risk of getting mixed up in crime, we're not-so-subtly told, but for the heroic local bobby checking up on their well-being, the very model of community-led policing by consent.

What *Cops UK*'s rose-tinted narrative doesn't cover, however, are the pre-dawn raids by Nottingham Police a few weeks later, targeting the family homes of the video producers who filmed Glockamoley and Lil Danny. 'It was really early in the morning, my whole family was sleeping,' explains one of them. 'They were beating on the door . . . they wanted to grab my Mac, memory cards, hard drives . . . they woke up my baby sister, brought everyone downstairs . . . they said they wouldn't give any of it back until they got to the bottom of things.' This, it turned out, was shorthand for the police demanding personal information on the artists they'd worked with. 'They treated us like we're criminals . . . but we thought giving a platform to the youth was a good thing.'

The three young men in question – Leon Matthews, Ephraim Morgan and Luke Fannin – had met a few years earlier in Birmingham while doing a media studies course, their shared love of music inspiring them to set up a production company named Krown Media after they graduated. Making music videos for aspiring artists in their local community, helping get their music on Spotify and other streaming services, and hosting freestyle sessions on their YouTube channel had been not just a business venture, but also a creative outlet and a way of supporting their community. In person they're earnest, softly spoken and professional, young businessmen helping to build precisely the type of cutting-edge creative industry the UK says it wants, but which in reality – at least when it comes to dance music – remains subject to to strictly enforced social hierarchies. None of the people in Krown Media were connected to any 'gangs' no matter how spuriously defined, they hadn't been in trouble before, they didn't even make drill music, but they were treated like a threat regardless, deemed fair game for the police's atttentions solely because their professional clients included rappers. After getting nothing out of Matthews, Morgan and Fannin, the police eventually backed down and returned their equipment. PC Browne makes a cameo appearance in Glockamoley and Lil Danny's video, watching on as the artists do their thing. In a wry twist on the dehumanizing and anonymizing grammar of reality TV cop shows, this time it's his face, rather than those of the young men around him, which is pixellated.

Arguably the biggest Black British music subgenre of the early 2020s, UK drill offers inner-city Black youth a chance to express themselves, after Brexit and a decade of Tory austerity has gutted their life prospects and the nation's urban centres. It's also attracted vast police and media attention as a catalyst of violence and disorder, lamented as the root cause of uncontrollable inner-city unrest. But these issues are not remotely new. In 1926, John Souter's painting *The Breakdown* — which depicts a naked white woman dancing ecstatically to the sounds of a Black jazz saxophonist, who's sat fully clothed on the shattered bust of a classical statue — caused uproar when it went on display in the Royal Academy. An attempt to, in the artist's own words, 'suggest the fascination exercised by the primitive and savage upon the over-civilised', it was also an assault on myriad fragile white sensibilities, from fears of Black virility to the threat of Renaissance culture being overtaken by illicit Black rhythms. The painting was lambasted by the media ('As a protest against the Jazz Age', wrote a scandalized *New York Times* review, 'the picture seems remarkably effective') and withdrawn from public view after the Colonial Office declared it 'obnoxious to British subjects living abroad in daily contact with a coloured population', before being destroyed by Souter himself. Two years previously the first editor of *Melody Maker* magazine had demanded on behalf of his fellow white jazz musicians 'that the habit of associating our music with the primitive and barbarous negro derivation shall cease forthwith.' A review of a jazz dance in the *Sunday Chronicle*, also published in 1924, follows a similar train of thought: 'The negro musicians knew well how to recapture the inflaming noises made by their far-back ancestors, and which are still enjoyed by cannibals during their most important ceremonies . . . [T]he animal devotees of jazz, who like to be maddened . . . [s]ee how it whips them about! They obey it like slaves . . . These women . . . shuffle round the room with striding legs too far apart, rigid bodies, and fixed staring eyes . . .' While the transparency of the racism on display and the precise terminology used to convey it may have changed over the ensuing century, the underlying sentiment — that Black music is a corrupting, dehumanizing force with either sex or violence at its core — has remained constant.

These same dynamics have accompanied UK dance music ever since its inception. In 1988, just as acid house was annexing warehouses, airfields and brownfield sites across the country, a parallel moral panic about Black violence was also taking hold. In tones which are highly reminiscent of scaremongering around raves, the *Daily Star* quoted an 'evil drug-crazed gang leader' claiming that he 'ate and slept crack . . . it became my God' in a piece dealing with 'Yardie drug fiends' while in 1989, the *News of the World* illustrated a piece titled 'Inside The Crack Castles' with photos of young Black men smoking the drug. Despite being largely portrayed as a problem of Jamaican-born gangsters exporting violence from the slums of Trenchtown and Tivoli Gardens, with specific immigration restrictions passed as a result of media scaremongering, a 2012 study found that 70 per cent of Black gang members – the term 'Yardie' is notably absent from serious studies of the topic – were in fact born within the EU, with the next most common places of birth being Somalia and West Africa rather than the Caribbean. These dubiously evidenced associations extended to Jamaican music, specifically dancehall reggae: when in 1992 Mark Burnett was shot on the dance floor at a show by dancehall artist Capleton at The Podium in South London, the police and media immediately blamed the killing on Yardies and the drug trade. Between long-standing and well-evidenced Black suspicions about the police, and the fear of reprisals which came with explicitly linking the murder to organized crime, the police's decision served to scare off potential witnesses: 350 people claimed to have been in the 750-person venue's toilets at the time of the shooting, while 90 per cent of the names and addresses given to police by attendees turned out to be fake. 'The dancehall music scene, where rappers flaunt guns, has had a huge influence on British youth . . . this is gun culture,' claims a Sky One documentary made in the aftermath of Burnett's death, alongside footage from the gig, recorded moments before the fatal shots were fired.

UK dance music's growing popularity in the early 1990s saw it splinter into countless new subgenres. One of these in particular, jungle, drew heavily on the sonic signifiers of reggae and dancehall, from half-time basslines to ragga vocal samples, and foregrounded specifically Black artists and audiences (though was also made and listened to by white and Asian DJs and dancers). The associations in mainstream white imagination between earlier Jamaican-influenced music, crack cocaine and Yardie violence transferred seamlessly across to this new scene. 'During the first weeks of BBC Radio One's One in the Jungle, broadcast Summer '95, a listener near the Welsh Brecon Beacons faxed the show with a complaint,' writes Brian Belle-Fortune. 'How could he persuade his friends that the Jungle scene was "safe" when MCs chatted about "Bad" and "Rude Boys" either on stage or on the radio?' 'Jungle makes people uneasy. Their prejudices are being confronted,' said John Peel in 1994, quoting an unnamed BBC producer who apparently dismissed the genre as 'music for black criminals and crack dealers'. Gang members' patois is adopted from 'jungle, the latest and loudest derivative of reggae', according to the *Daily Mail*, while *The Guardian* opens one 1997 piece about shootings at a club in Hackney with reference to its 'Jungle and Garage' music policy. Yet another *Guardian* piece from 2000 opens with a detailed description of the queue outside Chicago's, a 'soul and reggae' venue in Peckham, shortly before a shoot-out which would wound eight people. It's only some twenty-nine paragraphs later, buried deep at the end of the text, that we're told 'police [are] not linking the violence to Chicago's, which they described as well-regulated.'

As UK dance music's evolution continued, jungle was overtaken in the popular consciousness first by the skippy two-step rhythms of UK garage in the late 1990s, then the ice-cold beats and raucous MC clashes of grime in the early years of the twenty-first century: with each of these new Black-coded genres' rise in popularity, the drawing of dubious associations between UK dance music and inherent Black criminality by politicians and police forces was recycled and updated. In 2003, teenagers Charlene Ellis and Letisha Shakespeare were killed after a New Year's party in Birmingham, caught in the crossfire during a shoot-out between rival gangs. Rather than grappling with the complex questions raised by such senseless violence, Culture Minister Kim Howells took the easy option of blaming 'idiots like So Solid Crew' who were apparently responsible for 'glorifying gun culture and violence.' So Solid's popularity and criminal records made them obvious scapegoats: they'd reached Number 1 with '21 Seconds' two years earlier, while two members of the crew had recently been charged with assault and weapons offences. Despite having no connections to Birmingham and having been hundreds of miles away at the time of the shooting, the government chose to seize on them as soundbite-friendly cyphers for inner-city violence and moral decay. 'For years I have been very worried about these hateful lyrics that these boasting macho idiot rappers come out with,' opined Howells. 'It has created a culture where killing is almost a fashion accessory.'

Blair's ruthlessly disciplinarian Home Secretary David Blunkett joined in, vowing 'to crack down on violent lyrics in a bid to banish gun culture' rather than trouble himself with the material causes of crime, like inner-city poverty or social exclusion. Much as with the panic around US-produced gangsta rap in the 1990s, politicians like Howells and Blunkett confused cause and effect, wrongly assuming that the music spawned violence rather than merely reflecting the violent context of its creation. For starters, they and others failed to consider that So Solid Crew weren't scoring Number 1 singles with an audience made up of disaffected Black inner-city youth: their debut album sold 100,000 copies in its first week, and a minimum of 300,000 in total; every single Black British male between the ages of sixteen and twenty-four would have had to go out and buy multiple copies for the stereotype to even remotely fit. 'There's more rap music listened to and bought by white kids in Swindon than there is by black kids in Hackney,' said the then-*NME* editor Conor McNicholas, 'but nobody's talking about the gun culture on the streets of white suburban Britain.' If So Solid Crew's music was the root cause of UK garage violence, then their legions of white middle-class fans should have been attacking each other in equal numbers. If the music's siren call to self-destruction was being heard only by a narrow group of young Black listeners, then clearly the real issue lay elsewhere.

With Iraq and other scandals eroding New Labour's poll lead ahead of the 2005 General Election, Blair and his acolytes desperately needed a set of attention-grabbing domestic policies with which to seize back the moral high ground, and the political agenda. They found it in the 'respect agenda' – a lukewarm rebranding of the 'Back To Basics' slogan offered by John Major in 1993, promising to give power back to the upstanding moral majority, now apparently overrun by a sordid mob of litterbugs, lager louts and happy slappers being driven into an antisocial frenzy by contemporary folk devils like So Solid Crew. In practice, this 'radical new approach to restore the liberty of the law-abiding citizen' meant expanding state power to cover low-level anti-social behaviour, building on the example of the Criminal Justice Act, and exhuming the same old tropes to justify the same collective loss of personal liberty: crusty ravers and left-wing protestors replaced in the popular imagination by a feral underclass in tracksuits and hoodies. In 2008, the government's own REACH programme found that 70 per cent of media coverage focusing on young Black men and boys related to crime, with the only regular exceptions being stories about Premier League footballers. Throughout the 2000s and 2010s UK dance music produced by Black artists or for Black audiences became swept up in this narrative: the shadowy inverse of the 'creative industries', in which underground culture became not a proud emblem of British identity, but a threat to its existence.

As a result, UK garage and grime in particular continued to be treated as the simplistic cause of wider, infinitely more complex social ills throughout the 2000s. 'Is violence holding grime back?' reads one weirdly off-colour *Guardian* article from 2006, which calls on the genre to 'shake off its brutal past' – a legacy which covers everything from Crazy Titch's murder conviction and his infamous tussle with Dizzee Rascal in the rooftop studio of pirate station Deja Vu FM, to fights breaking out when Lethal Bizzle's 'Pow! (Forward)' is played in clubs. Even unequivocal statistics can get twisted beyond recognition when moral panics take root: Ned Beauman, the author of the *Guardian* piece in question, claims in it that grime's violence is the product of urban areas where 'gun crime is out of control'. He links to a *Times* study by way of evidence, which claims salaciously that 10 per cent of teenage London schoolboys admitted to carrying a gun in the preceding twelve months. A couple of paragraphs into that article, it's revealed that only 1 per cent of those responses related to an actual handgun, as opposed to far less lethal alternatives like BB guns or airguns: it seems that things are only 'out of control' if you don't read past the headlines. Elsewhere, Beauman argues that grime has 'failed to live up to expectations, and violence is partly to blame. Most promoters now find it impossible to put on grime in clubs, because grime nights have been unofficially outlawed by the police' – a framing which, by putting the violence first, suggests a causal relationship between disorder at grime events and the police's subsequent actions.

Both anecdotal and statistical evidence suggests that this wasn't in fact the case. No one would dispute that garage and grime nights have been marred by violence, but then so has basically every other form of popular music throughout human history. No one reacted to the onstage stabbing of Liverpool indie band The Kairos in 2020 or the mass brawl which broke out when the Eagles played Hyde Park in 2022 by claiming that jangly guitars and MOR ballads are responsible for skinny-jeaned hipsters and soft rock dads going feral. In 2018, researchers in the US studied data related to police call-outs over eight years in the Midwestern city of Madison, Wisconsin: they found that events featuring hip hop and other Black music genres were no more likely to attract violence than those involving country music or karaoke. Another academic study from 2012, this time in the UK, argues that there's 'no basis to infer anything but a coincidental link' between grime events and crime. Famously, the per capita arrest rate at Notting Hill Carnival, the only major event for which the police cite knife crime statistics as a matter of course, remains slightly lower than that of Royal Ascot.*

---

* Figures released via FOI requests reveal that there were seventeen arrests at Ascot in 2018 out of a crowd of 69,000 – one for every 4,000 attendees.

Despite this Black music events have continued to be seen as uniquely dangerous: any objective justification for those fears clouded by lazy assumptions, broad-brush demonization and heavy-handed policing. Beauman's comments in *The Guardian* fall victim to the same confusion of cause and effect as David Blunkett and Kim Howells: grime raves in 2006 weren't being shut down because they were uniquely violent; they were disproportionately understood as violent because they kept getting shut down. Two years later, the web of distortions and inequalities underpinning all of this would be laid bare, when the Metropolitan Police publicly acknowledged the existence of a document called Form 696.

Form 696 had been introduced by the Met in 2005, providing a secretive but highly formal basis for the unofficial ban on grime detected in *The Guardian* a year later. It was, on the surface, a perfectly reasonable piece of bureaucratic risk management: where particular events had been assessed as carrying the possibility of crime or disorder, venue licensees were asked to fill in several sheets of A4 and return them to the local police station, with sections demanding additional information about performers and audiences, including artists' real names and addresses and the type of crowd expected to attend, in order to better 'enable police to give you appropriate support and advice to ensure a safe event.' But the devil, as always, was in the details: it's made clear on the original version of the form that police are only interested in events featuring a DJ and MC, not live bands; one question asking about the 'music style to be played/performed' offers bashment, R'n'B and garage as examples; a request for the full names and dates of birth of all performers specifically mentions 'sound systems'. In that initial version of the form, the ethnicity of artists and attendees is also requested: 'I've got a nagging suspicion that "Irish" was not the answer they were looking for,' remarked Feargal Sharkey, CEO of industry body UK Music in 2009.

Notting Hill saw 374 arrests from a crowd of 1.75 million the same year, or one arrest for every 4,700 attendees.

The intentions behind Form 696 were clear: to submit any and all events playing Black music or catering to a Black audience to an additional layer of police and licensing scrutiny, thereby creating additional grounds on which they might be shut down. While this was justified with specific reference to violence at late-night venues – the Met's internal review of 696 in 2009 highlighted four shootings in late 2004 and early 2005 as prompting the form's introduction – a far blunter agenda is impossible to deny. In 2007, the *South London Press* covered a meeting between club owners and police at Ministry of Sound – it quotes Sergeant Mick Meaney telling the assembled group that: 'If you're playing a violin string quartet you're not going to get a steaming gang turn up. These people go to certain places and they are attracted by the music. If the music being played is attracting a certain type of crowd, don't play the music.' The form itself was voluntary, but if a specific venue was deemed a hotspot for crime, then a local council could order a review of its licence, adding a condition that all events had to be accompanied by a completed 696 form. Failure to submit a 696 form when requested could lead to six months in prison, or a £20,000 fine.

The practical effects on grime in particular were vast, detailed extensively in Dan Hancox's history of the scene *Inner City Pressure*: DJ Logan Sama was told by police that 'you can't have a grime room' at a festival he'd been booked to play; when MC Slinger was killed on the same night as journalist and promoter Chantelle Fiddy's grime event Straight Outta Bethnal in 2006, it was labelled a 'grime murder' and the event was shut down permanently, despite the murder and the rave having nothing to do with each other. Footage from a performance by Jammer and the Slew Dem Crew from Straight Outta Bethnal earlier in 2006 reveals what was actually going on in Shoreditch's 333 Club: Tempa T spits his bars, eyes closed, vibrating with the intensity of the moment; the tune is suddenly wheeled up, and the club dissolves in a cacophony of shouts and whoops; bodies surge across the stage, jostling the camera. To someone who hasn't been to a grime rave, it could all look terrifyingly chaotic and intense, suffused with barely-controlled anger or disorder. Of course, it's nothing of the sort. Skepta steps forward, grinning the same popstar grin which would become a fixture in the mainstream within a few years. 'Fuckin 'ell, I can't do nothing better than that right now,' he says, before dissolving in laughter along with the other MCs. 'Too much energy for me, way too much,' he admits gleefully, before passing the mic to Jammer. A year later, Jammer's own record release party was infiltrated by plain-clothes officers, who followed MCs out of the venue when the party finished, before stopping and searching them.

Even when raves weren't locked off they still suffered: those assessed as medium or high risk by the police were required to hire additional security or change their opening hours, making it harder to turn a profit. 'It doesn't take loads of shows being shut down for it to be a huge thing', said Logan Sama in 2014, 'because when one or two large events get closed down, everyone else sees it.' Before long, he explains, artists and others in the music industry affected by these additional pressures would be forced to conclude that 'making this type of music wasn't able to support them financially.' These monetary and policing pressures were deployed exclusively against the underground and grassroots spaces where grime lived and breathed – venues owned by large entertainment conglomerates like the O2 or Brixton Academy remained exempt from Form 696 in its entirety. This didn't stop larger business interests from contributing to the enforced silencing of Black music as well, though: when Giggs's UK-wide tour was shut down with minimal notice in 2010, he instead set up a series of CD signings in suburban shopping centres, before the Met Police leant on the premises involved and got those signings cancelled too. Between 2005 and 2010 the live grime scene in London (and eventually the rest of the UK) withered away to almost nothing.

In 2014, the aggressive use of Form 696 to shut down grime events reached a nadir, when it transpired that not even the prestigious Barbican Centre was immune from its chilling effects. The week before promoters Just Jam were due to throw a party of 'gritty beats and new media arts' at the central London arts venue, featuring a broad line-up ranging from Syrian dabke singer Omar Souleyman to electronic experimentalist SOPHIE and a handful of grime MCs, they were informed by the Barbican that the City of London Police had pulled the plug. 'We're struggling to understand why this has happened and will try to start a dialogue with the police so we can discuss whatever issues they have', said Just Jam's founders, but no explanation for cancelling the party was ever provided. Police referred cryptically – or perhaps just uncaringly – to not having 'adequate measures in place to address potential issues that might arise.' This opaque bureaucracy, the police's decisions presented with zero discussion or explanation, remained utterly infuriating to those affected – the same opaque use of policing powers as embodied in the Criminal Justice Act. If grime artists weren't even free to perform in a publicly funded space better known for ballet and opera, and no one would tell them why, then where else could they go?

What makes all of this even more baffling is that grime was not, by the Met Police's own account, a particularly prominent source of event-related violence. In a 2009 review of the effectiveness of Form 696 the word 'grime' appears precisely once, towards the bottom of a list of genres associated with violence at venues: several rungs below Cheesy Classics, and just ahead of Irish, Latin and Oldies. Contradicting the statement made by his colleague Mick Meaney at Ministry of Sound in 2007, one senior police officer told the BBC that 'it wasn't about the music, it wasn't about the venue, it wasn't about the promotion – it was because gangs were associated with those particular events', which merely raised more questions. If the music itself was irrelevant, then surely the police could assess the risks involved without asking for the home addresses of the artists in question. If genre didn't matter, then it's unclear why grime raves attracted so much more attention than other objectively riskier genres. Just as with the shutdown at the Barbican, no answers to these appear to have been forthcoming in the twelve years Form 696 remained in use. Indeed, as Dan Hancox notes, the whole procedure around Form 696 remained cloaked in secrecy, utterly impenetrable even to the artists and promoters whose livelihoods were being eviscerated by it, with 'walls of silence erected by anyone who actually knows what's going on.' The police would quietly lean on venues to cancel events rather than officially forcing them to do so, enabling senior officers to claim that it wasn't their decision, and refer all queries to the venues. Venue owners, meanwhile, were uunderstandably wary about rocking the boat with the police or local councils, fully aware of the attendant risk of having their licence revoked; so they stayed silent, leaving no accountability or oversight for the ongoing suppression of vital Black British musical culture. While the Met's use of Form 696 was eventually discontinued in 2017, through a combination of pressure from incoming Mayor Sadiq Khan and a drop in event-related violence, other forces in Leicestershire, West Yorkshire and Hertfordshire continued to use it, even retaining its most contentious questions about audience ethnicity.

Elsewhere in the UK, policing and licensing policies reflected the same suspicions and scapegoating as Form 696 without the need for paperwork. From its foundation in 1992 to its closure in 2005, Sheffield club Niche played a vital role in the development of bassline – a faster, harder style of UK garage with aggressively synthetic bottom end, borrowed from happy hardcore and dubstep – to the extent that the genre also ended up known as 'niche' in certain quarters. This tendency to 'thump up the bass a bit' gave the music a darker, headier feel, which in owner Steve Baxendale's words 'led to a change from a predominantly white crowd to a predominantly Black crowd.' Niche rapidly became the national home of this new sound: 'London never had bassline as we had it here,' Baxendale explained. 'It was our DJs at the Niche that created that sound. It went from an underground club with a smaller community to a massive UK-wide thing with people coming from all over the country': a level of popularity which attracted the attentions of ravers, police officers, Sheffield Council and more shadowy elements alike.

Some of the tales associated with Niche's early years suggest that its rough-hewn reputation was not entirely undeserved. Baxendale is described by long-time Niche manager and resident DJ Chris Bailey as 'like a dangerous version of Del Boy' – on arriving for his first shift as a sound engineer, Bailey was told by Steve Baxendale's brother Mick to 'Go stand over there and make sure nobody nicks the decks.' Bailey also recalls resident Mark Carr dropping the 'Loop Da Loop Uptown' remix of Todd Terry's 'Something Goin' On (In Your Soul)' early on in Niche's history, pitching it up to 135bpm, and inadvertently discovering a new sweet spot for the emerging bassline sound. The remix in question takes a classic chugging New York house tune – described in one review as 'emotional but not overdone' – and retools it to absolutely monstrous effect, with ferociously dirty low frequencies rubbing up against the original's sugary pop hooks. The Sheffield crowd responded by pelting Carr with anything they could get their hands on. 'They went mad, throwing cans and bottles at Mark,' said Bailey. 'I think they loved it so much that it sort of hit a nerve. It were almost like punk: if you like it, you spit on it.' Elsewhere though, the atmosphere at Niche tipped over from endearingly boisterous to genuinely frightening, with gangsters and dealers from across the North following ravers to Sheffield in search of a big night. 'They saw us as an easy target . . . [but] we had good lads, hard, working class lads that could handle a fight. The only things the dealers understood was violence.' Mick Baxendale was stabbed to death outside the club in 1998: police speculated that Manchester gangsters thrown out earlier in the night were responsible, but no one was ever charged.

Despite all of this, the police's response to Niche's majority Black crowd comes across at times as excessive, or detached from the realities of actually keeping clubbers safe. Tipped off about a stabbing at another Sheffield club, Niche's bouncers detained a young man matching the police's description; the police report, according to Bailey, ended up reading 'Response at Niche nightclub, to a youth involved in a stabbing incident.' Reforms to venue licensing in 2003 meant that Niche were able to sell alcohol for the first time, but they also provided greater latitude for unannounced council inspections. 'It was racism,' Steve Baxendale would later claim. 'They decided that because we were attracting a Black audience they would come down hard on us.' The raid which eventually forced Niche to close would certainly meet this description: Operation Repatriation (a somewhat dubious choice of code name given the venue's largely Black audience) involved 400 police officers descending on an 800-capacity venue, with armed response teams, mounted officers, road closures and helicopters. Despite briefing to the media that Niche was a 'crack house' ('I went mental when I saw that,' says Bailey. 'You don't apply to the council for a licence to run a crack house') the raid recovered a paltry volume of drugs. Their licence was suspended and then revoked nonetheless: 'The writing was on the wall, the police wanted it shut and they got their way,' says Baxendale.

If the justifications for closing Niche feel arguable, then the subsequent treatment of bassline elsewhere in Sheffield comes across as borderline vindictive. When Baxendale set up another venue in the city in 2007, he was banned from naming it Niche, or from allowing his DJs to play any bassline tunes. The same year, Leeds-based producer T2 hit Number 2 in the charts with bassline anthem 'Heartbroken' and a Ministry of Sound bassline compilation sold 150,000 copies, but in the city which had birthed the sound it remained essentially blacklisted: local DJ Jamie Duggan said in 2018 that, 'I couldn't get a gig. Promoters weren't allowed to book me, guys I'd worked with for years. Police wouldn't let them. That went on for a good couple of years.' While the grime scene eventually defied the restrictions of Form 696 to force its way back into the spotlight in the 2010s, with a period in the wilderness followed by the re-emergence of Skepta, Dizzee and others as mainstream pop stars, there would be no such happy ending for Niche. By the end of 2009 Steve Baxendale had given up entirely – the police's insistence that his new club operated a financially unsustainable member-only policy the final straw – while the bassline scene as a whole fizzled out, crushed by the same pressures which seem to accompany Black British music wherever it flourishes.

Just as the demonization and suspicion which lay behind Form 696 didn't exist in a London-specific geographic bubble, it was also one part of wider political approaches towards Black and inner-city communities, its introduction coinciding both temporally and ideologically with the 'respect agenda' and its enhanced state powers, specifically the expansion of anti-social behaviour orders. ASBOs had been introduced in 1998 and were retained until the mid-2010s with their highest year of usage coming in 2005, the same year Form 696 was drawn up. They criminalized behaviour which was not otherwise illegal – 'conduct which caused or was likely to cause harm, harassment, alarm, or distress, to one or more persons' – with the threat of criminal prosecution attached to any breaches. Where the Criminal Justice Act had cramped the legal boundaries of allegedly disruptive or undesirable behaviour undertaken as part of a large collective group, from an illegal rave to hunt sabotage, ASBOs extended that same ethical principle to far more personal and quotidian events: one man was banned from speaking sarcastically to his neighbours after they complained to police; another woman was accused of breaching her ASBO against excessive noise by groaning too loudly during sex. When used against musicians, as they were with depressing regularity, ASBOs became the dystopian inverse of New Labour's approach to the 'creative industries': where Ministry of Sound and Fatboy Slim were celebrated as the proud stewards of a forward-thinking globalized British industry, young kids making beats in the ends were threatened with prison sentences for engaging in their musical craft. Most famously, grime DJ and Rinse FM stalwart DJ Slimzee was given an ASBO preventing him from going on any rooftop higher than four storeys in Tower Hamlets for a period of five years, destroying his career and sending him into a spiral of depression.

But he was far from the only person affected. The UK's first gang protection order was served in 2011 by Southwark Council on a local rapper, his identity kept secret but referred to pseudonymously as 'Matt'. Southwark chose to deal with the complex, knotty problems of young Black life by banning Matt from walking down certain south London streets, being in the company of two or more people at any time, or making any music which they deemed 'might encourage violence'. Any breaches of these draconian conditions could have seen him imprisoned for up to two years. ASBOs were a direct extension of all the worst aspects of Form 696 and the Criminal Justice Act: the same confusion of symptom with cause, and cure with placebo, expanded from the nightclub to cover all aspects of civic life. Why engage with the material realities of poverty, disempowerment and anti-social behaviour, when you can just get a court order which makes it illegal for a specific person to say the word 'grass' or publish music recounting their experiences and expressing their emotions? The state's treatment of grime through Form 696 and ASBOs represent the political establishment doing exactly what they'd always done, from the Jazz Age to the reggae shebeen to the warehouse rave: blaming the disorder of a disenfranchised underclass not on the forces oppressing them, but the art they make in response.

Just as these forces stigmatized and constrained Black music from the outside, they also shaped UK dance music's internal relationships and characteristics. As the police's clampdown on grime began to bite, several DJs pivoted to playing UK funky and funky house – slower, poppier genres, largely free of grime's associations with violence or disorder – only to find the same suspicion of Black artists and dancers at play within those spaces too. In 2013 the funky house scene underwent something of a schism around the question of 'shuffling' – expansive, performative dancing to house music, associated largely with Black dancers and audiences. For those involved in shuffling, it was merely another form of dance floor expression, harking back to acid house and rare groove's close connections to breakdancing crews like the Mastermind Roadshow. For others, it was intrusive and threatening: 'The stereotypical shuffler brings aggression and a badman mentality to parties', wrote a spokesperson for a Facebook group called the Anti Foot Shuffling Campaign, while London house club Creche announced a ban on shuffling, before backtracking and claiming, somewhat unconvincingly, that the policy was a joke.

Similarly, by constantly reinforcing that jungle, garage and grime were inherently aggressive, confrontational and threatening, it made those male-coded characteristics an ever more integral part of perceptions within each scene, shaping expectations of them. The author and academic Julia Toppin had been going out raving to jungle since the early 1990s, but dropped out when the darker, more mechanical sounds of techstep drum'n'bass began taking over in the latter years of the decade, an experience which informed her subsequent research into the forgotten role of women within the scene.

> In my research, from looking at the literature and interviewing people, it was clear that the women had been turned off by the new sound: it was empty, it wasn't warm, it was cold and tweaky. Women were being tacitly told, "This isn't *really* for you." Somewhere in that sphere of Black masculinity and linking it to criminality is where the Black women get completely erased, because there isn't a space to market them or create narratives around them. There were always women in jungle raves, but that's the problem: all these *unsung* women. There were dancers, there were people managing their boyfriends who were DJs, there were women on the door. There were DJs like Dark Phoenix, who's been around for a long time. There were MCs like Chickaboo, who's been around since the days of Soul II Soul, right? They just didn't get covered.

As the Blair government was replaced first by coalition and then Conservative rule, this disconnect between Black British dance music's social function and its popular depictions became even more entrenched, reflecting the forces which would crack society apart over the ensuing decade. For the student protestors of 2010, occupying Conservative party headquarters in Millbank in fury at the government increasing tuition fees and scrapping the Education Maintenance Allowance, Lethal Bizzle's 'Pow! (Forward)' provided both an exhilarating soundtrack and a deeper expression of pent-up collective rage. 'How you gonna buss if there's no room?' asks

Fumin, one of several guest MCs on the tune, encapsulating the sense of claustrophobia and hopelessness felt by a generation watching their life chances being snatched away: dance music as a form of collective therapy. As austerity dismantled the support structures of British society piece by piece over the course of the 2010s – most noticeably the collapse of the UK's network of youth clubs serving marginalised urban communities – the social function of dance music became even more important, providing collective resources, opportunities, expression and meaning for communities too often left on the fringes of society (doubly so in the era of austerity, with public services for young people cut to the bone). Music enabled young Black men in particular to 'resist, in multiple ways, the marginal roles that have been mapped out for them', as the author Joy White puts it, '[placing] themselves at the centre of their own life stories' and '[showing] value for lives that are deemed to be disposable.'

When he was a child, grime producer and MC Jammer's parents had run the East London Rastafarian Information and Community Service, a grassroots organization providing support and advice for local Black communities. In the early 2000s, the basement of their family home in Leytonstone became a critical incubatory space for the grime scene, somewhere between a recording studio, video set and youth club, taking on the same communal and supportive function of the ELRIC a generation earlier. A documentary shot for a 2022 exhibition on grime at the Museum of London describes a queue of young rappers sat on the stairs leading down into the basement waiting for their turn on the mic; Jammer's own *Lord of the Mics* DVD series would record countless clashes against its graffiti-scrawled walls, not least one with an impossibly young-looking Wiley and Kano, years before either would break big, which has since passed into scene folklore. In 2019 the borough of Waltham Forest acknowledged the historical significance of the basement, unveiling a blue plaque on the house's frontage.

And yet at the same time, just over the council border in Enfield, dance music's ability to draw together groups of young Black men and help them develop a network of mutual trust and support was treated very differently. Like the aspiring rappers waiting in Jammer's basement, twenty-year-old Orlando Chinhemba looked up to the senior figures around him – Tyrone, Dee and Fish, owners of a local record shop, Boombox – and saw in his relationship with them a chance to better his own prospects. 'I had a conversation with Tyrone, how I want to help my community, how I want to stop crime,' Chinhemba would later say. 'I want to do big things.' That included making use of the affordable recording studio in Boombox's back room to cut his own tunes. Until, in 2009, he got a call from Tyrone, his friend and mentor: one of Tyrone's mates was visiting from Ireland, and was looking to score some heroin. Could Orlando help them out? He 'looked up to the undercover officers as "olders"' said his lawyer Abbas Nawrozzadeh, describing them as 'music producers who were able to make [Chinhemba] famous.' What could he do but say yes, call his mate who dealt a bit of gear, and sort out £75 worth of heroin for the guy his friend had vouched for? Except neither Tyrone nor the record shop's other owners were record producers: they were undercover police officers, part of the £500,000 Operation Peyzac; the record shop was an elaborate front, wired for sound and video, designed specifically to draw in criminals from Enfield and the surrounding areas and catch them in the act. In 2011, over 650 officers raided thirty-five addresses across the borough based on evidence obtained at Boombox, making multiple arrests; local and national media lauded the arrest of '30 gangsters for drugs and gun offences'.

Where Jammer's basement had functioned as an informal, emergent safe space in which the next generation of Black British stars might find community, aspiration and a chance to hone their craft, Boombox was its bleak inverse: Black music, and the creative coming-together of Black men, treated as an inherently suspicious incubator for criminality. Setting up a *studio* of all places, a space dedicated to self-expression, as a tool with which to incriminate its users feels like a profound transgression. While some of the arrests made as the result of Operation Peyzac were undoubtedly positive for the local community – several firearms and ammunition caches were amongst the items seized during the raids – others, like that of Chinhemba, seem to have been little more than entrapment. 'Essentially, these offences were manufactured by the police,' said Nawrozzadeh, arguing that the police 'entrapped [Chinhemba] to commit these offences under inducement and threats' which included 'a promise of advancement in relation to his music career.' In the end, scared by the possibility of an even harsher sentence if he tried to fight the charges, he pleaded guilty and spent fifteen months in prison.

Chinhemba was sentenced in September 2011, a little over a month after the fatal shooting of Mark Duggan by officers from Operation Trident sparked riots across the UK. Once again, grime and wider Black British culture were seized upon as a cheap, simplistic scapegoat by commentators from across the media spectrum. Disorder was the fault of 'the pernicious culture of hatred around rap music', spat the *Daily Mirror*, while historian David Starkey ranted on *Newsnight* that 'the whites have become black' and blamed 'a particular sort of violent destructive, nihilistic gangster culture' for corrupting good old-fashioned native English decency. More measured responses looked at grime and road rap, its slower and more menacing cousin, as both reflecting and contributing to a creeping sense of inner-city nihilism: veteran dance music journalist Joe Muggs lamented the road rap scene's 'apolitical grimness', embodied in road rapper Blade Brown's claim that 'I don't rap about Black Power / I'd rather hear a Mac shower,' as representing 'the mentality behind what we have seen these past few days.'

But the roots of the 2011 riots, and indeed of the parallel anger expressed in Black British music, ran far deeper. In the days after the riots subsided, grime MC Scorcher directly compared Mark Duggan's killing with that of his grandmother Cynthia Jarrett, whose death in 1985 from a heart attack followed a police raid on her home, igniting long-running tensions over aggressive policing of Black communities in Tottenham, and sparking the infamous Broadwater Farm riots. In a documentary filmed two years after

Broadwater erupted, a reggae DJ called Millard Scott – brother of stalwart Black community organizer Stafford Scott – talks about the upcoming christening of his son, and his plans for the boy's upbringing: 'He's got to do the best for himself. I'm not gonna tell him to do that because he's going to build a better world, I'm gonna tell him to do that because if he doesn't the system gonna get him.' Millard's son would grow up to become grime artist Wretch 32, whose knotty and cerebral lyrics drew directly from the violence and unrest he grew up with, and indeed continued to experience. In 2020 the then sixty-two-year-old Millard Scott was shot twice with a Taser after five officers stormed into his house, looking for another of his sons. 'I have to tell my children the same things about the police I was told by my dad and my uncle when I was growing up,' said Wretch 32 after the incident. 'It's the same story now that it was then.'

The experiences of Millard Scott suggest that whatever progress Britain might think it's made since Broadwater Farm, the Stephen Lawrence Inquiry or the Black Lives Matter protests, the demonization and mistreatment of Black communities remains as relevant today as it did forty years ago. But it also underlines the changing ways in which Black British music has fed into those debates, a constantly shifting cycle of marginalization, acceptance, and renewal. The reggae and dub soundsystems of Millard Scott's day were once depicted as a febrile source of disorder and licentiousness, before artists from UB40 to Aswad served to destigmatize the music in the popular white imagination. Acid house clubs and warehouse raves – which if not exclusively Black were clearly rooted in Black experience – took over from the blues dance as the cultural spaces most likely to corrupt Britain's youth, before being absorbed into the mainstream after the Criminal Justice Act. As rave and house became increasingly understood as white culture, attention pivoted to the Black-coded sounds of jungle and drum'n'bass. When, in turn, those genres attained their own level of respectability – from Roni Size winning the 1998 Mercury Prize to countless TV shows and video games adopting drum'n'bass as shorthand for late-1990s modernity – the baton was passed on to garage and then grime, bringing the issue right back to the doorsteps of the Scott family.

In turn, of course, even grime would become absorbed into the British pop firmament: Dizzee Rascal and Wiley turning to commercial dance music to score massive hits with 'Bonkers' and 'Wearing My Rolex', before 'That's Not Me' by Skepta and Meridian Dan's 'German Whip' brought grime back into the spotlight on its own terms in 2014. By 2016, Skepta's *Konnichiwa* would add a second grime Mercury Prize to Dizzee's win over a decade earlier, and in 2019 Stormzy headlined Glastonbury, the first Black British solo artist to do so. There were, it's worth noting, no reports of mass violence amongst the 100,000-strong crowd.

As grime's popular associations with disorder and societal collapse have receded, and its biggest names have been rehabilitated as genuine pop stars, so UK drill has taken its place as the sonic embodiment of establishment anxieties around perceived Black unruliness. On one level, some of the concerns around drill are understandable: where grime, garage, jungle and even road rap's rhetorical violence came with a certain level of self-aware theatricality (no one *really* thought Tempa T was threatening to steal the UK's CD collections, or that JME was actually going to assault you with his HSBC card reader), as each claimed on record, UK drill lyrics have regularly lacked any such artifice, offering an unfiltered account of the street violence experienced by young people across the UK's inner cities. A 2018 study by the right-wing think tank Policy Exchange claimed that over a third of the forty-eight gang-related homicides which occurred in London that year involved drill in some capacity: either the suspected perpetrator or victim were rappers, or drill lyrics were used as evidence during the trial. Two of the genre's biggest talents have ended up in prison at various points, with Headie One sentenced to six months for possession of a knife, and Digga D jailed after breaching a criminal behaviour order (or CBO, the successor to the ASBO), and his involvement in a multi-person knife fight outside Westbourne Park tube station. Clearly, whether or not drill is the root cause of violence amongst

Black British youth, it clearly exists in closer proximity to it than other genres. And yet the response to that problem from policymakers and police has regularly been absurdly heavy-handed. The CBO for which Digga D was convicted, for example, banned his group 1011 from mentioning real-life incidents of violence or London postcodes in their songs – the first order restricting the creative output of such a high-profile musician. 'It tries to control who he can talk about, what he can talk about, the areas that he can talk about,' complained his lawyer, to no avail. Digga was also arrested in 2020 on suspicion of inciting violence and breaching the terms of his CBO, after attending a Black Lives Matter march: an absurdly draconian and vindictive decision which mirrored the harassment experienced by grime MCs and soundsystem DJs at the hands of the police.

The treatment of Brixton drillers Skengdo x AM brings these worrying trends into even sharper focus. In 2018, two months after 1011 were hit with a pre-emptive CBO restricting their future lyrical subjects, the Met also attempted to censor AM's already-released single 'Attempted 1.0'. All future performances of the track by Skengdo, AM and their group 410 were banned on the basis that they could incite violence against rival gangs Moscow17 and Harlem Spartans. On one level, it's easy to see why, given the song's lyrics deal almost exclusively in simultaneously lurid and utterly impassive descriptions of the violence meted out to 410's enemies: the chorus talks about AM's 'opps' – or enemies – getting splashed, dipped and 'cheffed like onions', reduced to little more than slabs of meat on a butcher's table. And yet, just as with the panic around grime raves or So Solid Crew, the police's argument that drill is 'a particular genre of music being used specifically to goad, to incite, to provoke, to inflame, that can only lead to acts of very serious violence being committed' withers under closer analysis. Performing 'Attempted 1.0' as an encore at a sold-out show in London venue Koko in 2019, Skengdo, AM and two other 410 members were convicted of breaching their CBO and hit with nine-month jail sentences, suspended for two years. 'They have imposed something that will give us a criminal record just for making music,' they told *The Guardian*. 'We didn't contest the injunction, and the breach, because we couldn't afford it – we were forced into a corner, where we had to choose between our careers and freedom.' Footage of the Koko show shot by grime and drill YouTube channel Link Up TV shows a crowd that's rowdy but hugely diverse in terms of race and gender, albeit majority white and male, from moshpits of lads to glammed-up girls filling out the front rows; both groups know every tune word for word, holding up their phones to capture the action. Halfway through, a minute's silence is held for 'the brothers who couldn't make it'. Selling out Koko, one of the capital's most prestigious venues, is a serious career achievement. 'We've been working with the boys for two and a half years,' one member of their team tells Link Up TV, 'and their progression is absolutely amazing. I'm happy because they've shown that people from that kind of background, that kind of area can come a long way, despite the criticism, the police, even the media.' Before the show starts, Skengdo chats to the duo's DJ about the setlist, runs through his between-song banter, agrees which tunes to wheel up and when, giggling nervously at the thought of a capacity crowd going wild. And yet the government's case was that this entire event amounted to little more than a call to arms, inviting an 1,800-strong of teenage and early twentysomething rap fans to descend on South London and stab people.

    This treatment of individual drill rappers follows the same pattern as the earlier mishandling by police and politicians of grime, garage and road rap, but it also reflects wider systemic pressures involving young Black and working-class lives. Stop-and-search powers introduced back in 1994 as part of the Criminal Justice Act are now a regular part of everyday life for Black and Asian teenagers, already disproportionately targeted by the police's increased detention powers. Drill shows now get locked off pre-emptively, just as grime raves once were, often on extremely spurious grounds: Ian McQuaid, the label A&R who first signed Skengdo x AM, explained in a 2020 roundtable on racism in the music industry that one venue was banned from ever playing drill again, following a stabbing which took place a mile away from the venue, but occurred on the same night as a show by drill group 67. This clampdown has extended online, with the removal of hundreds of drill videos on the insistence of the police, despite video monetization and online sharing playing a crucial role in developing the careers of underground artists Krown Media (the video producers from Nottingham targeted by police following the Glockamoley video shoot were also, it's worth noting, hit by takedown requests both before and after their homes were raided). Just as with Form 696, the opaque nature of YouTube's content moderation leaves artists with no idea why a particular track has been removed, and no recourse to challenge the decision or agree edits which might make it acceptable. As result, things have slipped into the absurd, with drill fans re-uploading removed videos onto increasingly dubious hosting platforms less answerable to the Met's takedown requests (a few have eventually ended up on Pornhub), rendering the whole exercise pointless. And yet, as is so often the case, this merely made the police double down, with annual takedown requests almost trebling between 2020 and 2021.

Just as policing and political strategies have shaped UK drill, so the music has also fed back into the machinery of the UK's criminal justice system. A report by the charity JUSTICE in 2021 found that 'misunderstanding of drill music is leading to unfair convictions' largely through the use of police 'experts' – usually rank-and-file officers with no specific understanding of or background in underground music – arguing that specific drill lyrics function as direct threats or confessions, unfiltered by anything as ambiguous as artistic licence or crowd-pleasing sensationalism. The police officers and Crown Prosecution staff involved have, say JUSTICE, 'been blinded by literalism, and are unable to see drill as anything other than a dangerous means gangs use to incite violence.' One particularly depressing example of this was the conviction of ten young people in Manchester in 2022, charged under joint enterprise laws of plotting revenge attacks after their friend was murdered. Of those, four were convicted on the basis of what appeared to be little more than messages in a group WhatsApp chat, including the quoting of drill lyrics. Interviewed by *Rolling Stone* about the case, Goldsmiths lecturer Alex de Lacey pondered 'this idea that artists can't embody personas, they aren't afforded the realms to take on characters or role-play. Everything they do is taken as verbatim, or indicative of some sort of criminality.' This dubiously literal use of drill lyrics to secure convictions has become such a recurrent issue that a team of researchers at the University of Manchester, advised by criminal defence barrister Keir Monteith, have now begun providing alternative expert evidence from those with a grounding in drill as music, who appreciate the slippery ambiguities of creative self-expression. 'What is real and not real? What counts as truthful expression, and what counts as posturing? Can art be both?' writes one of those experts, the author and youth worker Ciaran Thapar, of his efforts to unpick the simplistic assumptions of the police. In one case, he pores over lyrics, YouTube videos and case files: in response to the defence team's submission of Thapar's evidence, the prosecution withdraws its claims around drill. 'The young man would be tried as a person', writes Thapar, 'not an assumed gang member.'

As drill moves into the mainstream – expect a driller to win the Mercury Prize in 2026, based on grime's timetable for the popular rehabilitation of previously demonized Black British music genres – there have been some tentative signs that things are changing, even if only in terms of the sound and focus of the music rather than its treatment by the authorities. In January 2022 Liverpool driller Hazey scored a massive viral hit with his first single 'Packs and Potions' – its skippy Afrobeats-inspired rhythm overlaid with playful football-heavy metaphors ('when they need more', Hazey says of his drug supply, 'I'm right back like I'm Trent.'). Given that drill's primary audience – young urban men – also tend on aggregate to be massive football fans, it's unsurprising that the tune was a colossal hit, both in terms of absolute numbers and heralding a shift away from the suffocating bass and dead-eyed directness of other drill styles. Despite still ostensibly being a tune about burner phones, cling-film-wrapped drug bundles and shots ringing out in the back streets, Hazey's fleet-footed bars and the tune's insanely catchy beat make the whole thing sound like cartoonish fun, miles away from the bloodied and entirely literal depiction of young inner-city Britain with which drill is more normally associated.

Elsewhere though, artists continue to fall foul of the police's refusal or inability to treat Black British music as an artform rather than a clunkingly literal call to arms, the same tired prejudices that have tainted Black music all the way from the days of blues dance and *The Breakdown*. A decade after Dizzee Rascal performed 'Bonkers' at the London Olympics opening ceremony to a rapturous reception, Coventry-based artist Pa Salieu was removed from the 2022 Commonwealth Games closing ceremony in nearby Birmingham after 'failing a background check'. Topping BBC Radio 1Xtra's charts in 2020, releasing one of the most critically acclaimed albums of that year, being signed to the major label Warner Music, and playing a show in a stadium full of athletics fans, for whom violent disorder was presumably not high on the agenda: none of this mattered. He'd admitted his involvement in a fight outside a bar during which his friend had been killed, and was awaiting sentencing,[*] so when the Commonwealth Games organisers put his name into the computer, it flashed red. Nothing more to be done. 'I have fully cooperated with the process. Attended court on time every single day. I've consistently been trying to use my career to show people where I'm from that there is another life for us,' Salieu said, clearly exasperated, 'but what can you do if the police, the justice system and the Home Office don't care about you?' Twenty years after Tony Blair's final election victory, and forty years after Broadwater Farm, the same old power structures remain solidly in place: those in authority calling endlessly for 'respect' from the people they govern, while offering none of their own in return.

---

[*] In December 2022, Salieu was sentenced to 33 months in prison for his involvement in the brawl.

GORDON MCNAMEE IN KISS FM'S FINAL PIRATE STUDIO, 1988

8. Pirates' Anthem

Kiss, Rinse and the evolution of dance music radio

The MC's voice swirls up from the past, through a fog of radio static, tape hiss and YouTube compression: '382a Lea Bridge Road, Leyton E10. Kiss FM going live, the Christmas '86 warehouse party. Get on down here if you can, we're gonna be rocking, shocking and everything else until 7 a.m.' Even at nearly forty years' remove and with only low-fidelity audio to go on, recorded off the radio onto cassette before being uploaded, you still get an unmistakeable sense of the party itself: a gloomy, low-ceilinged post-industrial space, in a corner of East London decades away from anything even approaching gentrification, knots of soul boys, rockers and hip-hop heads shuffling in the gloom. Things sound ramshackle, maybe even a little unsure of themselves, but bracingly full of the minutiae of life. At one point the MC refers to the DJ 'trying to get the people moving and grooving', as if tacitly admitting that they still need a bit of encouragement. 'If Lyndon C's around would he please reach,' says the MC of one of Kiss's then-resident DJs, 'there's a little question of some money you owe me.'

As UK dance music evolved from niche hipster interest to mass-market youth culture in the late 1980s, so the nature of the crowds it brought together, and the means by which it did so, shifted. As acid house and rave took over the pirate radio airwaves, they ceased to be cultures defined by people dancing in the same physical space; dance floors could now be geographically diffuse, made up of a community tuning into each other from afar rather than sharing a specific physical location. For many of its listeners, pirate radio provided all of the same cultural connections (and several of the social ones) as the rave itself, forming a crowd as potent and unified as any that gathered in person, without them ever necessarily stepping foot in the same room as each other.

The tune playing underneath proceedings tonight is the slow-motion boogie of 'Adventures in Success', by fictitious self-help entrepreneur Will Powers, its semi-robotic vocal a stream of nebulous banalities encouraging the listener to take charge of their life, and believe that anything is within their grasp, all delivered in a sardonic monotone. New York photographer, artist and celebrity scenester Lynn Goldsmith had conceived of Powers in 1983 as a satire on ubiquitous 1980s self-help babble, enlisting a bunch of her famous mates including Sting, Nile Rodgers and Steve Winwood to record glossy dance-pop backings for her tongue-in-cheek mantras. Picked up by club DJs and transported to the world of the warehouse rave and pirate radio broadcast, however, something shifts: Goldsmith's satirical intent evaporates, and the message of 'Adventures in Success' ends up feeling strangely earnest; it's as if

Powers is speaking directly to Kiss FM and the rest of the UK's pirate stations, cheering on their insurgent scrabble up the face of Britain's media edifice, urging warehouse dancers, distant listeners and everything in between – a shadowy thread of wires and radio waves, illicit transmitters and tower block relays – on to bigger and better things.

Kiss owed its entire existence to precisely this spirit of self-confidence and a willingness to dream big. 'I was DJing on this station called JFM,' recalls Kiss founder Gordon McNamee of the latter's creation in October 1985. 'JFM closed up because they was going for a community radio licence, and the guy that ran it said to me "Gordon, if you get a chance to go elsewhere, go there, because you don't speak well enough to come back on the station if we get a licence." I thought, fuckin' hell, I've just done *three years* for you.' McNamee combines a laid-back ease with an unmistakeable sense of steeliness: with several other pirates also shutting down in 1985 to apply for legal licences, he flipped the potential setback of being dumped by JFM into an opportunity, just as Will Powers' self-help platitudes might have advised. 'Everybody went off air: Solar, Horizon, JFM, LWR for a bit, there was no pirates on. And I thought, well, I'm not gonna get a fuckin' job when they come back on anyway. So George Power said to me, let's start a pirate up.'

Music had been in McNamee's blood from the very beginning, when his parents started throwing blues dances in their flat above a shop in Anerley, near Croydon. 'My stepdad had propped up all the floors with bricks, and him and a local soundsystem guy was running a shebeen there every Friday and Saturday night. There was just this one light in the middle of room, with a red and green lens on it, going slowly round and round. It was the first time I'd ever seen a soundsystem.' By the time he was in his teens, nothing else mattered. 'I was into reggae because my cousin Mandy used to go out with one of the top skinheads up at Chelsea, when skinheads weren't National Front or anything . . . she introduced me to discos at Butlin's and stuff like that, and once I'd been to disco, that was it . . . I wanted to be a disc jockey.' Having done his time in the reggae and soul clubs of South London and at more established soul pirates like JFM, starting Kiss felt like a natural progression, even if the decision itself was sudden. Seizing the airwaves at the precise moment they'd been cleared of any potential competition, Kiss cleaned up; by January of 1987 they were voted the second most popular radio station in London – encompassing both pirate and legal outlets – beating Radio 1 to a spot, just behind Capital FM.

The seeds for Kiss's creation had been sown several years earlier, not just with McNamee's life story but wider political and economic forces. Just as the ability of bedroom producers to churn out acid tracks had been catalysed by the mass affordability of drum machines, samplers and synths, the arrival of small-scale FM transmitters on the semi-professional and hobbyist market at the beginning of the 1980s sparked an explosion in pirate radio activity. For an earlier generation, broadcasting from boats anchored in international waters (and thus outside the UK's archaic and restrictive radio licensing regime) had been laborious and occasionally life-threatening: in 1980 the MV *Mi Amigo*, home to one of the original rock music pirates Radio Caroline, sank during a Force 10 storm; pop-pickin' DJs Stevie Gordon and Tom Anderson signed off in unsettlingly upbeat Smashie and Nicey fashion, before hopping from the studio directly into a lifeboat. But as cheaper and more portable transmitters hit the market, those financial and logistical barriers dissolved; within a few years a new generation of land-based stations playing reggae, dub, soul, jazz, funk, hip hop and electro had taken over. At the time, radio listeners had an almost comically limited set of legal options: four BBC stations and one local independent broadcaster, or two (LBC and Capital FM) in London. Music and editorial policy across all of these was overwhelmingly staid and almost exclusively white, leaving vast sections of the UK population ignored and silenced: a void filled by illegal broadcasters of every conceivable perspective and background.

Launched in 1980, Dread Broadcasting Corporation was the UK's first Black-owned radio station, spinning everything from dub to soca – including a hip-hop show with a pre-fame Neneh

Cherry – from a studio in Neasden. People's Community Radio Link started up in Birmingham as a direct response to the 1985 disorder in Harmondsworth, and a lack of cultural communication serving Black and Asian communities: 'We approached the BBC and the independent stations,' said its founder Cecil Morris, 'but they weren't interested. We realized that if they weren't going to do it, we'd have to do it ourselves.' Sheffield Peace Radio had been started by local CND members to cover the organization's national conference in December 1983, lasting only four months before being taken off air. London Greek Radio – founded like Kiss by McNamee's colleague George Power – broadcast everything from bouziki-laden Greek-language covers of Boney M's 'Rasputin', to Orthodox church services on Sunday. Across the UK the spirit of public service was met not by a BBC unable to see past the *celebridee* stylings of Tony Blackburn, Dave Lee Travis and their ilk, or legal independent stations focused myopically on the bottom line, but a vast black-market ecosystem of unlicensed operators doing whatever it took to make their voices heard.

Within the inner circles of Margaret Thatcher's government, this outbreak of grassroots community spirit was the trigger for vicious factional squabbling. On one side of the argument were free-market Tories who saw the wholesale flouting of the UK's radio regulations as merely a symptom of unmet demand, and one that justified the liberalization of Britain's airwaves. Set against them were the Tories' nativist and authoritarian wing, locked in a fight for survival once again with 'the enemy within' and highly resistant to the idea of Black, Asian and working-class communities being allowed to speak for themselves. In July 1985, the Home Secretary, Leon Brittan, outlined the details of a 'community radio experiment' originally promised by the government in 1984: twenty stations serving small local neighbourhoods or more geographically diffuse 'communities of interest' would be granted two-year licences, on the condition that they stopped broadcasting illegally while the decision-making process was undertaken. A dizzying 266 stations applied, 180 of them in London (including JME, leading to their firing of Gordon McNamee), each hoping to get on-air legally by early 1986.

A Cabinet reshuffle in the summer of 1985 saw Brittan replaced by Douglas Hurd, whose quibbles over licensing terms served to repeatedly delay the process. It was only in June 1986 that Hurd signed off on the list of successful applicants put forward by an independent advisory panel: a national patchwork of primarily talk-based stations (as opposed to the less contentious music-led stations Brittan had originally envisaged) serving marginalized and racialized communities, from the Afro-Caribbean Community Radio Project in London and Sunset Radio in Manchester, to Radio Gogarth in Wales, the Shetland Island Company Limited, and Cornish Waves Radio.

The response from Hurd's Cabinet colleagues to the proposed list of new broadcasters — who under the draft licence terms would be given substantial leeway to broadcast whatever they wanted — was apoplectic. 'Some of the chosen stations were judged to be politically "sensitive" (seemingly the ones with local authority grants)', wrote the pirate radio magazine *TX*, 'and it seems that the Conservatives were worried that stations with a left-wing bias, however slight, might damage their chances at the next election.' Welsh Minister Nicholas Edwards sent a scorching letter to Hurd: 'To say that [the selected applicants] pose political problems is to seriously understate the hazards ahead.' A meeting of 'H' committee — a sub-group of Cabinet ministers with interests in domestic policy — was arranged, at which Hurd was ambushed by Edwards, Malcolm Rifkind, Norman Tebbit and half a dozen others. 'To the Home Secretary's displeasure,' a subsequent briefing to Thatcher reads, 'his proposal to continue with the community radio experiment for a further 2 years was rejected.' Community radio was, in the majority's view, 'not a financially viable business, and consequently it needed subsidy and support from organisations that had a vested interest in putting out propaganda, such as local authorities, trade unions, and pressure groups . . . Community radio was not a matter of normal free speech.'

The entire plan for community radio was scrapped, with Hurd

forced to make a grovelling written statement to the Commons, which disingenuously blamed a lack of regulatory oversight and unsatisfactory licensing conditions, before announcing that 'the Government have therefore decided to give up the idea of an immediate experiment in community radio.' Pirate stations like JFM who'd come off the air in good faith over a year earlier, submitting extensive business plans and detailed cultural justifications for their applications, ended up with nothing to show for it but vague promises that the question would be revisited in an upcoming Green Paper.

There's a direct connection between the botched community radio experiment's undermining of Black, Asian and working-class sound, and the policing of marginalized communities in the period immediately before Kiss hit the airwaves. The 'H' committee memo which detailed Hurd's humiliation was written by an advisor to Thatcher, and later Conservative MP, Hartley Booth: he comments with snickering glee that 'we would switch off this radio'. A year earlier, Booth had co-authored a policy briefing for Thatcher on responses to the violent uprisings in Brixton, Harmondsworth and in particular Broadwater Farm; his co-author was another future MP, Oliver Letwin. Deriding the suggestion that public funding should be used to address chronic inner-city joblessness and poverty, Booth and Letwin claimed that 'entrepreneurs will set up in the disco and drug trade . . . and people will graduate from temporary training or employment programmes into unemployment or crime.' Attempts to provide for deprived inner cities were a waste, they said, on the basis of incipient Black malevolence. 'Riots, criminality and social disintegration are caused solely by individual characters and attitudes. So long as bad moral attitudes remain, all efforts to improve the inner cities will founder.' The arguments deployed here are a direct antecedent of the logic used to gut community radio a year later: if we give marginalized groups an inch of space or support, they'll take advantage and either undermine or attack the government. In their 1985 memo, Booth and Letwin call for 'a review of the other "voluntary bodies" to which the Home Office and other Departments give money, to see how far the funds are in fact supporting destructive far-left groups', citing with horror the potential scandal of a 'black "activist"' being indirectly funded by the government. Released under the thirty-year rule in 2015, the memo's unapologetic racism forced Letwin to half-heartedly apologize and claim that his views had changed. Booth, forced to resign in disgrace from the government in 1994 over an extramarital relationship with a junior Commons researcher, has since kept his opinions on 'bad moral attitudes' entirely private.

For better or worse, Kiss owed everything that came after to this repressive knee-jerk from the inner members of Thatcher's Cabinet. When Hurd announced that all 266 community radio applicants had been taken for a ride, several returned to pirate activity only to discover that Kiss had stolen a march on them in the year they'd been off-air, building an audience estimated to have peaked at half a million listeners. 'We came on, we had an amazing run for the first eight weeks,' says McNamee of his exploits with Kiss co-founder Tosca Jackson. 'We didn't get taken off air once, because me and Tosca put the transmitter on top of this rickety old roof in Carshalton, and no one could get it down. The fire brigade had to get one of those turnstile ladders and block off the whole road. So we had a non-stop run of eight weeks, which just boosted us into the stratosphere.' In addition to annexing the frequency dial in the absence of their competition, Kiss also moved to pick off the cream of the capital's DJing talent. 'Tosca had a *great* ear, he could pick a good DJ, y'know? So he went up to Trevor Nelson and said "You've got to be on the radio", went up to Norman Jay . . . between the pair of us we had a really good team of DJs.'

As the first flickers of pre-Ecstasy house began to filter through to the UK club scene (Kiss's 1986 Christmas broadcast features Adonis's 'No Way Back' mixed in with the prevailing sounds of soul, funk and electro) their edge over the pirate competition only sharpened. Danny Rampling, soon to launch Shoom, was already a resident on the station by the time he took his infamous trip to Ibiza in the summer of 1987, while Kiss's first rickety antenna had been hoisted in Carshalton opposite fellow station regular and 'Ibiza Four' member Nicky Holloway's flat. When acid house and rave began to take over UK popular culture in 1988, pirate radio – with Kiss as arguably its most visible proponent – formed a critical part of the nascent scene's infrastructure: between adverts for upcoming raves, its premiering of new tunes and its ability to build a DJ's career, it swiftly became UK dance music's primary marketing platform and national intelligence network. Pirate radio helped sell tickets for raves, those raves paid the DJs, then the DJs paid subs to the pirate stations, along with rave promoters buying airtime for adverts: a perfect, self-contained ecosystem powered by spiralling demand for dance music and the inability of the UK's licensed premises and legal broadcasters to keep up.

'Maggie Thatcher came along and said partying's banned,' says McNamee, his eyes lighting up, 'and we were like, fucking *thank you*. It couldn't have gone any better. We were all: fight for the right to dance, the sound of young London. It was a perfect storm.' Much like the raves they promoted, pirate radio stations ended up fighting a running battle with the state, in the form of the Department of Trade and Industry – the body responsible for radio licensing and enforcement – whose officers were empowered to raid premises alongside the police and seize transmission equipment. Shortly after the fire brigade had dismantled Kiss's transmitter eight weeks into their initial broadcasting run, the DTI hit their studio too, keeping them off the air until March 1986. This was not a new occurrence: according to former Kiss employee Grant Goddard,*

---

* Grant Goddard's book *Kiss FM: From Radical Radio to Big Business* is essential reading on two counts. On the one hand, it's a forensically detailed and hugely valuable first-hand account of UK pirate radio in the 1980s and early 1990s, from DTI raids to the intricacies of FM licensing. On the other, it's also an unintentionally hilarious piece of score-settling with anyone Goddard thinks has ever wronged him, chiefly Gordon McNamee but also numerous other Kiss employees, Radio 1 personality Tony Blackburn (whom Goddard witheringly accuses of only a superficial affection for soul music) and a malevolent ex-girlfriend who steals Goddard's toaster and throws out his last

the DTI made 231 raids on 80 different stations and brought 130 successful prosecutions against pirate radio operators in 1986, the first full year of Kiss's operation. Similarly, JFM's decision to apply for a community radio licence had been forced on them after a DTI raid at the beginning of 1985 seized not only their transmitter, but their entire broadcast studio; officers were allegedly tipped off by a rival pirate station keen to clear out the competition.

Much like rave convoys dodging Ken Tappenden's roadblocks, pirate operators played an evolving game of cat-and-mouse with police and prosecutors across the rooftops of the city. Where promoters used new technology to outwit the police, in the form of automated phone lines, so did pirate broadcasters, with the advent of microlinks allowing a signal to be bounced between multiple locations before reaching a main transmitter, making the process of tracking its source vastly more difficult. Occasionally, these tactics ended up in the courtroom: in 1984 the barrister Peter Corrigan had successfully argued, while defending members of JFM's crew, that the Wireless Telegraphy Act 1949 prevented police from confiscating a pirate transmitter unless there was a specific court order for its seizure; the same vein of legal cheek and creativity which would later enable Tony Colston-Hayter to categorize Sunrise's megaraves as 'private parties' and the free rave travellers to swerve the powers of the 1986 Public Order Act. Just as with the Bright Bill and the Criminal Justice Act, though, pirate radio loopholes were swiftly closed with the 1984 Broadcasting Act, and the DTI and police got back on with seizing transmitters, arresting operators and shutting stations down.

Their strategies played a key role in Kiss's growth. As increasing

---

pint of milk on the day Kiss gets its FM licence. It is fantastically, incomprehensibly petty: twenty years after the event, Goddard describes going out for lunch with McNamee by recalling that his rival's meal looked 'gruesome', before complaining that the wannabe DJs who sent demo tapes into Kiss were all rubbish and didn't know anything about dance music. Imagine the pirate station in BBC sitcom *People Just Do Nothing* hiring fellow comedy caricature Alan Partridge to host their drivetime show, and you're halfway there.

numbers of pirates rushed back into action in 1986 off the back of Douglas Hurd's community radio U-turn – and with outraged media coverage merely fuelling audience interest, much as with acid house parties and warehouse raves themselves – the overworked and under-pressure DTI decided to focus on stations broadcasting seven days a week, on the basis that the longer they were on air the more disruption they could cause. Kiss deliberately stayed under the radar by transmitting only at weekends: while twenty-four-hour soul stations like TKO ended up getting shut down once a week, Kiss got through a full month in July of 1986 with only one DTI raid to show for it. 'It makes you wonder if it is really worth it trying to broadcast twenty-four hours a day,' mused *TX Magazine*, 'if all stations end up with are raids which keep them off the air longer than they're on.' Kiss's limited hours also allowed for tighter quality control over their DJ roster, while anticipation for the big Friday switch-on gave them a sense of drama and occasion, swelling their audience even more. 'I learned a very big economic lesson,' says McNamee. 'Being on seven days a week, and guaranteeing your DJs five days, meant that you could easily lose five transmitters that week. Come on every Friday morning, come off Sunday night [and] leave people wanting more, I could earn the same amount from advertising and I'd lose a maximum of three transmitters.' But even this reduced level of DTI attention was gradually wearing McNamee down. 'You don't know what the government know about you, you don't know if they're gonna come and knock on your front door,' he says, 'which is why I never wanted to be a pirate for very long, because I actually didn't like that side of it.' Having bought out George Power and Tosca Jackson's shares in the promotion company which surreptitiously funded Kiss, by 1986 he was the station's sole owner. But within weeks, he was struggling to raise the money required to keep it all going, and anxious about being the only person on the hook if things went wrong. 'I thought fuck, this is stupid, owning it all . . . Billy Big Bollocks on me own with no fuckin' transmitters.'

In what would be a recurring solution to Kiss's problems, McNamee raised the money by sourcing outside investment in exchange for equity. He sold nine bundles of shares at £200 a pop, each worth 5 per cent of the holding company, to a group of core Kiss DJs including Trevor Nelson, Norman Jay and Tim Westwood: enough to buy ten transmitters and keep the station up long enough for it to become self-sustaining. 'But it also meant I had nine people who'd put 200 pound of their own cash into something that they really cared about . . . all of a sudden they owned something that they were proud of.' Strength in numbers was important not only to manage Kiss's finances, and ride out the attentions of the DTI, but also to see off their competitors. 'We never attacked [the DTI]. There's stories of us being up on the roof with baseball bats . . . and later on, when other stations were nicking our transmitters, yeah, we would have a team of people up there, but it was purely to protect you from the other pirates. If it's the DTI we used to hold our hands up and say, "Go on then."' By 1988, between the DTI raids and restricted broadcast hours, as well as Kiss's fervent and still-growing audience, it was clear to McNamee that going legal was the only way forward. 'It was getting darker out there. When we first came on, there was an unspoken code. No one would nick another station's transmitter, no one would broadcast over the same frequency, everyone pretty much kept to their own.

'By 1988, it was the fuckin' Wild West, I mean it really was.' In November of that year, Douglas Hurd announced that the previously aborted community radio experiment would be revived. On one level, this was clearly down to the tireless efforts of the pirates themselves, regularly making a mockery of the DTI and demonstrating that a massive audience existed for more diverse radio provision. But it was also indicative of the shifting mood of the country as it approached the 1990s: when Leon Brittan had first announced his plans in July 1985, it was only two months after the miners' strike had ended, with violent unrest in Black neighbourhoods across the country continuing through the summer. Thatcher's fear of 'the enemy within' was at the forefront of Conservative minds, and the idea of giving loony leftist revolutionaries or suspiciously foreign-sounding pressure groups a national broadcast system was unthinkable. By 1988, with Thatcher's surprisingly strong election result the previous year making her the first prime minister in 160 years to win three successive elections, and the newly formed SDP splitting the left, the perceived threat of opening up the airwaves had clearly receded. Applications for twenty community radio licences would reopen the following year, with a catch: anyone caught operating a pirate station after 1 January 1989 would be banned from applying for any form of FM licence for the next five years. Despite concerns from Kiss's DJs that this was 1985 all over again, and that once they went off-air there was no guarantee they'd ever come back, McNamee and the core team of resident DJs who'd bought shares in Kiss agreed to give up the pirate life, and go for a licence. The station's final illegal broadcast went out on New Year's Eve 1988 from Dingwalls in Camden, before falling silent on the stroke of midnight: 'Goodbye, London, thanks for tuning in,' McNamee told listeners before pulling the plug.

Unlike the venue owners, event promoters or record label heads who were also looking to ride the wave of UK dance music from illegal menace to legitimate business concern, McNamee's task was made exponentially more difficult by the convoluted regulatory regime around radio broadcasting, and the eye-watering costs associated with keeping a legal station on the air. The newly legitimate Kiss would have to hire consultants and produce endless reams of market research and compliance documents before they could even submit an application, much less switch the transmitters back on. Once they got on air, they'd be building a new studio, broadcasting twenty-four hours a day, seven days a week, paying salaries and taxes and licensing fees, swallowing all of those costs until their audience grew big enough to attract sufficient advertising income. It was clear that Kiss needed serious upfront investment to get it to that hoped-for break-even point: McNamee turned to the publishing mogul David Evans, who'd been a fan of Kiss in its pirate days and offered to help fund its resurrection. Initially, according to Grant Goddard, McNamee had planned 'to run the legalized Kiss FM along the lines of a pirate station that just happened to have a radio licence' – minimal overheads, no-frills studios, everything kept raw and rugged. Evans disagreed, and set in course a chain of events which would fundamentally alter the next decade of UK dance music. McNamee went to Evans with a draft business plan sketched out on 'the back of an envelope' and outlined what he thought he needed for a barebones Kiss, legally constituted but essentially managed as if it were still a pirate. 'He looked at me', McNamee recalls, 'and said "I think you're going to need a bit more than this."'

From that moment, everything changed: rather than the UK's biggest pirate radio station trying to go legal in unaltered and unapologetic form, it morphed rapidly from a ragtag bunch of scruffy outsiders to a highly formalized media company, one that became simultaneously more streamlined and more bloated. Staffing budgets were increased tenfold, the former head of the CBI was brought in as company chairman, and Evans's publishing contacts drew in magazine and radio conglomerate EMAP as major investors, who then appointed a young American called Tim Schoonmaker to manage their interests. According to McNamee, Schoonmaker 'could fuckin' start a row off in a room on his own . . . he'd walk into one of the floors of Kiss when it was all running, everyone would be happy, he'd walk out ten minutes later and five people would tell me they were going to resign.' Clearly there was no room any more for a familial, ramshackle spirit of a community doing things solely for the love of it. McNamee ended up in the middle of this cultural schism: he hunches up his shoulders to mimic the Kiss DJs' rudeboy swagger – 'We're still gonna play what we want, yeah?' – which he contrasts with the money men telling him that everything had to be playlisted. The prize justified putting up with these tensions, though. 'I fuckin' wanted it more than anything,' McNamee says of that first licence bid. He ended up so myopically focused that, driving up the A1 to meet an investor, his car blew up: he'd forgotten to put any oil in it for weeks.

And yet, all of this was for nothing: in July 1989, the decision came down from the Independent Broadcasting Authority. Kiss had been overlooked in favour of a rival bid from the safer and more genteel London Jazz Radio. The academic Richard Barbrook describes the IBA's intentions as '[incorporating] the pirates' style of radio programming while excluding their potential for cultural subversion.' McNamee dismisses any suggestion that Kiss's roots in Black music or pirate broadcasting counted against it, instead arguing that London Jazz Radio won simply because they had deeper pockets and stronger connections in the corridors of power: 'There's two reasons that we didn't get it. First, Jazz had even more MPs involved in their bid than the classical stations, and they had more money . . . after the decision I got a call from the IBA saying, "Promise me you won't go back on air [as a pirate], because your application was so good. You just needed more money. Your pockets weren't deep enough, and we can't have a failure."'

McNamee acquiesced, and Kiss stayed silent. Whether you see that decision as selling out the station's original principles, or merely a savvy adjustment to a changing marketplace, it's clear that attempts to go legal had fundamentally altered the station's culture and purpose, long before those same changes rippled out across the rest of UK dance music. This was only 1989, remember: the Bright Bill was yet to be passed, the Criminal Justice Act was five years away, and elsewhere in the rave scene people were up in arms about Tony Colston-Hayter apparently betraying the anti-establishment ideology of the rave scene by throwing parties which, while still wildly illegal, had apparently sold out to the Thatcherite mainstream by selling loads of tickets. Yet here was Kiss, securing multi-million-pound corporate backing and refusing to countenance breaking the law, the tenor and context of rave culture shifting in real time under their feet, a canary in the coal mine for the professionalization and corporatization which would mould the UK dance music scene over the course of the 1990s. Their diplomacy paid off faster than anyone hoped: in August 1989, two months after Kiss's first licence bid had failed, Douglas Hurd announced that two more independent radio licences would be made available for London by the end of the year. This time, there would be no half measures: Kiss beefed up their financial backing dramatically for this second bid, with Virgin Broadcasting, the radio arm of Richard Branson's business empire, taking a 15 per cent share in the company alongside previous investors EMAP. Between the increasing solidity of their accounts, the slickness of their presentation, and the widespread acceptance that one of the two new licences surely had to go to a youth-focused former pirate, of which Kiss was by far the biggest and most credible, there was enough to push their application over the line: in December 1989, just under a year after they'd come off air, Kiss were finally granted a legal licence.

The Channel 4 documentary *Radical Radio* charts the period leading up to its relaunch the following September: in one telling moment the camera pans through a huge, nondescript open-plan office, as we hear the voice of a senior manager from Independent Radio Sales, the consultants brought in to help Kiss secure more lucrative advertising deals. 'A lot of people remember Kiss as a pirate: there was a whole cachet involved, that kind of underground feel, that excitement generated by being a pirate station,' he says. 'A lot of the major advertisers are aiming their campaigns at London's youth, and Kiss provides them with an ideal way of getting that street cred to a much wider audience.' Here in microcosm is the same Faustian pact countless other forms of UK dance music would grapple with over the following thirty years: as underground scenes move from basement club to mass-market ubiquity, which compromises are worth making, and which serve to undermine the culture they're built on? There's a warning sign in the admission that Kiss's appeal to advertisers isn't its present or future, but its past reputation as a pirate: a facet of its existence which was rapidly being scrubbed clean. Channel 4's documentary ends right as Kiss goes back on air, Gordon McNamee leading cheers across the studio and amongst a packed crowd listening live back in Dingwalls, before selecting 'Pirates' Anthem' by Home T, Cocoa Tea and Shabba Ranks as Kiss's very first legally-broadcast tune. Even the ghosts of the past, in the form of a pirate station cutting across Kiss's new legal frequency ten minutes before they go on air, can't stop them. It's a triumphant and cathartic moment, but feels like something of a premature ending. McNamee and others had poured years of their lives into turning Kiss legal: what was it all for? What happens now?

The answer, sadly, was two decades of inexorable decline. In September 1991, Kiss's accounts revealed that they'd lost three quarters of a million pounds in their first year on-air: without serious changes they'd go bust within months. EMAP bought out Virgin's stake in December, making them the station's biggest minority shareholder; by August 1992 they'd expanded their stake sufficiently to take control of the company. Over the next few years, they steered Kiss towards profitability by reshaping it in the image of their other radio holdings, including easy listening staple Magic FM: specialist music shows were pared back, replaced by centralized playlist-led programming, while redundancies shrunk the back office to try to stem costs. 'I always knew that going legal would change things,' says McNamee, spelling out a gloomily mechanical view of how things worked under EMAP. 'Radio's not about music. Music's just something you chuck out there to attract an audience, and it doesn't care what type of audience that is, as long as they've got money in their pocket. If you've got a million of them and they're ABC1s, you can go out to Marks and Spencers . . . if you've got a hundred of them and they're C2DEs you're gonna find it hard to get advertising.' Despite this, McNamee is quick to defend his attempts to protect as much of Kiss's countercultural identity as he could. 'People thought I sold out because we played a playlist, [other] people thought I was too left-field for the investors because I didn't play Sam Cooke or whatever, so I learned very early on that you're never, ever going to please everybody. But if you can please the mass audience of that subculture, as fuckin' cheaply and cost-effectively as possible, then you can still make a living.'

But the tide was only pulling Kiss in one direction; McNamee handed in his notice in 1997, having been promoted to head of Kiss Enterprises – a far more corporate role overseeing various Kiss-related brands, which took him away from the radio studio where his passions really lay. The final straw, he says, was being told by an

EMAP executive that based on audience research amongst listeners under twenty-five, DJs on Kiss could no longer play any music that was older than six months, apart from three specific songs by Bob Marley. With McNamee gone, EMAP immediately rebranded the station, later changing its tagline from the implicitly politicized 'Radical Radio' to the pure pleasure-transaction of 'Live Sexy'. They reinvented its musical offering too, sacking a slew of pirate-era DJs (Radio 1, belatedly picking up on dance music, poached several others) while the daytime playlist was, in the words of EMAP's marketing director, 'smoothed out'. The most contentious of these decisions was the firing of Steve Jackson, the station's breakfast show host and the winner of 1998's Sony award for breakfast presenter of the year, who was accosted on arrival later that year, summarily fired and marched from the Kiss office by security guards. He was offered £10,000 in lieu of notice and another £10,000 if he agreed not to contest his sacking: he refused both, and in 1999 took Kiss to an employment tribunal on the grounds of breach of contract and racial discrimination, winning on the first point but not the second. Having been founded on playing Black music, operating with a roster of racially mixed DJs throughout its pirate years and helping to build the careers of leading Black musical figures like Trevor Nelson, Paul 'Trouble' Anderson and Norman Jay, by 1999 every single presenter on the station was white.

'I think it's fuckin' disgusting, it still sticks in the throat,' says McNamee of Jackson's sacking. 'Sure, he was a handful off air, but he was fuckin' brilliant. And so to do all that shit . . . I was glad I was out of it.' In 2007, EMAP sold its entire radio division, including Kiss, to the German multinational Bauer Media, owners of more than fifty other radio stations including Absolute 80s and Greatest Hits Radio. Tune in today and you'll hear the same rictus-grin patter and stats-driven playlists as every other one of their stations, just tuned to a highly targeted audience demographic. As I write this, a presenter is indulging in some stale on-air banter about TikTok, their cadence an eerily similar update on that of Smashie and Nicey all those years ago, before they segue smoothly into introducing the new Swedish House Mafia single. Kiss's journey stands as a parable for the rest of the UK dance music: in a little over a decade it went from the grimiest depths of illegality and menace, treated by figures at the very top of government as a threat which risked tearing the country apart, to a pliant mass-market product, indistinguishable from the dross it was supposed to replace. The story sits somewhere between inspiration and cautionary tale: here's where UK dance music can go with the right backing, and here's what can happen when it gets there. By the time it faded into irrelevance in the mid to late 1990s, a younger generation were ready to take over, determined not to make the same mistakes twice.

By this point, pirate stations had become so technologically sophisticated that the DTI's traditional methods of enforcement were rendered largely useless. While triangulating a pirate's broadcast transmitter was easy, the now-ubiquitous microwave link between studio and transmitter used a line-of-sight directional beam, which meant that the DTI could only hone in on the studio once they'd found the transmitter and scaled the tower block in question. 'The smarter pirate stations attached a cut-out switch to the door [onto the roof], which cuts the power supply and breaks the link,' writes Simon Reynolds. 'This ensures that the DTI can't trace the beam from the top of the tower block back to the studio, and that all the pirate station loses in the raid is a transmitter worth a few hundred pounds. The pirate can then switch its microlink beam to a back-up transmitter at the top of another building.' In response, the DTI switched from tracking pirate radio signals to tracking its operators: in late 1989 they arrested and charged the main players behind Centreforce FM on a variety of charges, from broadcasting offences to drug dealing and protection rackets, following six months of coordinated surveillance.

Station owner Andy Swallow was already well known to police as a key figure in West Ham's infamous hooligan crew the Inter-City Firm during the 1980s, but like Joey Wieczorek he'd been drawn away from terrace violence by the revelatory power of the rave, running a series of parties across Bethnal Green, Bow and into Essex before starting up Centreforce in May 1989, shortly after Kiss went off-air to apply for a legal licence. The case against them, Swallow recounted to Matthew Collin, 'was that we at Centreforce Radio were sitting there guiding people to these parties and at the parties we had all our drug dealers selling all the drugs, and we made the money from the drugs, money from the parties, and extortion from the parties that weren't ours.' With little more than circumstantial evidence, both the initial prosecution and subsequent retrial collapsed, but the repeated raids and continued pressure eventually saw Centreforce fold. During what turned out to be the station's final raid, the DTI evoked the sneering spirit of Hartley Booth MP by grabbing the mic, announcing: 'To all listeners of Centreforce FM, this is the last song you'll hear', and putting on the theme tune to cop show *Hill Street Blues*. Things were clearly getting nastier: a new Broadcasting Act passed in 1990 saw pirate operators face unlimited fines, up to six months in prison and the seizure of everything connected to the station, down to the DJs' record collections. And yet even this wasn't enough to deter people: in the first half of the 1990s pirate radio underwent another resurgence, as hardcore and jungle provided new creative impetus for working-class inner-city kids without the means or inclination to apply for a community radio licence.

Gordon 'Geeneus' Warren is sitting in the vast, tastefully appointed Hoxton offices of Rinse FM, the pirate station he started as a teenager in 1995, and which both extends upon and reframes the narrative arc of UK dance music radio established by Kiss.

> I went round to my older cousins' house one day – I remember it clear. And they had this mad, crazy music, it didn't make any sense. I mean, I knew what Bros was, and chart music, stuff on the radio or in the car. But in my cousin's bedroom they've got this mad, noisy, futuristic alien shit going on. Ever since I was young, I want information. I'm obsessed with information: what is it? Explain it to me. And I'm like eleven or twelve at this stage, and they told me: it's pirate radio.

'I guess I'm kind of the last one to achieve all of this from pirate radio, like Rinse is seen as the final chapter in that journey,' he says. Like his namesake Gordon McNamee, Warren's involvement in pirate radio was borne not only of inspiration, that flash of otherworldly sound in a cousin's bedroom or parents' blues dance, but of limited options growing up on an East London estate. 'I grew up with my mum, family issues, living in squats, spending a lot of time with my Nan, that kind of upbringing,' he explains. 'I didn't really agree with the school system from quite early on. I didn't agree that I should be taught religious education based on one religion, when I knew there's other religions out there . . . I never really believed that just because someone's an adult or a teacher, that they're more intelligent.' His attentions instead turned to music, leveraging precisely that same sense of youthful curiosity and anti-establishment impetuousness.

The pinnacle of young Geeneus's aspirations was getting a slot on Kool FM, the East London pirate which played a vital role in reshaping the post-rave sounds of breakbeat hardcore into the darker, faster, more ragga-influenced strains of early jungle: 'During 1993 – 95 Kool FM's unceasing dedication to Jungle undeniably helped move the music from the underground to the mainstream . . . During the summer of '94, every car stereo and open window in London's estates seemed to pump out Kool,' writes Brian Belle-Fortune. 'That was the station I listened to. There was a few other little ones, Weekend Rush from Hackney was good, but Kool was the one. They had all the best DJs,' says fellow Rinse figurehead DJ Slimzee, in a 2014 interview. 'We really wanted to get on Kool FM,' agrees Warren. 'We got on Pressure FM, we got kicked *off* Pressure FM because we was too young and a bit rowdy, and we couldn't get on another station.' Unable to break into the existing jungle pirate scene, a fifteen-year-old Geeneus teamed up with others he'd met through Pressure FM – DJ Fury, MC Beenie and Gary Mega[*] – and

---

[*] DJ Slimzee, who would go on to be a vital figure in Rinse's future, is listed as a founder of the station in most retellings. Warren underlines that, contrary

struck out on his own. 'The thought process from the beginning was – we're never gonna be like everyone else. Cos it was kind of cliquey and it doesn't bring everyone in. There's a lot of people out there that deserve a chance.' Earlier pirates had often been run by people with one foot already in the music industry, as with Gordon McNamee's DJ career, or Radio Caroline founder Ronan O'Rahilly's ownership of Soho club the Scene – they did it for love, sure, but there was also an implicit sense of pirate radio fitting into wider career ambitions. Rinse, on the other hand, was founded in the most marginal fringes of cultural and social life imaginable: a bunch of working-class kids rigging up a cheap transmitter on their estate, simply because they had no other options.

Where pirate radio's outsider status and anti-establishment kudos were celebrated by some, and repackaged in Kiss's case to help sell advertising, the question of illegality leaves Warren largely ambivalent.

> I grew up in an environment that crime was completely normal. I mean, I've got a criminal record that goes back for miles . . . from robbery to drugs to firearms to whatever, it's like, just part of life. So when you talk about pirate radio, and was the illegal side of it attractive, I'm like it was probably the tamest thing we done, in all honesty. D'you know what I mean? It was the nicest part, it was the community, the thing that brought our areas together. So, yeah, it was a crime, but it was the nicest crime we could have done.

That doesn't mean it was all plain sailing, though. Warren recounts being held hostage in a windowless squat in Hackney, a sharpened sword at his neck, watching all of Rinse's gear being robbed.

---

to those assumptions, Slimzee only took on a more central role within the station later on in its history, beginning as just a DJ.

We'd run out of spaces [to broadcast from] and someone told us about this place, but we got set up by another station. Some crackhead geezer kicked the door off, come runnin' in, put a sword in my neck, made us carry all the equipment out. Slimzee was hanging out of a window three floors up while I was held with a blade as long as my body poking in my neck, with a crackhead sweating all over me, thinking that he's gonna kill me at any second. And there was no one we could call because we're a pirate station . . . I was out of my comfort zone, I wasn't from Hackney, all of my support system and the friends I'd look to for protection, I wasn't near any of them. I remember going home and being completely freaked out.

Unlike Kiss, whose legal and illegal existences were strictly delineated in both chronological and conceptual terms, the two sides of Rinse's existence are far harder to separate from each other. Even as the station began to carve out its own sound – moving away from jungle, which had seen its best DJs pinched by Kool FM whenever they got sufficiently popular, and finding its own niche at the darker, more bass-heavy end of UK garage – they retained the same rough edges. 'It took quite some time for it to just become about radio,' Warren admits. 'I remember being maybe twenty or twenty-one, so that was about five years in, and we'd done a record deal with Pay As U Go, and that was the first time we'd seen that level of money from something legit. I remember getting a cheque for twenty grand. I took it home to my family and was like "I made *twenty grand* – it's right here written on paper." Up until then it had been a lifestyle of crime, poverty . . . when you make money in particular ways, it goes out as quick as it comes in.' And yet unlike their predecessors, for whom pirate broadcasting had only ever felt like a rung on the ladder towards some other form of legitimacy, for Rinse the shadowy rituals of breaking onto rooftops, rigging up transmitters and evading the DTI remained a core part of their identity long after they'd evolved from an adolescent hobby to become one of the most important platforms for underground

British music in the country. 'I went on a tower block for the first time, I climbed on the roof, and I was like, what is going on up here,' Warren explained in a 2019 interview. 'It was like a whole other life. What I imagined as a kid, it was a whole heap more, there was this next level of everything to do with radio. Straight away I was like: this is *amazing*.'

The numbers on a red LCD display tick upwards: 4, 5, 6. The camera pulls back to show a man standing in a yellow-lit metal lift, wearing a black New York Yankees cap. 'You're gonna be scared up there . . . it's bare floors, boy,' he says, before staring down at the floor, silent and still, as if in prayer or silent contemplation. The numbers tick up: 24, 25, 26. The doors slide open, and DJ Slimzee leads us out through unlit residential corridors to a thick metal door, the heavy clank of its lock suggesting non-standard workman's keys.* From there, into a low-ceiling maintenance room with deafening air ducts, ducking under concrete support beams and across to a ladder, leading up into a gloomy and impenetrable recess in the roof. The video cuts out, then back in with a view across East London, before panning up to show the thing we're here for: the Rinse FM aerial, silhouetted against a grey sky.

By the time UK garage began to mutate into grime in the early 2000s, Slimzee – real name Dean Fullman – wasn't just Rinse's most celebrated DJ but a key figure alongside Warren in keeping it on the air, breaking onto rooftops around Tower Hamlets and rigging up transmitters to replace the ones the DTI – or their successor Ofcom, who took over the policing of pirate radio in 2003 – kept shutting down. 'We was made aware that because of our success and because we'd made it virtually impossible to take our equipment that Ofcom had planned to really hurt us,' says Warren. 'I'd become more strict in the way we run things: you weren't allowed to drive from the

---

* 'In those days you could just buy the keys to get up the blocks in the shops, most of them were just fire locks with a standard key,' Fullman told NTS Radio in 2014. 'But then they started using all these other ones, like drop keys and girders. We knew the lift engineers though so they just used to let us use their keys.'

tower straight home, from the tower to the studio, the studio to the tower; you had to take multiple journeys and stop in places in between. That was me. But Slim, he thought it was all blown out of proportion.' This proved to be Rinse's undoing: they had indeed been under long-term and incredibly intrusive Ofcom surveillance, with tiny cameras placed around the block, in bottle banks, on the roof of the tower, even peering in through Fullman's windows to take photos of his girlfriend and baby. 'We knew the cameras were there, but we was going up, taping over them and cracking on,' says Warren, who remained masked while hitting the towers, in contrast to Fullman's more brazen approach. In 2005, having tailed the latter from the tower to the Rinse studio to his home, Ofcom hit all three simultaneously, seizing everything from multiple studios' worth of equipment to Rinse's account books.

Just as the police had placed Centreforce at the centre of a huge, spurious web of drug-dealing and gang activity, Fullman's undeniable role in helping to keep Rinse on their air saw him presented as a sinister, Machiavellian figure, the station's solitary mastermind, without whom the airwaves and streets would finally be safe. He was given a suspended sentence, a £500 fine and, prompted by Blair's respect agenda, an ASBO which infamously banned him from going onto the roof of any building higher than four storeys within Tower Hamlets. Despite this, Warren convinced him to join him on a fifteen-storey tower in North London a couple of weeks after his conviction.

> We got the aerial up, everything was going neat, then the police turned up. He panicked, jumped down straight away, left me holding five scaffolding poles. I ran down to find him, but he'd run straight into the police. He said he was me, straightaway gave them my name, so then I was like – who am I? We spent twenty-four hours in a cell for burglary cos they didn't know what we was doing, then we got interviewed by Ofcom. And it was bad for him, it really shook him. After that, he was out.

The ASBO effectively killed Fullman's career for the best part of a decade, and dragged him into the depths of a nervous breakdown. Not satisfied with this, or perhaps antagonized by Warren getting Rinse back on air within twenty-four hours of Fullman's arrest, plugging MP3 players into back-up transmitters in a show of last-ditch defiance, Ofcom set out to end Rinse once and for all. 'For the next thirteen days, we lost a transmitter a day,' says Warren. 'By the time we'd put one up, switched it on at 4 a.m., woken up at 9 a.m., it was gone. I've never, ever been attacked like that by Ofcom.' Relying on subscriptions from its DJs and on-air advertising to keep it going, if Rinse was kept off air it would die. If the Broadcasting Act's increased legislative powers and DJ Slimzee's conviction were pirate radio's own Criminal Justice Act, the legislative and physical force of the state used to crush underground culture, then Warren's desperate attempts to keep things running were the broadcast equivalent of Mother, the free party scene's final, abortive attempt at a Castlemorton-sized gathering after the Criminal Justice Act passed: one last fuck-you before things crumbled. And yet, unlike events a decade earlier, this time the state blinked first. 'We had fourteen transmitters, and we had no money. I was putting iPods into transmitters, they was trying to do studio raids, we was playing cat and mouse for two weeks,' Warren explains. 'We put in the last transmitter, I was like this is the end. And that's the one they didn't take. One more move, and we was out, because there was no way for me to get the money back.'

Within two years of DJ Slimzee's arrest, having come so close to everything falling apart, Rinse accepted that going legal was the only way forward. But, having seen Kiss's demise, they were determined to do things differently. 'To be honest, we never really had the approach of – we're going for a licence and that's the be all and end all,' says Warren. In a notable change from the landscape two decades earlier when Kiss first applied for their licence, Rinse straight-up refused to switch off their pirate broadcasts while their application was considered. Initially invited to apply for a small neighbourhood licence, Rinse instead pitched for the entire London-wide broadcast spectrum. 'I was like, mate, I'm already on a 300 watt transmitter, I can go from here to Southend no problem. I'm not jeopardizing that. We'll stay pirate if we have to.' This intransigence made some of the pitching meetings a little more awkward. 'I had a moment of panic,' admits Warren, at the prospect of sharing a meeting room with Ofcom. 'I did think, oh my God, I'm meeting the people that I've been dodging for ever. But there's no way out of this. We have to have a sit down because, well, you're not gonna beat us.'

At the same time, it was clear that certain aspects of the pirate lifestyle were wearing thin. 'People don't understand: everyone has the dream of being on the tower block, it's beautiful, *lovely* view. But no one takes into consideration that when you've got to cable it, I'm either sitting in a lift shaft on my own for hours, jumping out the way of lifts, or moving around under water tanks and my closest friends are thirty pigeons. I'd come out, I'd have shit all over me, I'd catch flu straight after and feel ill for days.' Even so, old habits die hard: it was only after they'd been awarded a licence in 2010 that Rinse finally agreed to shut their pirate broadcast down, recognizing at that point that they were beginning, ever so slightly, to take the piss.

Rinse's FM application had been steered in large part by Sarah Lockhart, whose industry experience across both the mainstream and underground – from running foundational dubstep night FWD>> to handling global A&R for major labels – provided the perfect foil for the station's rougher-edged pirate instincts. Lockhart left in 2019, and there are occasional hints of friction when I mention her name to Warren, but what's striking is how different this feels from discussing any of Kiss's former employees with Gordon McNamee: the clueless flailing of corporate vultures back in the 1990s, versus subtle differences in opinion about how best to keep an underground brand fresh as it grew. It feels like Kiss's mistakes and mis-steps paved the way for Rinse to do things differently – it's hard to see how they could have refused to go off-air before getting their licence, for one thing, had McNamee and Kiss not laid the groundwork – and have in turn gone on to inspire others.

In the decade since Rinse went legit, a whole spectrum of radio stations have followed their lead to creative and financial sustainability – aided, of course, by internet broadcasting usurping the infinitely more demanding and geographically limited world of FM transmission. The future success of stations like Reprezent, Radar Radio* and NTS – where DJ Slimzee made his first tentative steps back onto the air in 2014, before rejoining Rinse in 2017 – make clear Rinse's profound cultural and industry influence. After a few years away from running the station day-to-day, Warren came back to the company in 2019 and decided to reboot the whole thing. 'I got to the stage where I was like – I'm not sure what we stand for, I feel like we're taking a bit of a wrong direction, I don't agree with the way the company's being run . . . I completely switched the team out, I took my youngest team, who were interns and volunteers, and made them into the senior people and I was like – let's go again.' It's clear there were disagreements internally with this – a critical reading might note the effectiveness of culling senior staff as a means to head off potential power struggles – but it has undoubtedly kept Rinse sharp and relevant, finding a balance between the glossy media empire it now exists as, and the scrappy upstart it's always been. 'Change is important, it's disruptive, and not everyone is built for it,' says Warren. 'As we've changed, in each direction, there's been losses that, whilst at the time they feel painful, they're important for the progression of the company.'

In January 2023, Kool FM's founders Eastman and Susie G announced that they were stepping back from the station they'd founded in 1991: taking over their roles, and acquiring Kool in the process, were Gordon Warren and Rinse FM. 'To progress and make the platform bigger it needs youthfulness and energy, which

---

* Radar collapsed in 2018 after allegations of sexual harassment and financial mismanagement, under the ownership of Ollie Ashley, son of Sports Direct owner Mike Ashley, its ethically dubious ownership offset by the superb platform it provided for early career Black talent unable to get on other stations. Intriguingly, Warren says that he made an offer to buy Radar shortly before it shut down, so that it could be kept going, but Ashley rebuffed him.

I ain't got no more', said Eastman in his final Kool broadcast. 'And it needs money pumped in so our DJs are proud to walk into a studio, not worried about looking over their shoulder.' Having been originally born out of the teenage Warren's inability to get on Kool's decks, Rinse was now substantial and established enough to step in and save the station which first inspired it, the balance of power between the two comprehensively reversed.

There's a subtle nod to Rinse's journey in the building it now occupies: having started out broadcasting from teenage tower-block bedrooms, it now does so from a glossy office and studio complex wedged between Hoxton Street and a mid-century housing estate, in a building unmistakably designed as residential rather than commercial property. 'I consciously decided to get this place,' says Warren, leaning back into the sofa, a windowsill of Rinse merchandise and vinyl promos stacked behind him. Next to him is a clear plastic box of defunct FM transmitters, recently pulled out of storage for use in a scripted film set in the halcyon days of old-school pirate radio. On the other side of his desk sits a pile of self-help books on entrepreneurship and business: *The Intelligent Investor* by Benjamin Graham; *The Four-Hour Work Week* by Timothy Ferriss; *Antifragile* by Nassim Nicholas Taleb. 'I looked at the estate, then this place, and thought: yeah, that feels like home.'

DANCERS AT A JAMIE XX BOILER ROOM SHOW IN ICELAND, 2017

9. Real People Doing Real Things

Broadcast TV, digital platforms and the visual mediation of UK dance floors

The gloom suffusing the Eclipse in Coventry is impenetrable, the noise a cacophonous surge of distorted breakbeats and sirens, the dance floor a sinister throng of sweating bodies merging together into one indistinguishable mass. 'You might have noticed this isn't a normal *Hitman and Her*,' offers Michaela Strachan tentatively, her voice somewhere between affable reassurance and barely contained grief: the precise tone normally reserved by *Blue Peter* presenters for announcing the death of one of the show's beloved pets. Pete

Waterman, meanwhile, has completely lost the plot: drenched in sweat and struggling to get through his script, he breaks away repeatedly to complain about the suffocating heat. With his gold chain matted into a damp mess of chest hair, he looks like what he arguably is: a disco king out of time and out of his depth, watching his empire crumble around him.* In the four years since ITV's *The Hitman and Her* was first broadcast, Pete and Michaela have seen the Berlin Wall torn down, the Soviet Union collapse, Nelson Mandela released from prison and Thatcher forced from power: at a time when old orthodoxies are being dismantled and gatekeepers dethroned left and right, the revolution has finally reached the world of music-based late-night light entertainment programming.

Filmed on a Saturday night and airing early Sunday morning, just as weary clubbers were returning home, *The Hitman and Her*'s weekly format and style were drawn straight from existing entertainment TV staples – vox pops, location shoots, audience interaction and gameshow-like cheeriness. Pop impresario Waterman had come up with the idea after coming home late one night, and finding nothing on TV but a panel discussion about Northern Ireland. He then successfully pitched the concept to Granada TV and an industry friend, Nick Wilson, who owned a TV production company

---

* This perspective is perhaps a little unfair. The rise of dance music undoubtedly torpedoed Waterman's cultural relevance and credibility as a media personality, but the behind-the-scenes picture is more mixed. Despite his association with Kylie-adjacent pop music of the carpet and chrome variety, Waterman also released a slew of dance tunes in 1991 and 1992 through a PWL sub-label called Black Diamond. Another label co-founded by Waterman in Manchester, 380 Records, would go on to release the classic 'Set You Free' by N-Trance in 1993. 'I loved acid house and trance. I just absolutely adored it. For me it was like a breath of fresh air. Because I also loved punk which everybody forgets. I just loved the freshness of it,' Waterman told *The Guardian* in 2013. As with many other major labels at the time, dipping a toe into the rave scene in this way involved a certain amount of subterfuge: an absolutely relentless breakbeat hardcore remix of PWL pop starlet Mandy Smith was commissioned in 1992 from producer Mickey Finn, but released solely as a white label without any reference to Waterman's involvement.

called Music Box. Each weekend, Waterman and the perennially bubbly Strachan would rock up to a provincial nightspot to present a collection of interviews, audience contests, music videos, and extended sequences of packed dance floors doing their thing, all cut together with ramshackle charm. The incredibly short turnaround between filming and broadcast meant there was no time to smooth out the rough edges, but this also kept the show feeling immediate and lived-in: 'In the days before reality TV', wrote *The Guardian* in 2011, 'it was one of the few places in the schedules where you could see real people doing real things.'

Its first episode, broadcast from Mr Smith's Night Club in Warrington in September 1988 – the very moment acid house was taking hold across the country – feels like a time capsule from another century. The venue is a vision in carpet and chrome, the haircuts are back-combed and feathery, and every man in the building appears to be wearing a blazer and a tie. The music they're dancing to consists almost entirely of the kind of synthetic pop championed by Waterman's own PWL label, or produced under his Stock, Aitken and Waterman banner. The atmosphere is starched, deeply uncool, and riddled with end-of-the-pier silliness (another episode features a blindfolded woman kissing three men, and having to guess which one's her boyfriend). Strachan runs a karaoke competition set to 'I Should Be So Lucky' by Kylie Minogue;* before a 'live' performance in which a man in a leather jacket lip-syncs appallingly, flanked by four gyrating women in leotards and leg warmers. On the rare occasions when more contemporary sounds broke through this mainstream pop sensibiliity, the juxtaposition with the show's prevailing mood was unsettling: another 1988 episode features Humanoid's proto-rave acid banger 'Stakker Humanoid' accompanied by a dance routine from three glamorous lovelies in skimpy

---

* Like many of the artists featured in *The Hitman and Her*, Kylie was signed at the time to PWL: the show reflected the prevailing tastes across Britain's high street clubs, but also reinforced Waterman's hugely influential position within the industry by offering a national TV platform to the performers he had a stake in.

lingerie, and a topless hunk wearing Hammer pants and braces. *The Hit Man and Her* was a painfully accurate barometer of the naffest excesses of mainstream British clubbing in the 1980s, the antithesis of acid house's rebel energy and stripped-back futurism.

In January 1989, barely three months into their broadcast run, Waterman and Strachan ventured to The Haçienda in Manchester, and *The Hitman and Her*'s entire world began to unravel. 'We're in such a trendy venue that we're taking a back seat today, and just letting them get on with the music,' says Michaela, with perhaps a hint of ruefulness detectable under her usual cheerful veneer. Most of the episode is indeed taken up by footage from the dance floor, with Pete and Michaela's presence rendered largely peripheral. The weekly 'Showing Out' dance contest, usually presided over by the hosts from a stage in the centre of the club, instead becomes uncomfortably voyeuristic: Pete and Michaela appear only as disembodied voices, commentating on various unsuspecting dancers as the camera zooms in on them from a gantry in the building's rafters. In a rare presenter-led segment, Michaela asks a young man with razor-sharp cheekbones and an air of supercilious detachment what attracts him to the 'trendy' surrounds of The Haçienda (it's repeated over and over, to the point of defensiveness, that The Haçienda is 'trendy'). 'Because nobody wears stripey shirts or Topman suits,' is his reply, and his friends erupt with laughter. 'Well *we* don't wear that, do we?' grins Strachan in a game attempt to ingratiate herself. 'Come on,' replies her interviewee, gesturing off past the camera, 'Pete's wearing *leather trousers.*'

Recalling her visit to The Haçienda thirty-odd years later, it's clear that this uncomfortable banter wasn't being played up for the cameras. 'They were so unwelcoming . . . It was super trendy in the early 1990s and we were the wrong show for that club,' Strachan told *The Courier* in 2020. 'The last thing they wanted was Stock, Aitken and Waterman tracks being played. We tweaked the music, but they hated us: I got a glass thrown at me and they were rude to Pete and I couldn't wait to get out.' Pete and Michaela's visit to Coventry three years later would make it even clearer that they were no longer at the cutting edge, and in fact represented the opposite: the personification of a deeply uncool light entertainment industry, unable to get a handle on the raw, disruptive energy of rave culture. Within months of the Eclipse episode airing, *The Hitman and Her* would be taken off the air entirely.

In its four-year history, *The Hitman and Her* provided a real-time picture of rave's evolution, and its Darwinian domination and eradication of the UK's existing nightlife scene. But it also highlights the pivotal role that television and online broadcasting would play in shaping the nation's attitudes towards dance culture. If the story of pirate radio reflected UK dance music's evolving power relationships (as well as its ability to bring together geographically distributed communities), and its fictional depictions from *Inspector Morse* to *Kevin & Perry* reflected rave's mid-1990s transition from dangerous, illegal counterculture to mainstream acceptance, then the same is also true of more documentary visual approaches, from *The Hitman and Her* to the online streaming video platform Boiler Room. Much like radio, UK dance music's visual depictions on TV and the internet have involved a tug-of-war between underground credibility and mainstream acceptance: a repeated cycle in which legacy media platforms are outflanked by cooler, nimbler independent operators, themselves forced in turn to juggle financial stability and cultural vitality, before being superseded by the next generation. *The Hitman and Her* putting acid house and rave on television was crucial in initiating that process, bringing dance music to a mainstream audience for the first time: for the average suburban thirteen-year-old, huddled under their duvet in the early hours of 1992, the volume on their battery-powered portable TV turned down so as not to wake up their parents, the images beaming in through the static from the Eclipse must have felt like a transmission from a parallel universe, and an infinitely more exciting one at that. Who could resist chasing that dream, or having their reality altered by it?

By the time *The Hitman and Her* first aired, electronic dance music had already proved itself capable of assimilation into the language of prime-time TV: as early as 1986 the singer Darryl Pandy could be found belting out Farley 'Jackmaster' Funk's early Chicago house classic 'Love Can't Turn Around' to a rapturous reception on *Top of the Pops*.* But more direct depictions of being *inside* the rave struggled to gain the same traction. Orbital's sarcastic anti-spectacle while 'performing' 'Chime' on *Top of the Pops* in 1990 went down like a lead balloon, while The Shamen's pantomimic, call-and-response rendition of 'Ebenezer Goode' in 1992 was made possible only after a still-prudish BBC lifted their ban on the record. Faced with the sight of Mr. C in full bondage gear rapping the song's entirely unsubtle references to Ecstasy to a crowd of pop-hungry teens, the tabloid press went into meltdown. For several years after that, the only occasions on which you might see dance floors represented on TV (at least without Pete Waterman and Michaela on hand to mediate the experience) were pearl-clutching news reports lamenting the drug-fuelled disorder on display.

This would change by the end of 1992: *The Hitman and Her*'s final episode in December of that year had been preceded by ITV's launch of *BPM*, a magazine show covering similar club-based territory – and even made by the same production company, Music Box – but showing it in a very different light. Where Pete and Michaela had refracted rave through tired TV-presenter tropes and Waterman's pop industry connections, *BPM* was as close to a first-person perspective as you could hope to find within the confines of broadcast TV. Presenters Dave Dorrell and Brenda Tuohy – him a cheeky North Londoner in a baseball cap, her a suave New Yorker in thick-rimmed glasses – had all the offhand cool and nerdy enthusiasm of their peers on MTV, while the show's frenetic collage of gurning dancers in dingy basement clubs, knowingly ramshackle

---

* Pandy's performance – the first time UK television audiences had been exposed to Chicago house – helped the song hit Number 10 in the UK charts the same year. But its musical and cultural signifiers – all shiny shirts and Jheri-curled hair, glamorous backing singers and gospel-inspired vocal acrobatics – feel far more in keeping with soul, disco and R'n'B than what we'd now understand as club music: the world of James Brown or Michael Jackson, rather than Ron Hardy or Frankie Knuckles.

presenter links, and lo-fi interviews with producers and label owners, usually conducted in front of a bank of synthesizers or a massive cathode-ray PC screen, gave it a credible, insider feel. A 1993 interview with drum'n'bass DJ Grooverider is a particular highlight, Tuohy flirting outrageously with a bemused but good-natured Grooverider as the two stand in 'the hot, *sweaty* hallway' of Club Kinetic in Stoke-on-Trent. 'Soooooo then, Groooooove baby,' purrs Tuohy, flicking her hair over her bare shoulder, 'where's it all *going*?' Dorrell, meanwhile, came with serious dance industry pedigree: an *NME* journalist in the early 1980s before getting into DJing, he'd scored a Number 1 hit in 1987 as a member of MARRS with 'Pump Up the Volume' – arguably the first UK-produced house record – before running an influential early acid night called Love, at the Wag Club in Soho. Much as the *The Tube* and *The Word* had done for guitar-led alternative music, *BPM* marked the assimilation of rave culture into a mainstream TV format, its scrappy style and effortless tone reflecting 1990s youth culture in something like its real form, shorn of top-down editorializing. Where Pete Waterman's befuddled, sweat-drenched appearance in Coventry had served to reinforce rave's alien, intimidatory qualities, *BPM* made a Saturday night spent in front of a speaker stack feel like the most natural, uncontroversial thing in the world.

The overtaking of staid formats by hipper and more credible upstarts may have been a shared theme across TV and radio, but in other aspects the two could not have been more different. The original rise of pirate radio back in the 1960s had been triggered by the increasing availability of low-cost transmission equipment, enabling independent broadcasters to carve out a niche for themselves in the frequency spectrum and compete on the same footing as their more established competitors (albeit over a smaller geographical area). For a number of reasons, this didn't translate to TV: the broadcast equipment required for video rather than audio signals remained vastly more expensive, for starters, while home TV aerials were mono-directional, pointing at the nearest TV transmitter rather than receiving from all directions. Wannabe pirate TV broadcasters either had to place their transmitter in front of an existing legal tower, making it laughably easy to identify and shut down, or convince viewers to get up on their roof and point their aerial in a different direction, *then* go back inside and retune their TV set, something people did every day with their radio but rarely if ever for their TVs. As a result, while there were a handful of attempts to set up pirate TV stations between the 1970s and 1990s (including one by pirate radio station Thameside FM) none made it beyond the novelty stage.*

While the pirate radio ecosystem continued to evolve and diversify through the 1990s, dance music's visual presence on TV instead narrowed: *BPM*'s cancellation in 1995 and the wholesale incorporation of mass-market house and trance into the pop charts meant that DJs hoping to make it onto TV screens invariably did so via appearances on *Top of the Pops* and *CD:UK*, rather than anything with *BPM*'s rough-edged grassroots sensibilities. All of that changed in February 2003, though, when a new channel popped up on digital TV guides: a frenetic mix of zero-budget music videos, live freestyles and comedy skits, all rooted in Black British grime, hip hop and rap; it was called Channel U. The station had its roots in the DIY grime DVD scene which had flourished in the earliest years of the millennium. In the absence of suitable TV platforms, enterprising videographers and producers filmed live-to-camera sessions with grime MCs in whatever locations were available, from backstage at the rave to the backstreets of their estate, packaged them onto DVDs – Risky Roadz, Lord of the Mics, and Practice Hours were three of the best-known series – and sold them at clubs and festivals, or via rudimentary internet mail-order. The rawness of their production mirrored the music perfectly: in one Risky Roadz clip, Kano raps incongruously about 'chilling with a topless girl by

---

* Grassroots community-produced TV did of course exist, via the BBC's Community Programmes Unit, or Channel 4's work with film-making co-operatives; the distinction being that these programmes were still subject to gatekeeping and oversight from larger broadcasters, as opposed to pirate radio stations being answerable to no one but themselves.

the pool' while standing in his dressing gown on a sodium-lit East London cul-de-sac, with a white van visible in the background and a mug of tea in his hand. Building on the grime DVD scene's no-frills approach and direct, unfiltered access to underground artists, Channel U filled a cultural space about which mainstream broadcasters remained utterly uninterested. Even MTV Base, the UK's dedicated music channel for rap, R'n'B and Black music in general, stuck rigidly to a diet of major label US imports in the early 2000s: endless re-runs of Puff Daddy on a jetski or J.Lo grinding lithely for the camera, white satin sheets billowing in slow motion behind them, while even the most successful UK acts were restricted to late-night 'homegrown' segments. Mass-market TV had no interest in the world depicted on Channel U, with its zero-budget camcorder-shot videos from no-name rappers, and interviews with grassroots MCs under a railway bridge in Croydon.

Despite lacking the resources of bigger labels or global broadcasters, Channel U rapidly became the single most important visual platform for emerging UK dance music in the mid-2000s: a pirate TV station to go with its radio siblings. 'Out of necessity, grime at its inception was a decidedly non-visual genre, in that so much of it was hidden,' writes Dan Hancox. 'Digital cameras hadn't been widely adopted, smartphones didn't exist, the established media weren't interested in documenting it, and the hubs for all grime activity were pirate radio stations, which by their nature had to be hidden in the shadows.' Channel U changed all of that, bringing the leading lights of the grime scene into homes around the country – giving artists including Tinchy Stryder, Lethal Bizzle and Dizzee Rascal their first TV plays – and building wider programming off the back of the music, from animated comedy *The Booo Krooo* to endearingly ramshackle interview strand *Ill Out*, in which hosts Ace and Vis went from visiting MCs in the ends to asking 50 Cent whether he'd have sex with the Queen. When Channel U founder Darren Platt died in 2016, plaudits flooded in from across the Black British music industry: 'There was no way we could get on TV, but Channel U bridged that gap . . . it made the man across the street a celebrity,' said MC and TV presenter Poet (who would later go on to host *Yo! MTV Raps* and the *Gasworks* series for Boiler Room). 'Man's watching Kanye, and then all of a sudden he's watching Kano. And then you'd have stuff like *Ill Out*, so it's not just the music but you're also telling stories around it, Ace and Vis getting chased by a dog with Crazy Titch. It was *sick*.'

Operating in its own self-contained ecosystem, with the national reach of digital TV but without the deadening strictures of corporate broadcasting to hold them back, Channel U created its own pantheon of cult heroes, often tripping into surreal comedy rather than the po-faced aggression with which Black music (particularly grime) has long been excessively associated. 'Yo! Let's go to the WOOOOOOODS!' hollers Bearman by way of introduction to his grime cover of 'The Teddy Bear's Picnic': within minutes he's been surrounded by a bevy of gyrating babes, as he spits bars while dressed in a bear suit. Or there's 'Junior Spesh' by Red Hot Entertainment, a 2007 posse cut dedicated to a local chicken shop's cut-price meal deal, featuring the deathless poetry of bars like 'Want mayo? Fifty pence / Piss off wanker, ketchup's bless / Give me a napkin in case of mess.' In 2015, YouTube channel VPoint tracked down several of the channel's lost stars: Mr Wong, the 'self-styled Chinese Boi', had since become a mental health nurse; Napper, the voice behind perhaps the most aggressive verse on Lethal Bizzle's infamous 'Pow! (Forward)', was now working as a personal trainer.

'If we'd known back then what we know now', laments Scarz, another former Channel U star now studying for a degree in music management, 'I'd be rich!' But then, maybe that industry savvy would have undercut the very thing that made Channel U special. Brought back onto TV screens for one night in November 2020, the increased professionalism of proceedings – along with the enervating effects of Covid-enforced social distancing, and a certain retrospective self-awareness in the live performances (Tempa T performing his biggest tune 'Next Hype', by now almost fifteen years old, in a *Booo Krooo* T-shirt) – felt akin to an ageing rock band hitting the heritage circuit. But even in nostalgic and pandemic-restricted form, this exhumed version of Channel U merely underlined how brilliantly weird and unfiltered the original had been, and how far short mainstream broadcasters from BBC Three to Channel 4 have since fallen in trying to capture that same youth culture energy: the diminished 2020-era Channel U was still an order of magnitude more exciting and culturally relevant than other live music programming on linear broadcast TV, which today appears to consist of little beyond Jools Holland, *Songs of Praise* and the musical guests on *Sunday Brunch*.

Channel U went into liquidation in 2009, before being bought out and rebranded as Channel AKA. It never fully recaptured either its audience or its mojo, but its spirit would continue on the internet. YouTube had launched back in 2005, but it was only in 2007, following its acquisition by Google, that it began to scale at speed. The same year, a sixteen-year-old MC calling himself Smokey Barz – real name Jamal Edwards – uploaded his first video to the site, shot on a school trip to Cadbury's World in Birmingham. Raised on Channel U, grime DVDs and pirate radio, SB.TV managed to be even more lo-fi and no-frills than any of those: wind whipping across the mic in a West Midlands car park, unknown MCs shot on a budget camcorder or phone camera against graffiti-covered walls, or sat on the back seat of a bus, tinny beats accompanying them from an off-camera speaker. 'I realised I was never going to make it on any mainstream platforms or any DVDs as an MC,' recounted Edwards in 2017, 'so I saw a gap in the market and thought, "Where could people go that don't have these platforms?" Why don't I start the platform?' . . . 'People used to watch YouTube just for funny videos then, so when they saw people spraying bars they were like "What?" But the more we put it out the more people wanted it.'

Edwards combined the growing power of social media, using MySpace and Bebo to promote his videos, with old-school IRL hustle, hanging around outside raves and getting MCs to freestyle for him. Along with peers like Link Up TV, GRM Daily and Tim and Barry of Just Jam, Edwards's curation and promotion of Black British music and culture thrived on YouTube's low overheads and minimal barriers to entry – a visual equivalent of the circumstances which had created pirate radio forty years earlier, building on Channel U's example – providing an entry point for underground MCs and, as production values and audiences numbers increased, a credible platform for the scene's biggest names too. Just as with Channel U or a grime DVD, the removal of mainstream TV's rictus-grin glitz created more breathing room for the music's rough-edged sounds and street-level celebrities: SB.TV's videos might have been reaching hundreds of thousands of fans, but they still felt intimate and real, even as the channel's profile grew. YouTube's algorithm-driven audience, looking for the next shiny thing to click on, encouraged an increasing frequency of content, which in turn required a growing supply of fresh music, creating opportunities for young artists who wouldn't otherwise have got a look in, and fostering a breadth of style which extended beyond the standard template of a moody MC speaking straight to camera. YouTube grime performances could still be raw and intense, but just as with Channel U they could also be fun: Tempa T and JME trading bars on a snow-covered street while being pelted with snowballs by Tim and Barry; or Skepta standing outside a country mansion and pretending it belonged to Wiley, as part of an SB.TV-produced diss track riffing on Blur's 'Country House'. Edwards leveraged the burgeoning attention he'd garnered on YouTube into serious business clout: by 2013 SB.TV had racked up 150 million views, enough to secure investment from venture capital firm Miroma Ventures which valued the company at £8 million. The following year, aged just twenty-four, Edwards was awarded an MBE: a level of establishment recognition entirely out of keeping both with society's broader treatment of young Black men, and that of earlier dance music entrepreneurs, and a testament to Edwards's unique influence.

Jamal Edwards and SB.TV represented the future of dance music as a visual medium, just as pirate stations were once the future of radio. By the early 2010s, major investors and media industry players finally realized that young viewers had all but abandoned traditional broadcast TV in favour of digital platforms, and weren't coming back; at much the same time, metrics produced by Facebook — later found to have been systematically falsified — suggested that social video was drawing vast audiences, demanding that media companies shift their attention online. Just as filesharing had done with recorded music a decade earlier, huge corporations with layers of decision-makers and out-of-touch bosses had failed to anticipate or react to the changing tastes of extremely online young fans, and were now forced to fight a desperate rearguard action to stay relevant and profitable, largely by buying up the platforms and talent which had outflanked them.

Along with SB.TV perhaps the most notable — and certainly the most contentious — beneficiary of this goldrush for online video was a livestreaming dance music platform set up in 2010, called Boiler Room. Their set-up was even more bare-bones than your average grime YouTube channel: two webcams, an internet connection, a DJ and a room full of East London hipsters, beaming the latest sounds from the capital's underground dance music scene to an audience around the world. A DJ set from September 2010 by James Blake embodies the early Boiler Room aesthetic: an impossibly cool DJ showcased *just* before they break through — Blake had one single under his belt by this point, and was weeks away from dropping the debut major label EP which would make his name — performing in a nondescript, half-lit living room while presenter Thristian Richards shouts out various names from the online chatroom. This would be one of the last Boiler Room sets aired from their original warehouse in Hackney Wick; there's a sheet draped loosely over the wall behind the DJ, and a poster of Haile Selassie I on the adjoining wall; in-the-know scenesters drift in and out of the room, chatting to each other in loose knots or settling into a battered armchair and sparking a spliff. You've almost certainly been to student house parties with more considered visual presentation and a more excitable crowd. The broadcast set-up is similarly sketchy: a terrible webcam, blurry and regularly out-of-focus, with a frame rate that makes everything feel jerky and otherworldly, regular technical issues affecting the decks and mics, the messy unpredictability of pirate radio transferred to streaming video. If someone told you at the time that these were the seeds of a global media empire, I'm not sure you'd have believed them.

The idea for these weekly Tuesday night broadcasts had grown out of *Platform*, an online arts and music magazine owned by Boiler Room co-founder Blaise Bellville. Born to an aristocratic family and educated at the prestigious Wiltshire private school Marlborough College, by his early twenties Bellville had ingratiated himself with the *Tatler* crowd by running club nights with old Etonian and founder of the Young* label Caius Pawson (who would later become a shareholder in Boiler Room), promoting alcohol-free under-age raves and festivals under the All Ages banner, and franchising them across the country to highly lucrative effect. In 2011, the year after Boiler Room launched, Bellville was listed as one of the *Daily Mail*'s '50 Most Powerful Posh People Under 30' alongside economic advisors to George Osborne, pro-hunting activist Otis Ferry and aristocratic heir the Hon. Drummond Money-Coutts, founder of the Eton College Magic Society.

Bellville created Boiler Room alongside Thristian Richards, Chalin Barton and Femi Adeyemi, the latter also the founder of music blog turned internet radio station NTS. Bellville and Richards's relationship remained largely frosty following the latter's acrimonious departure in 2014: by that point, Boiler Room had gone from a niche webcast to one of the most powerful dance music platforms on the planet, supercharged by venture capital funding and massive brands desperate to attach themselves to the hottest thing in global youth culture. The reasons for its stratospheric success are myriad, and largely contextual rather than the result of a considered internal strategy. Increasing broadband speeds, the development of streaming technology and the rise of social media created an entirely new media ecosystem and audience waiting to be captured. Boiler Room's simple set-up and lack of overheads (a camera or two, a laptop and a skeleton crew) meant they could

---

* Initially known as Young Turks, the label changed its name in 2021.

churn out content at dizzying speed, meeting every new demand in an instant. On the musical side, the decline of minimal techno and the bubbling-up of newer global club sounds from UK funky to gqom, monochrome industrial techno and a new wave of house music DJs provided a whole generation of artists capable of scaling up from dingy basements to headlining festivals in perfect synchronicity with Boiler Room's own growth.

To give Bellville and others their due, their curatorial nous was also superb, identifying the hottest new talent in underground dance music and getting them in front of audiences with a speed and consistency that others could only dream of. By early 2011 things looked far more like the Boiler Room you'd recognize today, the party relocated from a dingy student living room to a darkened nightclub, with a massed crowd of ravers bringing the energy; by the end of that year Boiler Room would host its first overseas streams in Berlin and Spain, beginning their takeover of global dance music culture. Online audiences were expanding exponentially too: by its fifth birthday in 2015, Boiler Room had streamed over 3.5 billion minutes of music, attracting real-time audiences of close to half a million for their biggest sets, with the most popular uploads rewatched 50 million times. Boiler Room's appeal to both viewers and investors was obvious: aside from the dizzying audience numbers (particularly in the eighteen to twenty-four-year-old demographic so beloved of advertisers) they offered a real-time window into the cutting edge of global club culture, with an air of unstudied credibility which turned their streams from a mere video of a DJ into a golden ticket for the hottest party on the planet. Its ascent was both beguiling and unsettling: if the evolution of dance music's visual documentation and broadcast from *The Hitman and Her* to SB.TV, via *BPM* and Channel U, had been one of deconstructing old power structures, and grassroots culture seizing the means of production, then Boiler Room's journey would be one of recentralization: capturing the very best in UK and global dance music, but in the process annexing it under their own banner and taking ownership of the cultural and actual capital it generated; a form of enclosure and privatization which mirrored the earlier capture of dance music's physical spaces.

The music journalist Gabriel Szatan joined the staff at Boiler Room in 2013, at the tail end of its initial expansion in popularity and first round of venture capital investment. He'd originally met Bellville as a fifteen-year-old indie fan, getting paid £50 to book line-ups for All Age Concerts gigs, before reconnecting seven years later and being brought in to manage Boiler Room's social media. Short on staff for an event in Marrakech, Szatan was flown out to run and host the show, quickly becoming an integral part of the company's dance music programming and editorial, at a time when everyone in dance music wanted in. 'Every promoter was like, I want a camera on my festival: let's put you on top of a hill and shoot the people dancing below. Every manager was seeking to kick off their artist's new album campaign with a bang. You were overloaded with offers, so in the early years you could pick and choose without really having to curate much. As a twenty-two year old, it was a dream.' This embarrassment of riches might have powered Boiler Room's takeover of the global dance scene, but it also hinted at the curatorial inconsistency which would eventually come to undermine it. 'Let's film Jamie Jones in Ibiza, let's do Grimes and Richie Hawtin on acid at a pool party – why not?' says Szatan. 'No one really looks at this any more but there are tonnes of filler shows from Adam Beyer, Guy Gerber, Nicole Moudaber – people that are now regarded as commercial or just not very cool. Boiler Room was saying yes to all these people, but no one remembers Guy Gerber's set or the really iffy brand stuff, they remember Jamie xx and James Blake.'

This scattergun approach flowed directly downwards from Bellville himself. 'We'd arrive in the office on a Monday morning to surprise edicts from the exec team,' says Szatan. ' "OK, so Boiler Room's a radio station now, or we're going to reinvent the morning talk show, go and nab compelling hosts from our rivals", and we'd all be like – what the *fuck* are you talking about? Even if some of the concepts were fun to execute, it was so evident where Boiler Room's strengths lay, yet we kept being sent on side missions.' Having imported the trope of a globetrotting, highly creative CEO with an extremely flimsy grasp on reality from the tech industry, Boiler Room also copied the very worst of that sector's employment practices. Despite pride in the job and a strong sense of team unity, the inclement conditions sparked a revolving door of arrivals and departures, says Szatan. 'There was increasing pressure on junior staff – the video producers, the content team, the booking assistants, the audio engineers – to work insane hours, and always be on hand to clear up messes. Even during PR firestorms, some colleagues would abdicate responsibility as soon as the clock struck 5.01 pm,' he explains.

Anonymous reviews from former Boiler Room employees on the employment website Glassdoor appear to bear this out, with a remarkably consistent stream of allegations around unsafe conditions, constant burnout caused by unrealistic workloads, and clueless decision-making from senior executives: 'Severe mismanagement and constant change in strategy; a steady stream of calamitous decision making from management creates no job security and a business that feels like it's doomed,' reads one of the more measured contributions. Despite repeated management interventions to try to improve Boiler Room's internal culture, substantial issues clearly remained. In August 2022 a *Vice* investigation into sexual harassment and toxic working conditions at another music platform, Beatport, named former CEO Terry Weerasinghe – by that time employed as chief operating officer at Boiler Room – as a repeat offender. According to the testimony of multiple people employed at Beatport over several years, Weerasinghe simultaneously belittled and took credit for the work of female colleagues, made derogatory remarks about pregnant staff members, and bullied his subordinates to the extent that several left the company. In a statement made to *Vice* through his lawyer, Weerasinghe offered an extensive rebuttal of the allegations against him, denying that he had bullied anyone or discriminated against them on the basis of sex or race, 'but apologised if his conduct caused distress to others'. After the article was published, Boiler Room announced that, despite an internal review uncovering no allegations stemming from Weerasinghe's period of employment with them, he would be 'stepping down with immediate effect' from his role with the company.

The seemingly mixed experiences of staff inside Boiler Room were mirrored by an increasing volume of outside criticism as it grew. This rested largely on the unsettling optics and power dynamics of a company owned by an extremely privileged white man harvesting and monetizing the fruits of dance music genres rooted in queer and Black cultures. A long-running and obvious point of contention was Boiler Room's failure to pay the majority of performers, on the understanding that exposure would be enough – a decision for which it's been branded extractive and, where this has involved a white Anglocentric media platform co-opting music from the global South, colonial in both outlook and effect. Whether fairly or not, Boiler Room have regularly faced far more barbed criticism on this point than their competitors in the contemporary dance music industry.

There's pushback from both Szatan and (in a brief email declining to comment further) Thristian Richards against the charge that Boiler Room exploited its artists. The obvious contrast with its rivals in the 2010s music media ecosystem is that Boiler Room's reach was vastly more diffuse and global than any of those other entities, and thus far less able to claim an organic, grassroots connection to the cultures it was showcasing. Rinse FM will always have the tower blocks of Bow, NTS its studio in Dalston, and Fabric its club in Clerkenwell to ground and locate them: concrete roots in a specific local culture, even as their brands expand globally. Boiler Room has only ever existed in the digital ether, attaching itself to existing scenes in far more transitory and transactional fashion. It also clearly didn't help that Bellville was such a visible figurehead for the company, and so inarguably detached from the social identities and communities on which his increasingly lucrative business model had ultimately been built.

If there's a counterargument to all of this, it rests less on the actions of others than the experiences of the artists Boiler Room championed, who hugely benefited in many cases from the platform it provided. 'I think that Boiler Room ended up, not necessarily of its own volition, being the beneficiary of economies of scale and the overarching centralization of culture,' says Szatan. He goes on:

> It meant that when you got a request from a turntablist in Tokyo saying, hey come out, I'm doing a 10th anniversary of my record label, or a gqom or amapiano producer in South Africa, it would feel in some way *more* myopic to say, no, we're going to do another show with a white DJ in Europe . . . there was a sense of always wanting to push Boiler Room's horizons and incorporate music from outside the Anglosphere, because it was fresh and original, and because Boiler Room in its early years so repeatedly failed to consider anything else beyond the immediate UK post-dubstep, emerging house scene . . . the feeling was that we were finally breaking down our own white male Anglo status. The conveyor belt of eager applicants, success stories who enormously increased their stock through a breakthrough moment, and permanently ecstatic crowds greeting us in new locations, obscured the blatant need to wean the company off free labour. And only in the rear-view mirror did we truly realize the extractive nature of it.

It's clear that, for up-and-coming DJs from Manchester to Melbourne, and Glasgow to Guatemala, access to the massive global audience offered by Boiler Room was worth playing a free show for, and that denying them the chance to do so would not have been any more progressive a gesture. At the same time, Szatan also nods to issues around appropriation and creative equity which were clear at the time, and left depressingly unresolved:

> The great failing of Boiler Room, and this happened more than we'd have liked to admit at the time, was when there were shows in other territories – other cultures with different cultural conditions and sensitivities about being portrayed – Boiler Room

steamed in with half a b-team to run the show. Perhaps they hadn't been briefed properly or the hosts hadn't done their research, they'd just looked at a flyer, and this was Latvia's only chance to be on Boiler Room that year . . . why wouldn't you enlist a local film team? Why would you mispronounce artists' names? Why would you stream it at the same time as a brand-funded Skream set, which means they're obviously going to get no hits? . . . That rankled me really severely because then you're doing a terrible disservice to people.

All of these questions came to a head in 2017 when Boiler Room announced that they'd received nearly £300,000 in funding from Arts Council England to film the following year's Notting Hill Carnival – a grant three times larger than that given to the producers of Carnival itself. In fact, Boiler Room had been filming since 2016 as part of a plan to raise the media profile of soundsystems and parade floats, and to push back against mainstream media depictions of the event as a sordid morass of drug use and violent crime. The concept had been rooted in Bellville's deep and entirely genuine affection for Black music, and Carnival in particular, but it immediately became apparent that his efforts represented a colossal and calamitous misreading of the public mood. Szatan explains:

> Carnival had been Blaise's passion project for years, and there were months of planning meetings in the build-up to make this the pride and joy of Boiler Room's summer programming; to really do everything above board. There'd been conversations with local councillors, and with soundsystem owners who were very happy, after negotiations, to be broadcast. I believe there was a contract signed that said Boiler Room would give some of the money it made directly to the soundsystems. There'd also been extensive conversations with locals: hey, can we put a router in your house, can we film a short about your Mas band? The problem was that no one thought about the *crowds*.

He goes on:

> There was no consideration of the people who use Notting Hill as the one or two days a year where they get to be expressive, be themselves, get out of their nine-to-five and go and party on the streets and connect with their ancestry and their roots. And there we were, naively roving through the streets with an enormous HD camera in hand. I mean, put yourself in their shoes. 'No, I don't want to be filmed drinking Cherry B with a flag wrapped round my head, what the *fuck* are you *doing*? You're using a picture of me as your thumbnail on your YouTube channel, I didn't consent to this, I didn't sign any forms.'

If Pete Waterman sweating in the Eclipse in Coventry marked the moment when *The Hitman and Her* lost its grip on the cultural zeitgeist, then this was Boiler Room's equivalent; the moment at which the cracks in its cultural credibility became terminal.

The attempt to muscle into Notting Hill wasn't just a mis-step, but a transgression of the most corrosive kind: cutting across half a century of antipathy and violence towards Black culture from precisely the sort of people Blaise Bellville grew up with, and ignoring the vast web of communal needs, social rituals and unspoken rules which existed around Carnival. Where Carnival's radical Blackness had once been seen as a threat those in power, Boiler Room's intervention felt like a form of sanitisation, inadvertently reminiscent of the police's attempts to relocate the entire event to Stamford Bridge football stadium decades earlier. In an instant, it crystallized and amplified everything that was wrong with Boiler Room: an aloof media behemoth led by a well-meaning but deluded aristocrat and funded by global capital, haplessly trampling across grassroots Black culture in order to increase its market share and enrich its owners; an understanding of music solely as an exploitable resource rather than a living culture. 'Ultimately such coverage performs little to no public good, and will not stop the yearly conspiracy to shut down Carnival,' wrote one excoriating anonymous blog post. 'Instead this coverage feeds into Boiler Room's PR campaign, whitewashing black culture into a palatable consumer product and creating lucrative marketing opportunities for brands to infiltrate Carnival on a much larger scale than seen previously.'

As much as the Notting Hill farrago spoke to Boiler Room's cultural myopia, it also underlined the company's increasingly precarious financial situation. For years, it had comprehensively failed to turn a profit despite its colossal global audiences, requiring repeated injections of private cash to remain afloat. This, in turn, demanded an aggressive focus on the bottom line, protecting investments and delivering returns for its backers. Notting Hill was the result of Boiler Room both assuming that its cultural capital and audience reach made it untouchable, but also reflected its need to annex even more territory, harvest ever-increasing views, hoover up public funding, and ultimately begin turning a profit against the obligations it had accrued to its investors.

After the mishandling of Carnival closed off Boiler Room's strategy of extracting value from large-scale pre-existing events (they'd also lobbied hard to livestream from Glastonbury, but were turned down on the basis of the festival's pre-existing exclusive deal with the BBC) their focus turned inwards, to the untapped profit-making potential of the global music scenes they covered. In 2019, shortly after high-profile hires of several more business-minded executives, one of them emailed Philadelphia-based underground dance music promoter Aaron Clark with a profoundly unappetizing proposal. Clark was to organize and promote a club night in his home city: in exchange for an unspecified 'brand fee' he would be permitted to use Boiler Room's logo on marketing materials for the event in question; similar emails went out to promoters around the world, offering the same deal. While Boiler Room's business model had for years relied on precisely this kind of cultural piggy-backing, there was now one crucial difference: the event wouldn't be streamed online, thereby removing the only expense Boiler Room might have incurred, and the only means by which local promoters and artists might stand to benefit from the exchange. It was a plan of almost dizzying ineptitude and cynicism: you do all the work, take on all the risk, provide your labour and cultural capital to us for free – worse than that, *pay us* to effectively work for Boiler Room – and we will do absolutely nothing for you beyond putting our stamp on your work and claiming it as our own. Any lingering questions over Boiler Room's ethics, the benefits of their work for marginalized artists or the grey areas in which benevolent amplification bled into colonial appropriation were all resolved in an instant: this was nothing but extractive, a one-way transfer of capital and agency.

Clark promptly leaked the letter, describing Boiler Room's role within the industry as 'dance music cancer'. Where the PR disaster around Notting Hill had cemented Boiler Room's unedifying reputation with sections of the dancing public, the idea that Boiler Room now expected DJs and promoters to pay *them* for the privilege of handing over credit provoked much the same reaction behind the scenes. While Boiler Room's position as the world's pre-eminent dance music broadcaster meant that boycotting them was a non-starter, any sense of Bellville and co. operating as a force for cultural good was squandered in that instant. In a comment following the leak of the email, Boiler Room promoter Michail Stangl justified the proposed terms on the basis that Boiler Room's logo was enough to draw fee-paying dancers to any event: 'Over [the] years we found that BR has, no matter the region, an incredible pull when it comes to our events, which we are now trying to turn into something positive and financially sustainable for everyone involved.'

The 2019 email not only represented a head-spinning level of disdain for the music Boiler Room had built their business on, but also a last roll of the dice to finally achieve profitability. Instead of throwing free parties and streaming events to a worldwide audience, relying on brand funding to cover the costs, Boiler Room now turned to the last available source of disposable income in the food chain: the dancers themselves. Slowly but surely, fees started creeping in for previously free Boiler Room events, shifting their entire business model from one in which the music remained free at the point of use, to one where everyone involved was either a customer (the in-person attendees coughing up sixty quid a pop to see DJ EZ, at least twice what you might expect to pay elsewhere) or product (the artists subsumed into the Boiler Room brand, or the online viewers whose streaming views and page clicks could be sold on to advertisers and brand partners). Where the act of broadcasting up-and-coming artists to a global audience had once felt like a gesture of support and mutual exchange, it now began to resemble an inadvertent protection racket: artists and labels might no longer like what Boiler Room represent, but they remain a necessary evil; declining to work with them means shutting oneself off from one of the last remaining routes to visibility and ultimately profitability, in an industry where it's becoming harder to survive by the year. In October 2021, Boiler Room finally broke into the black, the result of a $6 million acquisition by ticketing company Dice (who clearly saw value in their pivot to paid events) allowing them to settle up with long-departed and underpaid staff members, healing several long-running wounds.

Boiler Room now exists largely in vestigial form only, its occasional moments of brilliance (like a 2021 broadcast from the British South Asian clubnight Daytimers) offset by broadcasts which serve much the same function for dance music fans as the Cavern Club in Liverpool does for Beatles-obsessed tourists: a heritage name, more lucrative and ubiquitous than ever, permanently severed from the underground cultures it purports to represent. 'It feels like a very special time for all of us . . . this is truly a piece of Boiler Room history,' announces a Boiler Room host in July 2022, introducing pop producer Fred Again (like Bellville, a descendant of minor aristocracy and alumnus of Marlborough College). The room is packed, the crowd consistently hyped throughout the ensuing seventy minutes, but the whole thing feels deeply unsatisfying: carefully stage-managed behind the scenes by Fred's record label, his DJ set of pedestrian pop-house bangers is a dead-eyed facsimile of Boiler Room-y moments, rather than an evocation of any kind of living, breathing culture. I'm reminded of Gabriel Szatan's descriptions of the cringe-inducing branded partnerships undertaken earlier in Boiler Room's history, including one in which a baffled Fiat executive threatened to pull a New York show unless a car was placed on the dance floor in front of the DJs. It's unclear what has changed in the interim, except for the product being sold: sensible four-door hatchbacks replaced by overpriced tickets to Boiler Room's own events.

Ultimately, Boiler Room ended up being to online video what Kiss FM had once been to pirate radio: the sharpest, most forward-thinking underground pioneers of their respective platforms, who broke big but compromised fatally on the principles which got them there, ending up hollowed out by commerce and ultimately retaining little of their original creativity or charm. Boiler Room's cultural decline also revealed just how far they'd diverged from their earliest streaming peers: SB.TV and Jamal Edwards might have signed deals with everyone from Google to the Department for Education, but in 2020 they were still studiously uploading freestyle videos, providing the same platform they'd always done for up-and-coming artists from the UK underground, maintaining the cultural ecosystem on which they ultimately relied rather than strip-mining it for a quick buck. Edwards's career as an entrepreneur might have taken him far away from the ends – sitting on the board of private members' club Soho House and acting as an ambassador for the Prince's Trust – but he also remained fastidious about giving back, volunteering at homeless shelters and youth centres in West London, and indeed launching a charity of his own, before his tragic death in 2022. The comparison with Boiler Room's social outreach efforts remain stark: read the latter's initiatives and statements on everything from electoral politics to Black Lives Matter, and they're always couched in the same tech-industry legalese, offering reassuring bromides without ever properly addressing their own role in whitewashing, extracting value from and undermining the underground scenes on which their success has been built.

In this, though, Boiler Room's narrative arc merely reflects wider trends across the music industry during the 2010s, with grassroots cultures swallowed up by increasingly sophisticated and aggressive commercial interests. In the physical realm, this has meant the centralization and corporatization of control over club spaces. Online, it has seen the balance of power shifting from the traditional centres of industry power – record labels, radio stations and the media – to tech companies. Six months before Boiler Room's first live stream, Spotify launched in the UK, its offer to artists even coarser than the worst Blaise Bellville could come up with: give us not just an hour of time but your entire discography for free, and we'll pay you a pittance in royalties. Streaming's primacy has distorted and disrupted the entire music industry, but has had particular effects within dance music, where recorded music as a physical medium had previously played a critical economic role: when the fledgling Warp Records put out LFO's self-titled debut single in 1990, it sold somewhere in the region of 150,000 copies and set them up financially, while grime artists like Wiley or Dizzee were able to build the foundations of their careers by selling white labels from the boot of their car. For artists trying to break through today, opportunities to generate the income required to sustain a creative practice are far narrower, as value continues to be skimmed off the top by a new generation of gatekeepers. Play a live show for Boiler Room, and maybe someone who watches it will buy your album. Give your album to Spotify for free, and someone who listens to it might buy a ticket to your live show – minus Dice's cut, of course. You may detect an issue here. In both cases tech companies and their investors get paid. Artists at the very top – those whose streaming numbers are substantial enough to provide a sustainable income, or whose profile means they can negotiate a hefty fee from Boiler Room for their time – are able to pay the bills. Everyone else is essentially working at a loss to keep the system running, the economic sustainability of underground music perennially treated as someone else's problem by those making the money.

This brand of 'platform capitalism' is not particularly new, though: for all the claims of innovation made by Spotify CEO Daniel Ek or other self-described tech industry disruptors, the exploitation of aspiring artists by industry gatekeepers and a reliance on free labour has always been a part of dance music. Aspiring producers give away their music for free via informal promo networks, in the hope that a DJ slightly higher up the food chain might like their work, and play it in a club set or radio show. From there, clout and name recognition trickle back down, allowing those on the bottom rungs to begin building a profile for themselves, and hopefully secure their own paid DJ gigs, for which they can then harvest their own supply of promo music. Mid-tier DJs and producers, meanwhile, perform a similar function for those above them: their position grants them access to a certain amount of exclusive music, which they can use to sustain their own careers, while also passing their own more desirable productions onto bigger-name DJs, in the hope of even greater patronage flowing down to them in turn, and ultimately elevating them to their own place in the lucrative festival headliner market. Those at the very top use these inbuilt social and professional advantages to protect their position: their access to the freshest and most in-demand music creates an automatic hook for fans to keep buying tickets to see them, and promoters to keep booking them. At the same time, the tight-knit social bonds which inevitably form within an industry based around nightlife, and the opaque mechanics of the music industry as whole, obscure the means by which the most prominent artists retain their headliner status; establish yourself as a legend, and you can retain that position long after your cultural relevance or creative spark has expired. DJ culture has for decades and by design functioned as an elaborate pyramid scheme, with the few who make it supported by the near-endless and largely under-remunerated cultural production of those who don't – a dynamic which has often served to reinforce existing disparities of class, wealth, gender, race, power and access, abetted by a coterie of managers, PRs, journalists, pluggers and ancillary staff whose own jobs depend on keeping the music and money flowing in the right direction.*

---

* This is obviously a simplification, and does a disservice to the many DJs, promoters, PR agents, journalists, bookers and other dance music workers

In 2017 Richard D. James, better known as abstract techno overlord Aphex Twin, played what was largely referred to as his first UK 'live' set in years at London festival Field Day. His performance interspersed his own productions with music by a host of younger and less well-known artists: the same pyramid scheme as enacted by superstar DJs for decades, now subsumed into a 'live' performance, and a form of culture still loosely branded or understood as countercultural. A decent chunk of his audience could be forgiven for not even realizing that they were listening to music made by other artists. Where a minority of reviews acknowledged the DJ-like quality of the performance, James's magpie approach was lauded for 'proving that a finger on the pulse has always been [his] way of operating' rather than questioning the optics of a big-name artist being paid colossal sums to effectively (if not necessarily intentionally) pass others' work off as his own. This is not a moral question – we have long since passed the point at which questions around the authenticity of the artist are relevant – so much as a structural one. What might lesser-known producers like Fis, Kamixlo or Chino Amobi have done with a proportionate share of the value they helped create for James and Field Day? What might the bedroom DJs and producers of Manchester, Liverpool, São Paulo or Kinshasa have done with a properly apportioned cut of Boiler Room's accrued cultural capital and cold, hard cash? How might the underground scenes which birthed and sustained this music be better strengthened and supported, at a time when the visual mediation of UK dance music has given way to its wholesale co-option by tech platforms, if we were to convince those at the top of the industry to reconsider their relationship with those at the bottom? Maybe this line of thinking is naive. Aphex Twin, having leveraged other artists' work for his 'live' performance, was himself co-opted in

---

who are driven by creative rather than financial concerns, or who support lesser-known talent regardless of their own interests. But it's worth acknowledging that these people are swimming against the tide, in an industry which is ultimately structured to funnel influence and money upwards.

turn, his set broadcast online in a branding exercise for Field Day. Sooner or later, everything ends up as a product to be sold.

But not everything is lost. Just as *The Hitman and Her* or Kiss FM's descent into cultural irrelevance created the space for new visions of UK dance music like *BPM* or Rinse FM to flourish, the same is undoubtedly true of Boiler Room's creative decline. Today, the most important visual platforms for breaking new British artists – certainly Black British MCs and rappers – remain curated YouTube channels like GRM Daily and Link Up TV, which have continued to plough the same steady furrow of freestyles and clashes for a decade or more, albeit with vastly improved production values. Central Cee, arguably the biggest UK rapper of 2022, got his break with a GRM Daily video for 'Day in the Life', which racked up 66 million views in early 2020, before the follow-up video for 'Loading' did double that number; within eighteen months he'd signed to a major label and his debut album *Wild West* had hit Number 2 in the charts. Meanwhile, startups like Resonate, a streaming platform owned cooperatively by the artists whose music it features, and Aslice, a software platform designed to track each of the tunes a DJ plays in a club set, and automatically distribute a percentage of their gig fee to the artists in question, offer us new ways to think about power relationships within dance music.

In the midst of the Covid pandemic in 2020, Black-owned online radio station No Signal found an opportunity to branch out into streaming video. The idea of using YouTube had originally come from co-founder Jojo Sonubi's dad – 'You know how it goes with Nigerian parents,' he told an interviewer in December of that year. 'They have an idea of what they want for you, they have their own plan and unfortunately, that's a struggle in itself.' But Sonubi's dad was right: when No Signal took their NS10v10 show onto YouTube, it blew up. The format was simple: the ten best tracks from two artists, played off against each other by No Signal hosts in a soundclash style, with listeners voting for their favourite on Twitter after each of the ten rounds, and discussing proceedings using the #NS10v10 hashtag. For the clash in May 2020 between Vybz Kartel and Wizkid, upwards of a million people locked in across YouTube and No Signal's own website, from ninety-nine different countries. 'It's evident that black people in particular are consistently engaged with organic content,' wrote Jumi Akinfenwa in advertising trade magazine *Campaign*, eulogizing the station's success. 'There are no strategists, marketing teams or break-out rooms, just pure, unadulterated fun, created by and for black people.' Initially, No Signal just used YouTube to livestream the radio station's audio feed, but by the end of August, and 2020's online-only edition of Notting Hill Carnival, they'd added video to the mix. In a stroke of curatorial genius, they reframed the NS10v10 concept for Carnival weekend to focus on steel pan bands, dividing 22-time Carnival competition winners Ebony into two teams, and having them go tune for tune against each other. It was a moment of pure synthesis: Black cultural ingenuity and heritage brought together to create something beautiful out of a moment of lockdown-induced struggle and uncertainty; the same grass-roots cultural energy and upstart defiance which had once catalysed *The Hitman And Her* or Boiler Room, and with which those earlier platforms had eventually lost touch.

Following the pandemic, No Signal returned to their core business of radio rather than Boiler Room-esque video streams, while much of the audio and video from NS10v10 has since been pulled from YouTube due to copyright claims, perhaps reflecting the difficulties facing upstart platforms without industry links or legal teams; 'Some of these white mainstream platforms are so lucky,' Sonubi said in December 2020. 'They're able to put money into something that nobody cares about. For black people, we're not always afforded that luxury of being able to have money pumped in.' But in the fragments of visual documentation which remain – sixty seconds of Ebony playing a steel pan cover of Kranium's 'Gal Policy' uploaded to Twitter, No Signal's presenters laughing and singing along, the song's melodies simultaneously euphoric and laced with an ineffable sadness – you can sense the cultural space available here once more, waiting to be reclaimed and reimagined by anyone daring and dedicated enough to do so.

CAVERNOUS LONDON RAVE VENUE
PRINTWORKS, 2022

10. Strictly Business Techno

Gentrification and resistance in the night-time economy

The experience is always the same. You buy your tickets from Resident Advisor, the global dance music website whose editorial content is bankrolled by the cut it receives from purchases made through its ticketing portal, and which now operates a near-monopoly on sales for UK dance music events. Maybe you heard about the party via an article on Resident Advisor or another online content platform – either editorially commissioned on its own merits, or manufactured as part of a branded media partnership with a big-name promoter – or via social media, after your account was algorithmically identified as that of a dance music fan and advertising space within it sold to those same promoters. Maybe you follow one of the DJs playing here, whose contract will have obliged them to undertake a specified level of pre-event social media promotion. Maybe you've previously bought tickets for another venue, festival or event owned by the same umbrella company catering to your needs tonight, through which your contact details and purchase history were fed into a huge marketing database. Either way, you're funnelled briskly through an online 'consumer journey' before reaching the Resident Advisor purchase page, which offers you a selection of tiered-price tickets: the cheapest ones sell first, with breathless updates on dwindling ticket numbers fed back onto the promoter's social channels to encourage others. You arrive earlier than you'd like – your reduced-price ticket is also time-limited, obliging you to get in shortly after the venue opens and spend more at the bar – to be searched by a dispassionate man in a hi-vis overcoat, who scans the QR code on your phone, then your photo ID, saving the latter onto a digital database retained by the venue.

When you get inside, the space is starkly post-industrial, its bricks and steel beams left exposed. It's named after the building's original function: a factory, warehouse, printing press or garage. A can of Red Stripe costs you £7. The dance floor is arranged to subtly funnel attention towards the DJ: they're dimly lit but raised on a stage or in a booth, able to be seen by everyone without ever making too big a deal of that fact. Visual needs are instead met by the lighting design, which switches between a mesh of spotlights playing over the exposed beams, pummelling strobes and soft washes of colour; depending on the size of venue, you might find sinuous, abstract visuals adorning a massive and unfathomably expensive LED screen at the back of the stage. The DJ playing when you arrive is local, a close friend of the promoters who supplements his day job as a graphic designer for a tech company with regular warm-up sets around the city and a monthly show on a highly regarded internet radio station. Following him will be a studiously hip twenty-something flown in from Berlin, sporting transparent-rimmed glasses and a selection of obscure tattoos. They're dating a bigger-name electronic music producer and share a flat with someone who does social media for a dance music festival, who connected them to a small but highly respected vinyl-only imprint as well as a booking and PR agency, all of whom are now pushing them furiously as the next big thing. They'll get their first big cover story in two months, and by the summer will be wedged firmly in the line-ups of a variety of electronic music festivals across continental Europe, each funded by their respective governments as a means of boosting tourism income. Headlining tonight will be a sixty-year-old man from the United States, who hasn't released a decent record in twenty years and barely even listens to dance music any more, but retains an absolutely consummate level of professionalism, mixing his way flawlessly through a two-hour set combining the requisite number of familiar classics with newer tunes harvested and pre-screened for him by a team of interns. His frictionless affect and mechanical precision sit somewhere between the automobile construction lines of Detroit and the flawless delivery of a classically trained concert violinist: his next UK gig, perhaps not coincidentally, will be an elaborate high-concept piece with a full orchestra performed at the Barbican. Across the eight hours the club is open these three DJs will play a functionally indistinct and entirely unbroken succession of tracks containing 4/4 kickdrums and synthetic effects at between 128 and 135bpm through a Funktion-One soundsystem to a crowd made up of urban professionals between the ages of twenty-two and thirty-eight wearing monochrome clothes. Six months later, you will read that the venue has been demolished as part of a multi-billion pound redevelopment project.

UK dance music has always been defined by the physical spaces in which it takes place, its history one of repeated ebb and flow between the densely packed inner city and the more open spaces of the suburbs and countryside, accompanied by a more gradual and linear centralization of financial and political power over these varied spaces. The arrival of acid house in late 1987 saw the epicentre of UK dance music relocate from grassroots community-controlled venues on the urban fringes – blues dances in the terraced houses of St Paul's, rare groove warehouses in Tottenham, and pre-Ecstasy house nights in Moss Side youth clubs – to licensed clubs in the heart of the city, from Shoom and R.I.P. in Southwark to Spectrum under the arches of Charing Cross. As the Second Summer of Love took hold, and it became impossible to contain rave's explosive energy within the walls of the city, rave burst back out into the industrial hinterlands of Blackburn, the verdant commons of Castlemorton and countless brownfield sites around the M25, before the Criminal Justice Act corralled the party back into bricks-and-mortar venues once again. UK dance music's canonical narratives *Energy Flash* and *Altered State* both draw to a close in the early 2000s with the shuttering or scaling-back of city-centre super-clubs like Cream and Gatecrasher, but this was arguably just another cycle of relocation: Britain's glossy high-street temples to hedonism replaced by the less glamorous pockets of suburbia where far more vibrant dance music was now being made, from grime in Bow to dubstep in Croydon. When, in turn, house and techno returned to cultural prominence in the early 2010s, they became the focus of commercial and spatial interests which rapidly came to dwarf even the biggest superclubs of the 90s.

This relentless push-and-pull between the inner and outer city, and the slow consolidation of spatial control by corporate rather than communal interests, have shaped UK dance music not just geographically but culturally, determining the audiences, aesthetics and politics which are privileged or marginalized on each new dance floor. The blues dance's soundtrack of lovers' rock, Sixties soul and roots reggae was tailored to tight-knit local communities of Black listeners who'd grown up with their parents' Blaupunkt stereo selections, a collective cultural understanding of the music inextricable from the domestic context in which it was played: 'There was an intimacy there, a sharing that you don't get in a club,' recounted Moss Side blues dance regular Owen Townsend in 2011. The chaotic, non-hierarchical and open-ended venues for 1990s free parties, from dingy suburban squats to temporarily autonomous pieces of common land, were filled with the sounds of breakbeat hardcore: a 'collage mess-thetic' of splattered drum loops and distorted basslines, its frenetic imprecision tailor-made for the free party's anarchic surroundings.* The physical space of the 1990s superclub, meanwhile, had precisely the opposite impact: its scale and spectacle were instead essential parts of a carefully designed mass-market sensory overload. To get the full effect of somewhere like Gatecrasher, you not only needed a dizzying light show and a brash soundtrack of hyper-euphoric trance bangers, but also a vast and overwhelming space crammed with thousands upon thousands of dancing bodies, glowsticks and lasers visible through a thick fog of dry ice. Berghain, the vast Berlin club opened in a former power station in the early 2000s, whose brutalist-hedonist aesthetic has been shamelessly borrowed by countless UK dance music venues since, has even birthed its own discrete subgenre of techno: tracks are engineered by producers or selected by DJs with specific reference to its cavernous and reverberant concrete spaces, just as polyphonic sacred music was composed to make use of cathedrals' natural reverb, or baroque chamber music was once written with the size of aristocratic drawing rooms in mind.

Either side of the financial crash of 2008, remorseless upward pressures on property prices and rents have continued to shape the spatial and sonic characteristics of UK dance music. From Soho to Shoreditch to Dalston to Hackney Wick to Tottenham, clubs have been both victim and harbinger of repeated waves of gentrification, radiating out from the city centre and pushing those affected towards its periphery. Muscled out of a given neighbourhood by office blocks and luxury residential towers, late-night activity relocates to cheaper and edgier neighbourhoods further from the

---

* This connection was further accentuated by the muddy sonics of truck-based rigs, which were punishingly loud but inevitably less precise than a club soundsystem calibrated to the layout of a particular room: space, sound and politics all pulling in the same raw and radical direction.

centre; new cultural activity in those areas drives new interest, and draws in new money; demographics slowly change, patterns of demand shift, and rents start rising; artists and venues find themselves priced out by the very people and processes they attracted to the area in the first place, and the cycle begins again. These nebulous economic forces have been amplified by more deliberate political choices, with austerity-induced budget cuts incentivizing local authorities and police forces to relocate or minimize the expensive and time-consuming mess and disorder associated with late-night venues, through stricter licensing rules and more assertive policing. At the same time, councils have encouraged the growth of larger daytime festivals in urban parks, on the basis that these are easier to police, and replenish rather than drain public coffers through promoters paying hefty fees to use public space: a budget-conscious inversion of the free party's annexation of the commons. In the second half of the 2010s and early 2020s, this relationship between gentrification, local politics and dance music became noticeably more intentional: despite occupying much the same kinds of brownfield sites as the orbital raves of 1989 or Spiral Tribe parties of 1992, venues like Printworks in London now work hand-in-hand with developers and councils on vast residential and commercial regeneration projects, operating on temporary leases in areas earmarked for demolition and reinvention as shiny new offices, shops and flats. Where dance music's interactions with physical space previously positioned it as an alternative to (or collateral damage from) wider economic and political power structures, it's now used quite deliberately to reinforce those same interests: a tool with which to erase a given neighbourhood's unwanted associations with post-industrial grot, and overwrite it with something sexier and more aspirational, before the bulldozers move in.

Over the last decade and half, these financial and political pressures have increasingly constricted and standardized the physical spaces in which dance music can operate, and thus the music itself. Threats of relocation and regulation have seen hundreds of small venues close across the UK (in the decade to 2015 more than half of the country's licensed clubs disappeared) allowing larger multi-venue operators and entertainment conglomerates, far better-equipped to handle such shocks, to expand into the space left behind: 'Every single change, every single licensing implementation leads to a cost. And it rules out the existence of a lot of venues,' Andy Peyton of the Columbo Group, owners of London clubs XOYO and Phonox amongst others, said in a 2016 Resident Advisor interview.

Peyton's comments are particularly unsettling given that the Columbo Group's multi-venue portfolio, along with interests in several London daytime festivals, means that they occupy the upper echelons of the dance music food chain, running from similarly sized national entertainment conglomerates like DHP Family (owner of Stealth in Nottingham and the Thekla in Bristol) to multibillion-pound developer-funded promoters like Broadwick Live (in charge of Printworks and Manchester's Depot Mayfield) and global entertainment behemoths like AEG. It's these businesses which have replaced the 90s superclub, their highly commercialized operations, revolving door of senior staff and corporate funding sources remaining largely hidden from dance music fans. In 2012, Cream owner James Barton sold up to American mega-promoter Live Nation, becoming the latter's first global President of Electronic Music. Live Nation's main competitor AEG followed them into the UK market in 2018 with the launch of All Points East, after winning a contract from Tower Hamlets Council to run events in Victoria Park, East London, forcing pre-existing dance music festivals Field Day and Lovebox to relocate. Founded as independent events, both Field Day and Lovebox had themselves been bought out in preceding years, the latter by events conglomerate MAMA, the former by promotion company Broadwick Live. In 2015, Broadwick signed a deal with Global Entertainment (owners of mass-market radio stations like Classic FM and LBC) for control of their festival portfolio, including Field Day along with South West Four, Boardmasters and a dozen others. In 2019, those events were sold on once again to Superstruct Entertainment, the LA-based company founded by James Barton after leaving Live Nation, with financial backing from private investment firm Providence Equity.

In addition to their insulation from financial and political pressures which might sink smaller competitors, it's these organizations who've benefited most from growth at the upper end of the UK dance music market, like day festivals and public–private redevelopment partnerships: opportunities which remain inaccessible to anyone but the biggest industry players. As these businesses have grown, narrower corporate interests increasingly dictate where, when and with whom we're able to dance, catering to the more affluent, cosmopolitan audiences who'll give their investors bigger returns, rather than the weirdos and the already-marginalized: a gentrification of the dance floor itself, not just the neighbourhood it occupies. Even as the dance music being made and played across the UK has continued to evolve and diversify at a thrilling rate, this consolidation of spatial control, under a decreasing number of increasingly wealthy, powerful and inter-linked entities, has served to homogenize the wider experience of being in a club, ultimately narrowing UK dance music's creative and social possibilities.

If the prototypical UK club or festival dance floor of the early 2020s has its own equivalent to 'the Berghain sound' or the chamber concerto of the 1700s, then it's one outlined broadly at the beginning of this chapter: a style loosely defined or derided as 'business techno'. This is dance music designed expressly for the exposed-concrete developer-funded superclub and the inner-city day festival, tailored specifically to the tastes and interests of the people attending those venues: predominantly young urban professionals, largely straight and/or white, majority male, looking for a reliable and accessible good time to share with their friends. Business techno does not, despite this particular audience focus, emerge organically from any specific geographic or cultural community, beyond identifying a specific target market to sell itself to: this is a club night for drum'n'bass heads between the ages of twenty-five and forty-two, that is a festival for queer clubbers who don't own a car.

One of the key identifying features of business techno is a

near-total absence of place-based specificity, allowing the same formats and sounds to be transplanted seamlessly between Brixton, Birmingham, Berlin, Brooklyn and Bogotá. That geographical transience is accompanied by tight vertical integration: unlike the superclubs of the 1990s, in which a promoter like Cream would collaborate with a venue like Nation, splitting ticket sales and bar profits between them, the new superclubs of the 2010s and 2020s keep everything inhouse, retaining all income and only paying for one set of back-office staff. Economies of scale kick in more dramatically for multi-venue operators, from relationships with the production companies who provide their lighting and sound, to exclusivity clauses for artists, which temporarily bar them from playing other shows in a given city, effectively locking competing (usually smaller) venues out of the market.

There are plenty of other telltale signs you can look out for if you're concerned you may have accidentally ended up at a business techno event. One of the easiest involves checking the proportion of dancers who are, at any given moment, taking selfies or filming proceedings on their phones. Between the extravagant light shows, the artfully distressed post-industrial chic of an indoor venue or the strictly demarcated pleasure zones fenced off within your local park, business techno is designed to be seen as much as heard, and the lure towards capturing the moment is incessant. Look, there are some lasers playing delicately over exposed steel beams in a breathtakingly vast turbine hall; wow, there's global dance music icon Peggy Gou sashaying elegantly as she drops a disco re-edit at sunset; oh my God, there's wistful house impresario Four Tet fiddling about with a sample of Ellie Goulding's voice while bathed in an infinite sea of blinking LED lights. Business techno caters with unerring accuracy to the contemporary need for social capital, and understands the pivotal role of photos and video in accruing it, recruiting us as unwitting and unpaid brand ambassadors in the process: the act of memorializing our presence, encouraged both implicitly and overtly by these events, bolsters our own sense of meaning and value while reminding the friends who missed out to buy a ticket next time.

Another key sign that you've stepped into the world of business techno is the music on offer. While this isn't always an exact science, and certainly isn't limited strictly to techno rather than other dance music genres, there's a certain sense of predictability and safeness to every set you hear: Detroit veterans booked to play the classics will play the classics; house and disco *selectors* (always marketed as such, as if the refinement of their record bag means that merely being a DJ is ever so slightly beneath them) will knock out the friction-free good-time vibes; fresh international faces booked to inject new energy into proceedings (and attract a new generation of fans and customers) will play the trippiest new sounds coming out of the bedsits of Kreuzberg and the lofts of Brooklyn. If anyone plans to deviate from the material you might reasonably expect from them — an industrial techno bludgeoner doing an hour of handbag house, say — this will be mined for novelty marketing value and trumpeted loudly ahead of time. There will be, to go all the way back to Theodor Adorno, a conspicuous sense of 'rhythmic obedience' — kickdrums will kick without interruption, hi-hats will fizz and sizzle on every offbeat, the technological advances of digital DJing, with tracks beat-mapped in advance and auto-synced in the moment, will ensure that every mix is flawless. The sound will of course be perfect, produced by row upon row of Funktion-One stacks — filling the room, thudding relentlessly into your chest, propelling you deeper and deeper into the music. None of this is to say that the experience will be *bad* — in fact it will usually be immensely pleasurable, rooted in consummate technical and curatorial skill on the part of the DJs, alongside faultless production chops and a keen understanding of the market from the organizers. But it will, almost subconsciously, be defined by a feeling of constraint: your expectations won't ever be challenged; your understanding of the sonic possibilities of the club won't expand; your sense of what a dance floor is ultimately *for* will not change.

Just as important as the music played by the average business techno DJ, though, is *how* they play it: a certain grammar of performance, difficult to explain but impossible to ignore once you see it, best explained by way of comparison. One of the great artefacts in UK dance music history is a thirty-minute segment of low-quality camcorder footage filmed at a club called Time & Envy in Romford on New Year's Day 2003, capturing the first UK appearance of New York garage producer and DJ Todd Edwards – indeed his first real club set of any kind. Having toiled away in obscurity in his home country throughout the 1990s, Edwards's productions became highly sought-after in the UK 'speed garage' scene at the turn of the century, his skippy beats and chopped-up vocal samples pounced on by British DJs looking for US import tunes they could pitch up to 130bpm. By the time the reclusive Edwards finally came over to play in the UK, garage producers inspired by him had taken over the British charts and he'd become a quasi-mythical figure: this video shows him realizing, in real time and with no prior warning, that he's a superstar. There's so much to love about it, from the crowd's gelled hair and shiny shirts perfectly evoking the suburban UK garage scene of the early 2000s, to the mass hysteria which breaks out before the beat even kicks in on Edwards's first tune, which is duly reloaded within seconds. But best of all is the reaction of Edwards himself: a rictus grin accompanied by some extremely self-conscious bopping behind the decks and awestruck glances back at his fellow DJs, his emotions somewhere between bemused affability and abject terror in the face of the mayhem unfolding on the dance floor. He cues up the next record with a mixture of studiousness and anxiety, like a nervous intern on their first day in the office: it's the opposite of a performance, and all the more powerful for it.

Fast forward to 2012, and DJ EZ – the person who'd booked Edwards to appear in Romford nine years earlier – is playing a set for Boiler Room, replete with all of the dizzying technical dexterity and hyperspeed mixing for which he's known. He punches a button on his CDJ, and a snippet of Wookie's 'Battle' is looped in perfect time with the beat. He reaches for the mixer, filtering the track down in the mix. Over the top, he repeatedly triggers a snatch of vocals from a bootleg grime remix of Cleptomaniacs' pop-garage classic 'All I Do' on the other CDJ while yanking its pitch fader back and forth, playing the sample up and down the octaves with all the craftsmanship and intensity of an 1980s rock star shredding an epic guitar solo. In a single fluid movement, his right hand whipping up over his head, he cuts the Wookie loop and drops the beat: the crowd becomes a seething mass of limbs, in a moment which has gone down in Boiler Room history and played a critical role in cementing its reputation as the epicentre of UK dance music, early on in its meteoric journey towards global domination. It's rooted in the diamond-sharp DJ skills EZ honed in clubs exactly like Time & Envy in Romford, but also a sense of visual spectacle, accentuated by the presence of a camera perched next to the decks: his dizzying hand speed akin to a close-up magician wowing you with feats of wizardry.

Fast forward another six years, and it's that feeling of artifice which has come to define the performative language of business techno, encapsulated in a UK garage set by dubstep producer Hatcha and house DJ Sam Divine at a festival in Croatia run by Defected – the UK house and garage label which originally put out 'All I Do', now largely synonymous with unadventurous mass-market house raves and lucrative chart-dance fodder. The music has barely changed from Edwards's day – 'Battle', released some eighteen years earlier, gets played forty minutes in – while the set itself is specifically marketed as a garage set, a novelty excursion from Hatcha and Divine's usual interests. Both DJs' body language is a carbon copy of EZ's, all tight-shouldered wiggling behind the decks and precise hand movements. But everything feels . . . off, somehow. They grip the knobs and faders in exaggerated fashion, arms flexing in time with the music, even when the close-up Boiler Room-style camera shows that they're not moving anything on the mixer or altering the sound in any way. When they let go of the controls, they flick their fingers away with over-the-top EZ-inspired suddenness, a practice jokingly referred to elsewhere as 'hotknobbing'. Stepping back from the decks, they dance with the lugubrious ease of people who are entirely comfortable with being watched, and gesture expansively to the dance floor: the camera pans over the crowd, their eyes collectively locked on the stage, smartphone cameras raised as a mediocre two-step remix of Whitney Houston's 'It's Not Right but It's Okay' plays.

This is dance music designed to be looked at and talked over, rather than listened to or lived within, the visual language of EZ's dizzying DJ flourishes stripped of the craft which gave them meaning: a change in performance style which speaks entirely to the narrowing effects of corporate capture. This is partly a question of audience expectations, the search for a perfect Instagram moment with a big-name DJ under the Croatian sun, but it's also about wider marketing strategies: the set is filmed in glossy high-definition by Defected's own video team, racking up a quarter of a million views on YouTube. For DJs, the increasing visual attention involved in business techno – from Boiler Room's career-making possibilities to the audience-building necessity of social media, and the tacit knowledge that your sets are being recorded, shared and rewatched as a matter of course – demands that you cultivate a visual presence as an artist, as critical a skill as knowing how to beatmatch. Once you spot this style of performance, you see it everywhere across contemporary UK dance music: a sense of self-aware and vaguely theatrical *busyness*, each DJ alternating between studied (and occasionally unnecessary) knob-twiddling, grand stagey gestures, and lithe shuffling performed for the gaze of others. It couldn't be more different from watching a sheepish Todd Edwards fumble his way around the DJ booth and, for all the stagecraft involved, tends to end up far less interesting or engaging.

The road leading to business techno's domination of UK dance music's physical and performative forms begins with the election of the Coalition government in 2010, and the austerity politics introduced by David Cameron and George Osborne. Students and other young people, always a key audience for dance music, were hit with drastically inflated tuition costs or the removal of their Education Maintenance Allowance: as they stormed Millbank and inner-city Britain burned during the 2011 riots, the Saturday night clubbing rituals memorialized in *Spaced* and *Human Traffic* began to feel less and less relevant to the lives of young Britons; between 2010 and 2015 annual visits to nightclubs dropped from 149 million to 115 million, with revenue falling by more than a fifth. But austerity also created substantial issues around managing and catering to the millions of people who were still going out dancing, with swingeing cuts to local government funding requiring councils to pare back non-essential spending with brutal efficiency. For many boroughs, the noise, disruption and anti-social behaviour associated with late-night venues rapidly became an unwelcome and distracting drain on resources: every pound spent hosing vomit off the high street or dealing with noise complaints felt like one taken away from more immediate priorities like social care.

In 2013, Hackney Council proposed new measures which would effectively bar new clubs from opening in areas they felt had reached 'saturation point', introducing a Special Policy Area in Dalston which made it next to impossible for new venues to get a late licence, or for existing spaces to extend their opening hours. This was followed in 2017 by an additional council tax levy on any venue serving alcohol after midnight, and the year after by doubling the size of the Special Policy Area and instigating a strict midnight curfew for all new premises. In 2016 the neighbourhood's pre-eminent dance music venue Dance Tunnel – a narrow, sweaty basement with a killer soundsystem and adventurous booking policy – closed its doors for good, explicitly blaming the 'licensing climate in Hackney [which] has made it impossible for us to get the [opening] hours we need' before going silent. 'The whole structure around licences is geared towards stopping bad things happening, when the reality is that licensed venues are generators of culture, and can be economically regenerative,' Dance Tunnel's owner Dan Beaumont told me in exasperated tones several years later. 'But none of those ideas can ever be reflected in licensing decisions.' Where clubs weren't actively forced to close as result of measures like these, their passive effects could still have an effect, draining the love and optimism out of spaces and reducing their existence to a mere fight for survival. While the 2013 closure of Plastic People, one of the most influential and beloved small clubs in recent UK history, didn't stem directly from state interference, a police-initiated review of its licence in 2010, resulting in restrictions on the volume at which its soundsystem could operate, undoubtedly marked the point at which the vibe began to shift.

Austerity played a pivotal role in undermining the UK's small dance music venues, but it had the opposite effect elsewhere in the industry. Despite substantial falls in nightclub attendance, house and techno remained big business, returning to media prominence having spent much of the previous decade eclipsed by garage, grime and dubstep, and assisted by the return of high-strength Ecstasy to the UK market. While fewer people might have been going out to clubs, they were still flocking to other events, dancing to more intense music and taking more potent drugs in the process; between 2015 and 2019 the amount spent on tickets for festivals across the UK more than doubled, spent across nearly 1,000 different events. 'Nightclub culture is dying out, definitely,' one young woman from Peterborough told a reporter from the BBC in a 2015 news segment. 'None of my friends go out to nightclubs, it's more festivals or bars. They'll save up for that big festival instead.'

Where disorder around late-night venues had caused headaches for local government, the same demand would also, when channelled into other forms, present an opportunity. Even as the number of high-street clubs across Britain went into freefall, the number of daytime festivals held in parks and other urban open spaces skyrocketed – Field Day, Sunfall, Parklife, Newsam Park, Boundary Brighton, All Points East and dozens of others joining 1990s stalwarts like Creamfields – actively encouraged, in many cases, by the same councils clamping down elsewhere on smaller venues playing largely the same music. The reasons for this are primarily economic: the nature of day festivals mean that councils can charge substantial fees for promoters looking to hire out the huge swathes of public green space required to host them; contracts also pass the costs of managing post-event crowds and clearing up mess onto the promoters, while entry points to the festival can be tightly controlled and monitored, making life easier for the police. If you gave public authorities the choice between ten high-street clubs with capacity for a hundred people opening every Saturday night of the year, or a 26,000-person festival running over one weekend, it's clear their interests would be better served by the latter. But there's also a subtler cultural influence at play here: festivals inherently attract a different crowd from a nightclub, shorn of the faintly sordid connotations of late-night spaces and rooted in a more laid-back, cosmopolitan vibe, tacitly if not overtly aligned with more middle-class experiences. Several day festivals place particular emphasis on their more upmarket qualities: the first edition of Gala in South London was promoted as 'a festival of independent music, food and drink' with artisanal food trucks and local craft breweries given equal billing alongside the DJ line-up. Festivals and clubs might play the same music, but the former invariably feel far more like something you might take your parents to.

This sense of aspirational glossiness and polite respectability is detectable elsewhere across the business techno landscape: dance music functioning not just as an end in itself, but as a subtle signifier of social status and cultural refinement. When a particular strain of monolithic, monochrome industrial techno came to dominate the UK's festival headline slots and post-industrial rave cathedrals during the mid-2010s, it was the clubbing scene in Berlin (and one club, Berghain, in particular) which was most often cited as its source, with a conspicuous number of increasingly prominent bookings accruing to European DJs as a result, along with Berghain itself becoming an international techno tourist destination. Despite playing broadly the same music, the UK's own industrial techno underground – like the long-running and hugely influential House of God night in Birmingham – seemed to remain far more peripheral in that conversation, its DJs largely left out of the genre's reabsorption into the dance music mainstream. Maybe imbalances like this are just the inevitable result of increasingly globalized networks of cultural influences, and the breaking down of regional and national borders. But it's also hard to escape the feeling that class signifiers, or at least the marketability of different visions of dance music, have played a role.

This suspicion is heightened by the treatment doled out to other regional UK dance music genres, from the uncompromising but bouncy 4/4 sounds of makina in Newcastle and the cartoon hardcore of donk in Liverpool, to the frenetic overload of Scotland's PCDJ scene: all heavily connoted with working-class audiences, all largely overlooked by the media and wider dance music industry in favour of glossier global sounds, treated as unserious and embarrassingly parochial, or granted attention only when filtered through the curatorial lens of more credible tastemakers. At the same time, a number of far more aspirational micro-trends have flourished: like high-profile DJs collaborating with experimental chefs, spinning a tastefully curated selection of tunes to accompany feats of molecular gastronomy in something approaching a rave-infused middle-class dinner party. Elsewhere, dance music has been subsumed into the wellness industry and late-capitalist productivity chic, with early morning alchol-free raves positioned as the perfect tonic to prime yourself for the working week; or it's been wrapped in audiophile fetishization, with strenous marketing attention placed on the sonic superiority offered by the presence of rotary mixers, valve amplifiers and time-aligned tweeter arrays.

This process of subtle class-based gatekeeping applies to the structures of the business techno industry as well as its changing tastes. With barriers to entry raised by an increasingly stratified hierarchy of commercial operators, breaking through requires not only talent and persistence, but also time spent building a career, connections within the industry and demonstrable marketability, all qualities which tend to accrue more readily to certain social groups. 'If you're a young artist who happens to be from a less-privileged background then you're probably not gonna have the time to focus solely on your music because you'll be working full-time,' the producer and DJ Pessimist told Resident Advisor in early 2023. 'Meanwhile there's a lot of mediocre talent about at the moment that has been propped up by financial backing, family support and the fact that these people have the time on their hands to fully commit themselves.'

While issues of class, financial agency and access remain critical, it would be foolish to assume that those at the top of the food chain are immune to risk: even the biggest and most influential nightclubs in the UK have faced threats from struggles over money, physical space and notions of social respectability. Founded in late 1999, Fabric is perhaps the last of the UK's original 1990s superclubs still operating in something like its original form, with its more ambitious curatorial decisions and ability to shift with changing tastes keeping it culturally relevant as its competitors have faded.* But none of this counted for anything when two drug-related deaths in June and August 2016 sparked an undercover Metropolitan Police operation to assess the extent of usage and dealing inside the club, which ended up with Islington Council rescinding their licence and forcing them to close. The internal documents produced by the police in arguing to the council that the club should be closed, along with the political and popular response to that decision, are a roll-call of antiquated and predictable policing tropes, de-emphasizing measures like drug testing and harm reduction in favour of archaic prohibitionism and stiff-armed spatial authority. A previous licence hearing in 2014 had seen the Met demand that Fabric implement (and pay for) a pack of sniffer dogs on the door, as well as scanning and retaining customers' ID; officers were knocked back in

---

* When it opened in 1999, Fabric's main competitor was expected to be Home, a superclub in Leicester Square originally earmarked as Cream's London venue; delays and disputes over the plans saw Cream founder Darren Hughes split off from business partner James Barton to launch Home as a separate entity. Stripped of the brand recognition Cream would have brought with it, outpaced by a changing market in which 1990s superclub glitz no longer held the same sway, and hounded by the police over drug use, Home lasted all of eighteen months before its licence was revoked and it went into receivership, leaving the way clear for Fabric to become the capital's pre-eminent clubbing venue.

humiliating fashion when both conditions were overturned in the local magistrates' court on the basis of cost and, in the latter instance, privacy. You can detect a faint hint of sniffiness around this in their 2016 report, which argues that in the absence of such measures, and given the overwhelming evidence of Fabric's capitulation to unchecked drug abuse, there's no option but to revoke the club's licence entirely.

Reading the statements of the two undercover officers sent in to investigate, it's hard to ascertain exactly what they're relying on to justify this. They note that Fabric's entry searches are conducted less exhaustively than would be ideal; once inside, one of the officers sees a dancer putting something in his mouth, but can't be sure what it was; a man goes into a darkened alcove and then comes back out again; someone else in the smoking area has his shirt off. The closest thing to actual evidence is a pair of empty plastic baggies found behind a bin in the toilets. Most of the report consists of recounting what other people say about drugs: someone's mate is a dealer who was apparently at Fabric last week; someone else confesses that they took their drugs too early, and they're now keen to find some more; a former work colleague of one of the two men who died recalls someone *else* saying that Fabric's a good place to score. The gravitas with which the police recount such unconvincing material gives the distinct impression that Fabric's guilt has been pre-determined, a feeling underlined by the code name given to the investigation: Operation Lenor, a glib pun on a brand of fabric softener. Despite the limited nature of the police's allegations and the 900-odd pages of public submissions submitted in support of Fabric remaining open, Islington Council voted to revoke its licence.

The fallout from across the dance music world was immediate and vociferous: open letters were written, petitions were signed, hashtags flooded social channels, press outlets voiced their outrage, and somewhere in the region of a quarter of a million pounds was raised to keep the club's lights on and pay for its legal bills. It was easy to see why Fabric had aroused such intense feeling: if a club this well respected and securely established could be brought to its knees, then what hope did anyone else have? But the reaction also inadvertently said something about the centralization and hierarchies of the business techno industry: hundreds of smaller clubs across the UK had closed without anything like the same reaction, including those of profound and unique cultural importance. But then they were only local community spaces rather than world-leading culture brands with millions of followers. Fabric certainly didn't deserve to close, but the imbalance in resources available to its owners to challenge that injustice, and the fates of other spaces unable to leverage the same resources in their own defence, remains stark.

Similar issues arose in 2020 when beloved Glasgow venue the Sub Club announced a fundraiser to help it battle development plans for a site next door whose owners – the pub chain Wetherspoons – wanted to build a hotel. However, it subsequently transpired that the plot in question had been sold to Wetherspoons by the parents of one of the Sub Club's owners for over a million pounds: punters were being asked to bail the club out of a property deal they themselves had been closely connected to. Shortly afterwards the club's other owner – whose family's wealth has been estimated at £90 million by *The Sunday Times*'s Rich List – was forced into a grovelling apology for a number of bafflingly tone-deaf social media posts, including photos of him flying to Berlin in a private plane to celebrate his celebrity DJ friend Peggy Gou's birthday. Questions about which venues occupy the most space in this conversation, and what that means for the sustainability of the wider UK dance music ecosystem, feel stark and uncomfortable.

This disconnect was reflected in political responses to Fabric's closure. For London's newly elected Mayor Sadiq Khan (the man to whom the Met Police were ultimately answerable), Fabric's closure was the perfect opportunity to live up to manifesto pledges around supporting London's nightlife. In November 2016, he appointed promoter, writer and DJ Amy Lamé as the UK's first Night Czar, with a remit to bring together various factions involved in the twenty-four-hour city, and improve the situation for cleaners, clubbers and cab drivers alike. 'The first thing Sadiq said to me when I started my role was, "You have to get Fabric reopened,"' Lamé explains, indicating the extent to which Islington and the Met's actions had become a political hot potato. Her appointment also pointed to the embrace by political decision-makers of a concept known as the 'night-time economy'. It's a line of thinking which connects back to the Blair government's concept of the 'creative industries' and the idea that theatre, art, even clubbing don't just matter because they make us feel good, but because they employ people and spark investment. The night-time economy extends that principle into the early hours of the morning: shadowy backstreets and late-night clubs are no longer treated as sordid or suspicious, but recognized as a key cog in the British economy and a potential source of both GDP and creative innovation: the business, if you will, of business techno.

Over the course of the 2010s, the idea of the night-time economy became increasingly notable in discourse around UK dance music, from the efforts of lobbying groups like the Night Time Industries Association to the appointment of Night Czars in Bristol and Manchester to help steer policy responses which might better support the night-time sector. While part of the appeal for this shift in priorities might have been cultural and altruistic, part of it was also sharply mercantile: in an era when the traditional UK high street has been ruthlessly gutted by online retail, nightclubs are one of few businesses still drawing people back into Britain's urban centres; by bringing nightlife into the political mainstream, Sadiq Khan and others promised to make our late-night experiences bigger, better, safer and more successful. With the priorities of the mayor made painfully clear to Islington Council and the Met, and with Lamé acting as a peacemaker, by the beginning of 2017 clubbers were gleefully streaming back through the doors of a reopened Fabric: a small victory to make up for years of loss and atomization. But even that success demonstrated the limits of the night-time economy as a concept – if dance music is valued primarily for its economic rather than cultural impact, those who boast the biggest turnover end up getting the most help.

While an increase in political engagement with UK dance music (and in particular the physical spaces it occupied) over the course of the 2010s was undoubtedly a good thing, the political and economic benefits produced by these new collaborations – much like the profits accrued in an increasingly centralized dance music industry – have not always been distributed evenly. Sacha Lord, Amy Lamé's counterpart in Manchester (under the slightly different title of Night-Time Economy Adviser), is a particularly interesting figure in this regard, combining political responsibility for the North West's night-time economy with his status as the region's most successful promoter. After a decade running clubs and bars across the North West of England, Lord made his name with the creation of The Warehouse Project in 2006, a wildly profitable series of events whose unvarnished post-industrial setting, consistently stacked line-ups of excellent if unadventurous names, and pummelling light and sound give it a decent claim as the UK's first post-1990s superclub, and the first real temple to business techno. Within a matter of years WHP was the most successful nightclub in Manchester: in 2007 Lord founded Parklife, which rapidly became the city's biggest festival too.

When the position of Night-Time Economy Adviser was announced in 2018 – a move for which Lord himself had been lobbying ever since Lamé had been appointed two years earlier – it came as no surprise whatsoever that Lord himself got the job. His advocacy for dance music and the wider night-time economy has been laudable, but invariably intertwined with his own commercial activity. In several cases, this has been a happy symbiosis: Lord campaigned successfully for the government's pandemic-era Culture Recovery Fund to be expanded to fully support nightclubs (it had initially only covered venues which featured at least some proportion of live music) providing essential financial backing for dance music spaces across the UK. Of course, this also included Lord's own interests, with The Warehouse Project securing a substantial grant from that same fund, alongside state support for smaller venues. At other times, the political and personal have pulled in different directions though: Lord has robustly defended the use of exclusivity clauses, despite their unpopularity among smaller promoters, and off-the-record mutterings about the particularly restrictive conditions imposed by big Manchester promoters like The Warehouse Project. Lord's close allies in the Night Time Industries Association have a similar track record, their advocacy regularly benefiting the night-time economy as a whole, but occasionally gravitating towards those at the top of the food chain. While they worked tirelessly and laudably during the pandemic to support and champion venues of all sizes, their initial response to the imposition of lockdown was subtly telling: a demand not for industry-wide support, but a mortgage and business rates holiday for large corporate landlords, on the basis that its benefits would then trickle down to others.

If political approaches to the night-time economy served – even if unintentionally – to increase the gap between UK dance music's haves and have-nots, then so did threats to independent dance music spaces which sat outside the sphere of political influence. The closure of LGBTQ+ venue XXL in 2019 wasn't caused by licensing subcommittees or police officers, but private developers building luxury flats, offices and a hotel. Emails and meeting minutes released under Freedom of Information legislation show Amy Lamé and her team taking XXL's plight seriously, and doing their best to get the warring parties around the table, but – unlike Fabric, and like hundreds of other venue closures driven by purely economic concerns – this was not a situation where political pressure had any real leverage. In an interview with *The Guardian*, XXL co-owner James McNeil described LGBT+ culture being 'socially cleansed' from the new development, while an email to Lamé reads: 'We asked the Mayor's office for help over two years ago and something should have been done then, before XXL becomes just another statistic.' The sad, unspoken truth remains that when it comes to conflicts between clubs and developers, political buy-in and appeals to the cultural importance of UK dance music aren't enough to challenge ravenous global demand for inner-city real estate. Instead, gentrification and redevelopment continue to push outwards, overwriting the local cultures which predated a given neighbourhood's newly desirable status, and relocating its previous inhabitants. More often than not, this ends up with economically, socially or racially marginalized groups being replaced by wealthier and more 'desirable' ones. One 2017 study into late-night venues in London found that closures in the city centre were being offset largely by openings further north and east – venues like Plastic People in Shoreditch, Dance Tunnel in Dalston, Cable in London Bridge and Madame JoJo's in Soho replaced by ones like Colour Factory in Hackney and Five Miles in Tottenham (itself since forced to close) – continuing to push dance music from the heart of the city to its fringes, and narrow the space in which grassroots clubs are able to survive.

And yet UK dance music has been an unwitting perpetrator of these processes as much as a victim. Just as the arrival of artisan coffee shops and a little Waitrose might signal the end of a particular neighbourhood's creative vitality, so the arrival of artists' warehouses and basement dance music clubs tend to threaten its previous communities too, driving property prices and rents upwards as people flock to areas where desirable cultural activity is happening. 'It's that magical something that [London boroughs] all want,' an employee of property developer Bouygues explains, his tone disconcertingly blithe, in a 2014 interview. 'They all want IT businesses and they all want creative industries, because it gives them that young, hip vibe. People take it very seriously, because it creates value . . . Of course, by the time they're successful, the place has been established, the property's gone up massively in value, and the owners have gone "Right, I'm turfing these people out, I want to convert it to [residential]."' The most obvious example of this might be the luxury flats built on the site of The Haçienda, with their glib nods to Peter Savile's interior design for the since-bulldozed club. Turnmills in Clerkenwell spent much of the 1990s as the capital's epicentre for pummelling, uncompromising dance music: its most famous night, Trade, was the UK's first licensed after-hours party (beginning at 3 a.m. on a Sunday and running until Monday morning) with an intense hard house soundtrack and heroically decadent LGBTQ+ crowd. The building was demolished in 2009 to be replaced by offices, but in a cringeworthy nod to the site's heritage each newly constructed meeting room was named after a DJ or club night connected to Turnmills: the Judge Jules room; the Tony De Vit room; the Trade room.

Even the opening of a new nightclub can sometimes serve these same dubious principles. At first glance, clubbers in Brixton might well have welcomed the opening in 2023 of The Ton of Brix, a new venue run by well-respected promoters Percolate, who promised to bring an enviable line-up of local and global DJ talent to South London. And yet this was an exercise in erasure as much as creation, given that the building housing The Ton of Brix was previously home to a venue called Club 414. One of Brixton's longest-running late-night venues, 414 had been a cornerstone of the local music community, home to everything from underground jazz nights to South London's surviving hard house and acid techno scenes; its communal, rough-edged charm and connection to under-served groups embodying the raw, original urgency of UK dance music as a social force.

In 2019, the club was bought by Hondo Enterprises, a property development company owned by Texan billionaire Taylor McWilliams, as part of his purchase of the adjoining Brixton Market; 414's managers were unceremoniously fired shortly afterwards. McWilliams's plans for Brixton have been hugely controversial, inflaming local concerns around gentrification and exclusion (Hondo's first project in London, a luxury apartment block, met with controversy in 2014 after installing segregated 'poor doors') with a succession of long-standing market retailers – most notably Nour Cash & Carry, a family owned grocer catering to the local community for over twenty years – threatened with eviction, or slowly replaced by a succession of cocktail bars and upmarket eateries. Hondo's plans for Brixton currently include the construction of a vast office block, wedged next to the market and towering over the town centre.

It's in this context that the opening of The Ton of Brix should be viewed: as part of a wider process of gentrification and profit-seeking, with profound consequences for the different communities and identities welcomed or excluded by competing visions of dance music and the night-time economy. Grassroots campaigners, opposed to Hondo's bland annexation of Brixton's cultural and commercial heart under the banner of 'Save Nour', have raised similar questions about The Ton of Brix. 'I'm really happy that a club will take over the space – it means music, it means jobs,' one campaigner told Resident Advisor. 'But at the same time, I'm really devastated that [the building] is owned by Taylor McWilliams, and I feel guilt and regret that the activism that was put to good use with Save Nour wasn't able to help save Club 414.'

McWilliams himself also moonlights as a DJ, playing pedestrian tech-house to his society mates in the private members' clubs of the West End as part of a four-strong group called Housekeeping, their vanity record label part-funded, according to Companies House, by generous interest-free loans from his property development company. The website for Tape London, the private members' club founded by McWilliams's Housekeeping partner and professional aristocrat Jacobi Anstruther-Gough-Calthorpe, speaks to the potential for dance music's gentrifying potential, not just its vulnerability to gentrification. 'Our policy at Tape is smart, elegant and on trend. To avoid disappointment at the door we strongly advise you to dress to impress. Avoiding flip-flops, shorts, athletic wear, baseball caps, hooded jumpers.' Interestingly, Tape also has an apparel store, selling a range of branded baseball caps and hoodies, all presumably prohibited by its own door policies: it's not hard to infer the two different audiences being addressed here.

In the late 2010s the relationship between developers, dance music and political actors over questions of spatial control and gentrification shifted from one rooted in conflict to one built on collaboration.

Rather than continuing to fight massive developers for control of contested urban space, the most successful dance music promoters in the UK now ask those same developers for a job. 'We see an opportunity to create something special in the interim of the regeneration phase,' Broadwick Live's managing director Bradley Thompson told *The Guardian* of their new 10,000 capacity Drumsheds venue, and its role in the wider £6 billion redevelopment of the surrounding Meridian Water area, undertaken hand-in-hand with Enfield Council. 'I want hipsters to come to Meridian Water, they bring money and that's a good thing,' former local councillor Alan Sitkin said of the project, neatly encapsulating the role performed by popular culture in softening up neighbourhoods for regeneration or gentrification. At the time the Drumsheds opened in 2019, it was surrounded by light industrial units facing compulsory purchase, and colossal gas holders scheduled for demolition; by the time of its closure in 2022, with work beginning on the first of the area's planned 10,000 new homes, it had successfully established Meridian Water as a 'destination' for young urban professionals, furnishing it with a conceptual gloss of creativity, culture and colour.

The pivotal role of the Drumsheds in shaping the cultural and social identity of Enfield follows a template laid down by another of Broadwick's mammoth cultural-redevelopment partnerships, Printworks. In 2012, the former *Daily Mail* and *Evening Standard* printing presses at Rotherhithe were purchased by developers British Land, whose other local interests include a £34 million rebuild of Surrey Quays shopping centre, and a multimillion-pound redevelopment project with Southwark Council at Canada Water. In 2017, Broadwick were brought in on a five-year contract to operate a clubbing venue in the building's cavernous printing hall, while its new owners worked on a masterplan for the surrounding area. Between line-ups stacked with big names – including a who's who of business techno talent – a reassuringly hefty soundsystem and the undeniable grandeur of the space itself, Printworks was ruthlessly effective at drawing in ravers looking for something more from their clubbing experience: a sense of occasion and otherworldliness, or just a unique visual setting to stick on social media. 'People want to experience things, there's a need for it, they want the social kudos that come with it,' explained Thompson in 2018.

But then, just as with the Drumsheds, it was all over. In the spring of 2022 – five years on from signing the original contract with Printworks – British Land announced that the printing presses would be demolished and replaced by a bland office block, residential towers, shops and carefully manicured green space (with the UK economy tanking once more during Liz Truss's brief and chaotic time as prime minister, they granted clubbers a temporary reprieve, keeping Printworks open until the spring of 2023). As with Fabric six years earlier, London's clubbers were outraged at the loss of yet another venue they'd grown to love, but their signing of petitions and gnashing of teeth were always going to fall on deaf ears: the whole point of Printworks was that it was temporary, clearing out the ghosts of the industrial past and forging a new identity for this previously unloved industrial site before graciously making way for the bulldozers.

By comparison, the same week that Broadwick's closure of Printworks was announced another club closure went almost unnoticed, underlining the imbalance in attention between mass-market spaces which didn't need or want help, and a grassroots one which did, when Studio 289 became another name on the list of the UK's lost venues. The Bethnal Green railway arch in which their 200-capacity space was located had originally been owned and managed by Network Rail: facing a steep drop in passenger numbers and a projected £53 billion in debts, they decided in 2016 to sell their entire property portfolio to a consortium of two hedge funds, Blackstone and Telereal Trillium for £1.5 billion. While Studio 289's rent remained fixed initially, when their contract came up for renewal their new landlords – entities based entirely on delivering returns for their investors – more than doubled it. 'As a small venue trying to push good music,' wrote Studio 289 founder Harry Follett after discovering the plans, 'it's not possible for us to generate enough income to survive such high rents. Nor do we want to begin the race to the cultural wastelands by putting on nights purely to make enough money.'

In the nine months between British Land going in for planning permission (with proposals which confirmed Printworks would be demolished) and Southwark Council granting approval, Broadwick made no attempt to alert clubbers or rally opposition. Why would they? Their occupation of the niche between deindustrialization and redevelopment had proved wildly lucrative, avoiding the wearying battles between developers and councils which had sunk so many other late-night venues, enabling them to draw income not only from the entertainment industry, but also from the far more lucrative worlds of redevelopment and construction. Following their success with Printworks and the Drumsheds, Broadwick secured investment from American video games studio Rockstar Games, the makers of Grand Theft Auto and Red Dead Redemption, whose annual turnover is counted in the billions and who currently make roughly $2.5 million a day from sales relating to Grand Theft Auto 5 alone. With that increased financial backing Broadwick began planning £200 million worth of projects across their portfolio of more than a dozen venues across the UK, from Depot Mayfield in Manchester – the home of Sacha Lord's Warehouse Project, and part of a £1.4 billion regeneration project backed by Manchester City Council – to Exhibition London (a former rail warehouse situated within the £8 billion redevelopment of White City, spearheaded by US behemoths Westfield) in West London, to The Beams and Dockyards (an old Tate & Lyle sugar factory and a patch of open-air industrial wasteground respectively) in the rapidly regenerating Royal Docks to the east of the city. The opening of The Beams in 2022 coincided with the launch of Newham Council and the Greater London Authority's £3.5 billion redevelopment plans for the Silvertown Quays area, including more than £300 million in public funding intended to subsidize affordable housing within the 1,500-home project. Broadwick MD Bradley Thompson was on hand once again to wax lyrical about 'a new centre of cultural gravity for London in the heart of The Royal Docks' as the cycle began once more. Broadwick's property portfolio now even includes the semi-cannibalistic repurposing of existing dance music venues: Oval Studios, launched by Broadwick in 2023 as a space for 'creative and corporate events', occupies a building which was previously the highly regarded nightclub Oval Space. At a time when the creative industries – one of the few areas in which the UK remains a world leader – are facing unprecedented pressures from Brexit, the pandemic and government under-investment, it's perhaps inevitable that sharp-minded operators would pivot instead to another area where Britain remains an outlier, namely its grotesquely over-inflated property market and land prices.

While this business model has proved hugely successful for Broadwick, its effects on UK dance music are harder to ascertain. It's clear that venues like Printworks are spectacular and exhilarating: their line-ups are always reliable, if not always adventurous, and their sound quality reassuringly bone-shaking. Find yourself a space in front of the speaker stacks, lose yourself in the volume and scale of the whole thing, as thousands of satisfied customers across the UK do every weekend, and the experience can be intensely pleasurable. But in truth, that's all it can ever be: the perfunctory, passive consumption of an (admittedly high-quality) entertainment product, stripped of the cultural, communal or historic associations formed when venues emerge and find their audience in more organic ways. But there's also something deeper here, a sense of dance music moving from a cultural end in itself to a mere stepping stone for grander political and financial ambitions. The ravers filling Printworks aren't just Broadwick's customers but also their *product*: the disposable income and cultural capital those thousands of young people bring to Enfield, Mayfield or Meridian Water are themselves being sold to Broadwick's commercial partners, and used as tools with which to erase and rewrite the historic connotations of these areas, and ultimately to sell nearby commercial and residential real estate.

Or at least, that's how it's supposed to work. Alan Sitkin sounded a note of caution about plans for the Drumsheds back in 2019: 'if it feels artificial and young people don't come then you're spending a lot of taxpayers' money on an ambition without it panning out.' His successors in council roles across London – particularly those on Newham Council involved in 'close collaboration' with The Beams – might be forgiven a dose of the same scepticism, given the issues which have befallen similar projects in the past. In August 2012 the London Pleasure Gardens, an open-air cultural venue within spitting distance of what are now The Beams and Dockyards, collapsed into administration, taking nearly £8 million of funding with it. The vast majority of that sum was public money: buoyed by the waves of optimism and investment washing over East London in the run-up to the Olympics, Newham Council had gambled their own financial reserves on the promise of culture-led regeneration. Despite being – along with Enfield – one of the most impoverished boroughs in London, Newham ended up forking out £3.3 million upfront, in exchange for 20 per cent of the Pleasure Gardens' profits once it was up and running. 'We're involved in the same way venture capitalists might be, and the return we get on our investment will go towards creating other jobs and "meanwhile" activities in the borough,' said their head of regeneration Clive Dutton in July 2012. Within weeks, those optimistic projections had turned to dust.

Featuring a wildly ambitious line-up, from Steve Reich and Snoop Dogg on the main stage to pounding techno on a German battleship docked in the Thames, the dance music festival Bloc was planned as the Pleasure Gardens' first big public event. Its organizers had sold more than 10,000 tickets by the time they were informed, two weeks before their event opened on the sixth of July, that large swathes of the site, including Bloc's entire second stage, wouldn't be ready in time: having discovered large volumes of asbestos on the site, £1 million of Newham's initial £3.3 million loan had to be spent on decontamination, causing delays and resourcing issues across the whole project. With the festival site hastily rearranged and reduced in size, thousands of would-be ravers arriving on the Friday evening were forced into terrifying bottlenecks outside the gates, with queues stretching back for over a mile. 'Hundreds of people were penned in, waiting for hours with no movement, and no security on hand to herd them through or control the situation,' one attendee told *The Guardian*. As frustrations and fears of serious injury mounted, things began to unravel: people rushed the barriers, and bouncers stopped scanning tickets. But the reduction in stage capacity meant that anyone making it through the crush merely found themselves cordoned once again outside already-full tents, further escalating the febrile atmosphere. A recording of Boddika's set aboard the MS *Stubnitz* captures the moment when the plug was finally pulled. 'Fuckin' 'ell . . . all right boys and girls, the police are shutting the party down,' says MC Chunky over the PA, clearly nonplussed by what's happening. 'So what's the procedure? Do we tell everyone to leave or what? Jesus Christ. All right, ladies and gentlemen, unfortunately everybody's got to exit the venue in a calm and orderly fashion . . . you know what the police are like when they shut something down. If we don't do things in an orderly fashion they're gonna pepper spray every motherfucker and get the dogs out.'

The second day of Bloc was cancelled by sunrise on Saturday, and by the end of the weekend two other festivals booked for the site had announced their intentions to relocate. Within weeks both Bloc and London Pleasure Gardens went into administration, with accusations of blame flying in all directions. A project which Clive Dutton had described as 'a no-brainer' ended up with everyone losing out: the vast majority of attendees received nothing in the way of refunds, while £2.6 million owed to suppliers and staff went unpaid. Having upped their investment to £5.1 million to try to keep the whole thing afloat, Newham Council were left on the hook for a further £1 million in post-administration costs, just as the most savage phase of Westminster's austerity-induced cuts to local government budgets began to bite. While the £6 million sunk into the London Pleasure Gardens was only a small fraction of the £100 million in cuts that Newham were forced to implement over the following years, it's hard not to wonder what else might have been done with that money.

In 2013, Newham served eviction notices on a group of twenty-nine vulnerable young mothers and children housed in emergency council accommodation, insisting that their only options for rehoming lay outside the borough; some were told to relocate to Manchester and Birmingham or be classed as voluntarily homeless. A 2018 report by the Child Poverty Action Group indicates that Newham's borough-wide budget for Discretionary Housing Benefit over the previous financial year was £1.2 million, or less than a quarter of what they'd once spent on the London Pleasure Gardens. Lessons appear not to have been learned: a year after the London Pleasure Gardens collapsed, then-Mayor Boris Johnson signed off on a £1.7 billion, 25-hectare development across the water of Gallions Point Marina on the other side of the Royal Docks, fifteen minutes' walk from The Beams. As of 2022 it remains largely unbuilt and almost entirely unoccupied – 'a row of pristine office blocks marooned in a sea of tarmac and overgrown scrubland' – after Chinese developers Advances Business Parks scaled back their plans following shocks to the property markets in both the UK and Asia. One architect described the project as 'a bombastic elevator pitch, short on detail, questionable and poorly conceived', when what the area needed was 'environments which are resilient, diverse and which respond to the needs of this part of east London.'

The rise of a new generation of business techno superclubs, the centralization of control over UK dance music's physical spaces, and the absorption of club culture into the business cycles of massive developers raises similar questions about cultural resilience and diversity. At their worst, this new high-volume high-spectacle developer–clubber model risks the loss or marginalization of smaller cultural spaces; a narrower focus on more lucrative audiences who don't always reflect the breadth and diversity of UK dance music culture; the stagnation of sounds and performance styles platformed on these larger stages; and in extreme cases the spectre of public–private dance music projects actively making life harder for cash-strapped local councils trying to provide essential services. It's a legacy as questionable as the most derided aspects of the original 1990s superclub era, and yet one which has attracted a fraction of the same criticism. This is partly down to the veneer of free party-era credibility granted by the reuse of spaces like abandoned factories and commonly owned green spaces, and partly it's the sense of novelty and renewal created by the industry's increasingly deliberate ephemerality: The Beams feels like a 'new' venue even if its ownership, intention and audience are all functionally identical to those of other Broadwick-controlled and developer-funded spaces. Partly it's because the experience of being in these spaces is still immensely satisfying despite their shortcomings: a day out at Printworks, with its smoothly repurposed concrete spaces and predictable soundtrack, feels like going to a 1990s rave theme park, both in its vaguely plasticky feeling of unreality and the fact that it's still heaps of fun regardless. It is pleasurable despite being stripped of the upended power structures which elsewhere define the dance floor: the carnival, just without the carnivalesque.

Other potential reasons for the relative lack of opposition to dance music's gentrification over the last decade and a half feel knottier: when the primary media platform for a culture is directly dependent on ticket sales for its financial survival, while countless others benefit more obliquely from event-related advertising and access, drawing attention to the flaws of the industry's biggest promoters might be considered unwise for cash-strapped editors. Business techno's acceptance as UK dance music's primary operating model has also been accompanied by laudable and overdue progress on deeply ingrained racism and sexism across the industry: while the increasing visibility of women, trans folks and people of colour in the DJ booth has been wonderful to witness, it's also inadvertently served to mask the fact that business techno's power and profits continue to accumulate in less equitable ways behind the scenes. 'Parklife Festival 2022 Took Lineup Diversity To A Whole New Level' crows one headline under a photo of business techno mainstay Peggy Gou, before fawningly detailing the only stage at the event which managed a 50/50 gender split, encapsulating both the positive changes occurring at the level of artist diversity, and the lack of deeper structural analysis beyond those identity-based signifiers.

There is an alternative though, forming in the spaces left unattended by monolithic business techno interests: it's encouraging to remember that if the narrowing of UK dance music's outlook has been influenced by its relationship with physical space, then the choices we make about where we go raving can reverse that same process, offering new avenues for unpicking current problems or imagining new possibilities. By and large, the most vital dance music in the UK isn't being made in business techno spaces, or with expansion to that scale in mind. Venues like The Cause and FOLD in London, Cosmic Slop in Leeds and Strange Brew in Bristol have been designed as community spaces first and foremost, their human scale and umbilical connection to local creative communities a critical part of their appeal, while boutique festivals like Field Maneuvers and Freerotation (the latter so committed to remaining small-scale, despite burgeoning demand for tickets, that it runs an annual lottery to get in) have set the template for outdoor events which don't feel like an exercise in market capitalization. Maybe this represents the model for the next cycle of UK dance music's spatial ebb and flow as the 2010s ended: parties defined not by geography but scale, dance floors populated by people you know, a sense of community and meaning impossible to communicate in a Resident Advisor puff piece, or to experience when the person throwing the party is ultimately some faceless residential developer.

As it turned out, all conversations to this effect would be suddenly put on hold when the Covid pandemic shuttered every (legal) dance floor in the UK for nearly two years, acting as a violent reset button for UK dance music as a whole, with particular impacts on its relationship to physical space. Stay-at-home orders may have temporarily dampened the debate over where and how we go dancing, but before long – both during the prolonged tail of pandemic lockdown and in its hugely challenging aftermath – these questions would return, more urgent now than ever before.

PROTESTORS AT THE 'SAVE OUR SCENE' MARCH IN CENTRAL LONDON, 2021

11. Plague Raving

Covid-19 and the eternal return of the illegal party

The early spring of 2021 could be mistaken for any other point in the preceding year-and-a-quarter of Covid-19 restrictions, so seamlessly have the weeks and months blurred into each other. We are still largely stuck in our homes, still separated from friends and family, still mostly trudging round in our pyjamas, playing Wordle and sitting stoically through another interminable round of Zoom calls. But beneath the surface something is finally stirring, a feeling of ambiguous potential, equal parts anticipation and precariousness.

By the end of April, increased vaccine availability means that more than half of the UK population have received their first dose, and rules on outdoor gatherings begin to soften: beer gardens are once again full, despite the grim weather conditions and ongoing prohibitions on indoor socializing. Over the May Day weekend, a photo goes viral of five middle-aged women huddled under umbrellas on the patio of a pub in Devon; soaked by a torrential downpour, they nonetheless cling grimly to their dampening chips and rain-diluted beer, with the *Daily Mirror* lauding their display of 'true "British Bulldog" spirit at its finest.'

Two weeks later, I'm treading down a muddy towpath somewhere outside Chingford on my way to an illegal rave, searching for a similar British sense of derring-do, only this time expressed through the medium of a dark, sweaty room with big speakers instead of a sodden Ploughman's lunch and a watery pint. On the opposite bank of the Lea river a waste incineration plant looms ominously, plumes of smoke drifting into the damp air. Undergrowth cramps the path, blocking light from the motorway above. After months spent either cocooned in my flat, or restricted to a tight, repetitive grid of permanently illuminated South London streets, the impenetrable darkness under the on-ramp of the North Circular feels otherworldly, and laden with both menace and opportunity.

Over the first half of 2021, reconnecting with the forgotten pleasures of the dance floor would come to play a critical role in the tentative and highly choreographed restoration of everyday British life. On that same May Day weekend, club promoters Circus took part in the government's Event Research Programme: a series of large-scale gatherings, from a Sam Fender concert in Newcastle to the World Snooker Championships, designed to map the spread of Covid through mass public gatherings and the effect of distancing and testing on that process. Dance music's contribution to the science saw 6,000 ravers, each clutching a negative lateral flow test, descend on Bramley-Moore Dock in Liverpool to watch The Blessed Madonna, Fatboy Slim and others smash out the big room bangers. For these young people – part of the generational cohort forced to bear the greatest Covid-induced disruptions to their education, careers, and social or cultural lives, in order to restrict a disease of far greater risk to those older than them — the reopening of live music felt like eighteen months of civic debt being paid back in full. 'This is the best day of my LIFE!' hollers a girl in a bucket hat and white tracksuit, grabbing a BBC reporter's microphone. 'It feels surreal,' a more measured attendee tells Sky News. 'Part of me feels like it's not been any time at all, and the rest feels like it's been for ever.'

For the wider nightclub industry, shuttered ever since March 2020 (unlike pubs or sports venues, clubs were afforded no opportunity to reopen even temporarily) and forced to lay off half its workforce, these events were seismic: the point at which it became possible to imagine something other than slow obliteration. 'The government has continually underplayed clubs significance during the pandemic . . . I'm certain some clubs won't survive this, and will never open their doors again,' Newcastle-based promoter Gabriel Day told *Dazed* magazine shortly before lockdown restrictions were eventually eased. 'But we'll be looking to balance the books by taking advantage of the increased demand for dancing, and providing the best quality nights for underground music fans in the city.' The government published their findings from the test events at the end of May: of the 13,000 people who'd attended Circus and other events, a grand total of eleven positive tests had been returned, paving the way for nightlife to reopen later in the year.

And yet the Liverpool test event was also hugely contentious, reflecting the fractious moral debates over 'responsible' behaviour, which defined both the pandemic and its immediate aftermath. The opportunity for thousands of young people to let their hair down for the first time in two years was unashamedly joyous, but it was also a nakedly political gimmick, orchestrated by a government desperate to distract from a chaotic handling of the pandemic as a whole. Their 'roadmap' out of lockdown, for which the reopening of nightclubs, football stadiums and other large-scale events functioned as hugely symbolic waypoints, had been announced back in

January at a point when over 1,000 people a day were dying, and almost 40,000 patients were gasping for air in hospital beds around the country. 'Once you announce clear dates you create facts on the ground which alter the reality, and create a situation where it's very difficult to shift from those dates,' social psychologist Stephen Reicher told *The Guardian*. These huge events ultimately took place not because a sober analysis of the data determined their timing and size were appropriate, or because they were scientifically rigorous – that oft-quoted figure of eleven Covid cases can be seen in a different light when you find out that only 6 per cent of Circus attendees returned post-event tests – but because not holding them would invite uncomfortable questions about the government's competence.

Circus's decision to add the veteran trance DJ Sven Väth to their line-up was similarly questionable, given that a mere three months earlier he'd been happily playing to colossal non-distanced crowds in Goa, Hyderabad and Bangalore. Like several other big-name DJs caught playing 'plague raves' during 2020, Väth largely evaded rather than engaged with criticism, his agent providing the functional but underwhelming explanation that he had 'adhered to the local guidances of any location he visited during the pandemic' – an argument which might insulate his client against strict claims of illegality, but failed to deal with the broader ethical questions. Väth was far from alone in this, with big-name DJs like Nina Kraviz, Amelie Lens and Tale of Us – as well as British artists like Dax J and Patrick Topping – all remaining similarly coy about playing to huge crowds across Europe whenever local Covid restrictions allowed.

In a tacit nod to the moral ambiguity of their behaviour, several began borrowing under-the-radar marketing tactics from illegal promoters: events would be advertised locally rather than online, and mentioned obliquely on social media only after they'd happened. 'I had an absolutely amazing time in Italy,' says Kraviz in one Instagram post, seen holding a bowl of pasta on a near-deserted beach. You might be forgiven for assuming she'd merely been on holiday rather than touring, but for a specific reference to the 'promoters and people who made it such a special one'. Dax J posted a since-deleted Tweet about a string of European dates only once he'd safely boarded his return flight to the UK, saying it was 'So good to be back on tour!' In the accompanying photograph his medical mask is pulled down below his nose and mouth, rendering it useless. While Dax might have been grateful to restore some limited semblance of his lucrative international touring schedule, smaller artists with merely national profiles were denied those same opportunities: much as the relative comfort of remote-working white-collar professionals contrasted with the risks borne by workers in public-facing industries from transport to healthcare, Covid highlighted and deepened economic inequalities within dance music. Very little appears to have been said by artists of Nina Kraviz's or Dax J's stature, for example, about the risks their events posed to bar or security staff, whose direct interaction with crowds was required to keep their Covid-era income flowing.

While it's difficult to draw direct causative or quantitative links between individual events and infection trends, there certainly does seem to have been some level of correlation between the reopening of dance music venues and spikes in infections. Sven Väth's Indian tour was possible because venues had been allowed to reopen early in 2021; within weeks case numbers across the country began to surge uncontrollably, overwhelming the country's fragile health system and precipitating the world's third-largest Covid death toll. By the time Väth played in Liverpool, over 400,000 new infections were being registered across India every day, with the country reaching a quarter of a million deaths soon after. The reopening of Italian and Spanish nightclubs during the summer of 2020 was also followed swiftly by a spike in Covid-19 cases amongst young people, forcing both governments to backpedal furiously and re-close all music venues. In the Czech Republic, 98 Covid-19 cases and nearly 300 enforced quarantines were linked to one asymptomatic person who attended a nightclub in Prague in July. The UK government's Event Research Programme was billed as a sober, responsible and evidence-led approach to studying Covid transmission and developing a plan for reopening the events industry. This may have been true, but its creation and implementation also inadvertently reflected the violent disparities in power, access and medical care which the pandemic laid bare. The health risks facing ravers and dance music workers in Liverpool were a secondary factor compared to political optics, or the crowd-pulling economics of booking the biggest names possible. In turn, the safety measures that were afforded to those Liverpool clubbers were conspicuously not available for gigs in India by the very same DJs, profoundly altering how the pandemic affected audiences in different countries: the feel-good power of the dance floor, control over its joy-giving potential and the management of its associated risks doled out in a strictly enforced global hierarchy.

The decisions to allow 52,000 fans into Anfield for the Champions League semi-final between Liverpool and Atlético Madrid on 11 March 2020, or 65,000 into Cheltenham races the following weekend, have become infamous as totemic and deadly evidence of government inaction in the early stages of the pandemic; epidemiological studies would later estimate that thirty-seven people died as a result of allowing Liverpool's game to go ahead. But dance music events faced similar ethical questions in those confusing early months of 2020. Hosted every spring in a dilapidated Pontins holiday camp outside Southport, the Bangface Weekender cleaves wholeheartedly to UK dance music's tendency for lairy, hyper-saturated irreverence, from the pantomime rave of Altern-8 and splattered breakbeats of Squarepusher to the crowd's own nonsensical cardboard signs and bizarre costumes. But where it's normally a space of frenetic excess and cartoonish abandon, the 2020 edition of Bangface – held from 12 to 16 March, the weekend between the Liverpool game and Cheltenham Festival – instead became a eulogy for dance music itself, and the collective experiences which were about to disappear for an indeterminate period. 'Was it ever okay to rave in the face of a pandemic?' asks Megan Townsend in a *Mixmag* review of the event published two weeks later, days after the UK's first national lockdown was imposed. It details the shifting mood amongst the festival faithful (or the Bangface Hard Crew as they refer to themselves) as artist cancellations, news of concurrent parties across the UK being shut down by local councils, and rumours of school and office closures each filter through the crowd. 'What had begun as a last hurrah had turned into a serious question of whether or not remaining at the festival was ethical,' writes Townsend. 'We'd left home to come to a festival, but would be returning to a situation that was changing beyond what we could have imagined.'

And yet it's not as simple as concluding – as many have done both at the time and since – that football fans and ravers alike therefore have blood on their hands. As revealed by Boris Johnson's closest confidant and Machiavellian power-broker Dominic Cummings in a series of tweets in 2021, it was only after Bangface had begun – roughly around the time Helena Hauff's set of furious electro closed out its opening night, to be precise – that policymakers at Number 10 first began to grapple with the concept of a UK-wide lockdown. Prior to that Friday night, the government had planned to simply let Covid tear through the unvaccinated British populace, hoping for 'herd immunity' to eventually bring it under control without the imposition of lockdown restrictions. It was only when the implications of doing so became clear – 4,000 people dying every day at the pandemic's peak, the NHS completely collapsing and becoming non-functional for months, and a death toll somewhere in the region of a million people (split evenly between direct Covid casualties and those dying through being unable to access other NHS care) – that perspectives began to shift. Whatever credibility you place in Cummings's recollections, and notwithstanding his own risible defence of lockdown-breaking around his notorious Barnard Castle trip, blaming a bunch of gurning ravers in Thomas the Tank Engine costumes for exhibiting no less foresight or self-awareness than our elected leaders would appear to put the moral emphasis in the wrong place.

These questions of balancing pleasure with principles implicate me too. Whatever appeals to journalistic integrity I could offer while making my way to tonight's illegal rave, or however strongly I could justify my attendance as a form of research, as I begin to notice others dotted along the canalside – little pockets of two or three people huddled under branches, illuminated only by their phone screens – I can't deny a mounting sense of nervous excitement. This realization makes me feel decadent and compromised, at a time when the country has only recently emerged from a third wave of Covid infections. While I'm out dancing, someone somewhere will surely be watching through a PPE visor or the small window of a hospital door as a diseased chest rises and falls, unable to hold their loved one's hand as they die in some starched, miserable room. I'm able to party tonight in relative safety only because I'm fully vaccinated, a privilege denied to billions elsewhere in the world. And yet, as with those attending Bangface at the pandemic's beginning or Circus at its end, those feelings of guilt only go so far. After spending eighteen months deprived of the soft, familial embrace of rumbling bassbins and burbling voices, the idea of spending four hours in the pitch dark, pressed against throbbing speaker stacks and warm bodies, elicits a surge of visceral, synaptic energy far beyond that of a dispassionate observer.

Earlier the same evening, I discover that my upstairs neighbours have also decided to flout Covid-19 rules with a drunken birthday party, blasting out a delightfully tuneless karaoke version of 'High' by Lighthouse Family. Where a year earlier people were anxiously shopping their neighbours to the police for standing fewer than six feet away from each other, now an unspoken disdain for the letter of the law appears to be increasingly, albeit tacitly, accepted. This is true even of those responsible for drafting the laws in question, as will gradually be revealed to the public more than a year later: three weeks before I set out for tonight's rave, Downing Street staffers spend the night before the Duke of Edinburgh's funeral getting obnoxiously wasted, staying up until 4 a.m. and smashing a child's swing set.

Equally indicative of our loosening collective grip on ethical responsibility is an opinion piece by *Times* columnist Matthew

Parris, published the same day that I'm making my way towards the rave. Society has barely re-emerged from months on end of solitary confinement, and yet Parris has deemed it necessary to return immediately to that most reassuringly everyday of right-wing hobbies: treating nomadic communities with pathological disdain. In an article titled 'It's time we stopped pandering to Travellers', Parris combines a wheedling and entirely unconvincing performance of concern and empathy for Gypsy and Roma families' endemic deprivation and exclusion with calls for a form of cultural cleansing. He suggests an end to the obligation on councils to provide Traveller sites, apparently unaware that this hasn't existed since the Criminal Justice Act of 1994, along with removing 'the "ethnic minority" rights of people who are not a race' and talking of a 'relentless squeeze' to force travelling communities into fixed accommodation. While it may not contain an overt call for violence (although how else could Parris's 'relentless squeeze' ultimately be enforced?), it is a clear framing of Britain as a property-based monoculture, just as was argued in the mid-1990s, albeit with even less apparent concern for the rights or well-being of those affected. 'There is simply no place for the true nomad in modern Britain,' Parris opines breezily. 'It cannot be otherwise.' From the twitching curtains of Middle England to the smashed windows of the Beanfield to illicit soundsystems on the fringes of the city, the story is the same.

It feels quietly thrilling, then, to reach the rave and find it in a location tied deeply to Traveller identity and itinerant histories. Tonight's venue is a narrowboat, moored against an unlit and overgrown part of the canal, well out of sight and earshot of polite society: a tiny but bracing gesture of defiance against Matthew Parris and those who share his views, and some small sign that nomadic pleasure-seeking still has a place in the Britain of 2021. Its interior has been stripped clean to make room for a soundsystem at the far end, a dance floor in the middle and a bar nearest the entrance hatch, a small self-governing enclave in which dreams of collective escape might still be entertained. Its appearance and location echo not only the nomadic lives of Bargee Travellers, but also the earliest offshore pirate radio stations, and the Thames frost fairs of the sixteenth and seventeenth centuries: memorializing and extending the long and storied history of British waterways functioning as a haven for illicit behaviours, and a reliable place to seek ephemeral release from systems of control.

In many ways, the form and frisson of illegal raving have barely changed since the early days of acid house, or indeed those of free festivals, blues dances or travelling Elizabethan players. You buy a ticket, then wait for a location. You slip the bonds of the inner city, arriving in a space that feels both foreign and eerily familiar, with people you've never met but whom you implicitly trust enough to collude with, in this temporary shared conspiracy. The fug of weed and cigarette smoke on the dance floor is a sensory portal, taking me back to clubs as they were before the smoking ban passed by New Labour in 2007. It's hard to describe this acrid waft of tobacco as pleasant, but it's got a certain romance to it: I'd take it in a heartbeat over the rancid mixture of sweat, farts and vape juice which have accompanied the legal dance floors of more recent years.

Where some aspects of the party feel like a wormhole back into the past, others are defined by the present moment: instead of calling an automated party line from a phonebox, punters are added to a private WhatsApp group in the early evening, before the location drops with a Google Maps link. We're repeatedly told not to discuss the party openly if we're getting an Uber there, as the police have been leaning on poorly paid gig-economy drivers and recruiting them as informants. There is an absolute ban on mentioning the rave on social media, or using our phone cameras on the dance floor, and a polite but firm request to make sure we've all taken lateral flow tests before we arrive (though no check of this is ever conducted). Stepping down from the deck of the boat to its interior, I'm struck by a contradictory and overwhelming mesh of emotions. There's the intimate thrill of making it into this secret, forbidden space, and a sense of disbelief at the audacity of its existence. There's also the pleasure of defying a tired, discredited Conservative government, and prioritizing my own needs and wants over fealty to a system that has been ruthlessly geared against youth, excess and hedonism for decades, but particularly during the pandemic itself. On another level, I feel a sense of historic connection to those at Castlemorton or the Blackburn warehouse raves: a proud and defiant lineage continued despite the atomizing, alienating and disempowering effects of Covid-19. Mounted against all of this euphoria is the nagging pull of reality. I see in every unmasked face and unsanitized surface a thread running out from the present moment, a web of cab rides and night-bus journeys, shared joints, breakfasting housemates, Monday morning commutes and weekend visits to someone's grandparents. Each one of these forms an opaque and potentially deadly link in a chain, a network of self-indulgence which pulls at the pandemic's fragile bonds of social responsibility. The rhythms swirl, the past and present collide, the lights fizz pink, purple and blue. I duck under the beams of the barge's cramped ceiling and join the throng.

For many, the societal and inter-generational responsibilities forced upon them by Covid-19 frayed far earlier than May 2021; for some, they went out the window almost as soon as restrictions were put in place. Barely eight weeks into a pandemic which would rumble on for nearly two years, 6,000 people around Manchester broke lockdown regulations to attend two unlicensed events over the same mid-June weekend, one in Daisy Nook country park and the other in Carrington. Snapchat videos from the first of these suggests that media descriptions of a 'rave' constitute something of a category error. The soundsystem is impossibly weedy, for a start: two semi-portable speakers of the sort more often used for part-time pub bands, with their output muffled even further by handmade cardboard depictions of the Angry Birds placed over their grilles. The music is tinny, distorted, and barely audible over the chatter of the crowd; while pockets of people closer to the DJ are dancing, elsewhere they largely prefer to converse amongst themselves and huff on nitrous balloons. Their energy is that of twentysomethings sitting in a park, drinking beers and smoking a joint, or teenagers huddled around a bus stop in some provincial town centre, their intent merely to share social space with each other rather than reaching for musically induced transcendence. Where the Criminal Justice Act used the free party scene as a scapegoat or stand-in for much broader forms of civil disobedience, so it seems that by 2020 the term 'rave' had come to be understood by the tabloids as useful shorthand for any suspicious gathering of young people, regardless of whether or not it involved the more specific rituals of collective dancing to electronic music.

Two weeks later, the *Daily Mail* ran a similar story about stabbings at a 'beach rave' and other illegal gatherings at Ogmore-by-Sea in Wales and Leysdown Beach in Kent; mobile phone footage from Ogmore is shocking, with a chaotic multi-person brawl rolling across the seafront, but features nothing even vaguely mistakable for a DJ or soundsystem, while photos from Leysdown suggest the same miserly set-up and unenthusiastic dancing as the clips from Daisy Nook. Even more tenuous is an unlicensed event at Camber Sands in August 2020, described repeatedly in a *Daily Mail* article as a 'rave' despite being organized by a chicken shop and focusing entirely on food rather than music; it appears to feature no amplified sound whatsoever. While all of these events were undoubtedly a breach of Covid rules, and some featured violent disorder from a small minority of attendees, efforts to collectively define them all as 'raves' feel uncomfortable, as if dance music is being cast as a sinister motivating force behind events which appear to have had little interest in or connection to actual raving.* The scapegoating of dance music as a vector for social ills continued to rear its head in other contexts throughout the pandemic: following the murder in 2021 of Sarah Everard, a raft of half-baked measures aimed at protecting women was announced by Boris Johnson, including the idea of placing plain-clothed officers inside bars and clubs. Critics rightly

---

* The uncomfortable cultural overtones of classing varied types of disorder under the banner of 'raves' feel doubly unsettling in the case of Leysdown and Camber Sands, given that the attendees at both appear to have been almost entirely Black.

noted that Everard wasn't attacked in a club (which were, of course, still shuttered due to the pandemic) and was in fact murdered by a serving police officer. 'How could the presence of more police, invisibly woven into the fabric of women's everyday lives, possibly make us feel safer?' wrote Micha Frazer-Carroll in *The Guardian*, underlining the absurdity of linking Everard's death to late-night venues.

While the media might have been quick to cry 'rave' for events entirely distinct from the heritage of Castlemorton or the blues dance, in a number of other cases the term was entirely apposite. The July 2020 edition of long-running West Country free party Scumerset went ahead regardless of lockdown rules, with a motley assortment of post-Traveller free party people fist-pumping to thumping, relentless techno in the pouring rain. In August, a fully fledged teknival – the same term first used by Spiral Tribe for their post-Criminal Justice Act parties in continental Europe – took place outside Banwen, a remote village deep in the forested valleys of south-west Wales, with hundreds of dancers, dozens of cars and multiple huge soundsystems pounding out an uncompromising twenty-four-hour soundtrack of gabba, garage, dubstep and drum'n'bass. Photos from lockdown London warehouse raves could easily date from Blackburn in 1989; others from an August 2020 lockdown party in Thetford Forest, with a bare-chested and bearded raver kneeling in front of massed shield-bearing riot officers, could just have easily been plucked from the anti-Criminal Justice Act or environmental protests of 1994.

Despite the government imposing fines of up to £10,000 on organizers, and using Covid regulations to temporarily extend the anti-rave powers of the Criminal Justice Act, lockdown raves persisted. In part this was driven by free party systems like Scumerset continuing to do what they'd always done, but in other cases they were joined by legal promoters unable to access their usual licensed premises. 'Once the clubs are allowed to open up, we'll immediately go back to legal events,' said one promoter in September 2020, at a point when bars had been allowed to reopen as long as they enforced strict social distancing rules, limits on volume levels and bans on dancing. 'I don't see much difference in what we're doing: it's just the volume restrictions. And I'm sorry, but I don't think that's worth devastating a full cultural scene for. I'm not young, but for god's sake man, if you were 18 this summer, how desperate you'd be by now . . .' Young people attending illegal lockdown parties shared that sentiment: 'I was so desperate for a night out,' one young woman told *Dazed*. 'It is a bit selfish, but young people need some sort of social life; some sort of release. For me, that's being in a space surrounded by people entranced in the music and moving together.' By the autumn of 2020, the media was awash with stories of Covid raves, from East London to Bristol and Edinburgh to Poole. In June, *The Times* declared that 'Illegal raves are back' and asked, 'If the hippies of 1967 celebrated the first one and 1988 was the second, is 2020 shaping up to be the third summer of love?'

And yet depictions of illegal raving as wildly endemic and 'impossible to police' during Covid remain frustratingly difficult to verify, largely because police forces across the country have failed to record, let alone publish, systematic data on the number of unlicensed music events, rather than just offering media-friendly anecdotes. '#WATCH | We shut down an illegal rave', crowed one post on West Midlands Police's Twitter page, alongside some highly shareable video content shot with thermal-imaging cameras from a police helicopter commandeered by Operation Reliant, the West Midlands' illegal rave policing taskforce. A mass of spectral figures huddle under a motorway overpass; we hear the distant thud of 4/4 kickdrums being broken up by urgent shouting and commands for people to stay where they are. 'If anybody has got possession of any sound equipment, make sure those details are firmly recorded,' advises dispatch over the radio, as we see people being led into waiting police vans. Elsewhere in the media Operation Reliant were lauded for breaking up twenty-eight events in one twenty-four-hour period, and afforded supportive coverage from an ITV reporter who follows them for a night of kicking in pub front doors and raiding teenage house parties. And yet the same force's stance on providing concrete figures – the number of unlicensed music events recorded or attended by police, and what happened to the people attending or organizing them – is met with silence. 'Information regarding illegal gatherings under Operation Reliant is not held centrally or in an electronically, or any other, searchable format,' I'm told. 'In addition, there are no central recording categories or markers on our systems to denote "unlicensed music events" and, therefore, we are unable to search force recording systems for this specific information.'

Elsewhere, this opaque approach has had more profound consequences. When Home Secretary Priti Patel first increased fines for party organizers to £10,000 in August 2020, she justified doing so on the basis that 'in London alone, the Metropolitan Police has responded to more than 1,000 unlicensed events – such as big raves and parties – since the end of June, receiving information on more than 200 events across the city in a single weekend.' These eye-popping figures were immediately and dutifully repeated across the media as evidence of Covid kids going rave crazy. But they were wrong, as a *Mixmag* investigation subsequently revealed: they referred not to the number of events taking place, but the number of *calls* received by the police about them. If one party was reported thirty times, each of those calls was recorded separately, and understood by Priti Patel as thirty separate events, forming domestic policy on the basis of the police failing (or choosing) to misunderstand or miscommunicate their own evidence. How many parties actually took place? It turned out the Met either didn't know, or wouldn't say.

Where statistics have been published on the policing of illegal gatherings during lockdown, they suggest that people of colour have faced disproportionate numbers of Fixed Penalty Notices (i.e. fines) under Covid regulations for attending illegal raves relative to their proportion of the UK population. The number of fines issued to people across England and Wales for attending events involving 'amplified music' between the introduction of lockdown rules in March 2020 and the lifting of restrictions in July 2021 is 441; Black,

Asian and mixed race people accounted for more than a third of these, despite making up less than 15 per cent of the overall UK population. Of the 342 fines issued across England and Wales where the ethnicity of the recipient was recorded by police, 18 per cent were issued to people listed as Black, 11 per cent to people listed as Asian and 6 per cent to people of mixed race. Only 60 per cent of 'amplified music' fines were issued to white people, despite this group comprising more than 80 per cent of the UK's population. The statistics appear to reinforce what anecdotal evidence exists around the police's responses to unlicensed lockdown parties. On the hottest day of the year in late June 2020, around a week before restrictions on socializing were eased, footage from West London shows a vast majority-Black crowd being forcefully marshalled away from a party by massed lines of riot cops; over the same weekend in Stokes Croft, Bristol, a much more mixed audience was left to proceed by officers who feared it was 'too big to shut down.'

This is not surprising: research into the imposition of all Covid-related FPNs by the human rights group Liberty in 2021 found that BAME people were 54 per cent more likely to be fined than white people for breaching lockdown rules in general; it would appear that illegal Covid raving was merely a particularly acute example of wider prevailing trends. 'The government's approach during Covid was too broad, and laid the foundations for overzealous and inconsistent policing,' said Emmanuelle Andrews, policy and campaigns manager at Liberty. 'We saw throughout Covid that marginalised communities, those in deprived areas and people of colour really bore the brunt of fines and over-policing in general . . . These disparities weren't created by Covid, but the pandemic certainly amplified existing racism and discrimination.' But the policing of lockdown raves also spoke to deeper trends in the targeting of Black and Asian culture and communities, from Form 696 to stop-and-search. 'Whenever Black music is policed, we see it associated with disorder. The notion that something doesn't belong, doesn't count as music or art, doesn't fit the mould of what we consider normal,' said academic Lambros Fatsis. 'Four cellists walking into a park to play music together wouldn't be seen as a threat, but four or five Black kids rapping over a track on their phones might be. It's a culmination of wider attitudes to cultural difference and notions of civility.'

Evidence elsewhere suggests that illegal raving – at least the side of it which connected back to the pre-CJA free party scene – was as likely to have contracted rather than expanded during the pandemic, despite repeated claims of a surge in numbers. In the late spring of 2020, several of the UK's leading free party soundsystems even went as far as issuing a statement promising to 'hold the line' on public safety during lockdown, and suspend their events. Chris Liberator is a stalwart of the free party techno scene whose career dates back to the days of Spiral Tribe. In Autumn 2020, he told *Mixmag*: 'If you're a raver connected to the free party scene with your ear to the ground you know when events of a certain size are taking place. But, if you compare this summer to previous years when there was no lockdown, there were far fewer big illegal raves taking place during the pandemic.'

There's one other notable trend which should perhaps encourage us to take the press coverage claiming that the pandemic marked the triumphant return of the illegal rave with a colossal pinch of salt. It can be found in a *Guardian* article from February 2020 – the month *before* lockdown regulations were introduced – explaining why 'illegal raves are flourishing'. It's also present in a *New Statesman* piece on 'The return of rave culture' from August 2019. A *Daily Telegraph* article argues the same in March 2018, followed by the *NME* a couple of weeks later and *The Times* in June. *Huck* magazine and *The Guardian* (again) both claim that illegal raves are back in 2017, while an *Independent* article talks about an 'illegal rave renaissance' in 2016. Go back further, and you'll find a *Times* article mentioning 'the return of the illegal rave party' in 2006, and another *Guardian* piece on 'the return of the ravers' in 2005. The *Daily Mirror* mentions police breaking up an illegal rave ahead of the solar eclipse in 1999 while in 1996 the *Horley & Gatwick Mirror* recounts the local scandal of a hardcore metal band from Reigate* being charged with

---

* The article notes that the charges against the band, Xaxtreth, were

'involvement in illegal raves.' As regular as clockwork, right from the moment that the Criminal Justice Act clamped down on illegal raving, we have repeatedly been told that rave culture has finally returned. The only reasonable conclusion we can draw is that it never really went away.

Despite this, the people running these parties have certainly changed over the intervening twenty-five years. As rising ticket prices and an increasingly corporate club landscape drained the grassroots accessibility and anti-authoritarian rush out of mainstream dance music, increasing numbers of young people were drawn towards rawer, freer and more underground alternatives. *Vice*'s 2016 documentary *Locked Off* offers a window into the thought processes and motivating forces behind this newer generation of illegal rave promoters. 'We started off doing raves in clubs, and they were all right,' explains a member of the North Wales crew Diztorshon, all wearing matching hockey masks to obscure their identity. 'But people want to come to a rave and have a good time without dickheads over their shoulders, off their heads on beer.' Punters attending an illegal Diztorshon party in a remote quarry in the Forest of Denbigh agree: 'Once you've been to a rave and felt the atmosphere, it's well better,' says one. 'You don't feel uncomfortable, you don't feel out of place, no matter who's there, whereas if you went into town, the lads like to fight and the girls look you up and down and make you feel like shit.' Imagine yourself as a penniless twenty-year-old under the Coalition or Conservative governments of the 2010s: why on earth would you spend thirty quid to get groped by a bouncer on your way into some soulless enormo-club, where you'll spend the night surrounded by coked-out management consultants in V-neck T-shirts, watching some overhyped nerd from Berlin knock out market-tested business techno crowd-pleasers, when you could

---

eventually dropped, and – with a Spinal Tap-esque flourish – that they're currently looking to add 'a competent guitarist with a crazy streak' to their line-up.

break into a warehouse with a bunch of reprobates, and do whatever you wanted, for as long as you wanted, for free?

As the barge fills up, I'm left with much the same questions: my mounting excitement no longer feels restricted to defying Covid restrictions, but like it's some kind of rejoinder to the UK's entire surrounding set of economic and social pressures, borne disproportionately by the young, and protected by a system geared overwhelmingly towards the interests of the old. The generation dancing in front of me have been saddled with unmanageable debt for their education, when their parents were given grants. They've been stuck paying outrageous rents in decrepit flats, while buy-to-let landlords profit from a lifetime of asset inflation. They're working in entry-level jobs at pay levels broadly comparable to the 1990s, while the generations above plan for retirements buoyed by triple-lock pensions. They've been blamed for everything from declining birth rates to diminishing diamond sales, simultaneously painted as hopelessly self-absorbed and annoyingly earnest, patronized and told to grow up in the same breath. Why shouldn't they – and I – be allowed one stupid night of partying? The DJ, whom I recognize from the legal dance music world, but who's never been publicly linked to the illegal 'plague rave' scene, mixes from the sinewy percussive sounds of Lisbon's DJ Lycox into Rinse FM founder Geeneus's UK funky remix of Benga and Coki's dubstep classic 'Night', and the place erupts. It's noticeable how much more friendly, chatty and open the crowd is here than in your average London club, perhaps related to its members' prodigious and entirely undisguised drug intake. To one side of me, a twenty-something guy in a Hawaiian shirt sucks on a nitrous balloon, slumped against the curved internal wall of the boat, his eyes half-open. To the other, a girl in a white dress does a bump of something from her mate's fist. We get chatting, and she tells me over the din that 'We can't live in fear for ever. I haven't been raving since December, I've missed it *so much*.' Before I can decide whether she's a fearless advocate for the pleasure principle or question her on her lockdown raving history – December 2020 would have been at the height of the second Covid wave, with extremely stringent restrictions in place – she disappears into the sweating masses.

As the evening progresses, I'm plagued by more doubts. The event's been promoted as 'an intimate party with a maximum capacity of 80 people', but by my reckoning there's at least 120 punters here, well before the midnight cut-off point for guaranteed entry. Escaping the crush and climbing above deck, I find a queue of at least fifty more people ranged along the towpath, each waiting to board the barge, all in varying states of annoyance. 'I've paid twenty-five quid for this, you're letting me in,' says one woman, before shoving her way past a bemused and entirely unofficial-looking security guard, who lets her onboard without protest. As the night progresses the air is squeezed from the barge by ever more tightly pressed bodies, and a succession of decreasingly recognizable DJs move from bass-heavy but rhythmically fluid global club sounds to hammering 4/4 techno, which only increases my feelings of anxiety. There's the obvious problem of what to do if the police turn up, and the background hum of Covid-related risks (a much older crowd starts arriving in the early hours, noticeably raising the median age of the dance floor), but also a set of extremely visible issues around safety: the line of drunk, frustrated people standing haphazardly next to an unprotected and unlit body of water; the boat's single entrance and exit and its wildly over-filled interior; the lack of any apparent infrastructure to manage the crowd if things go wrong; and the self-policing narcotic opportunities of the free party leaving several people looking ruinously wasted. By 2 a.m. the stress has got to me and I decide to leave, before finding that someone's stolen my coat while I've been dancing. I get to Walthamstow station, only to discover that the Night Tube hasn't yet reopened, so I check my phone for details of the two-hour, three-bus journey ahead of me. I look up, and see an advert for easy-listening station Magic FM which declares 'Stay At Home: Dance With Us!'

And yet, even in that lowest of moments, my enthusiasm for lockdown raving terminally degraded by realizing that I'm now exhausted, cold, and trapped on the wrong side of London, some small flicker of illicit glee remains. I'm not convinced that 'dancing at home' was ever really an alternative for some people.

Despite our need for the collective release of the dance floor remaining undimmed by legal or physical risks, nightclubs remained at the bottom of the government's list of priorities throughout the pandemic. Late-night spaces would ultimately reopen in July 2021, long after pubs, theatres, gyms, football stadiums and other sites of mass entertainment had all returned to at least limited normality. Unlike the billions spent on the restaurant and hospitality sectors via 'eat out to help out', nightclubs' only meaningful source of state support was a competitive funding pot administered by Arts Council England, announced months after lockdown began, shared across the entire cultural sector, and which didn't even cover dance music initially. Forced to compete against institutions with deeper experience of applying for public funds, from community art galleries to the National Theatre, a substantial number of applicants across the UK dance music industry, from venues and festivals to labels and promoters, missed out entirely.

Where others were successful, this seemed to have less to do with genuine governmental support for dance music, and more with the box-ticking bureaucracy of public sector funding applications: reviewing the grants handed out over the course of the pandemic, it was notable how often large-scale operators like Resident Advisor, The Warehouse Project and Boiler Room, skilled in communicating their value to funders and investors, got the money they needed, while smaller but no less culturally important venues, labels and promoters faced far less certain odds.* One of the names listed as a

---

* These imbalances between large and small operators in the dispersal of Covid support funds was replicated elsewhere in the pandemic. LS Events Ltd, founded in 2004 by the former head of Creamfields and responsible for producing a number of large-scale dance music events, were able to leverage their wider production experience and economies of scale to set up a sub-company called HUB Logistics, which won multiple contracts to run Covid testing sites: a pivot clearly beyond the reach of grassroots dance music promoters.

successful applicant from the first round of the Arts Council's Culture Recovery Fund raised particular eyebrows: Sundissential, a Birmingham-based hard house promoter who had been hugely popular in the 1990s and early 2000s, but had thrown only a handful of small parties in recent years. Further digging revealed that the people behind Sundissential Limited — a man named John Nolan and a woman called Karen Muench, neither of whom had been involved with Sundissential during its 1990s heyday — had first registered with Companies House as a dormant company in 2017, reviving the organisation only days before Arts Council England's deadline for funding applications in September 2020, filing its first (and so far only) set of accounts, and expanding its 'nature of business' to include elements such as educational services and venue management, which could conceivably have broadened its appeal or eligibility for something like the Culture Recovery Fund. Their application form, published begrudgingly by Arts Council England only after a lengthy Freedom of Information appeal process, repeatedly emphasizes Sundissential's apparent tickbox-friendly qualities, from being queer-friendly to offering unspecified 'educational opportunities', and claims credit for events produced under the company's previous ownership. The application appears skilfully written to elicit a positive response, but substantial questions remain over its credibility, and the process by which it was deemed deserving of the just over £223,000 which was awarded to Sundissential in October 2020.

The following month a National Audit Office review of the Culture Recovery Fund's assessment process corroborated claims made in *Private Eye* that applications were assessed solely using ACE's automated Spotlight software rather than being reviewed in person. Certainly, anyone looking at Sundissential's application who had even the faintest familiarity with UK dance music would have known something was amiss — following the announcement of Sundissential's successful application, several news articles in the dance music press asked why a promoter who'd been largely inactive for years was deemed worthy of vast sums of public money, while numerous other venues and promoters working at the cutting edge of today's scene were turned down. The overwhelming impression was of a funding process completely detached from the culture it was supposedly supporting, and incapable of performing the required due diligence as a result. Arts Council England announced they were investigating Sundissential's grant application, but no further information was ever made public. The removal of Sundissential's funding was only revealed via an FOI request in 2022, but an internal Arts Council report – explaining why the grant was withdrawn, and why Sundissential were considered suitable for it in the first place – continues to be withheld on the basis that it would damage Sundissential's business prospects.* The police announced in March 2021 that they were investigating one potential case of fraud relating to the Culture Recovery Fund, but neither they nor Arts Council England would confirm the name of the applicant in question.

By the end of lockdown, many people connected to dance music had grown sick of being left at the back of the queue for support by an uninterested government. At the end of June 2021, dance music took to the streets, with as many as 10,000 ravers descending on Whitehall for the Save Our Scene protest, a scale of mobilization unseen since the days of the Criminal Justice Act. The brainchild of multimillion-pound Ibiza club magnate Kai Cant and charity campaigner George Fleming, Save Our Scene billed the march as a chance to stick two fingers up at the government's continued indifference towards nightclubs and dance music, prompted by yet another delay to the reopening of late-venues. On the fourteenth of June, as punters in top hats and ballgowns returned to Epsom races and the Royal Opera House, and 140,000 spectators were confirmed for the upcoming British Grand Prix, Boris Johnson announced that due to the increased transmissibility of the new Delta variant the

---

* At the time of writing, Sundissential Limited have filed no further accounts, and undertaken no further public activity. In January 2023, Companies House began compulsory strike-off action to dissolve them as a company.

final remaining Covid restrictions – largely concerned with clubs, music venues and late-night spaces – would remain in place for an additional month, until late July rather than late June. It all felt like extremely thin gruel, youth culture once again dismissed in favour of equally risky pursuits more likely to appeal to Conservative voters.

Another round of Arts Council funding was announced to try to cover this gap, enraging applicants who either still hadn't received the money they were promised earlier in the year, or didn't get any in the first place; the Department of Culture, Media and Sport had previously confirmed in February 2021 that a measly £495 million of the £830 million it had awarded the previous autumn had actually reached applicants' bank accounts. Like so much of the government's decision-making during the pandemic, an uneven and poorly communicated process left many wondering why certain sections of society had been so transparently prioritized over others, and those involved in dance music feeling like they'd been hung out to dry.

Despite this, Save Our Scene's political ideology remained loose and ill-defined: standing amongst the crowds filling Whitehall with the sound of breakbeats and airhorns, it felt less like political action than a bog-standard street party, the most apolitical 'political' protest I can remember. Instead, people were primarily focused on the tunes, dancing, and being with their mates; plenty were huffing nitrous oxide balloons, doing little bumps of powder, or otherwise swept up in the sensory pleasures of the moment. Where other protests invariably build in a crescendo of outrage as they pass Downing Street, there was little to no shift in mood here; a slogan on the side of the lead truck in the convoy read RIOT SQUAD, with an anarchist A, but this turned out to be an advert for a brand of vape liquid rather than anything more radical. Other aspects of the march suggested not an absence of political intent, but something more uncomfortable. It was surreal to hear the MC of a protest designed to confront the actions of the state shouting: 'Make some noise for the police! You've been working really hard, we appreciate you!' and being met by entirely unironic cheers. At one point, the march crossed paths with a cluster of transphobic protestors; the mixed reception their bigotry received suggesting that dance music's roots in queer and trans communities had been forgotten by some. At repeated points during the march, I was told to take off my mask, suggesting that the crowd's grasp on public health was similarly flakey.

More worryingly, the day's DJ line-up featured a number of artists who'd either ignored lockdown safeguards to continue playing parties throughout the pandemic, or who'd engaged in unapologetic anti-vaccine rhetoric on social media. Hannah Wants, one of the most famous DJs appearing at the protest and quoted extensively in Save Our Scene's press materials, spent the week beforehand reassuring her followers that the march's organizers weren't troubled by her dubious anti-vaccine scepticism, and encouraged people to attend the preceding day's conspiracy-heavy 'Freedom March', which called for an immediate end to all lockdown restrictions. Wants was far from the only dance music figure to dabble in this sort of rhetoric during the pandemic. Later in 2021 several prominent DJs, including UK garage originator Norris 'Da Boss' Windross and Shoom founder Danny Rampling, voiced their support for the Together Declaration – a somewhat more vociferous campaign against vaccine passports led by Alan Miller, onetime founder of the Night Time Industries Association and owner of the Vibe Bar on Brick Lane. In addition to his work in the night-time economy, Miller is also a longstanding figure in the UK's libertarian fringe, centred originally around the Revolutionary Communist Party and its magazine *Living Marxism*, then the website Spiked, the Institute of Ideas think-tank and numerous offshoot groups. The NTIA's first policy report in 2015 was credited to another Spiked stalwart, the sociologist Frank Furedi, more regularly found writing for the *Daily Mail* on topics such as 'woke indoctrination' and the left-wing 'cultural Taliban'. Miller's appearances on behalf of the NTIA dried up during the pandemic, but he continues to campaign for Together alongside a motley assortment of middle-aged DJs, GB News pundits and failed Brexit Party election candidates.

Despite all of this, there was still something undeniably inspiring about watching soundsystems and dancers occupy the heart of the city during the Save Our Scene march. Standing in Whitehall, hearing the relentless thud of the trucks as they passed, and watching the crowds cut shapes as they weaved their way past the heart of the British government merely underlined that the political power of rave has always been emergent rather than deliberate, impossible to pin down in slogans and agitprop. The assertion of our right to hedonistic release remains an inherent threat to state control, regardless of whether it's expressed in radical left-wing terms by collectives like Spiral Tribe, or via the libertarianism of Hannah Wants and others. The sight of the guy next to you coming up on a pill and rinsing out jungle tunes as you pass the Cenotaph speaks for itself; no further rhetoric needed.

But the question of what Save Our Scene and the wider dance music industry could actually *do* with that subversive energy remained frustratingly unclear. In the lead-up to the protest, Save Our Scene's leaders demanded that all nightlife venues should reopen immediately: a complete political non-starter while the Delta variant continued to surge. In his opening address to the march, former Radio 1 DJ Judge Jules inadvertently revealed a subtle but important shift in Save Our Scene's objectives, calling not for the immediate reopening of nightclubs but for the government to stick to its revised 19 July opening date. This felt like an overcorrection, from an impossible demand to one that Westminster was already committed to delivering. This singular focus on reopening ignored issues where public pressure might have had a chance to change government policy: better support for creatives unable to work because of lockdown, public underwriting of events insurance for festivals, protection from eviction for venues, or the intersection of these questions with other challenges facing marginalized communities. The absence of any discussion on these topics reflected Save Our Scene's lack of campaigning experience, their seemingly limited coalition-building efforts with trade unions, community groups, political activists and the wider dance music industry, or perhaps just a lack of interest in the details. Save Our Scene largely disappeared into the background once venues reopened in July 2021, with no apparent attempts to build more permanent campaign infrastructure or coalitions, most noticeably with the Black Lives Matter movement which had also erupted during the pandemic. 'We are currently at this anxiety-inducing point where festivals are being announced, scouring line ups for praxis, to see if anyone has listened or did the reading,' wrote Frankie Decaiza Hutchinson, founder of female-led DJ booking agency Discwoman, in the summer of 2021. 'The pandemic provided a point of reflection and space to look at what's wrong and try to make it right to commit to antiracism, [and] explore how the current industry upholds white supremacy. The fear of that being met with nothing is extremely difficult to process.'

Instead, it seemed that as soon as the clubs reopened, Save Our Scene lost interest in these wider conversations. They successfully mobilized the biggest rave-related protest for a quarter of a century, and got thousands of dancers to understand that the music they love is intrinsically tied to systems of political power. But when those protesters shouted for 'Freedom!' it was unclear precisely what they were thinking of, or being encouraged to imagine. This moment could have been the starting point for rethinking and rebuilding post-Covid dance floors along genuinely liberatory lines, connecting them to wider fights against racism, sexism and other injustices; or it might merely signal a return to the pre-pandemic status quo. The day after the march Hannah Wants posted, then swiftly deleted, a tweet which summed up the work still to do. 'Y'know another great thing about yesterday?' she wrote to her 77,000 followers: 'No politics, just music.'

DJ YUNG SINGH
PERFORMS AT BRIXTON
CLUB PHONOX, 2022

12. Just Like We Never Said Goodbye

The past, present and future of UK dance music

'Fifty-one point five zero nine three two nine, minus zero point three two zero five six one.' Dry ice swirls around the head of composer and sound artist Venus Ex Machina: she's seated at a desk onstage, performing an experimental piece titled 'Strange Fruit'. Her voice cuts through a storm of electrical crackles and the sound of city streets as she reads a list of seemingly random GPS coordinates into a microphone. It's September 2018, and I'm standing in the Stygian gloom of South London venue Corsica Studios: around us, the former Heygate estate and the Elephant and Castle shopping centre are being gutted and bulldozed, council tenants long since 'decanted' to the outer limits of the city. Brutalist blocks and small businesses selling African fabrics and Polish pickles have been torn down, to be replaced by luxury flats, gyms and artisanal brunch spots. 'Fifty-one point five zero eight nine two six, minus zero point one three two one eight seven.'

The performance and location speak powerfully to the renewed political intent of UK dance music in the years immediately before and after the Covid-19 pandemic. Venus Ex Machina's list of GPS coordinates are not random or meaningless, but in fact refer to searches of Black men undertaken by the Metropolitan Police under stop and search powers (including the Criminal Justice Act), drawn from publicly available police data. 'Fifty-one point five six eight one seven nine, minus zero point zero six six seven six zero' – this represents the corner of Oldhill Street in Upper Clapton, Hackney. 'Fifty-one point five five six four six seven, minus zero point zero seven six three seven four' – a residential street just off Stoke Newington Road. The performance is described as 'a personal remembrance of the young black lives impacted by racial profiling . . . to redress the gap between the detached inhumanity of police statistics, and the life-altering brutality that they represent.' But it also speaks to the history of UK dance music – a thread connecting back through contemporary moral panics around UK drill and knife crime, to the passing of the Criminal Justice Act and attempts to disrupt free party soundsystems, and the use of 'sus' laws to target blues dances a generation before. 'One of the intentions behind the historic policing of Black British music is precisely because it has political potential,' says Shannen SP from the record label Hyperdub, who's curated tonight's event as part of a monthly series called Ø, placing this unsettling piece of political performance art on a bill next to DJ sets from UK garage stalwart El-B and dance-pop auteur Tirzah. 'Stopping people from congregating means you're stopping them from sharing ideas, you're stopping them from talking about things, you're stopping them from just being together.' Venus Ex Machina will continue reading for four hours, pushing herself to the point of exhaustion; in that time, the dance floor transforms from a place of joy to one of mourning, a litany for those whose humanity has been stripped out by the blunt machinations of the state.

If there's a single overarching theme which defines UK dance music in the later 2010s and early 2020s, either side of the Covid-19 pandemic, then it's a re-establishment of club culture's roots in queer, trans, feminist, Black, Asian and other marginalized experiences, and a recognition of its associated political power. Far from being diminished or diluted as a result of co-option by the Boiler Rooms and Broadwick Lives of the world, UK dance music has instead done what it's always done: mutated, refocused and found new ways to tease social and political meaning from the act of losing yourself in the crowd. This has not been an unalloyed success, as the continued prominence of straight white men at the top of festival line-ups and the continual barrage of narrow-minded invective across social media might indicate, but it's clear that things are – albeit slowly – beginning to change. UK dance music now is suffused with a sense of re-assertion and homecoming, the feeling of communities and voices who've been arbitrarily shut out of the culture finally able to reclaim what's always been theirs. On 2015's 'Just Like We Never Said Goodbye', the trans dance producer and pop artist SOPHIE sings a paean to lost and rediscovered love, the realisation that everything she ever needed was right here all along: backed by a flurry of hoover basslines, euphoric synths and chipmunk-like sped-up vocals, her words take on grander possibilities, a love song to rave culture's own radical and joyful re-liberation.

'For me, Blackness has always been defined in binary opposition to whiteness,' says Shannen SP, 'so I feel like Black culture *is* counterculture, just through that mechanism. We see that with rap and drill, where the reason it's so popular is because it's this countercultural, oppositional thing, but then a lot of the fans are, like, young white kids.' From working with Just Jam's Tim and Barry and producing shows for NTS Radio, Shannen was hired by Kode9 to do A&R for his label Hyperdub – home to Burial, Laurel Halo and others – and co-curate Ø, a night he described as 'an experiment in clubbing'. Merging DJs and live performances with art installations and performances – the latter often with an avowedly political slant – Ø sought to broaden both the sonic forms and creative concepts contained within London's club scene, and the people who might feel at home there: Venus Ex Machina and El-B in adjoining rooms one month, The Otolith Group giving a lecture on experimental Black composer Julius Eastman while Laurel Halo spun pounding techno the next. 'I wouldn't say that the curation and world-building was utopian in the sense of, like, creating some perfect world where we're all holding hands,' Shannen explains, 'but it was about bringing people to the club, showing them that you can learn in a club . . . trying to build a world that I might want to inhabit, musically, even if it's just for one night.' And yet even the immediate context around that space reinforced the need for it to exist: in a Zoom panel discussion hosted during lockdown by DJ and producer Scratcha DVA, Shannen talks about 'events I've run with an all-Black line-up, where Black kids turn up and just get harassed on the door'. When we speak she's quick to defend Corsica Studios' security staff – it remains unclear whether her bad experiences were related specifically to Ø – but the possibility of young Black men being disproportionately targeted while trying to attend a performance art piece about the overuse of police search powers remains bleakly ironic.

Elsewhere, the renewal or rediscovery of UK dance music's political dimension has been deeply felt amongst a new generation of UK-based DJs, artists, promoters and dancers of Asian and South Asian heritage. In the late 1980s DJs such as Radical Sista established a network of alcohol-free 'daytimer' parties in Bradford and around the North West, playing a mix of house, hip hop and bhangra to crowds of South Asian kids (initially from Punjabi communities specifically) in community halls and youth centres. One attendee recounts ducking into the school toilets at lunchtime to change out of their salwar kameez and into sportswear and make-up, ready for an afternoon rave: 'Our parents thought we had been at the library, it was like a secret club for us all.' Much like the Black crowds attending blues dances, the experiences of Asian youth at events like these were shaped inexorably by wider societal pressures: their daytime nature was in part a nod to more conservative parental expectations, but also the fact that venue owners largely refused to offer brown-skinned promoters night-time slots. At a time when the National Front and their allies in the Conservative party were running rampant in the streets and the statute books respectively, daytimers provided British Asians with a safe communal space, and the chance to build a cultural identity which wasn't reflected anywhere else in British society. 'There was a gap and there was a thirst for something to fill it, so daytimers just rocketed,' said Radical Sista. 'It was about creating a new identity for Asians in the UK that had not existed before.'

Released in 2014, Riz Ahmed's semi-autobiographical short film *Daytimer* provides a fictionalized account of a party in London one afternoon in 1999: teenage boys with gelled hair smoking weed and talking shit in the back of a cramped Volkswagen Golf; girls wearing Adidas tracksuits and petulant stares; a group of Muslim lads are pulled from a fight with a Sikh guy, before the muffled bass and two-step rhythms of 138 Trek by DJ Zinc draw them from the afternoon light into the windowless gloom of the club. By the time Ahmed was going to daytime parties at the end of the 1990s, the generation who'd grown up raving to DJs like Radical Sista and bhangra stars like Bally Sagoo a decade earlier had broken through into the dance music mainstream. Talvin Singh and Sweety Kapoor's Anokha clubnight at the Blue Note in Hoxton acted as the fulcrum for a loosely defined 'Asian Underground' stretching from the tabla-and-sitar-meet-jungle of 'IC408' by State of Bengal, to Nitin Sawhney's cinematic trip-hop, to Asian Dub Foundation's militant lyrics dealing with everything from the imprisonment of Satpal Ram[*] to Maoist uprisings in India in the 1960s.

---

[*] Ram had been convicted of murder in 1987 after being attacked with a broken bottle and stabbing his white attacker in what Ram consistently

But trying to corral such disparate sounds into a single category was always going to make for an awkward fit. A white-controlled music media remained unwilling to judge Asian music on its own terms, instead viewing and defining it solely through the lens of racial otherness. Sawhney outlined his ambivalence to the 'Asian underground' label in 2019, celebrating the sense that 'cultural change could occur and that Asians would feel they have a relevance and identity within the wider culture' while simultaneously dismissing the grouping together of all Asian music into one undifferentiated 'underground'. Others within the scene were more unambigiously focused on radical politics, and resistance to the Orientalising instincts of white society. 'I think we could easily be a thorn in the backside of a lot of liberal people, or people that think they're liberal. I think as Asian people we're kind of throwing back at them. They'll come up with their terms, but it's all bullshit,' said Aki Nawaz of Asian Dub Foundation, who were joined at the anti-Criminal Justice Act protests and on Rock Against Racism stages by acts like Fun^Da^Mental, the latter derided by *The Observer* as 'Belligerent Paki-fists'. Even Apache Indian, better known for 1993 hit single 'Boom Shack-A-Lack', released an explicitly anti-BNP single titled 'Movin' On'. And yet old orthodoxies persisted: following Talvin Singh's Mercury Prize win for his debut album *OK* in 1999, trends began to shift and popular attention moved on; with the September 11th attacks permanently altering the relationship between Western governments and diasporic communities, the willingness of mainstream media to champion Asian artists withered even further. While individual artists like Jai Paul, Steel Banglez or M.I.A. would occasionally break through, it would take until the 2020s for British Asian dance music to reassert itself as a collective force.

---

claimed was self-defence. A campaign to overturn his conviction focused on the lack of translation provided for Bengali-speaking defence witnesses, the ineffectiveness of Ram's court-appointed barrister, and the brutal treatment afforded him in prison: each argued as evidence of the criminal justice system's inherent racism.

If there's one moment which defines the return of South Asian dance music to the foreground, then it comes early in a set by Yung Singh, a DJ with Punjabi Sikh roots, streamed on Boiler Room in August 2021 – evidence of the diminished platform's intermittent ability to still engage positively with underground culture. The lineup curated by Singh, hosted at London venue Colour Factory, includes the collective Daytimers: a revival of the old name by a new generation of DJs, producers and promoters. The party begins with a re-edit of the Punjabi folk classic 'Kori (Giddah)' by Panjabi MC and Sarvjeet Kaur, which combines the original's uptempo middle section with the whistling synths and overwhelming bass pressure of Benga and Coki's dubstep anthem 'Night': a looped snatch of Punjabi vocals spirals upwards into the night sky, the pressure building, before the beat drops and the room explodes. On either side of Yung Singh there's a man in a Burberry turban and sunglasses, and a woman in elegantly embroidered salwar kameez, pushed forward by the crowd, arms flailing everywhere. The tune is wheeled up, and the predominantly South Asian audience roars as one. A few minutes later Yung Singh drops another bootleg, this time of Bollywood tune 'Dola Re Dola', laid over the propulsive grime of 'Forward Riddim' by Dexplicit (the instrumental version of the Lethal Bizzle tune which had soundtracked student protests a decade earlier); Singh ends up having to plead with the now uncontrollably rowdy crowd to stop jostling the decks. 'Part of my experience as a British Asian has been struggling with my identity,' reads the top comment under the YouTube upload of his performance. 'This set blended so much of the music that shaped me.'

A month later Daytimers would collaborate with two other crews – No I.D., the club night run by producer, DJ and former Boiler Room programmer Ahad Elley, and Chalo, a global label and diasporic creative community facilitated by Indian–Canadian culture writer Dhruva Balram – on a day-long festival of South Asian music in North London called Dialled In. Much like the 'Asian underground' of the 1990s, the line-up was hugely varied – from dreamy guitar-pop courtesy of Nabihah Iqbal to frenetic global club sounds from Chippy Nonstop – but this felt a million miles away from the top-down pigeonholing Sawhney and Singh struggled against. Instead, Dialled In underlined how South Asian artists from wildly different genres could share a communal space without being lumped together. For artists and attendees alike, the creation and occupation of a cultural space that felt like it belonged to them was revelatory: 'It was just huge for me being in a space where I could easily talk with people who were South Asian or had some kind of South Asian roots about our experiences in a really comfortable way,' said Debi Ghose, who performed under her DJ name DEBONAIR. 'When you're young and really trying to figure out you are, particularly in a tough landscape where things are majority white . . . being in a space with 1,800 other people who look like you and have the same kind of experiences must be really comforting,' says Balram. 'If you're 19 or 20 years old, you've maybe never had that before . . . that opportunity for people to grasp how similar their experiences are, and to be physically in a room together post-Covid.'

A key aspect of Dialled In, and a clear point of divergence from the Asian underground of two decades before, was the retention of creative agency and ownership. This was not an attempt to bargain with major labels, or to find a space in the white-controlled nightlife industry or music media, but to build something self-supported and self-sustaining. 'We're trying not to rely on the music press or other obligations too much, and just focus on our thing, building a platform which can outlast that,' says Elley. 'Because, you know, the way press cycles work we might be cool one summer, which might have been last summer, and then no one's interested the following year. We're trying to stay outside that and build our own structures which offer long-term development and our own platform.'

As a writer and journalist, Balram is even more suspicious of industry-dictated hype cycles: 'What happens with any kind of community is that they choose one or two artists to platform, and they continue platforming and uplifting them without necessarily uplifting the wider community,' he says. 'They go on what's reflected in the clicks and online virality, but there are people out there who are much more talented who maybe don't use social media as well' – a focus on individual over communal identity which makes it harder to challenge wider assumptions. 'I think the white gaze has moved on from the South Asian scene,' Balram continues. 'As a freelancer, last year if I was pitching a story I'd get a commission like *that*. But this summer it's been really hard. One national publication came back to me saying they were already profiling one South Asian artist this month, and so two would be too many.' The solution to this has involved building Dialled In, Chalo, No I.D. and Daytimers up into an integrated, community-focused creative network offering workshops, training, content platforms and mentorships focusing on strengthening and sharing the perspective of South Asian people with a connection to dance music. Bollywood-and-bassline bangers might go viral on Boiler Room – even as Bollywood's dubious representations of Punjabi Sikhs can create complex cultural associations for artists like Yung Singh – but what really matters is the social and political infrastructure which blossoms out from the dance floor. 'It's not just about doing it for a couple of months,' says Balram, 'it's about taking away power away from the people who rule the roost . . . instead of all fighting over the same piece of pie, we just go and bake our own.'

Where the work of Dialled In and the community around it underlines UK dance music's ongoing role in unpicking questions around race, others continue to use the dance floor to address issues around gender and sexuality, including the way those identities intersect with ethnicity. 'Even though we can see more women, it doesn't necessarily mean that they're getting through the door,' says Shannen SP. 'When you do see a Black woman on the line-up – and I know this from my own career and those of my friends who are DJs – she's getting paid a lot less. It's almost like she's just there for the optics.' In part, as with Black and Asian artists struggling to break through, this is because the generational transfer of industry knowledge, connections and inspiration from older generations to younger upstarts doesn't exist in the way it does for whiter, straighter, or more masculine artists. 'What you find when you look at the history of dance music is that it favours particular people,' says Julia Toppin. 'There have been a lot of Black women out there . . . people managing their boyfriends who were really big DJs, but when they broke up, they just went back to doing admin work or whatever, when they actually had all this skill and experience. If they were men, they would have just morphed into doing music management somewhere else, but didn't even realize they were doing music management, do you know what I mean?' Toppin recounts a conversation with Katherine Green, the leader of a research project covering the hyper-local history of early 1990s pirate radio stations in Waltham Forest, in which Green recalls a jungle DJ called Cheryl who was a huge name in the local jungle scene, 'and then she married some guy, went to Australia or Canada or whatever, and just disappeared. And that was it. Women have children, family . . . I think sometimes it's easier for men to just run off and do their thing.'

Perhaps the most visible recent attempt to break down some of these inconsistencies has been Pxssy Palace, a party unambiguously focused on London's queer, trans and intersex people of colour, whose increasing industry and media attention has been accompanied by a steadfast refusal to water down any of those principles. Where a clubnight like this would once have been relegated prudishly to the inner pages of mainstream dance music magazines (if they were covered at all) or accepted only to the extent that it consented to smoothing off its more radical edges, shifting societal narratives around race, sexuality and gender identity, along with less narrowly gated online media, have seen Pxssy Palace lauded and uplifted. 'It's more than just clubbing. It's about creating a sense of community where everyone really cares about each other,' says one narrator in a film about Pxssy Palace funded by sportswear brand Converse. Harking back to those very first queer blues dances in Pearl Alcock's basement, Pxssy Palace started off throwing house parties before taking things public: wherever they were held, though, their events were about more than just the rush of the dance floor, with a focus on chill-out spaces, shared food and communal safety within the club, and daytime meet-ups, workshops and mental health sessions outside it, all echoing the 'electric church' of the blues dance some forty years previously; not a transactional leisure activity, but an entire alternative social order. 'My favourite part of Pxssy Palace is seeing people transform,' said Scottish-born promoter Nadine Artois in a 2020 video interview. 'They become more free, and more confident in themselves. I understand what that's like, because that's exactly what I did.'

Eventually, this increased visibility collided with Pxssy Palace's commitment to their principles. Despite a queer POC rave in East London not being the place you'd expect to find the average *Daily Express* or *Daily Mail* reader, both newspapers were apparently *outraged* to discover that they weren't on the guestlist. 'Fury as nightclub charges straight men six times more for entry,' read a headline in the *Daily Express*, while *Daily Mail* commenters frothed about 'proof (if it was needed) that straight white males are the most discriminated against' and claimed that 'if this policy was reversed the woke brigade would be claiming to be downtrodden.' As always with the right-wing media's attempt to foment outrage and stoke wider culture war rhetoric, it remained bafflingly unclear who, if anyone, had been offended by Pxssy Palace's door policies prior to the articles appearing (the *Daily Mail* commenters above, hailing from Guildford and Horsham respectively, seem unlikely to have been regular attendees). This manufactured controversy glossed over the extremely clear and entirely reasonable explanations provided on Pxssy Palace's own website. Where people aren't from the marginalized communities Pxssy Palace is created for, or where they've consistently disrupted previous parties (in responding to the *Daily Mail*, Pxssy Palace mentioned several incidents of violence in the club involving straight cis men) they're invited to ask themselves: 'Why are they coming? Who are they coming with? And if they are coming, how are they contributing to the space?' While one of the suggested ways to address this is by paying more on the door, or donating for a fund which pays for taxis home for trans people of colour at greater risk of late-night violence, it's also made clear that the policy is not policed, and that it's up to each attendee to pick a tier which aligns with their ability to pay.

Following their tabloid coverage, Pxssy Palace had to have some uncomfortable conversations with E1, the venue where their parties were hosted, while Kickstarter cancelled a crowdfunding appeal being run by the collective. But for the most part the experience increased their profile, emboldened their approach, and spurred them on to bigger things. If it was already funny watching suburban reactionaries work themselves into a frenzy over an inner-city queer club, Pxssy Palace's reaction to their outrage – temporarily changing the amount charged to straight cis men from £112 to £1,120 – made it even more surreally hilarious. In September 2022 they launched their inaugural festival Overflo: the queer, trans POC dance floor moving from the model of the blues dance to that of the free festival (those higher ticket prices helping to provide *gratis* entry for those unable to pay) and its dreams of a self-contained society built on different, better and more equitable principles.[*]

Alongside race, sexuality and gender, wider notions of class and agency have also been a key part of UK dance music's post-Covid politics, requiring an expansion of the discussion beyond the fringes of the dance floor, or the identities of those on the line-up and the guestlist. In August 2022, London queer venue Dalston Superstore announced that its workforce had unionized: while a first for the capital (and possibly for the entire UK), it certainly felt unusual for the employment conditions of a relatively small independent venue to merit national news coverage. A statement from employees and union reps Ayanna van der Maten and Max Beecher lays bare the connections between the cultural impact of UK dance music, and more concrete solidarity: what good is a communal dance floor, if

---

[*] Overflo was postponed the week before it was due to take place, as a result of Queen Elizabeth II's funeral being scheduled for the same day, and requiring the reallocation of officers from other events across London. As of December 2022 Pxssy Palace have not confirmed a new date.

the workers facilitating it are being exploited? 'Working in hospitality is often under-valued as a career and as a result work conditions and expectations can be unreasonable,' they write. 'Being a unionised workplace is an important step in recognising the value of the hard work we all do and sets an example for others in hospitality. We are proud to work at Dalston Superstore as we believe it has improved the lives of many queer people and we see being unionised as a part of that.' Later the same month, bar staff at Boomtown issued a collective statement alleging systematic mistreatment by subcontractors Freemans Event Partners which alleged 'threatening, belittling treatment' from managers, seventeen-hour shifts without breaks, 'invasive full-body searches' and 'various forms of discriminatory behaviour'. In response, Freemans Event Partners issued a statement that confirmed that they were looking into the allegations, while also providing a detailed explanation of their staff procedures and policies, which they stated were 'put in place to ensure the welfare and safety of employees, and to maintain the highest standard of operations and event delivery'. If you were to imagine a dance music ecosystem which properly reflected the liberatory potential of the music itself, then staff welfare might be one place to start: applying pressure to DJs and dancers, calling on them to only play at or buy tickets for events which guarantee a certain level of pay and working conditions for the people making it happen, would seem like a fairly uncontroversial ask in philosophical or ideological terms, but one with the possibility to profoundly alter the wider role UK dance music plays sociopolitically.

Elsewhere, bonds of economic solidarity and social responsibility are increasingly being baked into the very function, structure and ownership of the club itself: if capitalism instinctively, remorselessly absorbs underground culture into itself, turning everything from Blackness to queerness into a sellable product, then one response involves building structures which are fundamentally incapable of being commercialised. Founded in 2009, Cosmic Slop has built a reputation as one of the best parties in the UK: with a superb crew of resident DJs and unannounced guests playing to a joyous and easygoing 200-strong crowd on a hand-built soundsystem, it imports the free-spirited communality of David Mancuso's loft parties to a red-bricked former foundry in Mabgate, a working-class area of Leeds. But the audience's experience of the party is only one part of the picture: the event also functions as the primary fundraising tool for Music and Arts Production, or MAP, a charity which provides arts courses and training for local young people, particularly those excluded from mainstream education. Tickets for the club night feed directly back into MAP's charitable work, while those on the courses gain practical experience, for example designing the space in which the parties take place; an ecosystem which both gives the charity cultural kudos, and protects its financial interests at a time when government funding for social ventures has been gutted. 'People say I should have gone to a bigger venue, should be doing this or that, but this is a long-haul thing,' Slop founder Tom Smith told Resident Advisor in 2017. 'I want to be here for 50 years. Seven years in, we've not commercialised or commodified it. We haven't dispelled that air of mystery. I think that's important if we're going to have a culture that's worth fighting for and don't just crumble at the slightest whiff of financial gain, even if it's for charity.' Cosmic Slop's example reflects a growing trend for underground UK dance music to engage directly with the politics of physical space, and the foundation of a number of community-owned clubs around the UK looking to safeguard cultural diversity and freedom, insulating themselves as far as possible from the pressures of property speculation and corporate co-option. Other independent dance music operators have done the same, securing community-led spaces in which to perform and party, feeding back into local economies and reducing their dependence on external venues. In 2021, Liverpool-based dance music radio station Melodic Distraction secured £36,000 in crowdfunding to found a studio, cafe and bar to act both as an income generator and creative hub. Another crowdfunding appeal in Bristol led to the creation of Strange Brew, an independent community space functioning variously as a bar, nightclub, record shop, art gallery, market and lecture hall. In Nottingham the promoter Lukas Wigflex, whose older sister was a DiY regular back in the 1990s, has been instrumental in the establishment of Fisher Gate Point, another community-focused dance music venue.

This utopian vision of UK dance music – rooted in tight-knit community values and control over physical space, freed from capitalist extraction or cultural compromise – is not a new invention. Where collectives like Daytimers or Pxssy Palace seek to carve out new self-sustaining spaces for themselves and their communities, they're also on some level retreading a path laid down by the radical ravers of previous generations: those like the Luton-based Exodus collective, who evolved from a free party soundsystem to something approaching a holistic social movement, encompassing everything from housing to urban farming. Although various members of the soundsystem and wider collective had known each other since childhood, Exodus as an entity was born in 1992, with the squatting of Long Meadow Farm in Luton – an agricultural site which had been compulsorily purchased by the Department of Transport as part of their plans to widen the M1 motorway, before both the project and the site were abandoned – and a series of free parties which quickly took on a life of their own.

In the early 1990s, Exodus built a remarkably broad community of ravers and activists, investing their work with a unusually robust collective identity and purpose: they weren't just interested in throwing parties and listening to music, but in creating entire networks of communal support and solidarity. Money from the rave collection buckets went to support squatters at a nearby derelict hospice (renamed the Housing Action Zone, in a nod to Hakim Bey) and to restore the renamed Long Meadow *Community* Farm to something approaching working order. From these beginnings, Exodus dreamed of a path to legitimacy and permanence, in the form of a community centre they pre-emptively named The Ark: monthly raves would fund a wealth of services and resources, from creative studios and a local newspaper to cut-price food and affordable housing. Combining the new Travellers' dreams of a truly alternative, self-sustaining society with a free party that never stopped, The Ark would be a self-contained ecosystem, carrying the Exodus collective out of the toxicity of Babylon.

Right from their earliest occupation of Long Meadow Farm in 1992, however, Exodus were the focus of aggressive police attention, from violent raids on the unused properties they'd squatted to multiple unsuccessful prosecutions of Exodus members for everything from noise pollution to murder. Following one raid, senior Exodus member Paul Taylor was charged with drug possession, but the prosecution collapsed due to inconsistencies in the police's account of where and how the drugs in question had been found: Exodus themselves claimed vociferously that they'd been planted. In April 1995, South Bedfordshire Councillors from all three major political parties responded to the police's continued raids, not – as you might expect – by providing additional support in order to secure convictions of Exodus members, but by instead setting up an independent inquiry into the actions of the police, chaired by veteran human rights lawyer Michael Mansfield QC. 'This remains the first and only example,' writes the journalist Tim Malyon 'of a local council voting to investigate its own police force.'

Despite the inquiry ultimately being kicked into the long grass by the Home Office, and amidst criticism of Exodus from local Luton MP Graham Bright (the man responsible in 1990 for the UK's first anti-rave legislation), the collective's community work continued to produce social benefits which stretched well beyond the boundaries of the dance floor. Their raves were found to coincide with a drop in local crime levels, while the wider collective provided housing and employment at little to no public cost. When riots broke out at the nearby Marsh Farm Estate in 1995, tensions were soothed only when residents decamped en masse to an Exodus party on the Saturday night. In 1998, Exodus members identified and began squatting a nearby abandoned factory, the perfect location for their long-dreamt-of community centre. Three years later, they secured a £50 million grant from the Blair government's 'New Deal for Communities' fund, payable over the following decade; they bought the factory site in 2003, and in 2011 opened Marsh Farm Futures House, achieving their dream of building The Ark.

The lessons left by Exodus for today's radical dance music collectives, from Daytimers to Cosmic Slop, are obvious: where the thing you need doesn't exist, don't wait around for the discredited and corporatized dregs of the mainstream UK dance music industry to provide it for you; go out and build it yourself. 'Gather up the resources around you. Involve your friends. The thing doesn't have to be big or significant and it definitely doesn't have to be perfect,' writes Emma Warren in *Make Some Space*, a history of the semi-legal studio and performance space Total Refreshment Centre, from which a new wave of London jazz would emerge in the late 2010s. 'Unless you tell your own stories then people who don't share your lived experience – the material that underpins all culture – are likely to.'

This principle feels especially relevant at a time when the connections between underground culture of all kinds, including UK dance music, and more traditional Westminster campaigning and electoral politics are weakening. In the lead-up to the 2017 General Election, a surge in youth voting – and the surprising success of Jeremy Corbyn – was attributed in part to the 'Grime 4 Corbyn' campaign, in which rappers including Stormzy and JME stepped up to voice their support for the first leader in living memory to treat the interests of young people with anything more than cursory lip service: on the day of Labour's manifesto launch, the hashtag associated with it (#labourmanifesto) attracted substantially less social media traction than the one dedicated to #grime4corbyn. For a generation disenfranchised by and disillusioned with the tired old theatre of electoral politics, this offered a unique moment to tie together a cultural movement that spoke to young Britain on its own terms, and a Labour party capable of more than the lukewarm liberalism of what had preceded it. Such hopes were misplaced: once the temporary high of *nearly* defeating Theresa May (but, of course, still losing) had faded, Labour largely cut ties with grime artists, and indeed youth culture as a whole. When Boris Johnson called another election in 2019 and the canvassers came crawling back, hoping for a repeat of the same goodwill from two years earlier, the response was markedly less positive. 'They didn't follow up. They weren't expecting a general election so soon, and it's a bit late to go to the grime community now after ignoring us,' one anonymous industry figure said. 'To be honest with you, it was bullshit. It made no difference to anyone.' AJ Tracey told the *NME* of his dalliance with electoral politics, which he now felt didn't remotely represent him, his community or his culture. 'I'm done with supporting political parties.'

This feeling of detachment from traditional political processes was reinforced in April 2022 when the Police, Crime, Sentencing and Courts Bill passed into law: a terrifying extension of the Criminal Justice Act's authoritarian tendencies, which expanded stop-and-search powers, curtailed the right to protest and further cramped the limited space in which Gypsy, Roma and Traveller communities might try to eke out an existence. While opposition to the bill dusted off 1994's 'Kill the Bill' slogan, 2022's patchwork coalition of squatters, Travellers, protestors and other countercultural groups notably lacked the cultural edge previously provided by the free party rave scene; judging by the vastly larger scale of UK dance music's Save Our Scene protests the year before, ravers as a whole were now more interested in their own freedom to dance than the wider framework those freedoms might exist within. Despite the Labour party mustering the courage to vote against the government's proposals rather than abstaining as they had in 1994, the wider campaign against the Policing Bill felt entirely unlike the earlier movement against the Criminal Justice Act. Protest marches across the UK in January failed to attract anywhere near the numbers drawn to Trafalgar Square nearly two decades earlier, and elicited little response from a dance music scene more interested in fighting other battles.

That's not to say that dance music has given up entirely on the political process, though. One of the most exciting developments in the post-Covid era has taken place in Northern Ireland, with a younger generation of clubbers, promoters and DJs taking on direct responsibility for lobbying the government, rather than outsourcing that work to a separate political class of Night Czars, 'night-time economy' experts or corporate property developers. With licensing powers devolved from Westminster, Northern Ireland retains arguably the most draconian restrictions on dancing anywhere in Europe, with clubs unable to open past 3 a.m. and drinking banned after 1 a.m. When a 2021 review of licensing laws by the government failed to deal with the issue, DJ and promoter Holly Lester formed the campaign group Free The Night with a number of other Northern Irish nightlife operators including techno veteran Sunil Sharpe, and started long overdue conversations with policymakers. 'The last time any of these rules were properly discussed was 25 years ago, and sadly the outcome of this recent amendment is just not the progressive approach we'd been hoping for,' Lester said at the time. 'What we're asking for as Free The Night is that entertainment licenses can be extended by one hour, meaning that if venues choose to, we can keep drinking until 2am and dancing until 4am. We don't think that's a lot to ask for.'

A direct, personal connection to Northern Irish dance floors has been a critical part of Free The Night's campaigning: when they meet with Assembly members at Stormont to put their case forward, it's Holly relating her own direct experiences as a DJ, not refracting those arguments through the priorities of others. In a political and social environment where older generations have been burnt out by decades of sectarian violence and political corruption, there is now space for a newer generation to articulate their cultural and political needs on their own terms. 'Almost everyone involved is under 30,' Lester explains. 'The pandemic has given creatives the space to find our voices politically, and some of the older generation of ravers in Northern Ireland are jaded, for want of a better word. The way politics works here is exhausting, and people here are really tired.' Free The Night's immediate demands for Northern Irish nightlife to operate on the same terms as the rest of the UK are simple and compelling. But they're also building a foundation for deeper and more searching re-evaluations of what dance music means to people in the region, and how it can be reimagined from a grassroots perspective. 'What I want to see, in five years' time, is that young people can live here and have all their creative, social and career needs met,' says Lester. 'This licensing part is the first step, but there are so many other issues that we want to target.'

The direction of travel has not all been positive, however: even as UK dance music has found new political purpose and meaning in recent years, it also remains highly vulnerable to the same reactionary politics and corporate co-option which have hollowed out so much of what's come before. Thirty-five years on from the Second Summer of Love, rave culture is rapidly approaching middle age, with its familiar myths and approved canon remaining hard to dislodge, alongside a reliance on nostalgia which risks fundamentally warping or limiting our understanding. In late 2022 the London Film Festival, with funding from the British Film Institute and Arts Council, hosts 'In Pursuit of Repetitive Beats' – a VR 'experience' located the National Theatre, which promises to recapture the thrill of attending an illegal rave in Coventry in 1992. On arrival, I'm strapped into a VR headset complete with headphones and a Subpac,* then loaded into the VR environment: I'm transported variously from a microscopic flight down the grooves of a vinyl record to a rave-obsessed teenager's bedroom, then the inside of a Vauxhall Nova gliding down a digitally reconstructed motorway, a phone booth next to a garage, waiting for the party line to activate, and then finally a massive virtual warehouse, spectral CGI figures dancing around me as 'Chime' by Orbital plays. Throughout, a collection of talking heads repeat largely the same familiar perspectives on UK dance music which have been circling since 1992. The whole

---

* A kind of music-triggered vest, which connects to an audio input and vibrates to replicate the satisfying low-frequency thud in your chest from kickdrums and basslines produced by a massive speaker stack, in time with the music being heard through your headphones.

thing is expertly produced and thrillingly immersive, but feels conceptually and creatively inert: the reification of 'rave' as a static, historical artefact, a fossilized thing trapped in amber rather than a vital and ongoing culture. I find myself comparing the public funding lavished on looking backwards, with the uneven support of dance music during the pandemic, and wonder why someone wanting to understand and experience dance music wouldn't just spend their money on going to an actual rave.

This narrowing canon and a deference to the totems of the past reflects contemporary UK dance music's inconsistent attempts to grapple with structural, political or economic questions about how that culture is produced and whose interests it serves. This is reflected clearly in the specialist dance music media which, despite making substantial and laudable strides in terms of diversity and political engagement – both in terms of the music being covered and their operations behind the scenes – remain hemmed in by a web of conflicting economic obligations. The financial precariousness of magazine and digital publishing means that dance music platforms are increasingly reliant on the parts of the industry which actually make money – which ultimately means big promoters and festivals – limiting their ability to fully interrogate the power structures at play beneath the surface, or handle topics which might implicate or threaten the people they depend on for advertising. 'Music publications operate as a kind of middleman in the larger distribution chain of the music industry', writes the critic DeForrest Brown Jr, '[whose] sole purpose is to distribute and sell music.' Whatever surface-level progress has been made on representation within the media or the artists it covers, these opaque financial interests continue to result in genres and artists catering to certain audiences being covered extensively, while other communities – largely those on the fringes – are still expected to make do with scraps. Kodwo Eshun writes in 1998's *More Brilliant Than the Sun* of a British dance music press whose 'hagiographies and its geographies, its DJ recipes, its boosterism, its personality profiles' constrict rather than empower the culture it's built on: however things might have changed since then, it's hard to argue that these criticisms aren't still relevant.

One particular piece published in August 2022 on Resident Advisor (a platform which, in fairness, also publishes plenty of exceptional investigative journalism) embodies this sense of superficiality and incuriousness. Titled 'How to Make It as an Artist' the piece is a fever dream of tech industry jargon and self-help blather, which claims that 'making it' is largely synonymous with going viral on social media, from which an endless stream of gig bookings, industry access and cultural capital are presumed to flow. No attempt is made is to grapple with knottier questions, like artists paying their rent in an increasingly unforgiving economy, establishing an engaged and sustainable fanbase when our attentions are under constant digital bombardment, or honing and communicating their craft, beyond suggesting that readers find a gimmick which goes viral on Boiler Room and TikTok, and vague bromides about '[remaining] true to your original intentions and essence.' One artist talks glowingly and seemingly unironically about being flown from one gig to another on a private jet, as if it's a perfectly normal thing for a grassroots artist to expect or aspire to. Lip service is paid to queer, trans, Black and Asian identities, and the structural inequalities at play in the industry, without making even the faintest attempt to explain how they might be overcome in practical terms.

It is more imperative than ever that the dance music media, and the wider industry, engage with those trickier and more uncomfortable questions. Like a tsunami following an earthquake, vastly more destructive than preceding events despite being less seismic, the highly visible traumas of austerity, Brexit, the pandemic and the war in Ukraine have been followed by a far quieter but potentially even more destructive squeeze on British people's living standards, careers and disposable income. 'It's far scarier now than it was during the pandemic,' promoter Rik-Ines Andrin told *Mixmag* in early 2023, citing a perfect storm of multiple intersecting polycrises. Nor are other threats on the horizon likely to recede any time soon. In the summer of 2022, scarily ornate and credible AI-created images flooded social media, the product of machine learning tools such as DALL-E and Midjourney. The obvious next step, gradually filtering through to the general public as the 2020s progress, is for the same principles and tools to be applied to audio material rather than still images. In April 2020, researchers at Cornell University published a paper describing their work on Jukebox, a machine-learning algorithm which could produce surprisingly convincing, if still deeply uncanny, approximations of various genres of music from country to pop; by early 2023 other AI models were producing passable impressions of Kanye West. Dance music is by its very definition synthetic, simplistic and strictly functional: almost preternaturally suited for artificial intelligence to replicate. Imagine DALL-E's auditory sibling, or a more refined version of Jukebox, being fed with a learning set of every single industrial techno 12-inch ever released, and told to produce a track with a steady 4/4 kickdrum and abstract electronic textures. How long do you think it will take to tweak and refine that algorithm before it's capable of producing sounds indistinguishable from the work of a real-life music producer? How long before clubs are wired up with sensors and cameras able to detect crowd intensity and dancers' heart rates, scrape their most-listened to tunes from the phones, and feed all of that into an AI system controlling the flow of music? What happens to the social and political function of dance music when the jobs of first electronic music producers and then DJs are entirely capable of being automated? Are today's hedge-fund and developer-backed mega-promoters likely to keep paying human performers when they don't have to, or will they train an AI on every Larry Levan set ever recorded, pair it with some holographic visuals which reanimate the long-dead legends of the past, and not have to worry about sorting flights and a hotel?

The second threat to UK dance music, dramatically less open to interpretation or speculation than that of AI, is climate change. It is by now an unavoidable fact that climate breakdown will cause catastrophic and lasting damage to human society, demanding entirely new ways of living and interacting with each other. Whether this comes in the form of comprehensive social breakdown as we are pushed into closer and less stable social configurations, or merely the slow death of a globalized dance music industry built on the free cross-border exchange of people and culture, from international superstar DJs to techno tourists popping over to Berlin for the weekend, remains unclear. What's certain, however, is that things are going to fall apart in some form at some point, and that both our society as a whole and UK dance music in particular demonstrably lacks the tools to manage the resulting upheavals. Since 2011 the international campaign group DJs For Climate Action have lobbied on precisely this question: their vision for the global dance music industry of 2030 involves a reimagining of the streaming model to properly compensate artists, allowing for slower travel and carbon offsets to lessen the environmental impact of touring DJs, and venues which offer more back to local communities. It is a beautiful, compelling vision which remains useless without the backing of major industry players who, by and large, appear unmoved – the carbon embodied in the countless tonnes of concrete used to redevelop the Printworks building after the club has served its regenerative purposes, to take but one example, cannot simply be wished away.

None of this, as implacable as it seems, should lead us to despair: if the constantly shifting historical relationship between money, power and the ecstatic communion of the dance floor should teach us anything, it's that there's always a new perspective to be found, from the loftily global to the grittily personal. Bolt cutters glinting in the spring moonlight, a square is cut in the perimeter fence of Stansted Airport, through which nine women and six men silently crawl. Making their way across the tarmac, they encircle a plane carrying sixty people due to be deported from the UK. Four lock themselves around the front landing gear, arms locked together inside tubes filled with expanding foam. Others construct scaffolding by the rear of the plane, unfurl a banner, and lock themselves to the fuselage. One of their number is Nick Sigsworth, otherwise known through his releases for R&S and his own label Tanum under the name Klaus. When I speak to him in the summer of 2022, five years after the action and eighteen months after the Stansted 15's convictions (under an anti-terrorism law brought in after the Lockerbie bombings) have been overturned, things initially feel bleak.

'I've always felt, and still do feel, quite torn,' he says of the connection between political protest and the dance floor. 'By and large I feel like resistance to the state and dance music are increasingly far apart. I'm not feeling particularly optimistic about dance music, to be honest. I think I'm on the verge of checking out.' Sigsworth had moved to London in 2007, where he ran the 1-800-Dinosaur nights at Plastic People with James Blake, Airhead and others, until the club closed. 'At that point I was like, I can't really be bothered to go out any more . . . it was also the time that I started squatting, and I guess being more indirectly involved in some housing occupations. Up until that point I'd had a fairly stable existence, pretty good work. And I made a conscious decision to be, like, I don't want to just carry on down this path, I want to see what's possible in the world.'

From his involvement in squatting and activist networks Sigsworth became increasingly drawn to direct action, and to the groups who'd eventually halt the deportation flight at Stansted. He also travelled to Greece in 2016 to volunteer on food distribution projects and support people crossing into Europe, witnessing border violence first-hand. Where squatting and political activism had once galvanized the cultural activities of the free festival hippies and free party ravers, now it seemed to diminish it; even Sigsworth's attempts to raise funds through throwing parties felt unsatisfying. 'In a way that was kind of naive, or that I wouldn't consider now, I thought this was a way to make the dance music community I'm part of aware of something,' he says. 'But it always felt like pushing quite hard and undertaking a lot of work for not much money. It's kind of like, well, I could just spend that time working and donate that amount of money. It's not anything special. And yeah, probably more people are aware of it and talking about it, but I don't really see that translating into more action.'

In a world where DJs, promoters, journalists and dancers alike seem remarkably content to post the odd hashtag, play the odd fundraiser, and then take the plaudits for even the most meagre shifts in perspective or optics, Sigsworth's self-criticism is bracing, admirable and saddening. At points, I want to give him a hug and reassure him that the failings of the UK dance music industry are not his alone to resolve. But then, this is what activism often is: a Sisyphean struggle to overturn monolithic forces well beyond the resources available to those oppressed by them. Sigsworth applies the same sense of scrutiny to his own creative practices as a DJ and producer:

> I was making some money and trying to pursue a career, I would be playing mostly Black music, I would be sampling mostly Black music to make my own music, but not feeling particularly connected to Black communities. It felt like an opportunity to . . . I don't know, I feel like I should be doing that anyway, you know? I should be trying to help people who are being fucked over by the state. I have a limit to what I can do, but I'm always going to be trying to do that in some way, but especially because of my music.

Sigsworth's exploration of his own politics and music is frank and pitiless, but not without hope. The more we talk, the more I begin to see some kind of synthesis emerge, and some tiny shoots pushing up through the concrete. Conceptually, this has involved a return to smallness: placing less emphasis on promoting yourself, attaining specific markers of career development or status, and just focusing on the people in the room. He says:

> A lot of it's just to do with scale in some way, like I just want to do small-scale things. I want to feel genuinely connected to people, not like I'm a celebrity, [with] that DJ / audience distinction. I want to be doing things in a way that I imagined things happened back in the nineties. I crave things that are more messy. Not in a hedonistic way, but just for people to be up for a bit more chaos, for people to feel more invested in things, because everything else is so homogenized.

Sigsworth's main vehicle for this has been through building his own soundsystem, Tanum, and making it available for community use, as well as collaborating and sharing knowledge with others. One of the groups he's worked with are Black Obsidian Sound System, a collective of queer, trans and non-binary artists of colour, who 'draw on the sound system as an archetype of Black expression' and identify 'the speaker as a totem for creating a sacred space, where one can be moved and experience collective pleasure and healing.' Nominated for the Turner Prize in 2021, B.O.S.S.'s more conceptual approach suggests some of the same pathways as Ø, Dialled In or Cosmic Slop: the soundsystem and dance floor functioning as physical and philosophical spaces which by their very nature and design pre-empt co-option or dilution. Everything, then, runs full circle: from disillusionment with an industry rotted from the top down by commercialism, Sigsworth has been drawn back to the very roots of UK dance music in Black soundsystem culture. Or even beyond that, into its pre-history: Sigsworth's other main musical interest now is his role as a member of the Mangrove Steelband, formed in the 1980s as 'a platform to create and exhibit the traditional carnival arts of steel pan and mas' by regulars of the Notting Hill cafe of the same name, the focal point of conflicts between Black creativity and police violence so many years ago.

Sigsworth is not alone in returning to the source, and craving musical experiences on a more human scale: one of the things which stands out across much of the most inventive and interesting post-Covid UK dance music, and particularly when considering its social or political elements, is precisely that same theme of *smallness*, of recognizing that gigantic revolutionary gestures on the scale of Castlemorton matter less today than a patchwork of tiny actions, each of them committed to serving a specific community, each small enough to evade censure, but (at least theoretically or potentially) knitting together to form something of immense power. From the vaulted heights of Kiss FM's launch as a legal station, Gordon McNamee now runs a small digital station called Mi-Soul, playing all the old classics (and even employing some of the same DJs), as he did back in Kiss's pirate heyday, to an ageing audience woefully under-served by contemporary corporate radio. Illegal raves continue to dot the hillsides, quarries and warehouses of the British hinterlands, operating at scales just small enough to stave off renewed media panic or police clampdowns. Cosmic Slop refuses to grow beyond its 200-person capacity, a sign above the door reading 'MUSIC IS LOVE'. In the near future, as AI and climate change begin to transform our understanding of dance music, this sense of personal connection and local communal identity may well become the only means by which to quantify its meaning.

In July 2022, I travel to Bristol to attend the premiere of *Free Party* – a beautiful documentary about the early 1990s illegal rave scene directed by Aaron Trinder, complete with an exhibition of photos from Alan Lodge and others, followed by various members of Spiral Tribe DJing late into the night (DiY play the exhibition's closing party a week later). The event takes place a stone's throw away from St Paul's, the very neighbourhood Ken Pryce ventured to almost half a century earlier as part of his sociological study into the blues dance: I wander the streets, and wonder which exactly of these squat terraced houses he stepped foot in. I imagine the deep throb of the bass, and young Black voices drifting out into the night sky. When Spiral Tribe play, the crowd is made up not only of the nostalgic Kill the Bill-era techno-punks I'd expected to see, but also a substantial number of dancers at least a decade younger than me, and some thirty years younger than Spiral Tribe themselves: inner-city youths in tracksuits and scuffed trainers, monochrome sports-goth techno heads, androgynous art-school kids in colourful make-up, each paying joyous homage to their forebears just as the Spirals themselves once did to the free festival hippies, Greenham Common protestors, rare groove warehouse promoters and blues dance soundsystem DJs. Who knows what this new generation will make of Spiral Tribe's story, a faded myth of which they lack even the faintest childhood memory? What strange new worlds might they imagine or build with that inherited knowledge?

In a 2016 essay Mark Fisher talks about the Criminal Justice Act functioning as a form of 'psychic privatisation' intended to destroy the liberatory power of the rave, and subjugate it mercilessly to the whims of capital – the same 'clean and definitive distinction between morally improving toil and decadent leisure' over which British society has struggled ever since the enclosure of the commons. Ranged against that, Fisher describes UK dance music – via a quote from Fredric Jameson – as a 'baroque sunburst' breaking into our reality from some other world, reminding us 'that Utopia exists and that other systems, other spaces are possible.' I stand at the back of the dance floor, watching the past, present and future dance with each other, coloured lights playing over my face. I experience precisely that same glimpse of some alternative social structure that so many before me have seen and, with luck, many more are still to discover. It feels tantalizingly, euphorically real.

Thanks and Acknowledgements

I owe a huge debt of gratitude to the many people who've contributed directly and indirectly to the writing of *Party Lines*.

First and foremost this includes my editors Paul Martinovic and Andrea Henry, and my agent Charlie Brotherstone, who've been tirelessly supportive, insightful and patient throughout the last two and a half years. Thank you also to Ebruba Abel-Unokan, Nick Blake, Martin Bryant, Connor Hutchinson, Stuart Wilson, Mary Mount and everyone at Picador, as well as anyone who's been involved in getting this particular copy of the book into your hands. I'm especially grateful to Dan Hancox for his help in developing the original proposal for *Party Lines*, without whose generosity and expertise none of the rest would have happened.

I'm immensely grateful to everyone who's shared their time and knowledge with me during the writing process, in particular those who didn't end up in the book themselves: Chris Brian, Matthew Collin, David Katz, Ben Mechen, Ellie Morgan, Joe Muggs, Neil Perch, Sara Sender, Aaron Trinder, Brenda Tuohy, Gibby Zobel, Marva at Rinse and Marcus at Hyperdub, as well as the staff of the British Library, Lambeth Libraries, the National Archives and the Hull History Centre for their help with research.

Thank you to the editors whose commissions laid the foundations for *Party Lines*'s narrative: Luke Turner at the Quietus, Lauren Martin at DJ Mag, Ben Beaumont-Thomas and Laura Snapes at *The Guardian*, and Charlotte England at Novara Media. Thank you also to Jacqui Edenbrow, Jeremy Deller, Gabriella Pounds and everyone at Frieze; to James Payne, Louis Melvin, Kerry Brandon and everyone at Lemonade Money; and to Thomas Dark at Manchester University Press.

I'm humbly grateful to those whose writing has inspired me over the years, including: Matt Anniss, Brian Belle-Fortune, Matthew Collin, Anwen Crawford, Kodwo Eshun, Angus Finlayson, Mark Fisher, Dawn Foster, Paul Gilroy, Dan Hancox, Dave Haslam, Fergal Kinney, Ian Penman, Will Pritchard, Chal Ravens, Simon Reynolds, Annabel Ross, Philip Sherburne, Ciaran Thapar, Gabriel Szatan, Julia Toppin, Emma Warren, Derek Walmsley and Joy White.

Thank you to the friends who've supported and encouraged me, in particular: Sally Bell, Dave Charlesworth, Paul Choy, Foujia, Rory Gibb, Katie Gibbons, Sid Gudka, Sian Haestier, Tilly Hawkins, Dan Jones, Mike Knowlden, Curtis Leonard, Lauren Martin, Rose Mosse, Nishola, Lauren O'Hara, Patrick and Anna (and Boy), Chal Ravens, Rosie Rockel, Rosalind (and Malka), Laura Snoad, Marko Starcevic, Terry Stephenson, Gabriel Szatan, Carla Thomas, and Scott Wilson.

And thank you finally to my family: the Gilletts and Macaulays, Milo and Yoshimi, my sister Hannah, Nick, Imogen and Max, Melissa, my dad Jim, Emma, Josh and Freya, and my late mother Jan.

Notes

Epigraphs

Gutzmore, Cecil, 'Carnival, The State and The Black Masses' taken from *Inside Babylon: The Caribbean Diaspora in Britain*, (eds.) Clive Harris and Winston James (London: Verso, 1993), p. 211

Ehrenreich, Barbara, *Dancing in the Streets: A History of Collective Joy* (New York: Metropolitan Books, 2006), p. 252

von Goethe, Johann Wolfgang, *Italian Journey* (New York: Suhrkamp, 1989), p. 390

Introduction

1 **theory of the 'Temporary Autonomous Zone'**: Bey, Hakim, *T.A.Z.: The Temporary Autonomous Zone* (Autonomedia, 1991)
1 **focusing unambiguously**: https://libcom.org/article/leaving-out-ugly-part-hakim-beypeter-lamborn-wilson
3 **Criminal Justice and Public Order Act 1994**: https://www.legislation.gov.uk/ukpga/1994/33/contents

Chapter 1: Beat Down Babylon

8 **sweaty mass of humanity**: Pryce, Ken, *Endless Pressure: a study of West Indian life-styles in Bristol* (Bristol: Bristol Classical Press, 1986), p. 100
10 **charged at the door**: Evaristo, Bernadine, *Girl, Woman, Other* (London: Penguin Books, 2019), Chapter 1 – Amma
10 **a space like no other**: https://gal-dem.com/remembering-pearl-alcock-black-bisexual-shebeen-queen-of-brixton/

10	**queer men in the 1970s**: Cook, Matt, Evans, Jennifer V. (eds), *Queer Cities, Queer Cultures: Europe Since 1945* (London: Bloomsbury Academic, 2014), p. 47	
10	**with a black person**: Avery, Simon, Graham, Katherine M. (eds), *Sex, Time and Place: Queer Histories of London, c.1850 to the Present* (London: Bloomsbury Academic, 2016), p. 75	
10	**like some African queen**: Cook, Matt, Evans, Jennifer V. (eds), *Queer Cities, Queer Cultures: Europe Since 1945* (London: Bloomsbury Academic, 2014), p. 47	
11	**to open and run**: https://www.youtube.com/watch?v=BPx6KqklIAg&list=PLqtJeR4QMMKu_wHo8z4WvYWzuXUZJWxPh&index=9	
11	**its spiritual associations**: https://www.cbc.ca/radio/docproject/bop-chaka-zinyemba-mbira-1.5879374	
11	**riots in Trinidad**: https://digitalcommons.buffalostate.edu/expoition/vol1/iss1/4/	
12	**member for black people**: https://www.youtube.com/watch?v=gHydegA_oPc	
12	**so I start me own**: https://www.youtube.com/watch?v=gHydegA_oPc	
12	**Blacks in that room**: Interview with author, 2021	
13	**to the public bar**: Waters, Rob, *Black London Histories: The Rise and Fall of the Drinking Club*, https://web.archive.org/web/20220729021822/http://www.blacklondonhistories.org.uk/uncategorized/the-rise-and-fall-of-the-drinking-club/	
13	**no Pakis, no sportswear**: Interview with author, 2018	
13	**Windrush hove into view**: Bradley, Lloyd, *Sounds Like London: 100 Years of Black Music in the Capital* (London: Serpent's Tail, 2013) p. 23	
14	**without a conviction**: https://www.vice.com/en/article/xy3de3/club-labyrinth-newton-dunbar-interview	
14	**encouraged to relocate**: https://www.theguardian.com/music/2014/jun/04/count-suckle	
14	**servings of curried goat**: Kew, Tom, 'Rebel Music in the Rebel City: The Performance Geography of the Nottingham 'Blues Party', 1957–1987', taken from *Narratives from Beyond the UK Reggae Bassline: The System is Sound* (eds), William 'Lez' Henry and Matthew Worley (London: Palgrave Macmillan, 2021) p. 192	
15	**Town and Country Planning Act 1962**: https://www.legislation.gov.uk/ukpga/1962/38/contents/enacted	
15	**Licensing Act 1967**: https://www.legislation.gov.uk/ukpga/1967/19/enacted	

15	**violence were commonplace**: Waters, Rob, *Black London Histories: The Rise and Fall of the Drinking Club*, https://web.archive.org/web/20220729021822/http://www.blacklondonhistories.org.uk/uncategorized/the-rise-and-fall-of-the-drinking-club/	
15	**flout the law**: 'Well Run Club Refused Permission to be Registered', *South London Press*, 29 June 1962, p. 4, quoted in Waters, Rob, *Black London Histories: The Rise and Fall of the Drinking Club*, https://web.archive.org/web/20220729021822/http://www.blacklondonhistories.org.uk/uncategorized/the-rise-and-fall-of-the-drinking-club/	
15	**dens of vice**: 'Well Run Club Refused Permission to be Registered', *South London Press*, 29 June 1962, p. 4, quoted in Waters, Rob, *Black London Histories: The Rise and Fall of the Drinking Club*, https://web.archive.org/web/20220729021822/http://www.blacklondonhistories.org.uk/uncategorized/the-rise-and-fall-of-the-drinking-club/	
15	**Commonwealth Immigration Act 1968**: https://www.legislation.gov.uk/ukpga/1968/9/pdfs/ukpga_19680009_en.pdf	
16	**Rent Act in 1957**: https://www.legislation.gov.uk/ukpga/Eliz2/5-6/25/contents/enacted	
16	**detected after the event**: Secretary of State. (1978), *Memo from Secretary of State to the Legislation Committee*. [Manuscript]. HO 376/206. The National Archives, quoted in Lawrence, Paul, 'The Vagrancy Act (1824) and the Persistence of Pre-emptive Policing in England Since 1750', taken from *The British Journal of Criminology*, Volume 57, Issue 3, 1 May 2017, p. 527	
16	**Police and Criminal Evidence Act 1984**: https://www.legislation.gov.uk/ukpga/1984/60/contents	
17	**you were up against**: https://vimeo.com/245380275	
17	**senselessness of pain**: https://www.theguardian.com/commentisfree/2015/feb/22/black-art-dangerous-personal-political	
17	**another unlicensed rave**: https://www.youtube.com/watch?v=v1kUhcPjMK0	
18	**laws were being broken**: Gillroy, Paul, *There Ain't No Black in the Union Jack: The Cultural Politics of Race and Nation* (London: Hutchinson Education, 1987) p. 101	
18	**sanity as carnage erupts**: https://daily.redbullmusicacademy.com/2017/03/linton-kwesi-johnson-five-nights-feature	
19	**shit out of them**: Bradley, Lloyd, *Bass Culture: When Reggae Was King* (London: Penguin, 2001), Chapter 18: Warrior Charge	
19	**tearing at her clothes**: *Workers' Action*, 10 March 1976, p. 2, https://	

www.marxists.org/history/etol/newspape/workers-action-uk/
Workers%20Action%20no9%20March1976.pdf

19 **without a back pocket**: *Workers' Action*, 10 March 1976, p. 2, https://
www.marxists.org/history/etol/newspape/workers-action-uk/
Workers%20Action%20no9%20March1976.pdf

19 **boys in blue?** *Never*: Bradley, Lloyd, *Bass Culture: When Reggae Was King* (London: Penguin, 2001), Chapter 18: Warrior Charge

19 **club as I liked"**: https://www.marxists.org/history/etol/
newspape/workers-action-uk/Workers%20Action%20no9%20
March1976.pdf

20 **to those coming in**: https://www.margaretthatcher.org/
document/103485

20 **very dangerous indeed**: https://api.parliament.uk/historic-hansard/
commons/1981/feb/11/all-night-parties

21 **with them directly**: https://www.socialist.net/the-new-cross-fire-
40-years-on-13-dead-nothing-said.htm

21 **involving his soundsystem**: https://daily.redbullmusicacademy.
com/2014/05/count-suckle-rip

21 **arson attacks in early 1959**: Waters, Rob, *Black London Histories: The Rise and Fall of the Drinking Club*, https://web.archive.org/
web/20220729021822/http://www.blacklondonhistories.org.uk/
uncategorized/the-rise-and-fall-of-the-drinking-club/

21 **twenty-two people**: https://www.theguardian.com/world/2021/
jan/17/forty-years-on-from-the-new-cross-fire-what-has-changed-
for-black-britons

22 **in Ladbroke Grove**: https://www.uncarved.org/blog/2008/09/smash-
the-national-front-part-two/

22 **in Deptford in 1971**: https://www.theguardian.com/world/2021/
jan/17/forty-years-on-from-the-new-cross-fire-what-has-changed-
for-black-britons

23 **bring your own,' he explains**: Interview with the author, 2018

23 **interact and collaborate**: Gilroy, Paul, *Between the Blues and the Blues Dance*, taken from *The Auditory Culture Reader* (ed.) Michael Bull (London: Berg Publishers, 2003), p. 388

23 **1986 Soul Control party in Moss Side**: https://www.youtube.com/
watch?v=BZDEZ2U2ueo

24 **or Family Funktion**: Melville, Caspar, *It's a London Thing: How Rare Groove, Acid House and Jungle Remapped the City* (Manchester: Manchester University Press, 2019), pg.111

25	**go to clubs together**: https://www.interviewmagazine.com/music/jazzie-b
26	**or audience members**: Rosenior-Patten, Lynda, Reid, June, 'The Story of Nzinga Soundz and the Women's Voice in Sound System Culture' taken from (ed), William 'Lez' Henry, *Narratives from Beyond the UK Reggae Bassline* (London: Palgrave Macmillan, 2021) p. 137
26	**response to those struggles**: https://writersmosaic.org.uk/content/nzinga-soundz-june-reid-and-lynda-rosenior-patten/
27	**losing his deposit**: Moore, Tony, *Policing Notting Hill* (London: Waterside Press, 2013), p. 62
27	**their tempers are up**: Kynaston, David, *Modernity Britain: Book One: Opening the Box, 1957–1959* (London: Bloosmbury, 2013), Chapter 8: Get the Nigger
27	**own words, 'nigger-hunting'**: http://content.time.com/time/subscriber/article/0,33009,821170,00.html
27	**murder the bastards**: https://www.theguardian.com/uk/2002/aug/24/artsandhumanities.nottinghillcarnival2002
27	**stabbed to death**: https://www.theguardian.com/artanddesign/2017/apr/14/turbulent-times-kelso-cochrane-police-search
27	**Cochrane's drinking habits**: https://socialistworker.co.uk/features/who-killed-kelso-cochrane/
28	**to do with racial conflict**: https://irr.org.uk/article/the-worst-kept-secret-in-notting-hill/
28	**demand for illegal blues dances**: Moore, Tony, *Policing Notting Hill* (London: Waterside Press, 2013), p. 29
28	**of the Communist Party**: https://www.nytimes.com/2021/02/18/world/europe/notting-hill-carnival-claudia-jones.html
28	**white people arrested**: Moore, Tony, *Policing Notting Hill* (London: Waterside Press, 2013), p. 143
28	**multi-racial working class**: https://www.versobooks.com/blogs/5030-the-forgotten-legacy-of-claudia-jones-a-black-communist-radical-feminist
28	**of Black resistance**: https://www.versobooks.com/blogs/5030-the-forgotten-legacy-of-claudia-jones-a-black-communist-radical-feminist
29	**abuse at the players**: Ferdinand, Nicole, Williams, Nigel L., 'The making of the London Notting Hill Carnival festivalscape: Politics and power and the Notting Hill Carnival' taken from *Tourism Management Perspectives 27* (London: Elsevier 2018) p. 36

29	**New Orleans-style marching bands**: https://tribunemag.co.uk/2019/11/a-peoples-art-is-the-genesis-of-their-freedom	
29	**they were nice people**: Gutzmore, Cecil, 'Carnival, The State and The Black Masses' taken from *Inside Babylon: The Caribbean Diaspora in Britain*, (eds.) Clive Harris and Winston James (London: Verso, 1993), p. 215	
30	**Afro-Caribbean leadership team**: Ferdinand, Nicole, Williams, Nigel L., 'The making of the London Notting Hill Carnival festivalscape: Politics and power and the Notting Hill Carnival' taken from Tourism Management Perspectives 27 (London: Elsevier 2018), p. 37	
30	**gauntlet had been thrown down**: Gutzmore, Cecil, 'Carnival, The State and The Black Masses' taken from *Inside Babylon: The Caribbean Diaspora in Britain*, (eds.) Clive Harris and Winston James (London: Verso, 1993), p. 217	
30	**reluctantly put up with**: https://www.ucl.ac.uk/racism-racialisation/publications/2021/feb/conversation-linton-kwesi-johnson	
31	**incompetence and corruption**: Ferdinand, Nicole, Williams, Nigel L., 'The making of the London Notting Hill Carnival festivalscape: Politics and power and the Notting Hill Carnival' taken from *Tourism Management Perspectives 27* (London: Elsevier 2018), p. 39	
31	**tourism product**: Ferdinand, Nicole, Williams, Nigel L., 'The making of the London Notting Hill Carnival festivalscape: Politics and power and the Notting Hill Carnival' taken from *Tourism Management Perspectives 27* (London: Elsevier 2018), p. 33	
31	**the right-wing press**: https://www.theguardian.com/culture/2002/aug/17/nottinghillcarnival2002.nottinghillcarnival	
32	**artistic and political order**: Gilroy, Paul, *Between the Blues and the Blues Dance*, taken from *The Auditory Culture Reader*, (ed.) Michael Bull (London: Berg Publishers, 2003), p. 383	
33	**control or cancel it**: https://www.theguardian.com/culture/2002/aug/17/nottinghillcarnival2002.nottinghillcarnival	

Chapter 2: British Tribal Music

35	**put him where he belongs**: https://www.ukrockfestivals.com/windsor73flyer1.html	
36	**people' to stay away**: https://www.telegraph.co.uk/culture/music/3619773/The-forgotten-festival-I-was-there.html	

36	**the middle of a field**: https://www.youtube.com/watch?v=GIyjvEUINx8	
36	**anything I've ever seen**: Bainbridge, Luke, *Acid House: The True Story: Britain's Last Youth Culture Revolution* (London: Omnibus Press, 2014), p. 91	
38	**fields are in the way?**: Interview with author, 2021	
38	**during the Bronze Age**: https://www.nationalgeographic.com/culture/article/cain-abel-reflects-bronze-age-rivalry	
38	**remote parts of the country**: Interview with author, 2021	
39	**a threat to civil order**: Ehrenreich, Barbara, *Dancing in the Streets: A History of Collective Joy* (New York: Metropolitan Books, 2006), p. 251	
39	**can be bothered**: *Kensington Post*, 4th May 1972, taken from https://www.ukrockfestivals.com/windsor72.html	
39	**seemed quite laughable**: *Kensington Post*, 4th May 1972, taken from https://www.ukrockfestivals.com/windsor72.html	
41	**as the need arose**: Christopher, David, *Mean Fields: New Age Travellers, Thatcherism and the English Countryside* (London School of Economics, 2003), p. 6	
42	**punched in the face**: Rimbaud, Penny, 'The Last of the Hippies', http://www.spunk.org/texts/places/britain/sp001297.txt	
43	**the public any easier**: *The Times*, 30 August 1974, quoted in Christopher, David, *Mean Fields: New Age Travellers, Thatcherism and the English Countryside* (London: London School of Economics, 2003), p. 77	
43	**about their lives revolved**: Hetherington, Kevin, *New Age Travellers: Vanloads of Uproarious Humanity* (London: Continuum International, 1999), p. 6	
43	**blocking outside noise**: https://www.rca.ac.uk/news-and-events/news/sonic-stones/	
44	*For the Kids x*: https://stonehengecampaign.com/sir-walter-wally-remembers-wally-hope/	
44	**a sordid encampment**: http://www.ukrockfestivals.com/henge-history.html	
44	**Stonehenge Monument, Salisbury, Wiltshire**: https://www.andy-worthington.co.uk/2009/06/20/its-25-years-since-the-last-stonehenge-free-festival/	
45	**strange random patterns**: Rimbaud, Penny, *The Last of the Hippies*, http://www.spunk.org/texts/places/britain/sp001297.txt	
46	**at their authority**: Rimbaud, Penny, *The Last of the Hippies*, http://www.spunk.org/texts/places/britain/sp001297.txt	

47	**line-up for 1984**: https://www.ukrockfestivals.com/henge-history-84.html
47	**named Winston Silcott**: https://www.independent.co.uk/life-style/focus-in-the-face-of-prejudice-1199525.html
48	**account of proceedings**: https://www.ukrockfestivals.com/henge-history.html
50	**partying around them**: https://www.ukrockfestivals.com/henge-history-80.html
50	**neighbourly disrespect**: https://squallmagazine.com/f/f-assemblies-of-celebration.html
50	**side of the road**: Interview with author, 2021
50	**on Salisbury Plain**: https://flashbak.com/the-last-stonehenge-free-festival-in-photos-1984-417008/
51	**police operations centre**: Festival Welfare Services 1981 Annual Report
51	**1985 or thereafter**: https://www.upi.com/Archives/1984/12/28/No-more-rock-at-the-rocks/3412473058000/
52	**you support the police**: Samuel, Raphael, 'Mrs Thatcher's Return to Victorian Values', taken from *Proceedings of the British Academy 78*, (ed.) T.C. Smout (Oxford University Press, 1990), p. 14
52	**respect for the law**: Hansard, 3 June 1986, https://api.parliament.uk/historic-hansard/commons/1986/jun/03/hippy-convoy-new-forest
52	**hepatitis and AIDS**: Hetherington, Kevin, 'Vanloads of Uproarious Humanity' taken from *Cool Places: Geographies of Youth Cultures*, (eds.) Tracey Skelton and Gill Valentine (London: Routledge, 1998), p. 338
52	**as hippy convoys**: Hansard, 5 June 1986, https://api.parliament.uk/historic-hansard/commons/1986/jun/05/engagements
52	**'giro gypsies' and 'scum'**: Christopher, David, *Mean Fields: New Age Travellers, Thatcherism and the English Countryside* (London School of Economics, 2003), p. 76
52	**Hordes of Marauding Locusts**: *Daily Telegraph*, 27 May 1992
52	**about that stuff!**: Chippindale, Peter and Horrie, Chris, *Stick It Up Your Punter!: The Uncut Story of the Sun Newspaper* (London: Faber and Faber, 2013), Chapter 9 – The Wend and Kel Show
53	**than a physical one**: Hetherington, Kevin, *New Age Travellers: Vanloads of Uproarious Humanity* (London: Continuum International, 1999), p. 164
53	**part of this community**: BBC Two, *Seven Days at Stoney Cross*, 10 July 1986, https://www.youtube.com/watch?v=sIlWi05I-mo
53	**piece of gentle England**: *Daily Mail*, 26 June 1989

53	**'garbage and filth'**: Hansard, 9 March 1990, https://www.theyworkforyou.com/debates/?id=1990-03-09a.1110.0&s	
54	**to majority culture**: McKay, George, *Senseless Acts of Beauty: Cultures of Resistance Since the Sixties* (London: Verso, 1996), p. 59	
55	**protest and the party**: *News of the World*, 18 July 1982	
55	**movement as a whole**: https://green-history.uk/articles/events/peace-events/counter-cruise-cosmic-carnival-july-1982	
55	**strictly all women**: https://green-history.uk/articles/events/peace-events/counter-cruise-cosmic-carnival-july-1982	
55	**almost entirely devisive**: https://green-history.uk/articles/events/peace-events/counter-cruise-cosmic-carnival-july-1982	
56	**others to join them**: McKay, George, *Senseless Acts of Beauty: Cultures of Resistance Since the Sixties* (London: Verso, 1996), p. 33	
56	**defeated in the Falklands**: https://www.margaretthatcher.org/document/105563	
56	**such volatile rhetoric**: https://www.theguardian.com/politics/2014/oct/03/thatcher-labour-miners-enemy-within-brighton-bomb	
56	**culture of resistance**: Christopher, David, *Mean Fields: New Age Travellers, Thatcherism and the English Countryside* (London School of Economics, 2003), p. 143	
57	**an elderly headmaster**: BBC Two, *Seven Days at Stoney Cross*, 10 July 1986, https://www.youtube.com/watch?v=sIlWio5I-mo	
58	**360 attendees arrested**: https://history-is-made-at-night.blogspot.com/2012/02/nostell-priory-festival-1984.html	
59	**five years later**: https://www.leeds-live.co.uk/news/history/illegal-leeds-party-love-decade-23813981	
59	**modern British history**: https://www.andyworthington.co.uk/2020/06/01/its-35-years-since-the-battle-of-the-beanfield-where-do-we-go-now/	
59	**planes and helicopters**: Worthington, Andy, *The Battle of the Beanfield* (London: Enabler Publications, 2005), excerpt at https://www.andyworthington.co.uk/2009/06/01/in-the-guardian-remembering-the-battle-of-the-beanfield/	
61	**senselessly on the floor**: https://www.youtube.com/watch?v=yKVn1C3qcqw	
61	**homes in pieces**: https://www.counterfire.org/articles/history/21264-the-battle-of-the-beanfield-an-important-anniversary-in-the-history-of-state-brutality	
61	**sake of the cameras**: https://www.theguardian.com/artanddesign/	

2016/jan/15/battle-of-the-beanfield-stonehenge-1985-rose-brash-photograph
63   **don't *reside* there**: Interview with author, 2021

Chapter 3: Dance Before the Police Come

65   **he was a stripper**: https://www.youtube.com/watch?v=SBzmbWLmaQI
66   **with the washing up**: https://www.pinknews.co.uk/2021/01/26/royal-vauxhall-tavern-lily-savage-police-raid-paul-o-grady/
67   **coal delivery carts**: Prince, Michael, *God's Cop: The Biography of James Anderton* (London: Fredrick Muller, 1988), p. 24
67   **he thinks it's sinful**: Prince, Michael, *God's Cop: The Biography of James Anderton* (London: Fredrick Muller, 1988), p. 28
68   **beyond my comprehension**: Prince, Michael, *God's Cop: The Biography of James Anderton* (London: Fredrick Muller, 1988), p. 202
68   **in God's creation**: Prince, Michael, *God's Cop: The Biography of James Anderton* (London: Fredrick Muller, 1988), p. 202
68   **make their own laws**: Cosgrove, Stuart, *Young Soul Rebels: A Personal History of Northern Soul* (London: Polygon, 2016), Chapter 2
68   **castration of sex offenders**: https://www.theguardian.com/uk-news/2022/may/06/sir-james-anderton-obituary
68   **punish people quite easily**: https://www.theboltonnews.co.uk/news/20122046.former-greater-manchester-polices-chief-constable-james-anderton-dies-aged-89/
68   **entered a secret pact**: Prince, Michael, *God's Cop: The Biography of James Anderton* (London: Fredrick Muller, 1988), p. 69
69   **of society to ransom**: *The Sun*, December 1986
69   **children at the time**: https://www.pinknews.co.uk/2021/10/10/royal-vauxhall-tavern-popppers-hiv-police/
69   **'almost or mostly' wrong**: https://www.bsa.natcen.ac.uk/latest-report/british-social-attitudes-30/personal-relationships/homosexuality.aspx
69   **ruddy gas chambers**: https://huw.substack.com/p/poove-power-part-ii
69   **sound start in life**: https://www.margaretthatcher.org/document/106941
70   **that went with that**: https://www.youtube.com/watch?v=SBzmbWLmaQI

70	**to entrap gay men**: https://galop.org.uk/wp-content/uploads/2021/06/galop-annual-report-1984.pdf
71	**police do not approve of**: https://galop.org.uk/wp-content/uploads/2021/06/galop-annual-report-1984.pdf
71	**'quarantine the city'**: https://www.gold.ac.uk/calendar/?id=13115
71	**that accompanies it**: *The Guardian*, 7 September 1991
72	**thousand of its patrons**: *Pink Paper*, 4 February 1994
72	**kicked people in the queue**: Warren, Emma, *Dance Your Way Home* (London: Faber and Faber, 2023), p. 166
72	**form of continuity**: *The Sun*, 17 August 1988
72	**police spotlights**: https://www.theguardian.com/world/2004/aug/07/gayrights.communities
73	**dancing with each other**: https://www.bbc.co.uk/bitesize/articles/zygbf82
73	**other dance music venues**: Warren, Emma, *Dance Your Way Home* (London: Faber and Faber, 2023), p. 195
73	**allowed to leave**: https://www.mdmarchive.co.uk/artefact/14698/NAPOLEONS_PRESS_1984
73	**twentieth-century living**: https://thepixelworkshop.com/the-rise-and-fall-of-the-hulme-crescents/
73	**howls of neglect**: Parkinson-Bailey, John J., *Manchester: An Architectural History* (Manchester: Manchester University Press), p. 195
74	**concrete balconies**: https://www.manchestersfinest.com/articles/hulmes-notorious-crescents/
74	**spectre of urban decay**: https://municipaldreams.wordpress.com/2014/03/11/the-hulme-crescents-manchester-a-british-bantustan/
74	**million miles away**: Robb, John, 'Hulme is Where the Heart Is', https://web.archive.org/web/20050430114348/http://www.playlouder.com/feature/+hulmeiswheretheh/
75	**became the focus**: Collin, Matthew, *Altered State: The Story of Ecstasy Culture and Acid House* (London: Serpent's Tail, 2009) p. 162
78	**New York Yankees T-shirts**: https://www.lancashiretelegraph.co.uk/news/18732226.remember-manhattan-heights-brought-bling-blackburn/
78	**the people that went**: https://www.acidhouseflashback.co.uk/testimonies/david%20f-full-interview
79	**part of the whole thing**: https://www.acidhouseflashback.co.uk/testimonies/jane-full-interview
79	**unwitting accompaniment**: https://www.youtube.com/watch?v=kJuRubcOgRY

79	**one, the best one**: https://www.acidhouseflashback.co.uk/testimonies/tony-full-interview	
80	**tangible that we can do**: https://www.acidhouseflashback.co.uk/testimonies/john%20&%20mark-full-interview	
80	**aggressive action against them**: Entertainments (Increased Penalties) Bill, https://publications.parliament.uk/pa/cm198990/cmhansrd/1990-03-09/Debate-1.html	
81	**any kind of social restraint**: National Archives, HO 300/245: Control of unlicensed acid house parties	
81	**know they were there**: https://www.acidhouseflashback.co.uk/testimonies/jane-full-interview	
81	**moor near Edenfield**: Collin, Matthew, *Altered State: The Story of Ecstasy Culture and Acid House* (London: Serpent's Tail, 2009) p. 164	
81	**work for us now**: https://www.theguardian.com/music/2020/may/28/pills-mills-and-bellyaches-how-blackburn-out-partied-manchester	
82	**of their hobnailed boots**: Hemment, Drew, 'Dangerous dancing and disco riots: the northern warehouse parties', in *DiY Culture: Party and Protest in Nineties' Britain*, (ed.) George McKay (London: Verso, 1998), p. 217	
82	**party without the people**: https://www.acidhouseflashback.co.uk/wp-content/uploads/2020/07/Dissy-and-conclusion-and-appendix..pdf	
82	**just wanted to dance**: Anniss, Matt, *Join the Future: Bleep Techno and the Birth of British Bass Music* (London: Velocity Press, 2019), Chapter 4	
83	**not happening not here**: https://www.acidhouseflashback.co.uk/testimonies/damo%201-full-interview	
83	**1988 Licensing Act**: https://www.legislation.gov.uk/ukpga/1988/17/enacted	
84	**travelled any further**: Silcott, Mireille and Push, *The Book of E: All About Ecstasy* (London: Omnibus Press, 2000), p. 57	
84	**threat to the peace**: East, Roberrt, Power, Helen and Thomas, Phillip A., 'The Death of Mass Picketing' taken from *The Journal of Law and Society*, Vol. 12 No. 3 (London: Wiley, 1985), p. 308	
85	**licensing of music and dancing**: http://libertarian.co.uk/2021/08/24/political-notes-055-acid-house-parties-against-the-lifestyle-police-and-the-safety-nazis-1991-by-paul-staines/	
85	**never even heard of**: Silcott, Mireille and Push, *The Book of E: All About Ecstasy* (London: Omnibus Press, 2000), p. 57	
85	**to party organizers**: National Archives, HO 300/245: Control of unlicensed acid house parties	

86	**black line crossing it out**: National Archives, HO 300/245 : Control of unlicensed acid house parties	
86	**work on everyone**: Interview with author, 2019	
87	**rabbit ears behind them**: Interview with author, 2022	
88	**West Ham and Millwall**: https://www.bbc.co.uk/archive/police-crack-down-on-soccer-hooligans-1987/zdbcgwx	
88	**or impossibly weak**: Collin, Matthew, *Altered State: The Story of Ecstasy Culture and Acid House* (London: Serpent's Tail, 2009) p. 145	
89	**saw it close in late 1991**: Collin, Matthew, *Altered State: The Story of Ecstasy Culture and Acid House* (London: Serpent's Tail, 2009) p. 127	

Chapter 4: Make Some Fucking Noise

92	**act of 'psychic privatisation'**: Fisher, Mark, 'Baroque Sunbursts' taken from *Rave: Rave and its Influences on Art and Culture*, (ed.) Nav Haq (London: Black Dog Publishing, 2016), p. 45	
92	**repetitive beats**: https://www.legislation.gov.uk/ukpga/1994/33/contents	
95	**do it ourselves**: Harrison, Harry, *Dreaming in Yellow: The Story of the DiY Sound System* (London: Velocity Press, 2022), Chapter 6	
96	**decks and a mixer**: Harrison, Harry, *Dreaming in Yellow: The Story of the DiY Sound System* (London: Velocity Press, 2022), Chapter 8	
96	**paradigm was born**: Harrison, Harry, *Dreaming in Yellow: The Story of the DiY Sound System* (London: Velocity Press, 2022), Chapter 8	
96	**you just didn't get it**: https://www.vice.com/en/article/xd38mq/diy-25th-anniversary-scott-oliver-125	
97	**behind that was**: https://www.vice.com/en/article/xd38mq/diy-25th-anniversary-scott-oliver-125	
97	**regenerate those tribes**: Interview with author, 2021	
98	**let him do it**: Interview with author, 2021	
98	**until you make some noise**: Interview with author, 2021	
99	**shouts an unseen MC**: https://freepartypeople.wordpress.com/2022/04/18/3rd-5th-may-1991-free-party-people-at-beltane-free-festival-hungerford-common-berkshire/	
99	**thud of kick drums**: https://freepartypeople.wordpress.com/2022/01/08/2nd-16th-august-1991-spiral-tribe-circus-normal-diy-and-circus-warp-at-camelford-free-festival-bodmin-moor-cornwall/	
101	**not in the area**: BBC Two, *Dance Energy*, 2 November 1992	
101	**any further than that**: BBC Two, *Dance Energy*, 2 November 1992	

101 **set up new ones**: https://datacide-magazine.com/spiral-tribe-interview/

102 **bring the necessary paperwork**: https://saladofpearls.wordpress.com/2014/09/30/spiral-tribe-a-calendar-of-police-harassment-at-free-parties-1991-1992/

103 **watching the house**: Interview with author, 2022

103 **vehicle you can imagine**: https://freepartypeople.wordpress.com/2022/01/08/18th-20th-april-1992-spiral-tribe-free-party-at-acton-lane-london/

103 **women and children**: McKay, George, *Senseless Acts of Beauty: Cultures of Resistance Since the Sixties* (London: Verso, 1996), p. 203

104 **playing music and dancing**: https://www.theguardian.com/music/2009/jul/12/90s-spiral-tribe-free-parties

104 **might otherwise have done**: https://www.vice.com/en/article/vd8gbj/anti-rave-act-protests-20th-anniversary-204

104 **a politicised underclass**: Collin, Matthew, *Altered State: The Story of Ecstasy Culture and Acid House* (London: Serpent's Tail, 2009) p.

104 **individuals or subgroups**: Waddington, David, *Policing Public Disorder: Theory and Practice* (London: Routledge, 1998), p. 6

105 **middle of their camp**: *Western Daily Press*, May 27 1991, available at https://freepartypeople.wordpress.com/2022/04/18/26th-29th-may-1991-avon-free-festival-at-chipping-sodbury/

105 **Chipping Sodbury area**: https://dreamflesh.com/essay/criminal-culture/

106 **to defy authority**: Blakey, David, 'Our common cause', taken from *Police Review No. 100* (London: Police Review Publishing Company, 1992) p. 1042

107 **and the festival appeared**: https://djmag.com/content/free-party-politics-castle-morton

107 **large-scale disorder**: *Sunday Mirror*, 23 August 1992

107 **it was a hopeless attempt**: Blakey, David, 'Our common cause', taken from *Police Review No. 100* (London: Police Review Publishing Company, 1992) p. 1042

107 **human rubbish tip**: *Birmingham Daily Post*, 27 May 1992

107 **command and signals system**: https://hansard.parliament.uk/Commons/1992-06-29/debates/a32c9153-a73f-430b-ab30-db7fed65cb9a/Travellers

107 **belong in a zoo**: *The Times*, 31 May 1992; quoted in https://

9090riginals.com/2019/05/22/the-storming-of-castlemorton-common-may-1992/

107 **deposited on them**: BBC Two, *Newsnight*, 27 August 1992
108 **happens in every town**: https://www.youtube.com/watch?v=T1CbKsu7Hlc
109 **and just turns up**: https://www.bbc.co.uk/news/uk-england-hereford-worcester-39960232
109 **English Shangri-La:** Harrison, Harry, *Dreaming in Yellow: The Story of the DiY Sound System* (London: Velocity Press, 2022), Chapter 8
109 **belligerent euphoria**: Reynolds, Simon, *Energy Flash* (London: Picador, 2008), p. 139
110 **death of free rave culture**: https://freepartypeople.wordpress.com/2022/05/10/may-12th-1992-castlemorton-common-free-festival/
110 **let's enjoy it**: Interview with author, 2022
110 **going our way**: Interview with author, 2022
111 **the doors open**: Interview with author, 2022
112 **might be bad in society**: BBC Two, *Dance Energy*, 2 November 1992
112 **apocalyptic mess**: Interview with author, 2022
113 **pushing nomadic communities into permanent housing**: National Archives, HO 558/25: Gypsy sites: submissions and policy papers on illegal camping and new age travellers and ravers
113 **events at Castlemorton**: National Archives, HO 558/25: Gypsy sites: submissions and policy papers on illegal camping and new age travellers and ravers
114 **with little enthusiasm**: National Archives, HO 558/25: Gypsy sites: submissions and policy papers on illegal camping and new age travellers and ravers
114 **Not in any age**: https://johnmajorarchive.org.uk/1992/10/09/mr-majors-speech-to-1992-conservative-party-conference-9-october-1992/
115 **neighbourliness, decency, courtesy**: https://www.theguardian.com/politics/1993/oct/09/conservatives.past
116 **problem of crime**: Card, Richard, and Ward, Richard, *The Criminal Justice and Public Order Act 1994* (Bristol: Jordans, 1994), p. 5
116 **taking place in the summer**: Card, Richard, and Ward, Richard, *The Criminal Justice and Public Order Act 1994* (Bristol: Jordans, 1994), pp. 69–70
116 **consultation or research**: https://api.parliament.uk/historic-hansard/lords/1994/apr/25/criminal-justice-and-public-order-bill

117	**harassment and intimidation**: National Council for Civil Liberties, *Defend Diversity Defend Dissent* (London: NCCL, 1994), p. 33
117	**trying to address**: National Council for Civil Liberties, *Defend Diversity Defend Dissent* (London: NCCL, 1994), p. 33
118	**because it wasn't sustainable**: Interview with author, 2022
119	**display of people power**: https://history-is-made-at-night.blogspot.com/2021/01/revolt-of-ravers-movement-against.html?m=1
119	**tagging along for the ride**: Interview with author, 2022
120	**where they came from**: Interview with author, 2022
121	**back to the drug squad afterwards**: Interview with author, 2023
121	**the right to party**: https://www.youtube.com/watch?v=RpJj4AjtOjw
122	**DIY culture, is about**: http://www.urban75.org/photos/protest/cjb.html
122	**where were you all?**: https://history-is-made-at-night.blogspot.com/2013/10/anti-cja-protest-july-1994-eternity.html
122	**into the wrought iron**: https://www.youtube.com/watch?v=RpJj4AjtOjw
123	**this is a peaceful fight**: https://history-is-made-at-night.blogspot.com/2010/05/
123	**Class War anyway**: Interview with author, 2022
123	**it just deteriorated**: Interview with author, 2022
123	**demonstrators by the police**: https://www.independent.co.uk/news/uk/the-park-lane-riot-how-park-lane-was-turned-into-a-battlefield-1442203.html
123	**a front of legitimate protest**: https://history-is-made-at-night.blogspot.com/2021/01/revolt-of-ravers-movement-against.html?m=1
124	**had to end sometime**: https://history-is-made-at-night.blogspot.com/2010/05/claremont-road-1994-rave-had-to-end.html
125	**British Police Service**: National Council for Civil Liberties archive, Hull History Centre
125	**thugs, wreckers and bullies**: https://squallmagazine.com/f/f07-25-real-criminals-hsa.html
126	**run through the night**: http://news.bbc.co.uk/1/hi/england/devon/8155441.stm
126	**camp in Runnymede**: https://www.bbc.co.uk/news/uk-england-surrey-34269232
126	**number of Black men**: http://news.bbc.co.uk/1/hi/uk/4584000.stm
126	**Human Rights ruling**: S & Marper vs UK, 2008, quoted in https://justice.org.uk/s-marper-v-uk-2008/

127 **their white compatriots**: https://www.theguardian.com/uk-news/2020/oct/27/black-people-nine-times-more-likely-to-face-stop-and-search-than-white-people
128 **the first Pyramid stage**: https://freepartypeople.wordpress.com/2021/05/15/26th-27th-june-1992-underworld-at-experimental-sound-field-glastonbury/
128 **mainstream British culture**: https://www.youtube.com/watch?v=KfCTtR_a_rE
129 **the baffling anti-spectacle on display**: https://www.youtube.com/watch?v=tg5eTjqefHM

Chapter 5: Tony and Gordon Go Large

132 **back towards electability**: https://www.politico.eu/article/feature-kinnock-the-passionate-moderniser-whose-reforms-sparked-a-revolution/
132 **inevitably into the uncanny**: https://www.youtube.com/watch?v=sE0FKGeHxYk
133 **verge on self-parody**: https://www.youtube.com/watch?v=gi5j7jjhm4M
134 **sipping wine in Kettering**: BBC Two, *The Century of the Self*, (dir.) Adam Curtis, 7 April 2002
136 **for a way out**: https://www.theguardian.com/music/2008/apr/20/electronicmusic.culture
137 **scorching spring morning**: O'Farrell, John, *Things Can Only Get Better* (London: Black Swan, 1999), Chapter 21
137 **I hated it**: https://www.theguardian.com/politics/2007/may/02/politicsandthearts.artsfunding1
137 **whose religion was music**: https://www.theguardian.com/music/2020/jan/01/sugar-sweet-rave-united-belfast-david-holmes-iain-mccready
138 **what background you are**: https://www.youtube.com/watch?v=dz0-42PpFLQ
138 **political bigots ruling us**: https://www.vice.com/en/article/pgw7p7/film-about-rave-culture-90s-sectarian-ulster
138 **Creative Industries Mapping Document**: https://www.gov.uk/government/publications/creative-industries-mapping-documents-1998
139 **spirit of modern Britain**: https://www.irishtimes.com/culture/anyone-for-cultcha-1.207768

139 **of intellectual property**: https://creativeconomy.britishcouncil.org/guide/what-creative-economy/
140 **what they mean is drugs**: ITV, *Inspector Morse* (Series 6, Episode 5, 'Cherubim and Seraphim'), 15 April 1992
141 **picture of wretchedness**: BBC Two, *Loved Up*, 23 September 1995
141 **tragedy, but as farce**: Morrison, Simon A., *Dancefloor-Driven Literature: The Rave Scene in Fiction* (New York: Bloomsbury Academic, 2020), p. 43
141 **soothed and reconciled**: Channel 4, *Spaced* (Series 1, Episode 6, 'Epiphanies'), 29 October 1999
142 **the sound of a pedestrian crossing**: Channel 4, *Spaced* (Series 2, Episode 4, 'Help'), 23 March 2001
142 **the best night of my life**: (dir.) Kerrigan, Justin, *Human Traffic*
142 **'avin it large:** (dir.) Bye, Ed, *Kevin and Perry Go Large*
143 **dreamless**: Adorno, Theodor, 'The Culture Industry: Enlightenment as Mass Deception', taken from *Dialectic of Enlightenment* (Stanford: Stanford University Press, 2002) p. 98
143 **the jargon into which it is absorbed**: Adorno, Theodor, 'The Culture Industry: Enlightenment as Mass Deception', taken from *Dialectic of Enlightenment* (Stanford: Stanford University Press, 2002) p. 100
144 **authoritarian collectivism**: Adorno, Theodor, 'On Popular Music', taken from *Cultural Theory and Popular Culture: A Reader*, (ed.) John Storey (Athens, GA: University of Georgia Press, 1998), p. 207
144 **it's about human spirit**: https://cmci-kings.org/2020/03/24/the-birth-of-the-creative-industries-revisited/
144 **the creative industries**: Banks, Mark, and O'Connor, Justin, 'After the Creative Industries', taken from *The International Journal of Cultural Policy*, Vol. 15 No. 4 (London: Routledge, 2009), p. 367
144 **a more successful one**: https://www.theguardian.com/politics/2007/mar/06/politicsandthearts.uk1
145 **doing things the right way**: https://www.youtube.com/watch?v=Ac_b1gCCu9A
146 **Victorian tea party**: https://909originals.com/2018/07/25/time-machine-please-fantazias-one-step-beyond-party-took-place-on-this-day-in-1992/
146 **from The Prodigy**: https://djmag.com/longreads/let-us-be-your-fantasy-how-fantazia-brought-uk-rave-masses

147	**joyous and spontaneous**: Interview with author, 2022	
148	**get high all the time**: Channel 4, *Peep Show (Series 5, Episode 2, Spin War)*, 9 May 2008	
149	**down to the South Coast**: https://www.theguardian.com/artanddesign/2002/jul/21/artsfeatures.features	
150	**he tried to get through**: https://www.theguardian.com/artanddesign/2002/jul/21/artsfeatures.features	
150	**to that happening**: https://eprints.whiterose.ac.uk/87064/7/EJSP%20paper%20as%20(re)submitted%20Jan%202015.pdf	
150	**them to help on land**: http://news.bbc.co.uk/1/hi/entertainment/2127259.stm	
151	**created a monster**: https://www.theguardian.com/uk/2002/jul/15/arts.artsnews1	
151	**themselves and each other**: https://www.theargus.co.uk/news/5147237.fatboy-i-just-want-a-chilled-party/	
151	**plucked from the sea**: https://www.dailymail.co.uk/tvshowbiz/article-127823/Clean-big-beach-bash.html	
152	**crowds are in place**: https://www.independent.co.uk/arts-entertainment/music/news/brighton-restricts-beach-parties-after-fatboy-slim-concert-chaos-136932.html	
152	**a coherent alternative to it**: Fisher, Mark, *Capitalist Realism* (London: Zero Books, 2009), p. 2	
153	**the end of capitalism**: Fisher, Mark, *Capitalist Realism* (London: Zero Books, 2009), p. 2	
154	**lifestyle of 1990s Britain**: Phillips, Dom, *Superstar DJs Here We Go!* (London: Ebury Press, 2009), p. 3	
154	**the previous spring**: https://www.youtube.com/watch?v=KYB-7Et11yM	
155	**the front of their frocks**: https://www.youtube.com/watch?v=mD9hpT62sVY	
155	**jeans and trainers**: Turner, Ben, *Cream x 10* (London: Carlton Books, 2002), p. 36	
156	**just to go to Cream**: Turner, Ben, *Cream x 10* (London: Carlton Books, 2002), p. 44	
156	**but I saw the seeds sown**: Turner, Ben, *Cream x 10* (London: Carlton Books, 2002), p. 44	
156	**get back in the game**: Turner, Ben, *Cream x 10* (London: Carlton Books, 2002), p. 10	

157 **the police viewed us**: Turner, Ben, *Cream x 10* (London: Carlton Books, 2002), p. 76
157 **become a legal culture**: Ottewill, Jim, *Out Of Space: How UK Cities Shaped Rave Culture* (London Velocity Press, 2022), Chapter 3
157 **got us through**: Turner, Ben, *Cream x 10* (London: Carlton Books, 2002), p. 78
158 **'Odds were it was spiked'**: https://www.timeout.com/newyork/nightlife/paradise-garage-the-oral-history-of-nycs-greatest-club
158 **banker for Merrill Lynch**: https://www.independent.co.uk/news/people/profiles/james-palumbo-there-s-only-money-sex-ndash-and-music-and-mellowing-1769708.html
158 **didn't really have one**: Phillips, Dom, *Superstar DJs Here We Go!* (London: Ebury Press, 2009), p. 226
159 **working-class youth culture**: John, Henry R. L., 'UK Rave Culture and the Thatcherite Hegemony, 1988–94' taken from *Cultural History*, Vol. 4 No. 2 (Edinburgh: Edinburgh University Press, 2015), p. 174
159 **£70 million trust fund**: https://www.independent.co.uk/news/uk/lord-palumbo-accused-of-benefiting-from-trust-1369228.html
159 **by James's grandfather**: https://www.independent.co.uk/news/uk/palumbo-fails-to-prevent-his-children-suing-him-bitter-family-feud-over-pounds-70m-trust-fund-enters-new-phase-as-high-court-judge-dismisses-application-to-have-the-case-struck-out-1381644.html
159 **to Peter Mandelson**: https://www.independent.co.uk/news/mandelson-defends-right-to-go-for-chauffeurdriven-spin-1315783.html
159 **Charter Mark applications**: https://hansard.parliament.uk/commons/1998-07-21/debates/0e229a79-c60e-40b0-a834-08be77559d15/WrittenAnswers
159 **ahead with the Dome?**: https://www.theguardian.com/politics/2007/may/02/politicsandthearts.artsfunding1
160 **provide the money**: Gilliat-Ray, Sophie, 'The Trouble with "Inclusion": A Case Study of the Faith Zone at the Millennium Dome', taken from *The Sociological Review*, Vol. 52 No. 4 (London: SAGE, 2017), p. 467
160 **the religion of the new Millennium**: *Daily Mail*, 26 November 1998
160 **changing the rules**: https://www.campaignlive.co.uk/article/profile-club-class-james-palumbo-founder-ministry-sound/52451
161 **to Sony for £67 million**: https://www.musicbusinessworldwide.com/ministry-of-sound-to-sony-music-uk/

161 **informing his politics**: https://medium.com/@alexworradandrews/tony-blair-was-not-cynical-a-history-lesson-on-blair-s-socialism-50079ab9253c

162 **commitment to, their issues**: Howard, Roland, *The Rise and Fall of the Nine O'Clock Service: A Cult Within the Church* (London: Mowbray, 1998), p. 5

163 **town in the country**: https://www.thetimes.co.uk/article/the-rise-and-fall-of-chris-brain-and-the-nine-oclock-service-ggknfzpvl?fbclid=IwAR373ARNH0X6xLJ_1pni4JHLEFMbTmI3Yb5uadzgqjLm7xv_EJZpmYv9XeE

164 **bodily chakras with spiritual absolution**: Howard, Roland, *The Rise and Fall of the Nine O'Clock Service: A Cult Within the Church* (London: Mowbray, 1998), p. 94

164 **postmodern religious art of the highest order**: Howard, Roland, *The Rise and Fall of the Nine O'Clock Service: A Cult Within the Church* (London: Mowbray, 1998), p. 95

165 **lead to instant action**: https://www.youtube.com/watch?v=QxwdyF3qZj8

166 **accountability and compensation**: https://www.churchtimes.co.uk/articles/2021/23-july/news/uk/nine-o-clock-service-survivors-approach-bishop-of-sheffield

166 **allegations around NOS**: https://www.thetimes.co.uk/article/christian-cult-nine-oclock-service-at-centre-of-sex-claims-s360nkvkk

166 **in a *club* in 1989**: https://www.youtube.com/watch?v=NquS59ZEdZs

167 **his drum machine here!**: https://www.youtube.com/watch?v=hdZBVbHCPXk

Chapter 6: Some Giddy Rite of Passage?

170 **drug busts in European history**: https://www.bbc.co.uk/news/world-europe-23817379

170 **protected from organised crime**: https://www.bbc.co.uk/news/world-europe-24642035

170 **vacant land separating them**: https://www.rtbf.be/article/chimay-un-des-plus-grands-labos-d-ecstasy-d-europe-demantele-8072696

171 **in Holland or Belgium**: https://www.ukdpc.org.uk/wp-content/uploads/Policy%20report%20-%20Tackling%20drug%20markets%20and%20distribution%20networks%20in%20the%20UK.pdf

172 **'it all made sense.'**: https://www.theguardian.com/music/2007/aug/12/electronicmusic

172 **barely conceivable without** drugs: Reynolds, Simon, *Energy Flash* (London: Picador, 2008), p. xxiv

172 **but didn't do any pills**: *It's a London Thing: How Rare Groove, Acid House and Jungle Remapped the City* (Manchester: Manchester University Press, 2019), p. 185

173 **an ideological function**: *It's a London Thing: How Rare Groove, Acid House and Jungle Remapped the City* (Manchester: Manchester University Press, 2019), p. 146

173 **it is false**: *It's a London Thing: How Rare Groove, Acid House and Jungle Remapped the City* (Manchester: Manchester University Press, 2019), p. 146

174 **taken Ecstasy in the preceding year**: Forsyth, Alasdair J. M., 'Places and patterns of drug use in the Scottish dance drug scene' taken from *Addiction, Vol. 91 No. 4* (London: Wiley-Blackwell, 1996), p. 513

174 **cannabis from 44,000 to 89,000**: National Archives, JA 632/181: Ecstasy: Research

175 **my best friends weren't**: Warren, Emma, *Dance Your Way Home* (London: Faber and Faber, 2023), p. 173

175 **both at the time and since**: *Sugar* magazine press release, National Archives, JA 632/181: Ecstasy: Research

176 **embracing each other**: https://mixmag.net/feature/ecstasy-island-this-is-how-ecstasy-reached-the-uk

177 **like Robert Hollemans**: Snelders, Stephen, *Drug Smuggler Nation: Narcotics and the Netherlands, 1920–1995* (Manchester: Manchester University Press, 2021), Chapter 8

178 **transit hub for other drugs**: Snelders, Stephen, *Drug Smuggler Nation: Narcotics and the Netherlands, 1920–1995* (Manchester: Manchester University Press, 2021), Chapter 8

178 **from Dutch laboratories**: Snelders, Stephen, *Drug Smuggler Nation: Narcotics and the Netherlands, 1920–1995* (Manchester: Manchester University Press, 2021), Chapter 8

178 **psychedelic circles around 1970**: https://www.erowid.org/references/refs_view.php?A=ShowDoc1&ID=1149

179 **nothing they could do**: Snelders, Stephen, *Drug Smuggler Nation: Narcotics and the Netherlands, 1920–1995* (Manchester: Manchester University Press, 2021), Chapter 8

179 **that had been exposed**: *The Golden Guru*, https://pgoodnight.files.wordpress.com/2020/09/the-golden-guru.pdf

179 **were flesh and blood**: *The Golden Guru*, https://pgoodnight.files.wordpress.com/2020/09/the-golden-guru.pdf

180 **and an EMS Synthi**: https://www.sannyas.wiki/index.php?title=Sw_Chaitanya_Hari

181 **half a million pills a day**: Snelders, Stephen, *Drug Smuggler Nation: Narcotics and the Netherlands, 1920–1995* (Manchester: Manchester University Press, 2021), Chapter 8

181 **MDEA and MDA**: Snelders, Stephen, *Drug Smuggler Nation: Narcotics and the Netherlands, 1920–1995* (Manchester: Manchester University Press, 2021), Chapter 8

182 **and users edgier**: *Drugs 2.0: The Web Revolution that's Changing How the World Gets High* (London: Portobello Books, 2013), Chapter 2

182 **embers of a large fire**: Power, Mike, *Drugs 2.0: The Web Revolution that's Changing How the World Gets High* (London: Portobello Books, 2013), Chapter 6

183 **smouldering bonfire**: https://www.thenewhumanitarian.org/report/79340/cambodia-ecstasy-tabs-destroying-forest-wilderness

183 **to a measly 6 tonnes**: Power, Mike, *Drugs 2.0: The Web Revolution that's Changing How the World Gets High* (London: Portobello Books, 2013), Chapter 6

183 **seven years earlier**: https://shaunlacob.com/wp-content/uploads/2020/12/Ketamine-use-a-review.pdf

183 **off-axis percussion**: https://www.theguardian.com/music/musicblog/2009/mar/05/wonky-ketamine-dubstep-zomby

184 **pacifically to the horizon**: https://pitchfork.com/features/techno/6178-the-month-in-techno/

185 **European producers today**: https://www.unodc.org/unodc/en/frontpage/2012/March/limitless-ways-to-disguise-ways-to-manufacture-party-pills-unodc-expert.html

185 **again on top of that**: https://www.emcdda.europa.eu/system/files/publications/2473/TD0116348ENN.pdf

185 **British shores dip again**: https://www.vice.com/en/article/xgx3ja/heres-why-theres-so-much-fake-mdma-in-the-uk-right-now

186 **from a different set**: London School of Economics, *Middle Market Drug Distribution*, http://eprints.lse.ac.uk/13878/1/Middle_market_drug_distribution.pdf

186	**charged to protect**: Police Research Group, *Clubs, Drugs and Doormen* (Home Office, 1998), p. v
187	**at me to help her**: *The Independent*, 1 February 1996
188	**twisted out of shape**: *Daily Express*, 1 February 1996
188	**as early as tomorrow**: *Daily Mail*, 15 November 1995
189	**would end up in court**: *Daily Mirror*, 29 January 1996
189	**giddy right of passage**: *Daily Mail*, 14 November 1995
189	**threat to youngsters**: *Daily Star*, 14 November 1995
190	**thirty-four-year-olds roughly doubled**: British Crime Survey data, available at https://beta.ukdataservice.ac.uk/datacatalogue/series/series?id=200009#!/access-data
190	**HEAD FOR THE JUNGLE**: *The Times*, 20 October 1994
191	**stop them earning**: Interview with author, 2022
191	**skateboarding gang Laigon Life**: https://www.dailymail.co.uk/news/article-6758255/Bestival-killer-Ceon-Broughton-carried-knives-told-ex-dreamed-murdering-her.html
191	**drugs then filming them**: https://www.thesun.co.uk/news/8534905/louella-michie-boyfriend-ceon-broughton-filmed-women-drugs/
192	**It was literally unlucky**: https://www.thetimes.co.uk/article/louella-fletcher-michie-drug-death-ceon-broughton-took-pictures-as-i-lay-bleeding-says-former-lover-7r6zlv0mm
192	**only risk-free option**: National Archives, JA 632/181: Ecstasy: Research
192	**demands for her resignation**: https://www.independent.co.uk/voices/a-heroine-amid-the-drugs-hysteria-1305332.html
192	**get away with what they're doing**: *The Sun*, 11 April 1996
193	**either tobacco or alcohol**: https://www.crimeandjustice.org.uk/publications/estimating-drug-harms-risky-business
193	**caused by horse-riding**: https://www.theguardian.com/politics/2009/feb/09/ecstasy-horse-riding
193	**be seen but not heard**: https://www.theguardian.com/politics/2009/oct/30/drugs-adviser-david-nutt-sacked
194	**commitment to public safety**: https://researchbriefings.files.parliament.uk/documents/RP97-2/RP97-2.pdf
194	**"No to drugs" message'**: https://hansard.parliament.uk/Commons/1997-01-17/debates/1c873de4-952a-4eb6-9104-4f34358a74bf/PublicEntertainmentsLicences(DrugMisuse)Bill
194	**involvement with drug dealing**: https://www.plymouthherald.

co.uk/news/plymouth-news/dance-academy-owner-jailed-nine-5560959
195 **clubs' resident DJs**: https://www.vice.com/en/article/59qxp3/how-a-city-closed-a-nightclub-and-destroyed-its-owners-lives
195 **and the sale of drugs**: https://www.vice.com/en/article/59qxp3/how-a-city-closed-a-nightclub-and-destroyed-its-owners-lives
196 **their redevelopment plans**: https://www.plymouthherald.co.uk/news/plymouth-news/full-story-dance-academy-closure-431775
196 **or emotional state**: https://www.legislation.gov.uk/ukpga/2016/2/contents/enacted
197 **wants to ban pleasure**: https://www.telegraph.co.uk/news/general-election-2015/politics-blog/11645354/Theresa-May-wants-to-ban-pleasure.html
197 **almost a quarter to 2,996**: https://www.ons.gov.uk/peoplepopulationandcommunity/birthsdeathsandmarriages/deaths/bulletins/deathsrelatedtodrugpoisoninginenglandandwales/2020
198 **pills or powders:** Interview with author, 2021
200 **lose them any votes:** Interview with author, 2021

Chapter 7: The Breakdown

203 **is escalating**: UKTV Really, *Cops UK: Bodycam Squad*, 3 December 2018
205 **a good thing**: Interview with author, 2019
206 **upon the over-civilised**: https://chronicle250.com/1926
206 **seems remarkably effective**: https://chronicle250.com/1926
206 **shall cease forthwith**: https://georgemckay.org/jazz-race-and-jb-souters-the-breakdown-1926/
206 **and fixed staring eyes . . .** : https://georgemckay.org/jazz-race-and-jb-souters-the-breakdown-1926/
207 **'Yardie drug fiends'**: *Daily Star*, 16 June 1989
207 **smoking the drug**: *News of the World*, 30 July 1989
207 **rather than the Caribbean**: Warenycia, M. G. 'Pandering to Prejudice: The "Yardie" Problem of the 1990s as a Media-Constructed Moral Panic' (Toronto: Ryerson University, 2015) p. 4
207 **turned out to be fake**: http://news.bbc.co.uk/1/hi/uk/371604.stm
208 **or on the radio**: Belle-Fortune, Brian, *All Crews: Journeys Through Jungle/Drum & Bass Culture* (London: Vision Publishing, 2004), p. 19

208 **criminals and crack dealers**: 'Oi, Tony, Give Us Back Our Generation Gap', *The Guardian*, 4 August 1994
208 **derivative of reggae**: *Daily Mail*, 27 July 1996
208 **Garage' music policy**: 'Vicious Circles', *The Guardian*, 22 September 1997
208 **described as well-regulated**: https://www.theguardian.com/uk/2000/aug/01/ukguns.jeevanvasagar
209 **culture and violence**: https://www.nme.com/news/music/so-solid-crew-30-1381968
209 **banish gun culture**: https://www.theguardian.com/media/2003/jan/06/radio.politics
209 **white suburban Britain**: https://www.theguardian.com/uk/2003/jan/06/ukguns.immigrationpolicy1
210 **law-abiding citizen**: https://www.theguardian.com/politics/2006/jan/10/immigrationpolicy.ukcrime
210 **boys related to crime**: https://orca.cardiff.ac.uk/id/eprint/28559/1/2113275.pdf
210 **holding grime back?**: https://www.theguardian.com/music/musicblog/2006/nov/06/isviolenceholdinggrimeback
211 **country music or karaoke**: https://blogs.lse.ac.uk/usapp-blog/2019/06/28/evidence-shows-that-live-hip-hop-is-no-more-linked-to-violence-than-country-music-or-karaoke/
211 **a coincidental link**: Fatsis, Lambros, 'Policing the Beats' taken from *The Sociological Review*, Vol. 67, No. 6 (London: SAGE, 2017)
212 **UK Music in 2009**: https://www.theguardian.com/culture/2009/jan/21/police-form-696-garage-music
213 **don't play the music**: https://novaramedia.com/2017/01/22/fuck-em-and-their-law-repression-and-resistance-in-rave-and-grime/
213 **or a £20,000 fine**: https://www.theguardian.com/culture/2009/jan/21/police-form-696-garage-music
213 **can't have a grime room**: Hancox, Dan, *Inner City Pressure* (London: William Collins, 2018), p. 171
214 **the mic to Jammer**: https://www.youtube.com/watch?v=_nM77oU7qVQ
214 **support them financially**: https://www.youtube.com/watch?v=eW_iujPQpys
215 **whatever issues they have**: https://thequietus.com/articles/14594-just-jam-cancelled

215 **Irish, Latin and Oldies**: http://policeauthority.org/metropolitan/committees/cep/2009/090910/07/index.html
215 **those particular events**: https://www.theskinny.co.uk/clubs/interviews/sound-of-the-police
216 **what's going on**: Hancox, Dan, *Inner City Pressure* (London: William Collins, 2018), p. 179
217 **nobody nicks the decks**: https://daily.redbullmusicacademy.com/2015/09/nightclubbing-niche
217 **but not overdone**: https://en.wikipedia.org/wiki/Something_Goin'_On_(In_Your_Soul)
217 **no one was ever charged**: https://www.thestar.co.uk/news/killer-sheffield-nightclub-boss-never-caught-two-decades-648903
218 **come down hard on us**: http://alexdeadman.blogspot.com/2010/07/feature-niche-true-story-from-steve.html
218 **run a crack house**: https://daily.redbullmusicacademy.com/2015/09/nightclubbing-niche
218 **play any bassline tunes**: https://www.vice.com/en/article/nnyjpw/the-rise-and-fall-of-bassline
218 **good couple of years**: https://ukf.com/words/banned-from-sheffield-how-jamie-duggan-fought-for-bassline-and-won/23070
219 **pseudonymously as 'Matt'**: https://www.bbc.co.uk/news/newsbeat-14717364
220 **badman mentality to parties**: http://www.josephjppatterson.co.uk/2012/12/mixmag-shuffle-trouble.html
221 **didn't get covered**: Interview with author, 2022
222 **deemed to be disposable**: White, Joy, *Terraformed: Young Black Lives in the Inner City* (London: Repeater Books, 2020) p. 49
223 **'I want to do big things.'**: https://www.vice.com/en/article/dy74jk/fake-record-store-operation-peyzac
223 **drugs and gun offences**: https://www.dailymail.co.uk/news/article-2036437/The-hip-hop-cop-shop-Police-opened-fake-rap-music-store-snared-30-gangsters-drugs-gun-offences.html
224 **hatred around rap music**: https://www.mirror.co.uk/news/uk-news/london-riots-is-rap-music-to-blame-146671
224 **whites have become black**: https://www.theguardian.com/uk/2011/aug/13/david-starkey-claims-whites-black
224 **these past few days**: https://theartsdesk.com/node/4287/view

224 **Broadwater Farm riots**: https://www.theguardian.com/music/2011/aug/12/rap-riots-professor-green-lethal-bizzle-wiley

225 **system gonna get him**: https://www.youtube.com/watch?v=F7bcYu6CODI

225 **now that it was then**: https://www.theguardian.com/uk-news/2020/jun/15/i-could-so-easily-have-died-wretch-32s-father-on-being-shot-with-taser

226 **evidence during the trial**: https://policyexchange.org.uk/wp-content/uploads/2021/10/Knife-Crime-in-the-Capital.pdf

226 **possession of a knife**: https://www.bbc.co.uk/news/newsbeat-51039235

227 **output of a musician**: https://www.nytimes.com/2021/01/11/arts/music/digga-d-drill-music.html

227 **that he can talk about**: https://www.bbc.co.uk/bbcthree/article/144838d0-6be6-4fdb-a919-0a38811741c3

227 **at the hands of the police**: https://www.clashmusic.com/news/why-was-digga-ds-black-lives-matter-protest-shut-down/

227 **Moscow 17 and Harlem Spartans**: https://www.theguardian.com/music/2019/jan/31/skengdo-and-am-the-drill-rappers-sentenced-for-playing-their-song

227 **serious violence being committed**: https://www.bbc.co.uk/bbcthree/article/144838d0-6be6-4fdb-a919-0a38811741c3

227 **suspended for two years**: https://www.theguardian.com/music/2019/jan/31/skengdo-and-am-the-drill-rappers-sentenced-for-playing-their-song

228 **South London and stab people**: https://www.youtube.com/watch?v=KU2JAQ8DnCA

229 **show by drill group 67**: https://www.youtube.com/watch?v=KSYGq40Pwlo

229 **between 2020 and 2021**: https://www.vice.com/en/article/bvnp8v/met-police-youtube-drill-music-removal

229 **leading to unfair convictions**: https://yjlc.uk/resources/legal-updates/justice-report-report-finds-misunderstanding-drill-music-leading-unfair

230 **the quoting of drill lyrics**: https://www.theguardian.com/uk-news/2022/jul/08/four-black-teenagers-manchester-jailed-text-messages-plan-appeal

230 **some sort of criminality**: https://www.rollingstone.co.uk/politics/features/prosecuting-uk-drill-rap-lyrics-court-20131/

230	**an assumed gang member**: https://ciaranthapar.substack.com/p/unsilent-witness
231	**'failing a background check'**: https://www.bbc.co.uk/news/uk-england-coventry-warwickshire-62401973
231	**involvement in the brawl**: https://www.theguardian.com/music/2022/dec/02/british-rapper-pa-salieu-sentenced-to-33-months-in-jail

Chapter 8: Pirates' Anthem

234	**money you owe me**: https://www.youtube.com/watch?v=n5euVsZwEcQ
235	**start a pirate up**: Interview with author, 2022
236	**directly into a lifeboat**: https://www.youtube.com/watch?v=FieBuF0A6Fc
236	**a studio in Neasden**: https://dbc1981.com
237	**to do it ourselves**: https://www.youtube.com/watch?v=BQBUqIuzghA
238	**the next election**: https://www.amfm.org.uk/tx/tx7/communityradio.html
238	**the hazards ahead**: National Archives, PREM 19/2024 f. 403
238	**normal free speech**: National Archives, PREM 19/2024 f. 390
239	**experiment in community radio**: https://hansard.parliament.uk/Commons/1986-06-30/debates/4b45689b-8128-453b-a164-f573aa13a0b2/WrittenAnswers
239	**switch off this radio**: National Archives, PREM 19/2024 f. 390
239	**unemployment or crime**: https://www.newstatesman.com/politics/2015/12/oliver-letwins-non-apology-his-racist-remarks-isnt-enough
240	**black "activist"**: National Archives, *PREM 19/1920*
243	**longer than they're on**: https://www.amfm.org.uk/tx/tx9/onairlondon.html
244	**"Go on then"**: Interview with author, 2022
245	**before pulling the plug**: https://www.youtube.com/watch?v=kWAxADoyEXo
247	**for cultural subversion**: Barbrook, Richard, 'Melodies or rhythms? The competition for the Greater London FM radio licence' taken from *Popular Music*, Vol. 9 No. 2 (Cambridge: Cambridge University Press, 1990), p. 217
248	**a much wider audience**: https://www.youtube.com/watch?v=kWAxADoyEXo

249 **still make a living**: Interview with author, 2022
250 **contest his sacking**: https://www.theguardian.com/uk/1999/aug/18/race.world
250 **but not the second**: https://www.theguardian.com/uk/1999/nov/13/8
250 **Greatest Hits Radio**: https://www.theguardian.com/business/2007/dec/07/emapbusiness.emap
251 **and breaks the link**: http://www.furious.com/perfect/simonreynolds.html
252 **parties that weren't ours**: Collin, Matthew, *Altered State: The Story of Ecstasy Culture and Acid House* (London: Serpent's Tail, 2009), p. 45
252 **it's pirate radio**: Interview with author, 2022
253 **to pump out Kool**: Belle-Fortune, Brian, *All Crews: Journeys Through Jungle/Drum & Bass Culture* (London: Vision Publishing, 2004), p. 65
253 **had all the best DJs**: https://web.archive.org/web/20140910195520/http://ntslive.co.uk/slimzee-interview/
255 **as quick as it comes in**: Interview with author, 2022
256 **I was like: this is *amazing***: Hancox, Dan, *Inner City Pressure* (London: William Collins, 2018), p. 93
257 **Rinse's account books**: Hancox, Dan, *Inner City Pressure* (London: William Collins, 2018), p. 92
257 **within Tower Hamlets**: https://www.standard.co.uk/hp/front/asbo-bars-pirate-dj-from-the-rooftops-7173468.html
257 **he was out**: Interview with author, 2022
259 **stay pirate if we have to**: Interview with author, 2022
261 **looking over their shoulder** https://djmag.com/news/rinse-fm-announces-acquisition-legendary-london-station-kool-fm
261 **feels like home**: Interview with author, 2022

Chapter 9: Real People Doing Real Things

263 **normal *Hitman and Her***: https://www.youtube.com/watch?v=u3HrIPOxpX0
264 **the freshness of it**: https://www.theguardian.com/music/2013/nov/11/stakker-humanoid-25th-anniversary-acid-house
265 **people doing real things**: https://www.theguardian.com/music/2011/jun/15/the-hitman-and-her
265 **a blazer and a tie**: https://www.youtube.com/watch?v=m7hrUEeTqz0

266 **get on with the music**: https://www.youtube.com/watch?v=yYZaNbwMJ2g
266 **couldn't wait to get out**: https://www.thecourier.co.uk/fp/past-times/1818994/michaela-strachan-my-memories-of-the-hitman-and-her-at-flicks-in-brechin/
268 **vocal acrobatics**: https://www.youtube.com/watch?v=sst2ks-P_I0
269 **where's it all going?**: https://www.youtube.com/watch?v=ZY02R-xFC_A
271 **mug of tea in his hand**: https://www.youtube.com/watch?v=vOxc65Wl8l8
271 **hidden in the shadows**: Hancox, Dan, *Inner City Pressure* (London: William Collins, 2018), p. 117
272 **Crazy Titch. It was *sick***: https://www.youtube.com/watch?v=s-t-OmnaA-Q
272 **as a personal trainer**: https://www.youtube.com/watch?v=7yta10-L8-c
272 **the heritage circuit**: https://www.nme.com/features/channel-u-2020-revival-best-bits-2822446
273 **more people wanted it**: https://www.vice.com/en/article/3kpvev/an-oral-history-of-sbtv-the-youtube-channel-that-blew-the-doors-open-for-uk-rap
274 **by Tim and Barry**: https://www.youtube.com/watch?v=VtO-YRejpQI
274 **Blur's 'Country House'**: https://www.youtube.com/watch?v=xLg2I9zgCi4
274 **£8 million**: https://www.theguardian.com/media/2013/oct/21/youtube-video-channel-sbtv
275 **systematically falsified**: sbhttps://www.theverge.com/2018/10/17/17989712/facebook-inaccurate-video-metrics-inflation-lawsuit
275 **from the online chatroom**: https://www.youtube.com/watch?v=pNRCLHq3ins
276 **an aristocratic family**: https://www.thepeerage.com/p64290.htm#i642897
276 **College Magic Society**: https://www.dailymail.co.uk/femail/article-1347610/Britains-50-powerful-posh-people-30-From-catwalk-Westminster.html
278 **it was a dream**: Interview with author, 2022
279 **several left the company**: https://www.vice.com/en/article/v7vvaa/beatport-electronic-dance-music-online-store-toxic-workplace

280 **his role with the company**: https://www.vice.com/en/article/v7vvaa/beatport-electronic-dance-music-online-store-toxic-workplace
281 **centralization of culture**: Interview with author, 2022
282 **disservice to people**: Interview with author, 2022
282 **of Carnival itself**: https://www.vice.com/en/article/599qdz/why-there-was-anti-boiler-room-graffiti-at-carnival
282 **no one thought about the *crowds***: Interview with author, 2022
283 **didn't sign any forms**: Interview with author, 2022
284 **than seen previously**: https://medium.com/@boil_the_room/babylon-room-ea3eb474d155
285 **'dance music cancer'**: https://5mag.net/features/boiler-room-is-changing/
285 **sustainable for everyone involved**: https://5mag.net/features/boiler-room-is-changing/
286 **living, breathing culture**: https://boilerroom.tv/session/fred-again-br
287 **death in 2022**: https://www.theguardian.com/media/2019/nov/03/jamal-edwards-youth-club-knife-crime-london-young-people-grime
290 **his way of operating**: https://mixmag.net/read/aphex-twins-set-at-field-day-was-the-completely-bonkers-comeback-we-had-all-hoped-for-blog/
291 **a struggle in itself**: https://www.yellwzine.com/post/jojo-sonubi
292 **and for black people**: https://www.campaignlive.co.uk/article/no-signal-shows-power-brands-tuning-black-culture/1682287
292 **money pumped in**: https://www.yellwzine.com/post/jojo-sonubi
292 **an ineffable sadness**: https://twitter.com/WrayAndNephewUK/status/1299722948329308160

Chapter 10: Strictly Business Techno

296 **Owen Townsend in 2011**: https://www.mdmarchive.co.uk/artefact/8709/OWEN_TOWNSEND_MOSS_SIDE_BLUESSHEBEENS_VIDEO_2011
297 **'collage mess-thetic'**: Reynolds, Simon, *Energy Flash* (London: Picador, 2008), p. 126
297 **reverberant concrete spaces**: https://www.electronicbeats.net/ideal-listening-space-house-techno/
299 **licensed clubs disappeared**: https://www.theguardian.com/commentisfree/2015/aug/11/clubs-closing-nightlife-uk

NOTES

299 **a lot of venues**: https://ra.co/features/2795
299 **President of Electronic Music**: https://www.thebusinessdesk.com/northwest/news/319556-live-nation-buys-out-cream-group-in-14m-deal
299 **a dozen others**: http://www.festivalinsights.com/2015/07/global-entertainment-acquires-strategic-stake-broadwick-live/
299 **sold on once again**: https://www.iq-mag.net/2019/04/superstruct-broadwick-global-festival/#.XMC3nZNKiCc
303 **club set of any kind**: https://www.youtube.com/watch?v=1UxY5LonBIc
303 **for which he's known**: https://www.youtube.com/watch?v=qQaEWVYuyXU
304 **chart-dance fodder**: https://www.youtube.com/watch?v=1oeYSG7ankM
306 **extend their opening hours**: https://news.hackney.gov.uk/dalston-special-policy-area-approved-by-hackney-council/
306 **for all new premises**: https://london.eater.com/2018/7/19/17587068/hackney-council-licensing-law-nightlife-licensing-restrictions
306 **[opening] hours we need**: https://ra.co/news/34256
307 **the vibe began to shift**: https://www.factmag.com/2015/02/17/plastic-people-an-oral-history-fwd-cdr-co-op-ade/
307 **UK more than doubled**: https://committees.parliament.uk/publications/6136/documents/68377/default/
307 **big festival instead**: https://www.youtube.com/watch?v=s6QnwOSemD4
308 **techno tourist destination**: https://www.rollingstone.com/culture/culture-news/berghain-the-secretive-sex-fueled-world-of-technos-coolest-club-111396/
308 **night in Birmingham**: https://daily.redbullmusicacademy.com/2019/01/nightclubbing-house-of-god
309 **more credible tastemakers**: https://www.theguardian.com/music/2020/jan/10/gift-of-the-gabber-the-return-of-dance-musics-gloriously-tasteless-subgenre
309 **middle-class dinner party**: https://ra.co/features/4107
309 **the working week**: https://www.theguardian.com/music/2017/jul/14/rave-health-wellness-festivals-djs
309 **time-aligned tweeter arrays**: https://www.wired.co.uk/article/despacio
310 **fully commit themselves**: https://ra.co/news/78312
311 **forcing them to close**: https://www.theguardian.com/music/2016/

sep/07/london-nightclub-fabric-close-permanently-licence-revoked-drugs

312 **closely involved with**: https://theferret.scot/sub-club-director-family-sold-hotel-wetherspoons/

312 **Peggy Gou's birthday**: https://www.glasgowtimes.co.uk/news/18569497.millionaire-sub-club-director-regrets-social-media-boats/

313 **get Fabric reopened"**: Interview with author, 2021

314 **proportion of live music**: https://www.attackmagazine.com/news/500-million-culture-recovery-fund-includes-dance-music-events/

315 **from that same fund**: https://www.vice.com/en/article/qj4gn5/which-clubs-received-funding-257-million-government-arts-fund

315 **trickle down to others**: https://www.ntia.co.uk/wp-content/uploads/2020/04/campaign-email.pdf

315 **just another statistic**: https://www.theguardian.com/uk-news/2019/jun/28/london-gay-nightclub-xxl-faces-closure-to-make-way-for-flats

316 **are able to survive**: https://www.nesta.org.uk/blog/the-clubbing-map-what-has-happened-to-london-nightlife/

316 **convert it to [residential]**: https://www.vice.com/en/article/vd8pgb/london-regeneration-videos-dan-honcox-374

317 **segregated 'poor doors'**: https://www.vice.com/en_uk/article/4w7m4q/londons-poor-doors-defeated-by-anarchists-910

318 **help save Club 414**: https://ra.co/news/78219

318 **property development company**: https://thequietus.com/articles/28302-housekeeping-faces-review

318 **caps, hooded jumpers**: https://tapelondon.com/contact/

319 **the regeneration phase**: https://www.theguardian.com/music/2019/apr/09/tottenham-gas-works-to-transform-into-drumsheds-mega-venue

319 **cavernous printing hall**: https://thespaces.com/printworks-is-a-16-acre-music-venue-london/

320 **kudos that come with it**: https://news.pollstar.com/2018/05/08/our-business-depends-on-selling-tickets-qs-with-broadwick-lives-bradley-thompson/

320 **to fall on deaf ears**: https://www.change.org/p/lb-southwark-save-printworks-nightclub-from-being-converted-into-offices

320 **Telereal Trillium for £1.5 billion**: https://www.theguardian.com/business/2018/sep/10/network-rail-sells-railway-arches-real-estate-investors-telereal-trillium-blackstone-property-partners

321	**to make enough money**:	https://crackmagazine.net/2022/07/londons-space-289-announces-closure-later-this-month/
321	**studio Rockstar Games**:	https://www.musicweek.com/live/read/rockstar-games-invests-in-promoter-and-venue-operator-broadwick/085963
321	**Grand Theft Auto 5 alone**:	https://www.tribalwarehouse.co.uk/magazine/articles/rockstar-games-invests-into-depot-mayfield-printworks-operator-broadwick-live
321	**the 1,500-home project**:	https://www.housingtoday.co.uk/news/300m-public-funding-package-agreed-to-kickstart-silvertown-quays/5118252.article
322	**nightclub Oval Space**:	https://spacesstories.com/space/oval-studios/
323	**in 'close collaboration'**:	https://lwe.events/news/thebeams-launch
323	**activities in the borough**:	https://www.propertyweek.com/london/lost-gardens-of-london/5053520.article
323	**across the whole project**:	https://thequietus.com/articles/09308-bloc-festival-london-pleasure-gardens
324	**control the situation**:	https://www.theguardian.com/music/2012/jul/09/bloc-weekend-2012
324	**get the dogs out**:	https://www.stubnitz.com/audio/by/artist/boddika_and_mc_chunky
324	**budgets began to bite**:	https://www.propertyweek.com/london/lost-gardens-of-london/5053520.article
324	**London Pleasure Gardens**:	Child Poverty Action Group, *Child Poverty in Newham, a guide for London councillors* (London: Child Poverty Action Group, 2018), p. 22
325	**and overgrown scrubland**:	https://www.theguardian.com/artanddesign/2022/jul/20/empty-promise-the-fantasy-city-within-a-city-that-turned-into-a-ghost-town
325	**part of east London**:	https://www.architectsjournal.co.uk/news/behind-the-story-how-did-boriss-business-park-become-a-ghost-town
326	**mainstay Peggy Gou**:	https://hypebae.com/2022/6/parklike-festival-2022-female-lineup

Chapter 11: Plague Raving

330	**spirit at its finest**:	https://www.mirror.co.uk/news/uk-news/thirsty-punters-brave-torrential-rain-24023815

331   **BBC reporter's microphone**: https://www.bbc.co.uk/news/av/newsbeat-56951642

331   **like it's been for ever**: https://news.sky.com/story/thousands-head-to-uks-first-club-night-in-more-than-a-year-for-covid-safety-pilot-event-12291528

331   **music fans in the city**: https://www.dazeddigital.com/life-culture/article/53224/1/what-clubbing-in-england-will-look-like-post-covid-according-to-clubs-june-21

332   **shift from those dates**: https://www.theguardian.com/politics/2021/feb/26/experts-criticise-boris-johnson-putting-dates-covid-roadmap

332   **visited during the pandemic**: https://selector.news/2021/05/13/misstep-sven-vath-first-dance-covid-19/

333   **made it such a special one**: https://www.instagram.com/p/CEU1_MapD29/

333   **good to be back on tour**: https://web.archive.org/web/20200816181125/https://twitter.com/DaxJ/status/1295060515622981632

334   **game to go ahead**: https://www.theguardian.com/sport/2021/oct/15/liverpool-v-atletico-placed-fans-in-danger-will-anyone-be-held-to-account

335   **we could have imagined**: https://mixmag.net/feature/bangface-weekender-last-rave-hardcore-review

337   **it cannot be otherwise**: https://www.thetimes.co.uk/article/its-time-we-stopped-pandering-to-travellers-2slbdvbvp

340   **induced transcendence**: https://www.facebook.com/watch/?v=938130606610644

340   **amplified sound whatsoever**: https://www.dailymail.co.uk/news/article-8610995/Illegal-rave-Kent-beach-sees-revellers-ignore-social-distancing-rules.html (The piece's original headline, since amended, read 'Violence on Britain's beaches as two men are stabbed at beach rave')

341   **death to late-night venues**: https://www.theguardian.com/commentisfree/2021/mar/20/undercover-police-bars-clubs-women-boris-johnson

341   **techno in the pouring rain**: https://www.youtube.com/watch?v=eeUwOHNRz-Y

341   **dubstep and drum'n'bass**: https://www.youtube.com/watch?v=vmwmBoVcxxY

341   **from Blackburn in 1989**: https://www.mirror.co.uk/news/uk-news/hundreds-pack-warehouse-illegal-rave-22907955

341   **environmental protests of 1994**: https://www.theguardian.com/

world/2020/aug/30/police-in-england-and-wales-break-up-illegal-raves-as-covid-fines-introduced

342 **desperate you'd be by now**: https://djmag.com/longreads/plague-raves-clubbing-pandemic-ever-ethical

342 **and moving together**: https://www.dazeddigital.com/life-culture/article/51143/1/inside-the-uk-illegal-rave-scene-flourishing-in-lockdown-coronavirus

342 **'Illegal raves are back'**: https://www.thetimes.co.uk/article/illegal-raves-are-back-will-lockdown-herald-the-third-summer-of-love-s9d2sphc7

342 **rave policing taskforce**: https://twitter.com/WMPolice/status/1376610107916607488

342 **teenage house parties**: https://www.birminghammail.co.uk/news/midlands-news/west-midlands-police-disperse-28-18737760

343 **in a single weekend**: https://www.telegraph.co.uk/politics/2020/08/28/will-not-allow-selfish-behaviour-bank-holiday-weekend-derail/

343 **know, or wouldn't say**: https://mixmag.net/feature/exclusive-priti-patel-incorrect-illegal-raves-data-emergency-powers-met-police

344 **80 per cent of the UK**: https://www.theguardian.com/world/2022/nov/13/people-of-colour-more-likely-to-be-fined-for-lockdown-raves-data-shows

344 **lines of riot cops**: https://www.youtube.com/watch?v=uLsEAvo1VtI

344 **'too big to shut down.'**: https://uk.style.yahoo.com/police-apologise-rave-bristol-170653227.html

344 **inconsistent policing**: https://www.theguardian.com/world/2022/nov/13/people-of-colour-more-likely-to-be-fined-for-lockdown-raves-data-shows

345 **notions of civility**: https://www.theguardian.com/world/2022/nov/13/people-of-colour-more-likely-to-be-fined-for-lockdown-raves-data-shows

345 **during the pandemic**: https://mixmag.net/feature/london-illegal-rave-scene

345 **raves are flourishing**: https://www.theguardian.com/music/2020/feb/05/austerity-gentrification-and-big-tunes-why-illegal-raves-are-flourishing

345 **return of rave culture**: https://www.newstatesman.com/culture/2019/08/the-return-of-rave-culture

345 **same in March 2018**: https://www.telegraph.co.uk/news/2018/03/04/illegal-raves-rise-traditional-nightclubs-close-doors-new-figures/
345 **a couple of weeks later**: https://www.nme.com/features/nme-investigates-rave-culture-2275118
345 **the *Times* in June**: https://www.thetimes.co.uk/article/what-are-the-new-illegal-raves-like-vzmrmrzx9
345 **illegal raves are back in 2017**: https://www.huckmag.com/art-and-culture/music-2/blackburn-raves/; https://www.theguardian.com/society/2017/nov/27/come-together-how-rave-returned-to-the-cultural-mix
345 **'illegal rave renaissance' in 2016**: https://www.independent.co.uk/arts-entertainment/the-ravers-return-how-underground-parties-are-making-a-comeback-a7036131.html
345 **rave party' in 2006**: https://www.thetimes.co.uk/article/infadels-dbxgn0mx5m9
345 **the ravers' in 2005**: https://www.theguardian.com/uk/2005/jul/16/arts.artsnews2
345 **solar eclipse in 1999**: *Daily Mirror*, 11 August 1999
346 **'involvement in illegal raves'**: *Horley & Gatwick Mirror*, 25 July 1996
346 **off their heads on beer**: https://www.vice.com/en/article/vvnwxb/locked-off-uk-clive-martin-illegal-warehouse-raves-london
349 **dance music initially**: https://crackmagazine.net/2020/07/nightclubs-eligible-new-500-million-relief-fund/
350 **thrown a party in years**: https://mixmag.net/read/cultural-recover-fund-grant-dormant-birmingham-club-night-sundissential-frozen-news/
350 **Culture Recovery Fund**: https://find-and-update.company-information.service.gov.uk/company/10519921
350 **being reviewed in person**: https://www.artsprofessional.co.uk/news/exclusive-due-diligence-checks-emergency-grants-were-automated
351 **the applicant in question**: https://www.artsprofessional.co.uk/news/dcms-and-ace-face-inquiry-culture-recovery-fund-following-due-diligence-issues
352 **applicants' bank accounts**: https://www.nao.org.uk/wp-content/uploads/2021/03/Investigation-into-the-Culture-Recovery-Fund-Summary.pdf
353 **'cultural Taliban'**: https://www.dailymail.co.uk/debate/article-

11301337/A-new-breed-cultural-Taliban-turning-universities-woke-factories-warns-FRANK-FUREDI.html

355 **extremely difficult to process**: https://dwellerforever.blog/2021/03/clubs-and-festivals-are-coming-back-but-wheres-the-industrys-fight-against-racism

Chapter 12: Just Like We Never Said Goodbye

358 **brutality that they represent**: https://ra.co/events/1135625
358 **it has political potential**: Interview with author, 2022
359 **just being together**: Interview with author, 2022
360 **just for one night**: Interview with author, 2022
361 **like a secret club for us all**: https://www.azeemamag.com/stories/daytimers
361 **had not existed before**: https://homegrown.co.in/article/805466/how-bhangra-daytime-discos-defined-an-entire-south-asian-generation-in-bradford
362 **within the wider culture**: https://www.theguardian.com/music/2019/jan/11/asian-underground-music-eastern-electro-drumnbass
362 **Belligerent Paki-fists**: *The Observer*, 3 November 1993, quoted in Huq, Rupa, 'Asian Kool? Bhangra and Beyond' taken from *Dis-Orienting Rhythms: The Politics of the New Asian Dance Music* (London: Zed Books, 1996), p. 69
362 **it's all bullshit**: Huq, Rupa, 'Asian Kool? Bhangra and Beyond' taken from *Dis-Orienting Rhythms: The Politics of the New Asian Dance Music* (London: Zed Books, 1996), p. 69
363 **music that shaped me**: https://www.youtube.com/watch?v=kSpRpBDrIFM
364 **in a really comfortable way**: https://thefortyfive.com/opinion/dialled-in-festival-south-asian-underground-music-london/
364 **in a room together post-COVID**: Interview with author, 2022
366 **cares about each other**: https://i-d.vice.com/en/article/7xgqz4/our-rules-our-roof-this-short-film-celebrates-the-impact-of-pxssy-palace-for-queer-people-of-colour
367 **that's exactly what I did**: https://www.britishcouncil.org/voices-magazine/pxssy-palace-club-night
367 **times more for entry**: https://www.express.co.uk/news/uk/1560460/Pxssy-Palace-nightclub-entry-prices-gay-straight-sexuality-London

367 **claiming to be downtrodden**: https://www.dailymail.co.uk/news/article-10462283/Party-club-blasted-112-man-tax-t.html
367 **contributing to the space?**: https://www.pxssypalace.com/policy
369 **expectations can be unreasonable**: https://dalstonsuperstore.com/unite-the-union-and-dalston-superstore-sign-recognition-agreement/
369 **discriminatory behaviour**: https://djmag.com/news/boomtown-bar-staff-report-poor-treatment-discrimination-and-neglect-2022-festival
370 **even if it's for charity**: https://ra.co/features/2909
372 **investigate its own police force**: Malyon, Tim, 'Tossed in the fire and they never got burned: the Exodus Collective', taken from *DiY Culture*, (ed.) George McKay (London: Verso, 1998) p. 198
372 **by the Home Office**: https://web.archive.org/web/20040624002225/http://www.squall.co.uk/squall.cfm/ses/sq=2001061944/ct=2
372 **on the Saturday night**: https://alanlodge.co.uk/OnTheRoad/exodus-to-rave-or-to-riot/
373 **all culture – are likely to**: Warren, Emma, *Make Some Space: Tuning into Total Refreshment Centre* (London: Sweet Machine, 2019), p. 124
374 **supporting political parties**: https://www.nme.com/news/music/grime4corbyn-movement-distances-itself-from-labour-as-general-election-nears-2574380
374 **Policing, Crime, Sentencing and Courts Bill**: https://www.legislation.gov.uk/ukpga/2022/32/contents
375 **that's a lot to ask for**: https://djmag.com/longreads/who-owns-night-complicated-reality-night-time-economy
377 **distribute and sell music**: https://mixmag.net/feature/how-the-dance-music-industry-failed-black-artists
377 **make do with scraps**: https://itsrosh.nfshost.com/letter/
377 **its personality profiles**: Eshun, Kodwo, *More Brilliant Than The Sun* (London: Quartet Books, 1998), p. 7
378 **original intentions and essence**: https://ra.co/features/4049
378 **during the pandemic**: https://mixmag.net/feature/cost-of-living-nightclubs-venues-promoters-manchester-liverpool-london-glasgow-cardiff-bristol
379 **from country to pop**: https://openai.com/blog/jukebox/

380 **DJs For Climate Action**: https://www.djs4ca.com
383 **of steel pan and mas**: https://mangrovesteelband.wordpress.com/history/
385 **other spaces are possible**: Fisher, Mark, 'Baroque Sunbursts' taken from *Rave: Rave and its Influences on Art and Culture*, (ed.) Nav Haq (London: Black Dog Publishing, 2016), p. 45

Index

References in *italics* indicate images.

acid. *See* LSD
acid house: origins of 3, 5, 8, 11, 23, 24, 25, 33, 36, 37, 40, 45, 47, 49, 53, 63, 65–90, 96, 96n, 98, 100, 101, 115, 136, 137, 145, 154, 155, 158, 162, 172, 179–81, 182, 206–7, 220, 295–6, 338; pirate radio and 234, 236, 240–1, 242–3; *The Hitman and Her*/Waterman and 264n, 265, 266, 267, 269
Acid House Flashback 75, 78, 83
acid techno 6, 317
Acidica 49
Acklam Hall 22
Acton Lane 103, 111, 113
Ade, DJ 25–6
Adeyemi, Femi 276
Adonis: 'No Way Back' 23–4, 240
Adorno, Theodor: 'Enlightenment as Mass Deception' 143–4, 302
Advance Party 119, 122
Advances Business Parks 325
AEG 299
Afro-Caribbean Community Radio Project 238

afro-cosmic 75, 179
Agony & The Ecstasy, The (documentary series) 172–3
Ahmed, Riz 361
AI (artificial intelligence) 378–9, 384
AIDS 52, 66n, 67, 68, 69, 70, 71
Ajamu X 10
Akinfenwa, Jumi 292
Albany Theatre 22
Alcock, Pearl 9–11, 366
alcohol-free parties 276, 360
Alfredo, DJ 75, 142, 172, 180
Alkali, Operation 81, 86
All Ages 276
All Points East 299, 307
Alternative Free Festival 50
Amnesia 75, 142, 172–3
Amobi, Chino 290
amphetamines 174, 175, 177–8, 179, 181
Amsterdam 188–9, 198
Anderson, Paul 'Trouble' 250
Anderson, Penny 87
Anderson, Tom 236

Anderton, James 67–9, 72–3, 74, 77, 78, 83–4, 90, 126
Andrews, Emmanuelle 344
Andrews, Tony 49, 128
Andrin, Rik-Ines 378
Androids of Mu 54
Anglicanism, rave 161–8
Anokha 361
Anstruther-Gough-Calthorpe, Jacobi 318
Anti Foot Shuffling Campaign 220
anti-roads movement 123
Apache Indian 362
Aphex Twin 290
Appadu, Sherwyn 363
Ark, The 371–3
arson attacks 21–2
Artois, Nadine 367
Arts Council 75, 78, 158, 282, 349, 350, 351, 352, 376
ASBOs (anti-social behaviour orders) 88, 219–20, 226, 257
Asian Dub Foundation 361, 362
Asian underground 361, 362, 363, 364
Asian youth 127, 176, 208, 228, 237, 239, 286, 343–4, 359, 360–6, 378
Aslice 291
Aswad 21–2, 225
Auld, Graham 145
austerity politics 205, 222, 298, 305–7, 324, 378
Autechre: 'Flutter' 118
Avon and Somerset Police 105, 106
Avon Free Festival 96n, 105

Babylon (film) 21
'Back to Basics' campaign 115, 210
Bahmanzadeh, Manoucehr 194–5
Bailey, DJ Chris 217, 218

Bakhtin, Mikhail 33
Baldelli, DJ Daniele 180
Balram, Dhruva 363, 364–5
Bangface Weekender 334–5, 336
Barbican Centre 214–15, 295
Barbrook, Richard 247
Bargee Travellers 337–8
Barton, Chalin 276
Barton, James 154–5, 156, 299, 300, 310n
basement clubs 3, 6, 10–11, 15, 27, 175, 181, 222–3, 248, 268–9, 277, 306, 316, 366
Bass Culture Research 17
Bauer Media 250
Baxendale, Steve 216–18
BBC 58, 79, 101, 109, 129, 141, 145, 165, 188, 208, 215, 236, 237, 242n, 268, 270n, 273, 284, 307, 331
Beams and Dockyards, The 321, 323, 325, 326
Beanfield, Battle of the (1985) 57–62, 66, 74, 92, 93, 97, 98, 113, 337
Beard, Roger 98
Bearman: 'The Teddy Bear's Picnic' 272
Beatport 279
Beauman, Ned 210–12
Beaumont, Dan 306
Beaumont, Michael 51
Beauvais, France 112
Bebo 273
Beecher, Max 368–9
Beenie, MC 253
Beer, Dave 82
Belgium, MDMA manufacture in 169–71, 177, 186
Bell, Desmond 138
Belle-Fortune, Brian 208, 253

Bellville, Blaise 276, 277, 278, 280, 282, 283, 285, 286
Benga and Coki: 'Night' 347, 363
Berens, Camilla 117–19, 120, 123
Berghain 184, 297, 300, 308
Berkmann, Justin 158
Bernays, Edward 134
Betts, Janet 192
Betts, Leah 141, 157, 187, 188–9, 189, 191, 192, 193, 194
Betts, Paul 188–9, 192
Bey, Hakim 1–2n
Bez 95, 96
Bhagwan Shree Rajneesh 179
bhangra 360, 361, 363
Bicep 185
Big Beach Boutique 146–53, 167
big beat 146–9, 148n, 151, 162n
Big Beat Boutique 147, 148
Black Lives Matter 225, 227, 287, 355
Black Obsidian Sound System 383
Blackburn 74–5, 77–8, 79–84, 86, 89, 90, 100, 296, 339, 341
Blackburn, Tony 237, 241n
Blackstone 320
Blair, Tony 4, 81, 116, 131–2, 131n, 133, 133n, 134, 135, 136n, 137, 138, 140, 144–5, 152, 156, 157, 160, 161, 164, 167, 168, 188–9, 192, 197, 209, 210, 221, 231, 257, 313, 372; *A Journey* 161
Blake, James 275, 278, 381
Blakelock, Keith 47, 47n, 48n
Blakey, Chief Constable David 106, 107
bleep techno 77, 162
Bloc 323–4
Blue Note 361

blues dance 8–33, 9n, 47, 66, 71, 73, 95, 96, 96n, 100, 127, 173, 225, 231, 235, 251, 253, 296–7, 338, 341, 358, 361, 366, 367, 368, 384
Blunkett, David 209, 212
Boddika 324
Boiler Room 263, 267, 272, 275–92, 303, 304, 305, 349, 359, 363, 378
Bonobo 184
Boombox 223
Boomtown 369
Booth, Hartley 239–40, 252
Bouygues 316
Bovell, Dennis 18–19, 32, 71, 83
Boyle, Danny 140
BPM 154, 268, 269, 270, 277, 290
Bradley, Lloyd 4, 13, 25
Bradley, Peter 10–11
Brain, Chris 162–6, 167
Bramley-Moore Dock 330–1
Branson, Richard 18, 247
Brash, Rose 60, 61
breakbeat hardcore 162, 190, 253, 264n, 297
breakbeat techno 99, 118
breakdancing 23–4, 220
brew crew 50
Brexit 185, 199, 205, 322, 353, 378
Bright, Graham 80–1, 82, 372
Bright Bill (1990) 80–1, 82, 83, 84n, 93, 96, 100, 115, 145, 157, 242, 247, 372
Brighton 56, 146–53, 155–6, 167, 194, 307
British Film Institute 376
British Land 319, 320, 321
British Social Attitudes Survey 69
British Tribal Music 40
Brittan, Leon 237–8, 244

Brixton 9–10, 15, 21, 119, 227, 301, 317–18, 357; riots (1981) 16, 31, 57, 68, 104, 239
Broadcasting Acts: (1984) 242; (1990) 252, 258
Broadwater Farm riots (1985) 47, 47n, 224–5, 239
Broadwick Live 299, 319, 320, 321–2, 326, 359
Brookes, Basil 48
Broughton, Ceon 191–2
Brown, Blade 224
Brown Jr, DeForrest 377
Browne, Karl 203–4, 205
Brownhill, Bill 69–70
Burnett, Mark 207
business techno 300–27
Busta Rhymes 31
busyness, theatrical 304–5

Cable 316
Cage, John 118
Camber Sands 340, 340n
Cambodia 169, 182–3, 184, 185, 196
Cameron, David 305
Canada Water 319
Canboulay riots, Trinidad 11
Candescence 161–2
cannabis 8, 47, 74, 121, 174, 175, 338, 361
Cant, Kai 351
Capital FM 236
capitalism 5, 12, 28, 33, 93, 124, 143, 146, 149, 152, 153, 164, 167, 267, 309, 323, 369, 371
Capleton 207
Card, Richard 116
Cardamom Mountains, Cambodia 182

Carey, George 163
Carib Club 18–19
carnival traditions 11, 28–30, 33, 39, 45, 55, 135, 326
Casey, Jayne 157
Castle Donington 146
Castlemorton Common free party (1992) 90, 93–4, 102, 103, 105–18, 125, 140, 146, 147, 151, 152, 154, 175, 187, 296, 339, 341, 383
Cause, The 327
CD:UK 270
Central Cee 291; 'Day in the Life' 291; 'Loading' 291; *Wild West* 291
Centre for Crime and Justice Studies 192–3
Centreforce FM 88, 251–2, 257
Chalo 363
Chambers, Quentin 158
Channel AKA 273
Channel 4 130, 137–8, 141, 146, 147, 149, 166, 248, 270n, 273
Channel U 270, 271–3, 274, 277
Chemical Brothers 49
chemical generation 174
Chicago, US 2, 8, 22, 23, 24, 36, 40, 73, 75, 135, 136, 161, 162, 184–5, 204, 208, 268, 268n
Chicago-After-Midnight 21
Chicago house 24, 36, 73, 135, 161, 184–5, 268, 268n
Child Poverty Action Group 325
Chimay, Belgium 169–70, 177, 182
Chinhemba, Orlando 223–4
Chipping Sodbury 105
Chippy Nonstop 364
Circus 330, 331, 332, 336
City Life 72

City of London Police 215
civil disobedience 3, 89, 93, 122, 340
Class War 123
Cleptomaniacs: 'All I Do' 303
climate change 379–80, 384
Club 414 317, 318
Club Kinetic 269
CND 59, 237
Coalition Against the CJB 119
coalition government (2010–15) 160, 221, 305, 346
cocaine 132, 174, 178, 185, 190, 208, 346
Cochrane, Kelso 27–8
Coldcut: *70 Minutes of Madness* 6
Collin, Matthew 39*n*, 75, 104, 120, 174, 252; *Altered State* 2, 75, 85*n*, 172, 172*n*
Colour Factory 316
Colston-Hayter, Tony 76, 84*n*, 93, 100, 145, 153, 158, 242, 247
Columbo Group 299
Commonwealth Games (2022) 231
Commonwealth Immigrants Act (1962) 15–16
Commonwealth Immigration Act (1968) 15–16
community radio licences 235–45, 252
Conservative party 56, 70, 84*n*, 94, 100, 105, 107, 113, 114, 115, 134*n*, 137*n*, 138, 158, 193, 221, 238, 239, 244, 338, 352, 361
Control of Pollution Act (1974) 15
Converse 366
Cook, Robin 132
Cook, Norman. *See* Fatboy Slim
Cops UK: Bodycam Squad 203–5

Corbyn, Jeremy 89, 373
Cornell University 379
Cornish Waves Radio 238
Corrigan, Peter 242
Corsica Studios 357–8, 360
Cosmic Counter-Cruise Carnival 54
Cosmic Slop 327, 369–70, 373, 383, 384
Costelloe, Tom 194–5
counterculture 3, 37, 42, 45, 47, 93, 97, 124, 145–6, 160, 267, 359
Cousins, Janet 193
Covid-19 pandemic 4, 185, 199–200, 272, 291, 327, 329–55, 358, 359, 364, 368, 375, 383; Arts Council funding for venues during 349–52; Bangface Weekender and spread of 334–5; Event Research Programme 330–4; Fixed Penalty Notices issued during 343–4; lockdown parties/illegal raves during 33, 330–1, 336–49; plague rave scene 332–4, 347; reopening of venues (July 2021) 349; Save Our Scene march 329, 351–5; Together Declaration 353
Coxsone, Lloyd 21
Coxsone Outernational soundsystem 21, 47
crack cocaine 190, 208
Cramlington 145
Crass 42, 49
Crazy Titch 210, 272
Cream 4, 142, 143, 153–7, 174, 176, 296, 299, 301, 310*n*
Creamfields 157, 167, 307, 340*n*
'creative industries' 4, 131, 138–40, 143, 144, 148, 156, 164, 188, 210, 219, 313, 316, 322

Creative Industries Task Force: 'The 1998 Creative Industries Mapping Document' 138
Creche 220
Creft, Tony 79
criminal behaviour order (CBO) 226
Criminal Justice and Public Order Act (1994) 4, 5, 36, 37, 49, 55, 81, 88, 90, 91–130, 138, 152, 153, 154; Castlemorton Common free party and 93–4, 102, 103, 105–18, 125; demonstrations against *91*, 118–24; DNA data and 126; first people arrested under 125; flawed nature of 116–17; *Music for the Jilted Generation* and 91–2, 94; opposition to 116–25; origins of 92–115; police ideology and conveniences, moulded by 126; 'psychic privatisation' 92–3, 385; 'repetitive beats', clampdown on 3, 92, 114, 118; spy cops and 119–21; stop and search powers and 126–7; UK dance music's social and political identity and 94–5, 127–30
Critchlow, Frank 14
crowdfunding 368, 370–1
Cultural Herb Festival 47
Culture Industry 143
Culture Recovery Fund 314, 350, 351
Cummings, Dominic 335
Curtis, Adam: *The Century of the Self* 134
Cyrus 104

Daily Mail 53, 123, 151, 159, 177, 188, 189, 191, 197, 208, 276, 319, 340, 353, 367

Daily Mirror 100, 146, 189, 224, 330, 345
Daily Telegraph 196, 345
Daisy Nook 339, 340
DALL-E 379
Dalston Superstore 368, 369
Dance Academy 194, 195
Dance Tunnel 306, 316
dancing licence, first twenty-four-hour 83
Dancing On Narrow Ground 138
Darby, Robert 88, 89, 145
Davies, Nick 61
Davies, Philip, Assistant Chief Constable 107
Davis, Angela 28
Dax J 332–3
Day, Gabriel 331
daytime festivals/parties 286, 298, 299–300, 307–8, 327, 360–1, 363, 365, 371, 373, 385
Daytimer 361
Daytimers 286, 363, 365, 371, 373, 385
Dazed 331, 342
DEBONAIR 364
Deconstruction 155
Deep Dish 155
Defected 304, 305
deindustrialization 79–80, 321
Deja Vu FM 210
Deller, Jeremy 5; *Everybody in the Place* 5, 124
Department for Culture, Media and Sport (DCMS) 138–9, 144, 146, 199
Department for National Heritage (DNH) 138

Department of Trade and Industry (DTI) 17, 241–4, 241n, 251, 252, 255, 256
Department of Transport (DoT) 371
Depot Mayfield 299, 321
Devon and Cornwall Police 126, 195
Dexplicit: 'Forward Riddim' 363
DHP Family 299
Dialled In 363, 364, 365, 383
Digga D 226–7
Diggers 102
dimethylformamide 181
Disclosure 184
Discretionary Housing Benefit 325
Discwoman 355
Divine, DJ Sam 304–5
DiY 93, 95, 96, 96n, 97, 100, 106, 109–10, 112, 122, 145, 371, 384
Diztorshon 346
Dizzee Rascal 210, 271; 'Bonkers' 226, 231
DJ Mag 106, 146
DJs For Climate Action 380
DNA profiling 115, 126
Docklands 112
'Dola Re Dola' 362
donk 309
Donnelly, Anthony and Christopher 81
Dorrell, Dave 268, 269
Draper, Derek 134
Dread Broadcasting Corporation 236–7
D:Ream: 'Things Can Only Get Better' 132–3, 134, 136, 136n, 161
drill 19, *203*, 204–5, 226–31, 358, 359
drinking clubs, black members-only 15

drug trade 169–201. *See also individual drug names*
drum'n'bass 6, 121, 221, 225, 269, 300, 341
Drumsheds 319, 320, 321, 322
dub 8, 18, 22, 73, 96n, 184, 225, 236
Dubplate Pearl, DJ 17
dubstep 183–4, 216, 259, 281, 296, 304, 307, 341, 347, 363
Duggan, Jamie 218
Duggan, Mark 224
Duke, John 53, 57–9, 61
Duke Vin 12, 13
Dunbar, Newton 14
Dunn, Kevin 105
Dutton, Clive 323, 324
Dwyer, Bill 'Ubi' 41, 42, 61–2
Dynamic Meditation 179

East London Black Women's Organisation 26
East London Rastafarian Information and Community Service 222
Eastman 261
Eastman, Julius 360
Eat Static 48
Eavis, Michael 128
Ebony 292
Eclipse 263–4, 267, 283
Ecstasy 45, 73, 96, 150, 162, 268; distribution networks within UK 185–6; fatalities 141–2, 156, 186–94; harm reduction/drug-checking services 197–201; Ibiza Four and 3, 75, 76, 171–3; importance of to dance culture 169–77; manufacture, Belgium 169–71, 177, 186; manufacture, Netherlands 177–82, 185, 186;

Ecstasy – *cont.*
    musical styles, effects on 183–5, 190; numbers of people taking 173–4; Nutt paper on varying harms associated with major drugs and 192–3; origins 178; polydrug culture 174–5; precursor chemicals, governments clamp down on 182–3, 185, 196; Psychoactive Substances Act and 196–7; Public Entertainments Licensing (Drugs Misuse) Act and 193–6, 200; purity 181–2, 185, 199–201, 307; Rajneesh and spread of 180–1; supplies dry up in UK/search for alternatives 183–4, 196
Education Maintenance Allowance 221, 305–6
Edwards, Jamal 273–4, 287
Edwards, Les 94
Edwards, Nicholas 238
Edwards, Todd 303, 304, 305
Ehrenreich, Barbara: *Dancing in the Streets: A History of Collective* vii, 38–9, 39*n*
Ek, Daniel 288
El-B 358, 360
Elley, Ahad 363, 364
Ellis, Charlene 208
EMAP 246, 248, 249–50
Empire Windrush, HMT 13
enclosure 38, 42, 54, 152, 196, 277, 385
Enfield 222–3, 319, 322, 323
Enfield Council 319
English Heritage 51
E1 368
Equinox 158
Eric B. & Rakim 6

Eshun, Kodwo: *More Brilliant Than the Sun* 377
Essex Boys, The 188
Eternity 122
Eutylone 199
Evans, David 245–6
Evaristo, Bernadine: *Girl, Woman* 10
Event Research Programme 330–4
Everard, Sarah 340–1
Exhibition London 321
Exodus 371–3
Extinction Rebellion 124, 164
EZ, DJ 286, 303–4

Fabio, DJ 136
Fabric 6, 184, 194, 280, 310–14, 310*n*, 315, 320
Facebook 120, 126, 220, 275
Falconer, Charles 197
Family Funktion 24
Fannin, Luke 205
Fantazia 140, 146, 153
Farley, Terry 36
Farley 'Jackmaster' Funk: 'Jack Your Body' 135; 'Love Can't Turn Around' 268
Fassiaux, Françoise 170
Fatboy Slim 146–53, 155–6, 219, 330; *You've Come a Long Way, Baby* 148
Fatsis, Lambros 4, 344–5
Fauna and Flora International 182
feminism 10, 26, 359
Festival Welfare Services 37, 41
festivals: Covid-19 and 334–5; daytime 298, 299–300, 307–8, 327, 363; diversity and 326–7, 368; free 3, 35–63, 35, 89, 93, 96–7, 96*n*, 98, 99, 100, 101, 105, 106, 112, 117, 127, 138, 173, 338, 368, 384; future of

INDEX

199–200; ticket spending 307;
under-age 276
Fiddy, Chantelle 213
Field Day 290, 299, 307
Field Maneuvers 327
Fis 290
Fisher, Mark 4, 92, 383–4; *Capitalist Realism* 152, 153
Fisher Gate Point 371
Five Miles 316
Fixed Penalty Notices 343–4
Fleming, George 351
Fletcher-Michie, Louella 191
Flynn, Paul 194, 196
FOLD 327
Follett, Harry 320
football exclusion orders 87–8
football hooligans 67, 86, 87, 88, 115, 176, 251
Forbes-Leith, Detective Superintendent Ian 27–8
Forgemasters 162, 162n
Form 696 212–20, 229, 344
Four Aces 14, 22, 87, 89
410 227
Four Tet 184, 301
Frankfurt School 143
Frazer-Carroll, Micha 341
Fred Again 286
Freedom Network 123
Free Party 384
free party scene 74, 93–4, 96n, 97, 99, 100, 101, 105–8, 112, 114, 117, 119, 120, 121, 122–3, 124, 128–9, 145, 146, 153, 167, 297, 298, 326, 340, 341, 345, 348, 358, 371, 372, 374, 384
Free The Night 375–6
Freemans Event Partners 369

Freerotation 327
Freud, Matthew 134
Freud, Sigmund 134, 135, 168, 179, 248
Frontline 119
Fulltime, Operation 88
Fumin 222
Fun^Da^Mental 362
Funktion-One systems 49, 128, 295, 302
funky house 220
Furedi, Frank 353
Fury, DJ 253
Future 3, 22, 75–6, 98

Gala 308
Galaxy Soul Shuffle 47
Gallions Point Marina 325
gangs 19, 81, 186, 203–4, 205, 207, 208, 213, 215, 217, 223, 224, 226, 227, 229, 230, 257; gang protection order 219–20
garage 8, 208, 209, 210, 211, 212, 216, 220–1, 225, 226, 228, 255, 256, 286, 294, 303–4, 307, 341, 353, 358, 376
Garside, Richard 193185,
Gatecrasher 296, 297
Gay London Police Monitoring Group (GALOP) 70–1
general elections: (1959) 27; (1983) 52; (1987) 244–5; (1992) 113; (1997) 131–2, 136, 193; (2005) 210; (2017) 373; (2019) 373–4
gentrification 4, 10, 30, 100, 185, 234, 297–8, 300, 316, 317, 318, 319, 326
Gerbeau, Pierre-Yves 160
Giggs 214
Gilliat-Ray, Sophie 160

Gilroy, Paul 4, 18, 30, 32; 'Between the Blues and the Blues Dance' 23
Giorgis, Hannah 17
Glastonbury Festival 46–7, 62, 95, 96n, 97, 100, 127–8, 129–30, 175, 226, 284
Glenn Underground: 'Do It' 135
Global Entertainment 299
globalization 79–80, 124, 139, 219, 308–9, 380
Glockamoley 204, 205, 229
God in the House 166–7
Goddard, Grant 241, 241n, 245
Goethe, Johann Wolfgang von vii
Goldsmith, Lynn 234
Gong 48
Good Friday Agreement (1998) 137
Gordon, Stevie 236
Gou, Peggy 301, 312, 326
Gould, Philip 134
Granada TV 264
Greater London Authority 321
Greater Manchester Police 67, 73, 74
Green, Damian 114
Green, Katherine 366
Greenham Common 53–5, 384
grime 8, 19, 88, 208, 210–15, 218, 219, 220–1, 222, 224–8, 230, 256, 270, 271, 272, 273, 274, 275, 288, 296, 304, 307, 363, 373–4, 380; DVDs 270–1, 273
Grime 4 Corbyn 373
Grimes, Gareth 195
GRM Daily 273–4, 291
Grooverider, DJ 269
Guardian, The 71, 73, 127, 136, 137n, 149–50, 151, 159, 183, 208, 210, 212, 227, 264n, 265, 315, 319, 324, 332, 341, 345
Gutzmore, Cecil vii, 29, 30

Haçienda 22, 24, 73, 74, 76, 77, 81, 87, 100, 176, 266, 316
Hackney Council 306
Hadfield, Pete 155
Hague, William 197
Halo, Laurel 360
Hancox, Dan: *Inner City Pressure* 4, 213, 215–16, 271
Happy Mondays 69, 73, 87, 95, 96
Harlem Spartans 227
Harris, Leroy 18
Harrison, Harry: *Dreaming in Yellow* 95–7, 96n, 100–1, 102–3, 110–12
Harrison, Mark 101–2, 103, 111, 119–20
Hartnoll, Mary 192
Hartnoll, Paul and Phil 128–30, 192
Haselden, Rupert 71–2
Hatcha 304–5
Hauff, Helena 335
Hawkwind 36, 40, 47, 48–9, 56, 96n, 121
Hazey: 'Packs and Potions' 230
'H' committee memo 239
Headie One 226
Health Education Authority 193
Heaven 72, 75–6
Hemment, DJ Drew 81–2
heroin 50, 171, 189, 192, 223
Heseltine, Michael 59, 113–14
Hetherington, Kevin 53
Highways Act (1980) 57
Hillsborough 104
hip hop 22, 23, 31, 47, 147, 211, 234, 236, 270, 360

hippies 5, 35, 37, 39, 40, 44, 45, 49, 50, 55, 56, 59, 98, 101, 106, 112, 121, 127, 145–6, 171, 178, 180, 342, 384
Hitman and Her 263–8, 265n, 277, 283, 290
Hollemans, Robert 177–9
Holloway, Nicky 3, 75, 76, 172, 241
Holmes, David 137
Home Office 16, 85, 86, 100, 113, 115–16, 174, 186, 193, 199, 200, 231, 239, 372
homosexuality 69–70, 72, 90, 115, 136
Hondo Enterprises 317
Hope, Wally (Philip Russell) 43–5, 61–2, 86, 112
Horizon 235
Horley & Gatwick Mirror 345–6
hotknobbing 304–5
Housekeeping 5, 318
house music 2, 3, 5, 11, 22, 23, 24, 25, 48, 93, 97, 136, 137, 141, 154, 164, 166, 204, 220, 269, 270, 277, 281, 296, 302, 304, 307, 360; acid house *see* acid house; Chicago house 24, 36, 73, 135, 161, 184–5, 268, 268n; deep house 97, 163; funky house 220; handbag house 302; hard house 141, 317, 350; ketamine house 184; outsider house 184
House of God 308
'How to Make It as an Artist' 378
Howard, Michael 100, 114, 116, 125
Howard, Roland 162, 164
Howe, Darcus 14
Howells, Kim 208–9, 212
Hudson Mohawke 184
Hughes, Darren 154, 157, 310n

Hulme 22, 73–4
Hulme Crescents 73–4
Human Traffic 142, 306
Humanoid: 'Stakker Humanoid' 265–6
Hungerford Common 98–9
hunt saboteurs 115, 125, 219
Hurd, Douglas 52, 238–9, 240, 243, 244, 247
Hutchinson, Frankie Decaiza 355
Hyperdub 358, 360

Ibiza 3, 66, 75–7, 142, 143, 171, 172, 173, 179, 180, 240, 278, 351
Ibiza Four 3, 75–7, 173, 240
'In Pursuit of Repetitive Beats' 376
Independent 123, 151, 345
Independent Broadcasting Authority (IBA) 246–7
Independent Radio Sales 238
Independent Scientific Committee on Drugs 183
Inspector Morse 140–1, 267
Instagram 305, 332
Institute of Ideas 353
Inter-City Firm 251
International Opium Commission (1909) 177
Iqbal, Nabihah 363–4
Iraq War (2003–11) 167
Islington Council 310, 311, 313
ITN 61
ITV 61, 154, 188–9, 264, 268, 342

Jackson, Steve 250
Jackson, Tosca 240, 243
Jamaica 7, 8, 9, 10, 11–12, 22, 26, 26n, 30, 207, 208
Jameson, Fredric 153, 385

Jamie XX 263, 278
Jammer and the Slew Dem Crew 213; *Lord of the Mics* 222
Jarre, Jean-Michel 48
Jarrett, Cynthia 47n, 224
Jay, Norman 24, 240, 244, 250
Jay-Z 31
Jazzie B 24–5
JFM 235–6, 242
JME 226, 274, 373
Johnson, Boris 325, 335, 340–1, 351–2, 373–4
Johnson, Linton Kwesi 24, 30; 'Five Nights of Bleeding' 17–18
Jones, Claudia 28–9
Jones, Jamie 278
Jones-Lecointe, Althea 14
Judge Jules 155, 317, 354
Jukebox 379
jungle 3, 6, 8, 147–8, 182, 184, 190, 207, 208, 220–1, 225, 226, 252, 253–4, 255, 354, 361, 362, 366
Junior Byles: 'Beat Down Babylon' 19
Just Jam 214–15, 273, 359
JUSTICE 229

Kairos, The 211
Kamixlo 290
Kano 222, 270, 272
Kapoor, Sweety 361
Kaur, Sarvjeet: 'Kori (Giddah)' 363
Kay, Janet: 'Silly Games' 32
'Kennedy, Mark' 121
Kent Police Pay Party Unit 65, 83–6, 89, 90, 97, 98
ketamine 132, 183–4, 190
ketamine house 184
Kevin & Perry Go Large 142
Key, Robert 52
Khan, Mayor Sadiq 216, 312, 313
Kinnock, Neil 132
Kiss Enterprises 249
Kiss FM 6, 172, 233–52, *233*, 241n, 254–5, 258, 259, 265, 287, 290, 383–4
Kitchen, The 73, 74, 77
Klaus 380–1
KLF: 'What Time Is Love?' 5
knife crime 19, 27, 191, 203, 211, 226, 358
Knight, Jill 20–1
Kode9 359–60
Koko 227–8
Kool FM 253, 255, 260
Kranium: 'Gal Policy' 292
Kraviz, Nina 332–3
Krown Media 205
KU Club 171–2

Labour party 27, 56, 70, 116–17, 130, 131–9, *131*, 132n, 133n, 136n, 138n, 144, 148, 159, 161, 167, 179, 192–3, 194, 200, 209–10, 219, 338, 373, 374
Labrynth parties 86
Lacey, Alex de 230
Lambeth Council 15
Lamé, Amy 312–15
Laslett, Rhaune 29–30
Lawrence, Stephen 27, 89, 120, 225
Leftfield: *Leftism* 164
Legg, Barry 193–6, 200
Lehane, Ant 200
Lenor, Operation 311
Lens, Amelie 332
Lester, Holly 375–6
Lethal Bizzle 271; 'Pow! Forward' 210, 221–2, 272, 363

INDEX

Letwin, Oliver 239–40
Levan, Larry 158, 379
Levellers 38, 42, 102
Levellers, The (band) 38
Leysdown Beach 340, 340n
LFO 162, 288
LGBTQ+ culture 315, 317
Liberator, Chris 345
Liberty 117, 118, 123, 125, 126, 344
licensing laws 12, 15, 17, 18, 28, 70, 73, 77, 78, 83, 89, 145, 146, 153, 157–8, 195, 212, 216, 217, 238, 239, 241, 241n, 245, 296, 298, 299, 306, 315, 317, 375, 376; dancing licence, first twenty-four-hour 83; Licensing Act (1967) 15; Licensing Act (1988) 83; Public Entertainments Licensing (Drugs Misuse) Act (1997) 193, 194–6, 200
Lil Danny 204, 205
Link Up TV 228, 273, 291
Live Nation 299, 300
Living Marxism 353
Locked Off 346
Lockhart, Sarah 259
Lodge, Alan 37, 38, 40–2, 46–7, 50, 51, 53, 56, 59, 62–3, 97, 101, 120, 384
London Film Festival (2022) 376
London Greek Radio 237
London Jazz Radio 247
London Pleasure Gardens 323–5
Long Meadow Farm 371, 372
Loop, The 198–9
Lord, Sacha 314, 321
Lord Kitchener 13
Lord of the Mics 222, 270
Lord Tokyo: 'Ladbroke Grove Riot' 31

Lost Village 199
Love, Wag Club, Soho 269
Love Decade 59, 82–3, 84, 92
Love Parade 149
Lovebox 299
Loved Up 141
Lovers Rock (film) 32
lovers' rock 21, 23, 296
LSD 45, 175, 178, 180, 278
LWR 235
Lycox, DJ 347

Mabgate 370
McKay, George 56
MacKenzie, Kelvin 52–3
McNamee, David 18
McNamee, Gordon 233, 235, 236, 237, 238, 240, 241, 241n, 243–50, 253, 254, 259, 383
McNeil, James 315
McNicholas, Conor 209
McQuaid, Ian 228
McQueen, Steve 32
McWilliams, Taylor 317–18
Madame JoJo's 316
Madison, Wisconsin 211
Magic FM 249, 348
Major, John 113
makina 309
Malyon, Tim 372
MAMA 299
Manchester 13, 22, 23, 36, 67, 68, 69, 72, 73, 74, 75, 76, 77–9, 80, 84, 87, 126, 156, 166, 217, 229, 230, 238, 264n, 266, 281, 290, 296–7, 299, 313, 314, 315, 321, 325, 339
Manchester City Council 74, 321
Mancuso, David 24, 370
Mandelson, Peter 132, 159, 160n

Mangrove restaurant, Notting Hill 14
Manhattan Heights 77–8
Mansfield, Michael 372
MARRS: 'Pump Up the Volume' 269
Mark, Louisa: 'Caught You in a Lie' 21
Marsh Farm Estate 372–3
Mastermind Roadshow 24, 220
Maten, Ayanna van der 368–9
'Matt' 219–20
Matthews, Leon 205
May, Theresa 113, 120, 196, 373
MDA 181, 182
MDEA 181–2, 181n, 190
MDMA. *See* Ecstasy
Meaney, Sergeant Mick 213, 215
Measham, Fiona 199
Mega, Gary 253
Melodic Distraction 370
Melody Maker 206
Melville, Caspar 4, 17, 173
Men Behaving Badly 141
mephedrone 183, 196
Merck 178
Mercury Prize: (1998) 225; (1999) 362; (2016) 226; (2026) 230
Meridian Dan: 'German Whip' 226
Meridian Water 319, 322
Merseyside Academy 154
Metropolitan Police 5, 14, 16n, 29, 69, 70, 72, 86, 89, 103, 119, 212, 213, 214, 215, 216, 227, 229, 310, 311, 312, 313, 343, 358
Mi Amigo, MV 236
M.I.A. 362
Mid-Journey 379

Milan, Mirik 198
Miles, Robert 155, 167
Millbank 221, 305
Millennium Dome/Millennium Experience 144, 159–60, 160n, 161
Miller, Alan 353
Mills, Chief Inspector Peter 150
Miners' Strike (1984–5) 80, 82, 84, 84n, 88, 92, 244
minimal techno 184, 190, 277
Ministry of Sound 4, 83, 145, 148n, 153, 157–61, 174, 213, 215, 218, 219
Minogue, Kylie 155; 'I Should Be So Lucky' 265
Miroma Ventures 274
Mi-Soul 383
Misty In Roots 47
Monteith, Keir 230
Moore, Tony, Divisional Commander: *Policing Notting Hill: Fifty Years of Turbulence* 28
More (film) 171–3
Morgan, Ephraim 205
Morris, Cecil 237
Morris, Olive 10
Moscow 17 227
Mosley, Oswald 27
Moss Side, Manchester 22, 23, 36, 68, 73, 296–7
Mother festival 127, 258
MTV 268, 271, 272
Muench, Karen 350
Muggs, Joe 96n, 224
Museum of London 222
Music and Arts Production (MAP) 370
Music Box 265, 268
MySpace 273

INDEX

Nation 154
National Front 13, 14, 21, 25, 68, 235, 361
National Police Chiefs' Council 201
National Theatre 349, 376
National Trust 51
NATO 53, 54
Nawaz, Aki 362
Nawrozzadeh, Abbas 223, 224
Naylor, Liz 'No City Fun' 69
Nelson, Trevor 240, 244, 250
neo-liberalism 140, 152, 167–8
Netherlands, drug manufacture in 170, 177–82, 185, 186
Network Rail 320
New Age Travellers 33, 36–7n, 53, 55, 106, 107, 114
New Cross fire (1981) 21, 26
New Labour 130, 132, 133, 133n, 134, 135–9, 137n, 144, 148, 159, 167, 179, 209–10, 219, 338
New Musical Express (NME) 87, 128, 129, 209, 269, 345, 374
New Statesman 345
Newbury bypass 124, 125
Newham Council 321, 323, 324
News of the World 55
Newsnight 55, 207, 224
Niche 194, 216–18
Night Czars 312–13, 375
night-time economy 313–15, 318
Night Time Economy Advisor 314
Night Time Industries Association 313, 315, 353
Nine O'Clock Service 161–6, 167
Nocturnal 145
No I.D. 363, 365
No Signal 291–2

Noise Abatement Act (1960) 15
noise pollution 15, 372
Nolan, John 350
Nomad, Operation 105, 114
nomadic groups 37–9, 43, 51, 53, 88, 94, 96, 97, 113, 337–8
Norfolk Police 17
Northern Ireland 137, 138, 264, 375
Nostell Priory festival (1984) 58–9
Notting Hill Carnival 7, 26–33, 36, 104, 211, 212n, 282–5, 291
Nottingham Police 204–5
Nour Cash & Carry 317
NS1ov1o 291–2
NTS 179, 256n, 260, 276, 280, 359
Nurses Association of Jamaica UK 26
Nutt, Professor David 192–3
Nzinga Soundz 25–6

Ø 358, 360, 383
Oakenfold, Paul 3, 66, 72, 75–6, 98, 155, 171, 172–3
Obi, Liz 10
Observer, The 61, 362
Occupy movement 124, 164
O'Farrell, John 136–7
Ofcom 256–9
Ogmore-by-Sea 340
O'Grady, Paul 65–6, 70, 71
Olympics (2012) 231, 323
1–800-Dinosaur 381
Opglabbeek, Belgium 170
O'Rahilly, Ronan 254
Orbison, Joy: Sicko Cell' 185
Orbital 128, 130, 175; 'Are We Here' 118; 'Belfast' 142; 'Chime' 128, 129, 130, 268, 376
orbital raves 93, 138, 298

organized crime 76, 81, 89, 93, 120, 181, 185, 207
Orgreave violence (1984) 5, 33, 57, 59, 62, 92, 104, 124
Osborne, George 276, 305
Otolith Group 360
Oubridge, Brig 55
outsider house 184
Oval Space 322
Oval Studios 322
Overflo 368, 368n
Ozric Tentacles 48

Pa Salieu 231
Palumbo, James 158–61
Palumbo, Peter 158
Pandy, Darryl 267–8, 268n
Panjabi MC: 'Kori (Giddah)' 363
Paradise Garage 158
Parklife 307, 314
Parris, Matthew 336–7
Patel, Priti 197, 343
Patrick, Albert 88–9
Paul, Jai 362
Pawson, Caius 276
Pay Party Unit 65, 83–6, 89, 90, 97, 98
PCDJ 309
Peace Convoy 53–5, 59
Peech Boys: 'Don't Make Me Wait' 40
Peel, John 208
Peep Show 148
Pendragon, John 50
People's Community Radio Link 237
People's Free Festival 41, 46, 62
Percolate 317

Perkins, James 146
Pessimist, DJ 309–10
Peterson, Gilles 172
Peyton, Andy 299
Peyzac, Operation 223–4
Phonox 299, 357
Phuture: 'Acid Tracks' 40; 'Work It' 135
Pickering, Mike 24
piperonyl methyl ketone (PMK) 183, 185, 196
pirate radio 4, 6, 33, 88, 139, 210, 233–61, *233*, 267, 269–70, 270n, 271, 273, 274, 275–6, 287, 337–8, 366, 383–4. *See also individual radio station names*
plague raves 332, 347
Planetary Mass 163, 164
Plastic People 307, 316, 381
Platform 276
PMK-glycidate 185
Pod 117, 119
Podium, The 207
Poet 272
Police, Crime, Sentencing and Courts Bill (2022) 374
Police and Criminal Evidence Act (1984) 16–17
Policy Exchange 226
Poll Tax riots (1990) 95, 104, 129
polydrug culture 174
Powell, Enoch 16, 20
Power, George 235, 237, 243
Power, Mike: *Drugs 2.0* 182
Powers, Will: 'Adventures in Success' 234–5
Practice Hours 270
Prescott, John 132
Pressure FM 253

Printworks *293*, 298, 299, 319–22, 326, 380
Private Eye 350
Prodigy 146; *Music for the Jilted Generation* 91–2, 94
property: prices/rents 16, 41, 74, 153, 163, 297, 316, 320, 378; rights/land ownership 11, 37–9, 42, 52, 54, 55, 59–60, 130, 152, 196, 277, 317–18, 320–2, 325, 337, 370, 375, 385
Providence Equity 300
Pryce, Ken 384; *Endless Pressure* 8–9
Psychoactive Substances Act (2016) 196–7
Public Enemy 6
Public Entertainments Licensing (Drugs Misuse) Act (1997) 193, 194–6, 200
Public Order Act (1986) 57, 62, 63, 85, 87, 97, 100, 113, 114, 115, 242
PWL 264*n*, 265, 265*n*
Pxssy Palace 366–8, 368*n*, 371

Q Club 14
queer venues 3, 8, 10, 33, 66, 67, 70–2, 158, 173, 280, 300, 350, 353, 359, 366, 367, 368, 369

Race Relations Act (1968) 11, 15
Race Today Collective 26
racism 7, 8, 12–13, 14, 17, 18, 22, 25, 27, 28, 30, 31*n*, 80, 136, 206, 217, 228, 240, 326, 344, 355, 362, 362*n*
Radar Radio 260
Radical Radio 248
Radical Sista 360, 361
Radio Caroline 236, 254
Radio Gogarth 238

Radio 1 149, 172, 231, 236, 241*n*, 250, 354
RAF Molesworth 59
Rahman, Provhat 363
Railton Road, Brixton shebeen 9–11
Rajneeshpuram 180
Ram, Satpal 361, 361–2*n*
Rampling, Danny 3, 75, 171, 172, 240, 353
Randall, Stuart 53
Rankin, Junie 25–6
rap 191, 209, 224, 228, 270, 271, 359
raves 1*n*, 2, 3, 23, 24, 33; alcohol-free 309; Covid-19 and 5, 33, 330–55; Criminal Justice Act and 92–130, 138; grime raves 212–15, 227, 228; illegal rave scene, origins of 73–90, 141; orbital raves 93, 138, 298; pirate radio and 234, 240–1, 242–3, 247, 251; popular culture adopts 140–68, 267–9; proto-rave 37, 43, 48, 49, 50, 53, 54, 55, 56, 57, 59, 60, 62, 63, 66, 67, 71, 265; reification of 376–7; semi-legal 22; under-age 276; warehouse 6, 11, 24, 80, 82, 83, 93, 95, 225, 233, 234, 242–3
Rawle, Sid 41, 42, 98
REACH programme 210
Reclaim the Streets 120, 124, 164
Red Hot Entertainment: 'Junior Spesh' 272
reggae 7, 8, 12, 21, 22, 23, 30, 47, 96*n*, 190, 207, 208, 220, 224, 225, 235–6, 296
Reicher, Stephen 332
Reliant, Operation 342–3
Rent Act (1957) 16
Repatriation, Operation 218

Reprezent 260
Resident Advisor 293, 294, 299, 318, 327, 349, 370, 378
Resonate 291
respect agenda 210, 219, 257
Revolutionary Communist Party 353
Reynolds, Simon: *Energy Flash* 2, 39n, 109, 172, 172n, 175–6, 183–4, 251
rhythmic obedience 302
Richards, Thristian 275, 276, 280
Rifkind, Malcolm 238
Riley, Mykaell 12
Rimbaud, Penny 42, 44, 45–6, 50
Rinse FM 219, 252, 256, 260, 280, 290, 347
R.I.P. 296
Risky Roadz 270
Roach-McFarlane, Ashley 28
road rap 224, 226, 228
Roaring Twenties 14
Robb, John 74
Rock Against Racism 362
Rockstar Games 321
Rodgers, Nile 234
Rogers, George 27
Rolling Stone 230
Rough Trade 87
Roundhouse 102
Royal Docks 321–2, 325
Royal House: 'Can You Party' 79
Royal Vauxhall Tavern 65, 66, 69, 70, 71, 85
Ryder, Shaun 69

Sabido, Kim 61
safrole oil 169, 170, 181, 182, 185, 196
Sagoo, Bally 361

St Clair, Ian 98
St George's Hill 102–3
St Paul's, Bristol 7–8, 16, 296, 384
Sama, Logan 213, 214
sannyasin music 172, 179–80
Save Our Scene march, London (2021) 329, 351–5, 374
Savile, Peter 316
Sawhney, Nitin 361, 362, 364
SB.TV 273, 274, 275, 277, 287
Scarz 272
Scene 254
Schoonmaker, Tim 246
Schroeder, Barbet 171
Scorcher, MC 224
Scott, Millard 225
Scott, Stafford 225
Scratcha DVA 360
Scumerset 341
SDLP 244–5
Second Summer of Love (1988) 76, 90, 93, 296, 376
Section 28 20, 66, 70
Self Help Group 79, 80, 81, 82
Serious Organised Crime Agency 171
Sett End 78–9, 81
sexism 326, 355
Shake And Fingerpop 24
Shakespeare, Letisha 208
Shamen, The: 'Ebenezer Goode' 268
Shannen SP 358, 359–60, 365
Sharkey, Feargal 212
Sharpe, Sunil 375
Shaw, Jamie 125
shebeen 9–11, 9n, 127, 220, 235
Sheffield 77, 161, 162–3, 162n, 164, 165, 166, 194, 216, 217, 218
Sheffield Council 216

INDEX

Sheffield Peace Radio 237
Shenzen, China 185
Sherburne, Philip 184
Shetland Island Company Limited 238
Shoom 3, 22, 36, 75, 86, 154, 175, 240, 296, 353
shuffling 220
Shulgin, Alexander: *PiHKAL* 178–9, 180, 181*n*
Shut Down, Operation 15
Shut Up and Dance: 'Dance Before the Police Come' 82
Shy FX: 'Movin' On' 362; 'Sound of the Beast' 17
Sigsworth, Nick 380–3
Silcott, Winston 47, 47–8*n*
Silvertown Quays 321, 322
Sinclair, Carolyn 113
Singh, Bob Balraj 82
Singh, Talvin 361, 362; *OK* 362
Singh, Yung 357, 363–4
Sitkin, Alan 319, 322–3
Size, Roni 225
Skengdo x AM 227–8; 'Attempted 1.0' 227
Skepta 214, 218, 274; 'DTI' 17; *Konnichiwa* 226; 'That's Not Me' 226
Skint 146–7, 148, 148*n*, 149, 152–3
Slimzee, DJ 219, 253–4, 253*n*, 256, 258, 260
Slinger, MC 213
Smith, Chris 137*n*, 139, 159
Smith, Jacqui 193
Smith, Tom 370
Smith, Tommy 81
Smith & Mighty 32
Smokey Barz 273

Snail, The 181
Snowballs 182
So Solid Crew 209, 210, 227
Socialist Workers Party (SWP) 119, 120, 121–2, 125
Soho 14, 33, 254, 269, 297, 316
Solar 235
Sonubi, Jojo 291, 292
SOPHIE 215; 'Just Like We Never Said Goodbye' 359
Soul Control soundsystem 13, 22, 23–4, 25, 73
Soul II Soul 24, 25, 221
Souleyman, Omar 215
soundsystem culture: acid house and 93, 94, 95, 96, 96*n*, 98, 99, 100–5, 109, 110–13, 117–18, 119–20, 129, 145, 152, 153, 258, 298, 341, 345, 354, 384; Notting Hill Carnival and 26–33, 282; origins of UK 3, 7–33, 36, 37, 47, 62, 67, 73, 74
Souter, John: *The Breakdown* 206
South London Gay Liberation 10
South West Four 299
Southern Syncopated Orchestra 13
Southwark Council 219–20, 319, 321
Spaced 141–2, 306
Special Policy Area, Dalston 306
Spectrum 3, 72, 75, 98, 296
speed garage 303
Spencer, Tim 125
Spicer, Michael 107
Spiked 353
Spiral Tribe 93, 99, 100–5, 109, 110–13, 117–18, 119–20, 129, 145, 152, 153, 258, 298, 341, 345, 354, 384
Spotify 205, 288

spy cops 119–21
squatters 10, 41–2, 41n, 45, 73, 74, 92, 95, 97, 102, 103, 111, 115, 117, 119, 124, 253, 254, 297, 371–2, 374, 381, 384
Stansted Airport 380
Stardust 21
Starkey, David 224
State of Bengal: 'IC408' 361
Steel Banglez 362
Steel Pulse 12, 22; 'Blues Dance Raid' 17
Stephen Lawrence Inquiry 225
Stevens, Anthony 13, 22–3, 25, 73
Stewart-Cleary, Alex 107
Stock, Aitken and Waterman 265, 266
Stonehenge 5, 33, *35*, 43–9, 50, 51, 53, 57, 60–1, 62, 96n, 98, 99, 128
Stoney Cross 57–8
stop and search powers 8, 16, 115, 126–7, 228, 344, 358, 374
Stormzy 226, 373
Strachan, Michaela 263–6
Straight Outta Bethnal 213
Strange Brew 327, 370–1
Straw, Jack 81
Stubnitz, MS 324
Studio 289 320
Sub Club 312
Suckle, Count 11, 12, 13, 14, 21
Sufferer HiFi 18
Sugar Sweet 137
Sumner, Geoffrey 6
Sun, The 35–6, 52, 68–9, 72, 133, 133n
Sundissential 350–1, 351n
Sunrise and Energy 40
Sunset Radio 238

superclubs 4, 8, 33, 100, 127, 129, 142, 153–4, 296, 297, 300, 301, 310, 310n, 314, 325–6
Superstruct Entertainment 299–300
'sus' law 16–17, 18, 88, 115
Susie G 260
Swallow, Andy 251
Szatan, Gabriel 278, 279, 280, 281, 282, 286

Tale of Us 332
Tanum 383
Tape London 318
Tappenden, Ken 83–7, 84n, 90, 102, 242
Taylor, David 55
Taylor, Paul 372
Tebbit, Norman 238
techno 2, 6, 48, 77, 93, 97, 100, 101, 111, 122, 130, 175, 297, 348, 360, 375, 379, 380, 384; acid techno 6, 317; bleep techno 77, 162; breakbeat techno 99, 118; business techno 300–27, 346; minimal techno 184, 190, 277
teknival 112, 341
Telereal Trillium 320
Tempa T 213, 226, 272, 274
Terra Technic, DJ 101
Territorial Support Group 103–5, 122
Terry, Todd: 'Something Goin' On (In Your Soul)' 217
Thapar, Ciaran 4, 230
Thatcher, Margaret 3, 5, 20, 21, 42, 45, 51, 52, 56, 57, 65, , 66, 67, 69, 70, 76, 84, 85n, 88, 93, 104, 112, 115, 136, 139, 152, 156, 237, 238, 239, 240, 241, 244, 247, 264

INDEX

theories of disorder 104
The Tube 269
Thetford Forest 341
Thomas, Leslie 88, 145
Thompson, Bradley 319–20, 321–2
Thomson, Peter 161
333 Club 213
Time & Envy 303, 304
Times, The 42, 107, 191, 336–7, 342, 345
Tirzah 358
TKO 243
Together Declaration 353
Tomlinson, Ian 105
Ton of Brix, The 317–18
Tong, Pete 155
Tonka 96, 96n, 100
Tonto's Exploding Head Band 48
Top of the Pops 129, 268, 270
Toppin, Julia 4, 190, 221, 231, 366
Topping, Patrick 332
Total Refreshment Centre 373
Town and Country Planning Act (1962) 15
Townsend, Megan 334, 335
Townsend, Owen 296
Tracey, AJ 373
Trade 317
Trainspotting 140
transgender 326, 353, 359, 366, 367–8, 378, 383
Travellers 35–63, 66, 67, 71, 74, 87–8, 90, 93–100, 105–8, 113–15, 119, 127, 187, 242, 337–8, 341, 371–2, 374; New Age Travellers 33, 36–7n, 53, 55, 106, 107, 114
Tribal Gathering 146, 153
Trident, Operation 224
Trim, MC 380

Trinder, Aaron 384
Trip, The 3, 75
T2: 'Heartbroken' 218
Tuohy, Brenda 268–9
Turbosound 49, 128
Turnmills 316–17
2C-P 191
TX Magazine 238, 243

UK Drug Policy Commission 171
UK funky 220, 277, 347
UK Music 212–13
Underworld 128

Vangelis 48
Väth, DJ Sven 332, 333
Venus Ex Machina 357, 358–9, 360
Vice 96, 279, 346
Victoria Park 299
Villalobos, Ricardo 184; *Fizheuer Zieheuer* 184
Virgin Broadcasting 248
Virgin Records 18
Virgo: 'Free Yourself' 135
Volteface 200
Vybz Kartel 291

Waddington, David 81, 109
Wadham, John 125
Walker, Johnny 3, 75
Waltham Forest 222, 366
Wants, Hannah 353, 354, 355
Ward, Richard 116
warehouse parties/raves 6, 8, 11, 24, 59, 75, 76, 77, 78, 79, 80, 82, 83, 90, 92, 93, 95, 98, 100, 101, 103, 141, 146, 154, 185, 220, 225, 233, 234, 235, 242–3, 339, 341, 347

Warehouse Project, The 6, 314–15, 321, 349
Warner Music 231
Warp Records 288
Warren, Gordon 'Geeneus' 252–61, 253n, 260n, 347
Warren, Emma 4, 175; *Make Some Space* 373
Waterman, Pete 263–5, 264n, 265n, 266, 268, 269, 283
Waters, Rob 13
Way Out West 155
Weatherall, Andy 156
Weekend Rush 253
Weerasinghe, Terry 279
West Ham United 88, 251
West Mercia Police 106, 111
West Yorkshire Police 82, 83
Westwood, Tim 244
Wetherspoons 312
White Goddess free festival (1991) 99
Wieczorek, Joey 86–7, 88–9, 251
Wigflex, Lukas 371
Wigoder, Lord 116
Wiley 222, 226, 274, 288
Wilson, Nick 264–5
Windross, Norris: 'Da Boss' 353
Windsor Free Festival 35–44, 98, 121
Winterbottom, Jane 78–9
Winwood, Steve 234
Wireless Telegraphy Act (1949) 242
Wizkid 291
women: business techno and 326; DJs 301, 312, 326, 355, 365–6; feminism 10, 26, 359; jungle raves and 221; Notting Hill Carnival and 28; Peace Convoy and 54, 55; soundsystems and 25–6; spy cops and 120–1
wonky 183
Woods, Neil 121
Wookie: 'Battle' 303–4
Word, The 269
Wretch 32 225

XOYO 299
XXL 315

'Yardie' 207, 208
Young 276
Younge, Gary 33
YouTube 5, 205, 228, 229, 230, 233, 272, 273–4, 275, 283, 290, 291, 292, 305, 363

Zinc, DJ: 138 Trek 361
Žižek, Slavoj 153
Zorch 48–9, 128